Que's Computer Buyer's Guide

1992 Edition

Joseph Desposito

with

Jamey Marcum
Doug White

Que's Computer Buyer's Guide, 1992 Edition.

Library of Congress Catalog No.: 91-62312

ISBN 0-88022-759-1

93 92 91 4 3 2 1

Interpretation of the printing code: the rightmost double-digit number is the year of the book's printing; the rightmost single- digit number, the number of the book's printing. For example, a printing code of 91-1 shows that the first printing of the book occurred in 1991.

Publisher: Lloyd J. Short

Associate Publisher: Karen A. Bluestein

Acquisitions Manager: Rick Ranucci

Product Development Manager: Mary Bednarek

Managing Editor: Paul Boger

Book Designer: Scott Cook

Production Team: Jeff Baker, Brad Chinn, Sandy Grieshop, Audra Hershman, Betty Kish, Phil Kitchel, Bob LaRoche, Anne Owen, Howard Peirce, Tad Ringo, Linda Seifert, John Sleeva, Bruce Steed, Johnna VanHoose, Lisa Wilson, Phil Worthington

Product Director
Timothy S. Stanley

Senior Editor
Jeannine Freudenberger

Editors
Frances R. Huber
Greg Robertson
Anne P. Root

Special Contributor
Linda Fox

Editorial and Technical Assistance
Brenda Carmichael
Heather Fitzgerald

Composed in Garamond and MCP Digital by Que Corporation

About the Authors

Joseph Desposito

Joseph Desposito has a degree in electronic engineering from Manhattan College. He is a microcomputer consultant and free-lance writer specializing in microcomputer topics. He is a revision author for *1-2-3 Release 3.1 Quick Reference; Using 1-2-3 Release 3.1*, 2nd Edition; *1-2-3 Macro Library*, 3rd Edition; and *Using 1-2-3 Release 2.2*, Special Edition.

Jamey Marcum

Jamey Marcum holds a degree in journalism from Ball State University, Muncie Indiana. He is currently a sales representative of LMB Microcomputers in Indianapolis, Indiana.

Doug White

Doug White is currently employed by LMB Microcomputers in Indianapolis, Indiana, where he is a Certified Apple Systems Engineer. Doug holds a B.S. in marketing from Indiana University, Bloomington, Indiana.

Acknowledgments

Many people were instrumental in the completion of this book. Que would like to acknowledge the efforts of those involved.

Linda Fox spent many hours on the telephone and at the FAX machine contacting vendors for the information gathered into the data tables in this book. In fact, she was renamed "Linda Fax" by the many Macmillan Computer Publishing employees who patiently waited for her to complete her transmissions or who had to find another FAX machine.

Heather Fitzgerald entered all the data into the many necessary databases. Heather spent long hours deciphering handwriting on the specification sheets sent to us by the vendors.

Appreciation goes to Brenda Carmichael, who jumped in at the last hour to correct typos and help format the data tables. Brenda also pulled together the vendor listings in Appendix B.

Also, acknowledgements are fitting for Jeannine Freudenberger, who found the typos that Brenda corrected, as well as led the excellent editing team who made this book extraordinarily readable.

Thanks, too, goes to Tim Stanley, Product Director for this book. Besides providing technical answers to many questions, he formatted all the data tables, a task that became his worst nightmare.

Most important, an extra big thanks goes to the many vendors who took their time to fill out our forms and send us specification sheets so that we could provide the tables of specifications. Special thanks to Bill Stevens of IBM and Pam Jamison-Lenz of Zeos, International, LTD., for going the extra mile to make sure that we had the most up-to-date data for our tables.

Trademark Acknowledgments

Que Corporation has made every effort to supply trademark information about company names, products, and services mentioned in this book. Trademarks indicated below were derived from various sources. Que Corporation cannot attest to the accuracy of this information.

1-2-3 and Lotus are registered trademarks of Lotus Development Corporation.

Apple, Apple II, AppleCare, AppleTalk, Macintosh, and StyleWriter are registered trademarks and Disk First Aid and TrueType are trademarks of Apple Computer, Inc.

AutoCAD is a registered trademark of Autodesk, Inc.

Bitstream is a registered trademark of Bitstream, Inc.

COMPAQ is a registered trademark and COMPAQ DeskPro 386 is a trademark of COMPAQ Computer Corporation.

CompuServe is a registered trademark of H&R Block, Inc.

Crosstalk is a registered trademark of Digital Communications Associates, Inc.

dBASE and dBASE IV are registered trademarks of Ashton-Tate Corporation.

DeskMate is a registered trademark of Tandy Corporation.

DESQview is a trademark of Quarterdeck Office Systems.

DIALOG is a registered trademark of Dialog Information Services, Inc.

Disk Express II is a trademark of ALSoft, Inc.

Dow Jones News/Retrieval is a registered trademark of Dow Jones & Company, Inc.

EPSON is a registered trademark of Seiko Epson Corporation.

FASTBACK, Fastback Mac III, FASTBACK PLUS, and Mace Utilities are registered trademarks of Fifth Generation Systems, Inc.

Gateway is a trademark of Gateway 2000, Inc.

GEnie is a service mark of General Electric Company.

Hayes and Hayes Smartcom II are registered trademarks of Hayes Microcomputer Products, Inc.

HP and LaserJet are registered trademarks and DeskJet 500 and ScanJet are trademarks of Hewlett-Packard Co.

IBM, AT, Micro Channel, and Quietwriter are registered trademarks and PS/2 and XT are trademarks of International Business Machines Corporation.

MacTools Deluxe and PC Tools are trademarks of Central Point Software, Inc.

MCI Mail is a registered service mark of MCI Communications Corp.

Microsoft, Microsoft Mouse, Microsoft Works, and MS-DOS are registered trademarks and Windows is a trademark of Microsoft Corporation.

NEC is a registered trademark of NEC Information Systems, Inc.

Norton Utilities is a registered trademark and Sum II is a trademark of Symantec Corporation.

PC FullBak is a trademark of Westlake Data Corporation.

PostScript is a registered trademark and Adobe Type Manager is a trademark of Adobe Systems Incorporated.

Premium is a registered trademark of AST Research, Inc.

PROCOMM PLUS is a registered trademark of Datastorm Technologies, Inc.

Prodigy is a registered trademark of Prodigy Systems.

SpinRite II is a trademark of Gibson Research Corporation.

Tandy, Tandy 1000, and TRS-80 are registered trademarks of Radio Shack.

Virex is a registered trademark of Microcom Systems, Inc.

WordPerfect is a registered trademark of WordPerfect Corporation.

Xerox is a registered trademark of Xerox Corporation.

Zenith is a registered trademark of Zenith Electronics Corp.

Trademarks of other products mentioned in this book are held by the companies producing them.

Contents at a Glance

Contents

II Getting the Facts

III Making the Purchase

List of Tables

Introduction

Buying a personal computer for the first time is both an exciting and a daunting experience. You have the fun of deciding which computer will let you do all those things you have dreamed of doing. You have the excitement of learning about a new subject. But you also may feel uneasy and a bit insecure. Not only do you have many different brands from which to choose, but after you decide on a particular brand, you also have to figure out which model to buy. After you select a personal computer, you must make decisions about what kinds of equipment to connect to the computer. You have to determine which monitor and printer suit your needs, as well as choose other accessories, such as a modem or mouse. When you have decided on equipment, you must choose software, the programs you need to accomplish your personal computing goals. Choosing the right software takes as much thought as choosing the right hardware.

Designed to guide you through all the steps necessary to reach a purchasing decision, *Que's Computer Buyer's Guide*, 1992 Edition, covers all the computer hardware and software you will require to get started. This book provides the background information you need to make intelligent purchasing decisions and also offers advice about what to buy and what not to buy.

Rarely has the information required to make the right decisions about purchasing a computer, peripherals, and software been put in only one place; usually, the information is scattered around in various books, magazines, and other sources. Unlike many other computer books and magazines, this book is not specific to one brand of personal computer. *Que's Computer Buyer's Guide* deals with a wide spectrum of personal computers—computers powerful enough to meet your business and personal computing needs.

Unlike buyer's guides that appear in computer magazines (or in other consumer magazines), *Que's Computer Buyer's Guide* does not consist only of long lists of technical features so that you must tediously compare dozens of products in the same category. Instead, this book explains, without technical jargon, what different types of products can do and which types of products are best for particular applications. The authors then recommend one or more products in each category—recommendations based on years of experience using these products. Finally, this buyer's guide offers specification tables of computers and peripherals, organized by category, so that after you have decided on a category, you can select the best items for your needs.

Que's Computer Buyer's Guide provides the information you need to make intelligent purchasing decisions about computers, peripherals, and software. This book helps you select a computer manufacturer and model, a display and adapter, a printer, accessories, and software programs appropriate for your personal requirements. The book also gives you tips on buying, maintaining, and upgrading your system.

Who Should Read This Book

Anyone planning to buy a personal computer for the first time, for use in a business or at home, should read *Que's Computer Buyer's Guide*, 1992 Edition. Whether you are interested in an IBM or compatible or an Apple Macintosh, this book teaches you how to select a model appropriate for your needs—all without inundating you with technical details.

Que's Computer Buyer's Guide also is helpful to anyone new to personal computing—maybe you are working with computers for the first time at your job or in school. This book provides the information you need to understand the equipment you are working with. The information in this book helps you put your computer system into perspective and lays the groundwork for any purchase you may make: a computer system (including a monitor), a printer, a peripheral (such as a modem or scanner), or a software program.

Much time has been spent collecting and tabulating data specifications for this book. As the reader of *Que's Computer Buyer's Guide*, you will benefit by having a wealth of comparative details so that you can select the right hardware for your needs.

Finally, *Que's Computer Buyer's Guide* is appropriate for anyone who already owns a computer but wants to understand more about peripherals and software or wants to purchase a newer, more powerful computer system. Chapters 7 through 9, for example, are dedicated to printers, and Chapter 11 covers many popular software programs.

How This Book Is Organized

Que's Computer Buyer's Guide is structured logically so that information to help you determine what you want to do precedes recommendations on what you need to accomplish your goals. The book is made up of five parts and two appendixes. The first part, "Learning What I Need," is designed to familiarize you with the entire computer system. Part II, "Getting the Facts," gives you more specific information about the computer itself and about displays, printers, accessories, and software you may purchase to use with the computer system. This part includes useful tables filled with the specifications from many computer systems, displays and adapters, printers, and other peripherals. These tables give you the information you need to compare products so that you can find just the computer system you want. Part III, "Making the Purchase," is devoted to considerations you must make before you purchase a computer system. For example, you learn how to determine just how powerful a system you really need for word processing as compared to computer-aided design. Finally, the appendixes give you helpful information not directly related to your purchasing decisions.

Now, look at the contents of the individual chapters. First, by reading Part I, you gain a general knowledge of computers and what they can do.

Chapter 1, "Understanding What a Personal Computer Can Do," describes the benefits of using a computer. The intent of this chapter is to help you decide what you want your computer to do.

Chapter 2, "Understanding the Computer System," provides a basic overview of the major parts of a computer system and shows you how the parts work together. The chapter defines basic terms and presents the material in a nontechnical way so that you get the information you need to help you make a purchase decision.

At this point, you are ready to consider all the facts about computers, presented in Part II.

Chapter 3, "Deciding What Type of Computer You Want," builds on the information in Chapter 2. This chapter describes similarities and differences among various components and makes recommendations based on what those components are best suited to do. Included in this chapter is an overview of many computer manufacturers, pinpointing their strengths and weaknesses.

Chapter 4, "Listing of Computer Systems," contains 10 specification tables covering IBM and IBM-compatible computers based on the 8086, 80286, 80386SX, 80386, 80486SX, and 80486 microprocessors. Also listed are IBM and compatible laptop and notebook computers and Macintosh computers, including Macintosh and compatible laptop computers.

Chapter 5, "Deciding What Type of Monitor You Need," increases your knowledge of different means of displaying information on a video monitor. You learn about the different video standards available for IBM and compatible computers. The text also explains what you need to know when selecting a display and adapter for Macintosh computers and for IBM and compatible computers.

Chapter 6, "Listing of Monitors," gives you specifications of displays, adapters, and combination displays and adapters. You can use these tables to select a display and adapter that best suit your needs.

Chapter 7, "Reviewing Types of Printers," provides an overview of the different types of printers available. You learn the meanings of special terms and get an understanding of the different printing technologies.

Chapter 8, "Deciding What Printer Model You Need," continues the discussion begun in Chapter 7. Information in this chapter helps you think clearly about what you will be printing. After you have read the information in this chapter, you will be ready to select one of the technologies discussed in Chapter 7.

Chapter 9, "Listing of Printers," provides three specification tables. The tables compare different models of dot-matrix printers, inkjet printers, and laser printers. Each table gives you information specific to that type of printer and provides data vital to choosing the best printer for you.

Chapter 10, "Deciding What Extras You Need," discusses some of the add-on accessories that you may purchase with your computer system. The chapter discusses mice and trackballs, scanners, modems, CD ROM drives, and backup devices. Although these devices are not absolutely essential to the functioning of your computer, they offer helpful features. And these devices are becoming increasingly popular in specific areas. For example, scanners are used in desktop publishing. This chapter also includes specification tables for many of these devices. You can use these tables in your selection of accessories.

Chapter 11, "Determining What Software You Need," gives you an overview of the different types of software available. You learn about the different operating systems, such as DOS, OS/2, and System 7, and about popular operating environments, such as Microsoft Windows and DESQview from Quarterdeck. You also see what software can do for you and learn the differences among programs so that you can decide what features you need.

Part III takes you into the actual purchasing considerations and process.

Chapter 12, "Choosing a System To Fit Your Needs," discusses how to select the best system for your specific needs. Even though many people use the same type of software—for example, a spreadsheet—each person may use the program differently and demand a different response from the software. This chapter helps you select a technology of computer, based on how you will use it. For example, a person who uses a word processor does not want the same type of computer as the person who does desktop publishing or computer-aided design. This chapter helps you "fit" into the correct size computer.

Chapter 13, "Making the Purchase," discusses how to go about purchasing a computer. You learn how to research different systems and needs. You also are given questions to ask before making a purchase. Because there are many avenues to purchasing a computer system, ranging from mail order to full-service retail computer stores, you must know which is right for you.

Finally, the appendixes give you information you will need after you purchase your computer system and more data related to information in the rest of the book.

Appendix A, "Planning for the Future," helps you prepare for the future of your system. This appendix discusses service and repair and upgrades to your system. Appendix B, "Vendor Information," provides the names, addresses, and phone numbers of companies listed in the specification tables in this book. Get in touch with these companies for further information about products mentioned in this book.

Other Reference Sources

Although *Que's Computer Buyer's Guide* tells you what you should know in order to make an intelligent computer purchase, no book can fill all your personal computing needs. Que Corporation publishes a full line of microcomputer books that complement this one.

If you want general information about computing fundamentals, look through *Introduction to Personal Computers*, 2nd Edition, and *Que's Computer User's Dictionary*, 2nd Edition. For IBM and compatible computers, *Using MS-DOS 5* and *Using Microsoft Windows 3*, 2nd Edition, provide information about the most popular operating systems and environments. For Macintosh computers, *The Big Mac Book*, 2nd Edition, is an all-in-one reference source.

If you are interested in finding out more about how to use a particular software application, you can choose from many Que books for IBM and compatible and Macintosh computers. Que books on some of the more popular applications include *Using 1-2-3 for DOS Release 2.3*, Special Edition; *Using WordPerfect 5.1*, Special Edition; and *Using WordPerfect for Windows*, Special Edition. You also may consult *Using dBASE IV* (for IBM and compatibles) and *Using Excel for the Macintosh*, *Using Microsoft Word 4: Macintosh Version*, and *Using FileMaker* (for Macintosh computers).

If you are interested in further technical details about computer hardware, examine Que's *Upgrading and Repairing PCs*. This informative text shows you how to get the most from your current hardware and how to upgrade your system to achieve better performance from your software.

PART I

Learning What I Need

Includes

Understanding What a Personal Computer Can Do

Understanding the Computer System

CHAPTER ONE

Understanding What a Personal Computer Can Do

When you think of all the possible purchases you can make in your lifetime, a personal computer has to be one of the most exciting and frustrating. You have finally decided to take the plunge. You are ready to buy a personal computer. You have seen what personal computers can do to make your work easier, to calculate your budget, to keep track of inventory at work and at home, to entertain your kids. You have seen friends and coworkers using computers; perhaps you have used a computer yourself at work or elsewhere. You are excited, but you have many questions. This book can help you make intelligent decisions so that your computer purchase will be wise and relatively painless.

A computer costs a significant amount of money, more than you probably would spend for a good stereo sound system and sometimes as much as you would spend for a low-priced automobile. Because a computer costs so much, you want to make the right decision the first time. This objective pressures you to collect and assimilate all the information you can about the purchase.

As you collect information, the purchase decision becomes even more confusing and intimidating. You have many types of computers with many different features from which to choose. You are bombarded with advertisements and reviews comparing the types and features so that making sense out of the material is difficult. What is RAM? What does MHz stand for? What is an 80386 CPU? All you want to know is the bottom line—what computer do you need to get the job done (if you need a computer at all)?

A personal computer purchase is just the beginning of a series of purchases you must make to do work with your computer. Besides the computer itself, you need programs to run it and equipment to connect to it (for example, a printer).

The goal of this book is to take some of the mystery out of purchasing a personal computer and related accessories. The book explains what computers are and guides you through making an intelligent purchasing decision. Terms are defined and related to performance. For example, how does the amount of RAM affect the computer's capability to calculate a company's budget? By understanding the different terms and features, you can make an informed purchasing decision.

The first step in making that decision is deciding what you want the computer to do. A person who uses a computer to do financial forecasting may not need the same computer that someone who uses the computer to type letters needs. Your first task is to define in specific terms the tasks you want the computer to do.

This chapter begins by explaining some of the benefits of using a personal computer. (Note that this book uses PC generically to refer to any type of personal computer.) This book also shows you some of the tasks you can accomplish with a computer. Today you may want the computer to do a home budget, but tomorrow you may want to use the computer to publish a company newsletter. As you make your list of the tasks you want the computer to do, consider all possibilities. This chapter helps you determine specifically what you need the computer to do.

Understanding the Benefits of a PC

A personal computer may be expensive, but it often pays for itself. You can realize these benefits in many ways. A PC can save you time and money, help you do repetitive work, increase accuracy in your work, and open new avenues of opportunity for you.

Saving Time and Money

Computers can save you time and money. Any project that involves the calculation of numbers is done more efficiently on a computer because it can calculate much faster than the human mind. If you enter incorrect numbers on a simple list of expenses to be totaled, you can make the corrections, and almost simultaneously the computer recalculates the total.

More complex tasks also are simplified. For example, in business, you may want to make a five-year projection of sales versus expenses and develop graphs that highlight important areas of interest. Doing this task manually—gathering the figures, performing the calculations with a calculator, typing them into a report, drawing a graph—takes a good deal of time. Using a computer greatly simplifies these tasks. With the right program, you enter the figures once, and the program calculates the results and creates a graph.

A computer also speeds your work by eliminating repetitive tasks. You enter information (numbers, text, pictures) once and then store it permanently on a disk for future reference. You can access any saved information and change, rearrange, remove, or add to the existing information.

Besides saving time, a personal computer can save you money. One way is by helping you avoid mistakes. Depending on what you are doing—for example, adding a long list of figures—one mistake can cost you hundreds or even thousands of dollars. Computers can help you avoid this kind of error by doing calculations quickly and correctly. (Of course, if you type numbers incorrectly to begin with, a computer is not likely to catch the mistake.)

Another way in which a personal computer can help you save money is by providing you with alternative ways to do a job. For example, you may be using outside sources to typeset and print your company newsletter. With a PC and the right software, you can publish the newsletter yourself.

Handling Repetitive Work

If you have ever been stuck with a punishment of writing "I will not talk in class" 100 times, you know how boring a task like this can be. Although this kind of task may bore you, it does not bore a computer. A PC performs a routine task quickly and without making errors (even if you increase the punishment to 1,000 or 10,000 times).

Computers are perfect for tasks like typing the same letter to 10,000 people (and even personalizing it). A PC also is perfect for doing math problems that involve numerous repetitive calculations.

Quality can be improved because the time you save by not doing mundane tasks, such as retyping or recalculating, gives you more time to concentrate on the content of the task.

Increasing Accuracy

A computer can help you do your work more accurately. If you work with words, a spelling checker can help you weed out most or all spelling mistakes, and a grammar checker can alert you to incorrect grammar. If you work with numbers, a spreadsheet program can improve the accuracy of your results. For example, a change to one or more numbers of a budget forecast usually affects many numbers throughout the budget. A spreadsheet program can recalculate the entire budget quickly and accurately.

Opening New Avenues of Opportunity

No matter what career path you pursue, owning a personal computer can open new avenues of opportunity for you. With talent and the proper training and qualifications, you can write a book or a magazine article with a PC; you can design ads or newsletters with a PC; or you can connect your electronic music keyboard to a PC.

You may be thinking about a career change. You may want to pursue computer-specific areas such as PC consulting, programming, training, or technical repair. By purchasing a computer and the right software, you may pursue these areas. Some college courses even provide you with a computer to use during the course, with the option of purchase. You may pursue this option before buying a computer.

Determining Your Uses for a PC

CHECKLIST

For a computer to save you time and money, you must know what you want the computer to do. What tasks do you want to automate? What types of items do you want the computer to create—letters, graphs, reports, mailing lists? The following list describes many tasks you may want to do with a personal computer:

Working with words
Working with numbers
Working with information
Handling finances
Communicating with other computers
Working with symbols and images
Working with sound
Playing games
Enhancing education
Creating programs

To do any of these tasks on a computer, you need an *application program*, often referred to as software. *Software* gives the computer the instructions it needs to perform a task. A large variety of application programs are available in each of these categories. (Chapter 11 addresses the question of software.) Learn the personal computer's capabilities from this book and then apply this knowledge when deciding on a PC of your own.

Working with Words

You can use a computer to type letters, reports, manuscripts, or term papers. To work with words, you need a kind of program called a *word processor*. In many ways, you use a word processor as you use a typewriter, but a word processor offers significant advantages.

If you often make mistakes when you type, a word processor will help you because it increases accuracy. You see on-screen what you type. As characters appear on-screen, you can check them for accuracy. If a character is not correct, you can delete and replace the incorrect character with the correct character—you need no erasers or correction fluid.

If you have to make changes to the text you type, a word processor can help. With a word processor, you can rearrange text. If you type a paragraph with a typewriter and then decide later to move the paragraph to a different page in the document, you have to cut out the paragraph with a pair of scissors and paste it with glue or tape in the appropriate place on another page. You then must retype the affected pages. With a word processor, you simply mark the paragraph to be moved and then indicate the place to where you want the paragraph moved. The program does the actual moving. This method is simple and neat, and you do no retyping.

Most good word processors also check the spelling in your work when you issue the appropriate command. You can check spelling when you finish the manuscript or when you are stumped on a word. You can correct spelling errors—or any other type of error—before you print the document. If the printed document contains errors, you can return to the program, make the necessary changes, and print the document again. A word processor also may have a built-in thesaurus, which enables you to find just the right word.

You can use a word processor to create documents ranging from simple letters to complex manuals. Depending on the word processing program, you can get features with which you can create document headers, page numbers, footnotes, and so on. Some word processors also enable you to insert graphics into the document.

If you need presentation-quality output, you may need a desktop publishing program in addition to a word processor. With this type of program, you can create brochures, reports, newsletters, and similar documents. You can place text in one or more columns; add pictures; and use different typefaces for headlines, initial capitals, and captions. A document created with a desktop publishing program can look professional—as if you had the job printed at a print shop. All these capabilities are available to you with the right computer and software combinations.

Working with Numbers

You can use a computer to work with numbers, as in financial statements, budgets, and cash reports. You need a software program called a spreadsheet. A *spreadsheet* is the electronic representation of a page in an accountant's pad. The difference, however, is that a spreadsheet can contain as many as 8,196 rows and 256 columns. (As a comparison, note that a 40-column ledger book is considered large.) These dimensions give you enough room to enter data for even the most complex financial reports.

To perform mathematical operations on data, you enter the appropriate formulas. When you enter a new figure into a spreadsheet, the program recalculates all the formulas. If you make a change, you do not have to redo any of the calculations—the program recalculates for you.

If you are interested in figuring out different financial scenarios, you can enter different numbers and then recalculate the spreadsheet. This what-if feature of a spreadsheet gives it a tremendous edge over other calculating tools.

If you want to see a graph of the numbers, you easily can create line, bar, pie, and other types of graphs. The spreadsheet uses the numbers you have already entered to create graphs for you.

You can even enter small amounts of data—such as names, addresses, and phone numbers—into a spreadsheet and sort the data, create reports, and perform statistical calculations on the data.

Managing Data

If you want a program that helps you track names, inventory, or any other kind of information, you need a *database* program. You can use a database to perform simple tasks, such as managing your Christmas card list, or complex tasks, such as developing a complete order-entry system.

A database enables you to find information quickly and easily. Rather than searching through your filing cabinet, you can type a command and have the database program find and display the record you want.

A database program enables you to extract information from the database file in many ways. For example, you can print a report that contains information about all the people listed in the file who live in the state of New York, or you may want information only about New Yorkers between the ages of 21 and 29. Whatever your needs, a database program can help you prepare reports quickly and easily.

Working with Finances

Because PCs are adept at working with numbers, computers are excellent at tracking business and personal finances. For businesses, many accounting programs are available to manage your company's books. Some accounting programs are powerful, meant to handle a good-sized business. Others are less powerful, specifically designed to help a small-business owner track his or her finances. For personal finances, programs are available to help you track your assets and debits. You can find a financial program to handle almost any situation you encounter.

Communicating with Other Computers

Communications programs enable you to connect to other personal computers or to much larger computers called mainframes. If you connect to another personal computer, you can exchange messages and files. When you communicate with a mainframe computer, you usually are linking to an on-line service.

On-line services contain information on many subjects. For example, you can shop or make plane reservations through your personal computer and this kind of service. Some services, such as MCI Mail, are dedicated to electronic mail. Anyone who is a member of a service like this one can send an electronic letter to any other member. Other services, such as Dow Jones News/Retrieval, are dedicated to providing business users with up-to-date news and financial information.

You also can use a personal computer to communicate with business locations that have fax machines. By adding the appropriate fax product to a PC, you can send or receive faxes.

Working with Symbols and Images

You need *presentation graphics software* if you often display information in graphical form. Presentation graphics software enables you to create high-quality charts and graphs for documents, slides, and transparencies.

Presentation graphics programs give you a wide variety of graph types, including line, bar, stacked bar, pie, high-low, and others. With these programs, you can put special effects into your graphs (such as arrows or comments) or create graphs with symbols. For example, you may create a bar graph with five automobile icons stacked on top of each other to represent 500 cars sold.

Using a presentation graphics program is just one way to manipulate symbols and images with a PC. You also can use paint programs, draw programs, animation programs, and computer-aided design (CAD) programs.

If you are artistically inclined, you can create sophisticated electronic paintings with a paint program. If not, you can modify pictures that the program provides.

If a particular paint program doesn't provide a large assortment of pictures, you can enter pictures into a computer yourself. *Video frame grabber circuitry* is the technology that enables you to "capture" a video image and convert it to a digital image, which you store on and retrieve from a computer disk. With video frame grabber circuitry connected to a PC, you can capture video image(s) from a television or VCR, bring the video image(s) into a PC, and modify the image with a paint program.

Another way to enter pictures into a computer is by connecting a *scanner* to a PC. You run the picture through the scanner as you run a sheet of paper through a fax machine. The scanner sends a copy of the picture to the computer where you can modify the image with a paint program.

Computer-aided design programs generally are directed toward technical professionals, such as mechanical engineers, electrical engineers, architects, and industrial designers. With these programs, you can create any kind of drawing that you can do by hand with drafting tools. Additionally, you can create 3-D technical drawings.

Working with Sound

With the proper combination of software and hardware, personal computers can talk, listen, or even play music. PCs talk through electronic speech circuits, built-in or added to the computer and connected to a speaker. Some people use a PC as a telephone-answering machine. Not only can the PC answer the calls and store messages, but the computer also can route a call based on the caller's preferences (indicated by responses on a touch-tone phone). Available products provide the software and hardware necessary to perform these functions.

Most people communicate with a PC through a keyboard or mouse, but a PC equipped with the appropriate voice recognition software and hardware can accept voice commands. Instead of typing or pointing to commands, you speak them into a microphone. You can buy products that provide the software and hardware needed to implement voice recognition on a PC. The use of voice recognition software and hardware is not common, but this technology may become widespread in the future.

Working with sound on a personal computer often means working with music. You can write and play music with a personal computer if you have the right equipment. A common configuration is a personal computer connected to a keyboard synthesizer through a *musical instrument digital interface (MIDI)*. More information on this topic is given in Chapter 11.

Playing Games

If you are the kind of person who enjoys arcade games, you can use a PC to bring the arcade home. A PC equipped with a joystick or a mouse can provide some of the finest arcade action available.

PCs, however, can entertain you with much more than arcade games. For example, you can try simulations. Do you want to see what it's like to be in the cockpit of a plane? Would you like to try dealing with problems concerning the earth's environment? Would you like to try to run a business—without having to invest your own money? These experiences—and many others—are possible with your PC and the right software.

A wide selection of adventure games for PCs also is available. Whatever your interest—knights of the round table, the old West, outer space—you can become involved in the life and times of fictional characters as you try to ward off danger and achieve your goals.

Enhancing Education

A PC is an excellent educational tool for all ages—from preschool to adult levels. Preschoolers can learn how to count or add with games that feature syndicated cartoon characters, such as Charlie Brown, Bert and Ernie, and Mickey Mouse. School-age children can learn about chemistry or electronics by working with computer simulations of technical labs. Adults can learn to type through practice and feedback about errors or to understand popular computer programs through tutorials.

No matter what the instructional method—games, simulations, practice, or tutorials—thousands of educational software programs are available to enhance your learning experience, and most educational programs require just a standard PC and an inquisitive mind.

Creating Programs

Every computer software program that ever existed was created by a person who knew how to write in a language the computer can understand. You can learn a large variety of languages a PC can understand. If you have a great idea for a computer software program, you may want to spend the time and effort needed to learn a programming language. Many of these programming-language software packages include tutorial programs from which you can learn, and you also can take courses at a college or vocational school.

Making a Decision

Now that you have a basic knowledge of what a computer can do for you, you need to determine your requirements. Follow these steps:

1. Make a list of your needs.

   What do you want the computer to do? Define your objective with focused statements—for example, "To keep track of inventory in the book department," "To help my daughter improve her spelling," or "To improve the corporate image when producing proposals by incorporating graphics and other illustrations."

2. Collect data about your current way of doing things.

   You may want to computerize a small business or a home office, or you may want to use a computer for personal improvement or for entertainment. If you want to use a PC in a business or home office environment, first think about the way you do things now. Think about the reports, forms, and invoices you create. Are you dealing with text, numbers, or graphics? How do these reports, forms, invoices, and so on, look now? Do you use color? You should collect samples of what you are doing now or what you would like to do. If you don't have samples available, try to create by hand the kinds of things you want the computer to do for you.

3. Do a little brainstorming based on what you know computers can do.

   How could your work be done better on a computer?

After these three steps, you should have a detailed list of what you want the computer to do. This list gives you a head start in finding a computer best suited to your needs. To fine-tune the list, you should consider other issues before you make a purchase decision:

- Set priorities.

  If you haven't already done so, look around in computer stores to get a general idea of what is available. What features seem most important? What do you think you will need immediately? What can you buy later? For example, you may want to purchase a printer right away but purchase a modem (used for communication with other computers) later.

- Think of other users.

  Who will be using the computer? Other users may have different skill levels, and a program should accommodate the needs of beginners and more advanced users.

- Consider compatibility issues.

  Do you need to share your data with other people? If so, you need to gather information about their computing environment.

- Take into consideration your experience.

  What are your abilities? What is your previous experience and typing ability? Have you used a computer before?

- Determine your working environment.

  Where will the computer be used?

- Establish a budget.

  How much money can you spend?

- Plan for the future.

  What do you want the computer to do in one year and in three years? For example, do you want the system you purchase now to be capable of running the more advanced graphics software coming out in the market? If so, you may need to purchase more advanced hardware or hardware that can be changed easily.

The following checklist summarizes these issues. This list can start you on your way to making the right purchasing decisions.

- What do you want the computer to do?

  Help run a business

  Help manage a home office

  Enable you to do at home what you do on the PC at work

  Help with schoolwork

  Entertain

- How will you use the computer?

  Only for business-related work

  Only for pleasure

  For business and pleasure

- Where will you use the computer?

  At the office

  At home

  At home and office

  At school

  On the road

- Who else will use the computer?

  Employees

  Family members

  Friends

- What do you want a computer to do several years from now?
- How much can you spend?

  Less than $1,000

  Between $1,000 and $3,000

  Between $3,000 and $5,000

  Between $5,000 and $10,000

  More than $10,000

- What features are most important?

Chapter Summary

In this chapter, you have learned some of the benefits of personal computers. You have learned that personal computers can open new opportunities for you, save you time and money, and do repetitive work for you. You have also learned some basic information about working with words, numbers, information, finances, other computers, symbols and images, sound, games, education, and programs. Finally, you have learned how to lay the groundwork for making an informed purchasing decision.

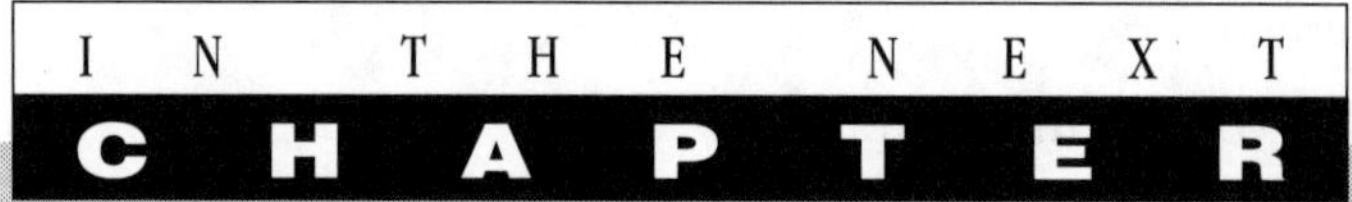

The next chapter provides you with an overview of the major parts of a computer system in terms that you can understand. The chapter defines each part and shows you how the parts work together.

CHAPTER TWO

Understanding the Computer System

Understanding a personal computer system is often simply a matter of understanding the individual hardware and software components that comprise the system. The hardware components are the system unit, monitor, keyboard, mouse, and other peripheral equipment. The software components of a computer system are ROM software, operating system software, and application software. This chapter defines these hardware and software components and describes how each works. Understanding a computer's hardware and software components can help you purchase a system appropriate for your needs.

Understanding Personal Computer Hardware

A typical computer system consists of the following hardware components:

System unit
Monitor (video display)
Keyboard
Mouse

Figure 2.1 shows how these components fit together to make up a computer system. The keyboard usually sits in front of the system unit, the mouse to the right side of the unit (for right-handed users), and the monitor on top of the unit. The system unit houses the system board (motherboard), one or more floppy disk drives, and one or more hard disk drives. Slots for floppy disk drives are visible because they must be accessible, but hard disk drives usually are stored inside the system unit. Some systems, laptop computers for example, squeeze all these components into one unit.

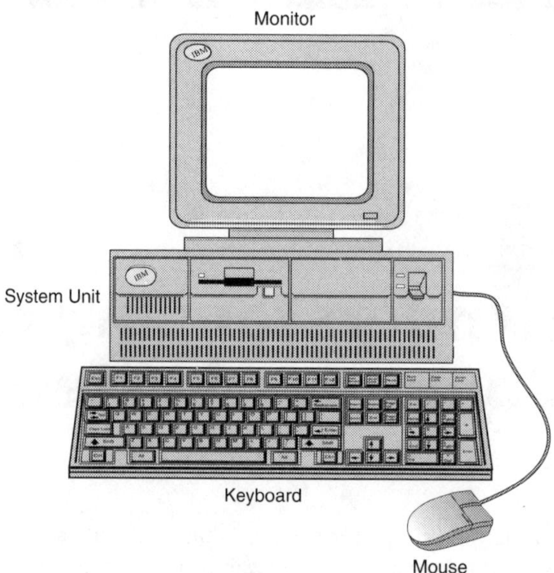

Fig. 2.1. A typical personal computer system showing the system unit, monitor, mouse, and keyboard.

The more you know about the components of a computer system, the better the decisions you can make when you shop for a computer system. The following sections explain these computer components in detail.

System Unit

The *system unit* of many personal computers is a rectangular case that can sit horizontally on a desktop (as in fig. 2.1) or stand vertically (see fig. 2.2).

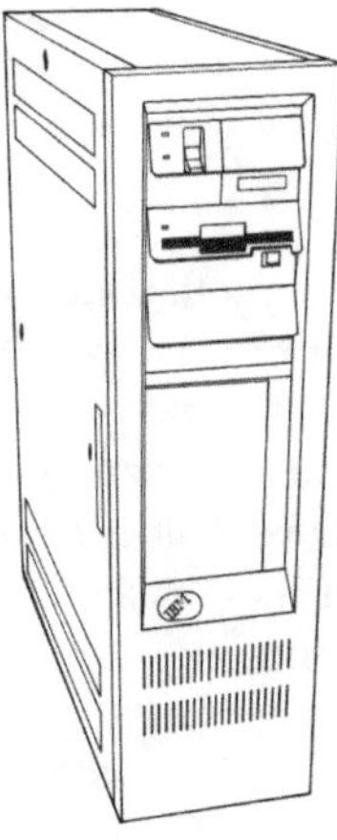

Fig. 2.2. This system unit is a floor-standing, or tower, model.

In order to shop wisely for a computer system, you need to know some basic facts about the system unit. All system units have a power switch for turning the computer on and off. The power switch is in the front of the system unit shown in figure 2.1, but the switch may be at the side or back of some units.

Many system units have a lock like the one shown in figure 2.3. Locking the system unit does not prevent theft of the unit, but locking the unit can stop someone from taking the cover off and tampering with the unit components. Some system unit locks also prevent people from entering information into the computer through the keyboard; other locks simply lock the cover in place. If no one else has access to your computer, the lock may be superfluous; but if you are concerned about someone tampering with your system or your data files, a lock provides some security.

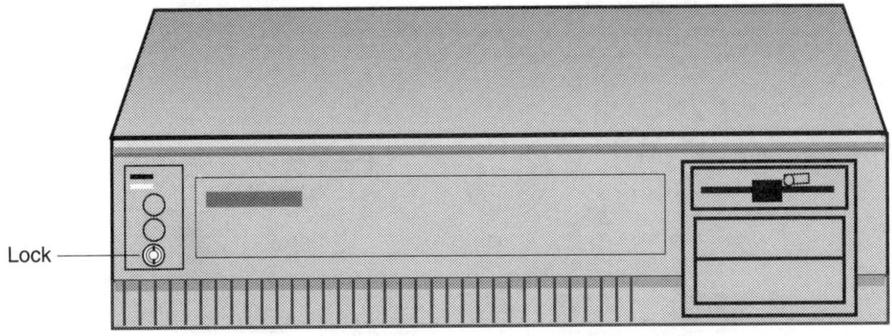

Fig. 2.3. *Locking the system unit prevents access to hardware components.*

Floppy disk drives and tape drives are located in the front of the system unit for easy access. In figure 2.1, you can see the slot for inserting a 3 1/2-inch floppy disk. You use the button on the disk drive to eject the disk from the drive. Some system units have 5 1/4-inch drives with a lever to open and close the drive when you insert or remove a disk. Some of the new 5 1/4-inch drives have an ejection button. With Macintosh computers, you issue a command to eject the disk.

Although many system units have hard disk drives, you usually can see only one or two indicator lights from the outside. Often, one light indicates that power is on, and another flashes when the hard disk is working.

If you look at the back of a system unit, such as the one shown in figure 2.4, you see many connectors. The power cord and most input and output devices, with the possible exception of the keyboard, are connected to the back of the system unit. At the back of the system unit, you may find connectors for the keyboard, the video monitor, the modem, the mouse, the printer, and other types of peripheral equipment.

The keyboard connector is often a round plug with 5 pinholes. The connector for the monitor usually has 9 or 15 pinholes. The connector for the serial port (also called the RS 232 or asynchronous communication port) may have either 8,

9, or 25 pins. The connector for the mouse is sometimes a small circular plug with 5 or 9 pinholes. The connector for the Centronics parallel port usually has 25 pinholes. These connectors are shown in figure 2.5.

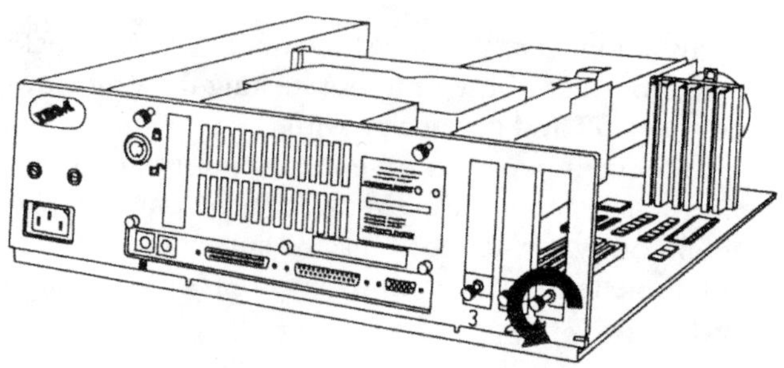

Fig. 2.4. Connectors at the back of the system unit.

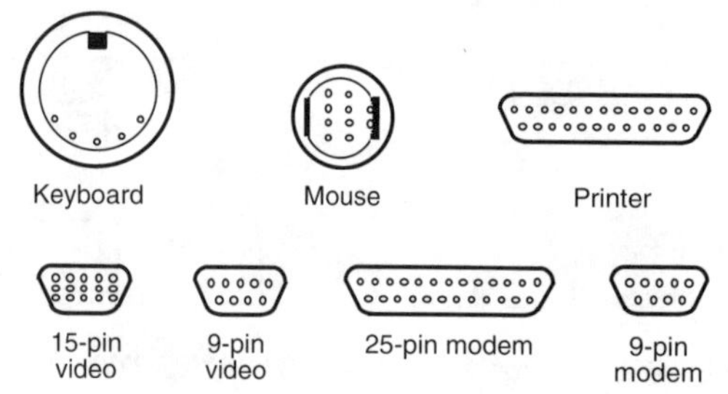

Fig. 2.5. Typical connectors for the keyboard, video monitor, modem, mouse, and printer.

Serial and parallel ports are an IBM-compatible computer's main avenues to the outside world. Although the Macintosh has two serial ports, the main connection is the Small Computer System Interface (SCSI, pronounced "scuzzy"). The serial port can be connected to many different kinds of devices, including a modem, a mouse, a printer, and a plotter. The parallel port is used primarily for printers. Some computers have built-in serial and parallel ports; other computers don't. If a computer doesn't have any ports, or if you need more ports than are built into the computer, you may need to purchase a serial port or parallel port *expansion board*. (*Multi-i/o boards*, which are generic boards for IBM-compatible computers, normally have two serial ports and a parallel port, as well as other features—a clock or a game port, for example.)

Different types of computers have different connectors. For example, printers connect to the serial port on the Macintosh computer, so a Macintosh does not have a parallel port. Make sure that the computer you purchase has connectors for each device you plan to attach. If you are considering an IBM-compatible computer, for example, make sure that the system unit has a parallel port for printing, a serial port for a modem, and a second serial port or a mouse port for a mouse.

The only other items of interest at the back of the system unit are the slots, shown in figure 2.4. These slots are reserved for electronic circuit boards that expand the capabilities of the computer. These boards are placed inside the system unit and are used to add enhanced memory, increase the computer's speed, enable special graphics features, and so on. Connectors and some switches on the board protrude out of the slot opening, as shown in figure 2.6. The connector may be for a video monitor, a modem, a printer, or some other kind of input or output device. The switches may be used to enable or disable features of the board. Some circuit boards have neither a connector nor switches showing through the slots. Although the slots are oriented vertically in figure 2.6, they may be placed horizontally in some system units.

Fig. 2.6. *Expansion boards with externally visible connectors.*

You are often warned not to open the cases of electronic products. It's common, however, to take the cover off a computer's system unit, usually to install additional circuit boards. Be careful to follow the safety procedures given in the unit's documentation any time you open the system unit case. Whether or not you install the circuit boards yourself, you need to know what is inside the system unit, where components crucial to the operation of the system are housed.

Among other items, a large circuit board resides inside the system unit. This board is the *system board*, or the *motherboard*. The black rectangles on the board are *chips*, the electronic devices that are the heart of the computer. One of these chips, usually the largest on the system's motherboard, is the *microprocessor*. Other important chips on the board are the *RAM* (*random-access memory*) and *ROM* (*read-only memory*) chips. Some newer units will have a main logic board and a bus board (horizontal slots), and units such as COMPAQ's 386/33L have processor boards. When you purchase a computer, you need to know the type of microprocessor, the amount of RAM, and the version of ROM the computer uses. The microprocessor, RAM, and ROM are explained in more detail in the following sections.

The system motherboard also has a socket for a *math coprocessor chip*, which is almost as large as the microprocessor chip. A math coprocessor speeds the computer's capability to do floating-point arithmetic operations. On some of the more powerful computers using the 80486DX microprocessor, the coprocessor is built into the same chip as the microprocessor. However, the 80486SX does not have a coprocessor built into it.

Expansion slots are important parts of a system unit. These slots hold additional circuit boards, which expand the capabilities of the computer. You need to know how many and what kinds of slots (8-bit or 16-bit) are available on the system board. The more slots, the more you can expand your computer. The type of expansion slot is an important factor in personal computer purchasing decisions. Having too few slots may limit your capability to expand your computer.

An equally important component in the system unit is the power supply. It must produce enough wattage to run the system plus any adapter cards you place in expansion slots. The power supply in many computers is on the right rear side of the system unit (looking at the unit from the front). The power switch that you can see from outside the system unit is an integral part of the power supply.

Besides the board with its chips and slots, the system unit houses the *disk drives*. The *floppy disk drives*, which you can see from outside the system unit, connect to the system board or to an expansion board. Although either method works, connecting a drive to an expansion board uses up one of the expansion slots. The hard disk also resides in the system unit. Like floppy disks, a hard disk can connect either to the system board or to an expansion board.

By now, you should have some understanding of a personal computer's system unit. Remember, however, that not all system units are exactly alike, and not all PCs have a separate system unit. Sometimes the video monitor and the system unit are combined into a single unit; the Macintosh Classic and the IBM PS/2 Model 25 are constructed this way.

The following sections describe the microprocessor, memory, expansion slots, bus, floppy disk drive, and hard disk drive in more detail.

Microprocessor

The microprocessor is the most important hardware component of a personal computer. The microprocessor determines how well the computer performs and what software you can run. Because the microprocessor usually resides in the system unit, your PC's specifications should tell you about the microprocessors. Many different companies manufacture microprocessors, which differ in speed, number of bits (data lines), and software compatibility.

Speed

In computer terminology, microprocessor speed refers to the time necessary to perform program operations, such as adding two binary numbers. Microprocessor speed is measured in megahertz (MHz)—millions of cycles per second. Generally, the higher the megahertz rating, the faster the computer performs. The speed for personal computers described in this book ranges from 4.77 MHz (the slowest) to 50 MHz (the fastest).

Speed is important. No matter what kind of software application you use, the computer takes time to process information, send and retrieve the information from disk drives, and perform other operations. Speed is especially important when a computer has a graphics user interface, which makes the computer easier to use but slows the speed of operation. Whether you are thinking about the microprocessor or any other component of a personal computer system, consider how fast that component works. Unfortunately, the fastest computers usually cost the most. For example, the fastest IBM and Apple Macintosh systems cost well over $10,000. Most buyers have to make a trade-off between speed and price.

For around $2,000, you can buy an IBM-compatible computer system that offers good performance ($3,000 for an IBM or Apple Macintosh system). If you cannot spend that much, you can purchase a slower system for $1,000 or less. Depending on what you plan to do with a computer, a slower system may meet your needs.

Number of Bits

The performance of a personal computer also depends on the way the microprocessor processes information. Microprocessors send and receive information 8, 16, or 32 bits at a time. A *bit* is a *binary digit*—a 0 or a 1. Computer bits are like the lanes on a highway. Some computers have 8 lanes to move data around; some have 16 lanes; and some have 32 lanes. More information can be processed and moved around more quickly on 32 lanes than on 8 lanes. Depending on the application, this greater processing capability enhances computer performance.

In theory, a 16 MHz microprocessor moving data around 32 bits at a time should outperform a 16 MHz microprocessor moving data around 16 bits at a time. In practice, however, you may see only a minimal difference in performance, depending on the software you use. For example, if you are simply typing letters, you will notice nearly no performance difference between a 16- and a 32-bit microprocessor. If you will be using software that does much calculation, such as a spreadsheet or computer-aided design software, however, you will benefit from the performance of a 32-bit computer over a 16-bit computer. In fact, some programs require a 32-bit microprocessor in order to run.

Purchase a system with the maximum performance you can afford. Knowing the number of bits at which a processor moves data around helps you make a smarter purchase today and prepares you to take advantage of new software designs in the future. In the sections that follow, notice the number of bits in the data path of each microprocessor.

Microprocessor Compatibility

Personal computers generally use microprocessors manufactured by Intel or Motorola. Intel makes microprocessors for IBM and compatibles. Motorola microprocessors are found in Apple Macintosh, Commodore Amiga, and Atari Mega and Atari ST computers. Personal computers with Motorola microprocessors are not compatible directly with computers that use Intel microprocessors. (Various ways of linking one type of computer to another type of computer are available. These links can be costly, however, and they don't guarantee complete compatibility.)

Software plays a big role in your choice of the computer and microprocessor you want. Your choice of software determines your choice between companies—Intel or Motorola—and among microprocessors. Most companies produce software for only one type of microprocessor. Some programs, such as Microsoft Excel, have versions for Macintosh as well as for IBM compatibles. You cannot run the Macintosh version of the software, however, on an IBM compatible. Many of the major software applications now have software on both platforms, ensuring ease of transfer of information between platforms.

To make an intelligent choice of microprocessor, therefore, you must have a clear idea of what applications you want to run on a personal computer. This chapter suggests some guidelines, based on your software requirements, for selecting a microprocessor and other computer components.

Intel Microprocessors

Introduced in 1981, the IBM PC used one of the most powerful microprocessors available, the 8088 from Intel. The IBM PC quickly became the standard for business computing. Many sophisticated programs were developed to run on the IBM PC. Since then, IBM has developed faster and more powerful personal computers—all using the latest model microprocessor from Intel. Other companies climbed on the bandwagon, manufacturing personal computers that used Intel microprocessors. Each time a new computer was introduced, whether from IBM or another company, businesses expected the new computer to run the same software—only faster. Intel, in effect, was forced by its customers to improve its microprocessors and at the same time keep them compatible with older units.

Intel succeeded in producing a line of compatible microprocessors with ever-increasing speed and power. This family of microprocessors, developed by Intel and used in IBM and IBM-compatible computers, includes the 8088, 8086, 80286, 80386SX, 80386, 80486SX, and 80486. (With microprocessors, you can assume that the higher the number, the higher the performance.)

Software that runs on personal computers equipped with 8088 and 8086 microprocessors also runs on computers using any other microprocessor from Intel. Some earlier versions of Intel's microprocessors, including 8088, 8086, and even 80286 microprocessors, however, do not run some newer programs.

You usually can spot programs that work only on 80286 through 80486 microprocessors by reading the system requirements information on a software package or by taking note of the name of the program. Paradox/386, for example, requires at least a 386.

8088 and 8086

The 8088 has an 8-bit data path. Originally, the 8088 worked at a speed of 4.77 MHz, but current models also have speed options of 8, 10, and 12 MHz. IBM used the 8088 in two computers: the IBM PC and the IBM PC XT. Although the 8088 was fast when it was first introduced, the 8088 is slow by today's standards, even at 12 MHz. The major attraction of a personal computer with an 8088 microprocessor is its low price. You usually can recognize these computers by the designation XT—for example, the Laser Turbo XT.

Personal computers with 8088 microprocessors run many popular software packages, including best-sellers like WordPerfect 5.1 and Lotus 1-2-3 Release 2.3. Most MS-DOS programs run reasonably well on an 8088 computer, especially programs, such as word processors or spreadsheets, that deal mainly with text. Programs, such as paint programs, that use graphics tend to operate slowly on an 8088 computer. Even a word processor takes a long time to complete tasks like checking the spelling of a long document.

Some newer programs are designed specifically for more powerful microprocessors and do not run on a computer with an 8088 or 8086 microprocessor. Examples of these programs are Lotus 1-2-3 Release 3.1 and Paradox/386. Microsoft Windows 3.0, the popular graphical user interface for IBM and IBM-compatible computers, does not run well on these computers.

The 8088 and 8086 microprocessors were designed by Intel at about the same time (1978). Companies like AT&T and COMPAQ were the first to use the 8086. In 1987, IBM introduced the PS/2 Models 25 and 30. The 8088 and 8086 are similar in most respects, except that the 8088 has an 8-bit data path, and the 8086 has a 16-bit data path.

Two other microprocessors, the V20 and V30, were manufactured by NEC to compete with Intel. These microprocessors share the same limitations as the 8088 and 8086. Software that doesn't run or work fast enough on an 8088 doesn't improve much on computers with V20 or V30 microprocessors.

You should not consider a personal computer that uses one of these microprocessors unless cost is of critical concern. A complete 8088, 8086, V20, or V30 system including monochrome monitor, hard drive, and printer can cost less than $1,000. You can use a system like this for word processing, spreadsheet analysis, and similar tasks and for educational and game software. You may, however, experience long delays when working with such low-end systems.

Table 2.1 lists representative systems that use 8088, 8086, and similar microprocessors.

Table 2.1. 8088 and 8086 Systems

Microprocessor	*Computer*	*Bits**	*Speed (MHz)*
8088	IBM PC XT	8	4.77
8088	EPSON Equity I+	8	4.77 and 8
V20	CompuAdd 810	8	4.77 and 10
8086	Tandy 1000 RL	16	9.5

*Microprocessor has an 8-bit or 16-bit data path.

80286

The first personal computer to use the Intel 80286 was the IBM AT, which had a speed of 6 MHz. An advanced microprocessor for its time (1984), the 80286 still is popular. But in spite of its 16-bit data path, advanced features, and capability to work at speeds up to 20 MHz, the 80286 has become the black sheep of the Intel family. Computer programmers have had difficulty using the advanced features of the 80286.

Programs run significantly faster on a personal computer with an 80286 microprocessor than they run on computers with 8088 or 8086 microprocessors. The 80286 microprocessor can address more memory than can an 8086 or 8088 microprocessor. More sophisticated operating systems, such as Microsoft Windows or OS/2, or more sophisticated applications, such as Lotus 1-2-3 Release 3.1 Plus, have been developed because of the increased features of the 80286. This performance advantage costs more, though. Before you settle for a computer with an 80286 microprocessor, you may want to consider buying an PC with an 80386SX or higher-performance Intel microprocessor.

Table 2.2 lists representative systems with 80286 microprocessors.

Table 2.2. 80286 Systems

Microprocessor	*Computer*	*Bits**	*Speed (MHz)*
80286	IBM AT	16	8
80286	IBM PS/1	16	10
80286	Leading Edge D-2 Plus	16	12
80286	CompuAdd 220	16	20

*Microprocessor has a 16-bit data path.

80386SX and 80386

Although IBM was the first personal computer maker to use the 80286 microprocessor, COMPAQ was the first to use the 80386. The 80386 established COMPAQ's reputation as a leading supplier of high-performance computers. The 80386 (sometimes referred to as the 80386DX) has a 32-bit data path and runs at speeds as high as 33 MHz.

Besides being speedy, the 80386 microprocessor also is excellent at *multitasking* (performing several tasks at the same time). Operating environments like Windows and operating systems like OS/2 take advantage of multitasking. Using Windows on an 80386 computer enables you to load several programs into memory at one time and have them all readily available and working. While you are typing a letter, for example, your spreadsheet can be performing a long calculation. When the calculation is finished, you can move immediately from the word processor to the spreadsheet and then back again without having to quit or close either program.

The 80386SX, which was introduced by Intel after the 80386, is less powerful than the 80386. Like the 80286, the 80386SX has a 16-bit data path. Unlike the 80286, the 80386SX's advanced features run smoothly, like those of the 80386. The 80386SX and the 80386 are similar in some ways—the most important being the capability of the 80386SX to run any software designed for the 80386. The differences are that the 80386SX has a 16-bit data path, compared to the 80386's 32-bit data path; and the maximum speed of the 80386SX is currently 20 MHz, compared to a top speed of 33 MHz for the 80386.

The choice between PCs with 80386SX and 80386 microprocessors is often a matter of price. A manufacturer's 80386SX computer usually costs significantly less than its 80386 model. Because you can run the same software with both microprocessors, the lower cost can be enticing. An 80386 computer, however, usually has better all-around performance than an 80386SX computer.

COMPARISON

When you compare the 80286 microprocessor to either the 80386 or the 80386SX microprocessor, you will find the major difference to be what software you can run. A computer with an 80286 microprocessor can run programs designed to run on 8088, 8086, and 80286 microprocessors. A computer with an 80386SX or 80386 microprocessor can run all these programs plus programs specifically designed for 80386 microprocessors: Paradox/386, Q&A/386, AutoCAD/386, and Interleaf, for instance. These programs take advantage of the features of an 80386SX or 80386 microprocessor.

The 80386 and 80486 microprocessors have the capability to process data 32 bits at a time. An 80386SX microprocessor can process 32-bit data but accesses memory only 16 bits at a time. The 80286 microprocessor can handle only 16-bit data blocks.

Another difference between the 80286 and 80386 microprocessors is speed. The 80386 microprocessor is faster than an 80286 microprocessor for two major reasons. First, although an 80286 microprocessor can run at up to 20 MHz, an

80386 may operate at 33 MHz. Another reason is that an 80386 accesses twice as much data at a time. The 80386 accesses 32 bits at a time instead of 16 bits at a time, as the 80286 does.

Why is speed important? Graphics-based programs (desktop publishing or CAD programs) and large applications (spreadsheets or databases) require a great deal of processing time on a slow computer. For these applications, you need a fast computer if you don't want to spend large blocks of time waiting for your programs to work.

Table 2.3 lists representative systems with 80386SX and 80386 microprocessors.

Table 2.3. 80386SX and 80386 Systems

Microprocessor	*Computer*	*Bits**	*Speed (MHz)*
80386SX	IBM PS/2 Model 55SX	16	16
80386SX	AST 386SX-20 Premium	16	20
80386	Northgate Slim Line 386/20	32	20
80386	Dell System 325D	32	25
80386	COMPAQ DeskPro 386/33L	32	33
80386	Club American Falcon Series 3/40	32	40

*Microprocessor has a 16-bit or 32-bit data path.

8087, 80287, 80387SX, and 80387

Each Intel microprocessor can perform many different functions. Besides performing operating system tasks and input/output tasks, the microprocessor also performs the calculations that the program you are using requires. Even though a CPU is fast, the application you are using can be even faster if a microprocessor is dedicated to doing nothing but calculations. That way, while the main processor is performing tasks, specific math functions can be passed off to a second processor. That convenience is the purpose of Intel's math coprocessors, the 8087, 80287, and 80387.

The 8087 is the partner of the 8086 and 8088, the 80287 is the partner to the 80286, the 80387SX is the companion of the 80386SX, and the 80387 is the match to the 80386. These microprocessors are designed to perform specific math functions. The software must be capable of accessing these math coprocessors, however. And many programs are. For example, most spreadsheet programs, such as Lotus 1-2-3, Microsoft Excel, and Borland's Quattro Pro, can take advantage of the math coprocessors. In fact, some programs require the math coprocessor be installed; one of these programs is AutoCAD, a sophisticated computer-aided design program.

When purchasing a math coprocessor, you should make sure that the speed of the chip matches the speed of the main microprocessor. For example, if your computer uses a 16 MHz 80386SX, you should purchase a 16 MHz 80387SX. Purchasing a math coprocessor that operates at a faster speed will cost more without giving you the benefit of the greater speed, and a slower coprocessor will not give you the performance you get from a chip of the correct speed. Before you purchase a coprocessor, make sure that your software actually will benefit from the chip.

80486SX and 80486

The 80486 is the current top-of-the-line microprocessor in the Intel family. Several features give the 80486 a performance advantage over the 80386. One advantage is special circuitry to do floating-point arithmetic, a feature that makes the 80486 ideal for running CAD programs. By inserting a special 80387 coprocessor chip on the motherboard of an 80386 computer, you can achieve the performance, but not the speed, of the 80486.

Another feature of the 80486 is *cache RAM*, special circuitry that helps process instructions faster. Cache RAM provides a way for the microprocessor to anticipate the next instruction and minimizes the time needed to process the instruction. Extremely fast memory is built into the CPU, where information is stored. Rather than having a fast CPU wait for information going to or from RAM, the CPU can place information into or retrieve information from the fast cache. The CPU keeps working instead of waiting. The cache RAM feature is one reason programs run faster on an 80486 than they run on an 80386.

A computer with an 80486 microprocessor has a premium price tag. Manufacturers tend to load an 80486 computer with high-performance components. The price, therefore, often is much higher ($500 to $2,000) than the price of an 80386 computer.

To lessen the price shock associated with 80486 computers, Intel has released the 80486SX, a version of the 80486 processor with the floating-point circuitry disabled. Currently, the top speed of the 80486SX is 20 MHz, compared to 33 MHz for the 80486. Computers using the 80486SX can cost considerably less than those that use the 80486.

Just the fact that the 80486SX has the arithmetic circuitry disabled does not mean that you cannot use a coprocessor. Intel also offers the 80487SX chip, which is the companion of the 80486SX. The 80487SX is really nothing more than an 80486 with the coprocessor enabled. When you insert the 80487SX chip into your computer, the 80486SX chip is disabled, and the 80487SX chip performs the normal CPU functions and the math coprocessor functions.

If you want an 80486 computer and think that you will at sometime need math coprocessor functions, purchase an 80486 computer for two reasons. First, purchasing an 80468SX and the additional 80487SX chip brings the total 80486SX system cost to nearly that of an 80486 computer. Second, you get more speed from an 80486 computer, because it runs at a faster speed than the 20 MHz of the 80486SX microprocessor.

Find out whether the 80486 you are thinking of purchasing is an upgraded 80386 computer. Some manufacturers, including IBM, replace the 80386 microprocessor circuit board with a circuit board (called a power platform) that has an 80486 microprocessor. Other manufacturers design their computers to be upgraded. Rather than installing the microprocessor on the system board, the manufacturer connects to the system board a board that may have an 80286, 80386SX, 80386, 80486SX, or 80486 microprocessor. If you want to run your applications as fast as possible, investigate the design of the system board.

Table 2.4 lists representative systems with 80486SX and 80486 microprocessors.

Table 2.4. 80486SX and 80486 Systems

Microprocessor	*Computer*	*Bits**	*Speed (MHz)*
80486SX	ALR Business VEISA 486ASX	32	20
80486	Northgate Elegance 486/25	32	25
80486	COMPAQ 486/33L	32	33

*Microprocessor has a 32-bit data path.

AMD Microprocessors

With demands being placed on Intel to produce microprocessors, the company looked to other sources that could manufacture its microprocessors. Advanced Micro Devices (AMD) was one company Intel contracted to produce Intel-compatible microprocessors. AMD made good use of its experience and began making and selling Intel-compatible chips on its own. AMD has produced an inexpensive 80287-compatible microprocessor. The company gained notoriety by selling the chip for $99, while Intel was charging several hundred dollars for the same chip.

Of late, AMD has claimed even more attention with a compatible 80386 chip. Not only does this chip open an additional source for 80386 chips, a move that brought prices of 80386 computers down, AMD made its 80386-compatible chip to run faster than Intel's fastest 80386. The 80386 compatible from AMD operates at 40 MHz, while Intel's 80386 operates at 33 MHz.

This 40 MHz microprocessor may offer you the performance you desire, without your having to pay the extra price for an 80486 computer. Before purchasing a computer based on AMD's 80386, compare the price difference between this computer and an 80486 computer. If the price is less than a few hundred dollars difference, the performance advantage of the 80486 may be worth the extra money.

Motorola Microprocessors

Motorola microprocessors 68000, 68020, and 68030 are currently used in Macintosh personal computers. Like the Intel microprocessors, each new Motorola microprocessor improves on the speed, capability to handle information, and special features of older versions of the microprocessor.

The Macintosh Classic uses the Motorola 68000 microprocessor, which has a 16-bit data path that runs at a minimum speed of about 8 MHz. The Macintosh portable uses a 16 MHz version of the 68000.

The 68020 microprocessor has a 32-bit data path and runs at a speed of about 16 MHz. One important feature of this microprocessor is cache RAM built into the chip (similar to the Intel 80486). The Macintosh LC and some older Macs, such as the Macintosh II, use this microprocessor. The Motorola 68020 is competitive with the Intel 80386, although the Intel 80386 is more powerful.

The Motorola 68030 has a 32-bit data path and a current maximum speed of 40 MHz, a built-in cache RAM designed to process data and program instructions faster than the 68020 or 68000 process, and a built-in memory management unit that enables programmers to implement multitasking (running more than one program at a time). The Macintosh SE/30 uses a 16 MHz version of the 68030 microprocessor; the Macintosh IIsi uses a 20 MHz version; the Macintosh IIci uses a 25 MHz version; and the Macintosh IIfx uses the 40 MHz version. The Motorola 68030 is more powerful than the Intel 80386.

Because Motorola designs new microprocessors to be compatible with older versions, software that runs on the Macintosh Classic (the low end of the Apple line) also runs on the Macintosh IIfx (the high end of the Apple line). Because of this concept, users have a highly compatible upgrade path and don't need to purchase new software when they upgrade.

Choosing among models in a product line is a price versus performance decision. If you use desktop publishing software on the Macintosh, you are likely to be dissatisfied with the performance and features of a 68000-based computer like the Macintosh Classic. If you are using word processing, spreadsheet, and educational software, however, you may find the Classic quite acceptable—for a monochrome system. If you want a color system, the low-end Apple model is the Macintosh LC.

The 68040 high-performance Motorola microprocessor is not used currently by personal computer manufacturers. This processor is used, however, on accelerator boards that can be added to certain Apple Macintosh computers.

Table 2.5 lists representative systems with 68000, 68020, and 68030 microprocessors.

Table 2.5. 68000, 68020, and 68030 Systems

Microprocessor	*Computer*	*Bits**	*Speed (MHz)*
68000	Macintosh Classic	16	8
68000	Macintosh Plus	16	8
68020	Macintosh LC	32	16
68020	Macintosh II	32	16
68030	Macintosh SE/30	32	16
68030	Macintosh IIsi	32	20
68030	Macintosh IIfx	32	40

*Microprocessor has a 16-bit or 32-bit data path.

ROM

ROM (read-only memory) permanently holds programs needed to operate the computer. For computers other than IBM compatibles, you don't need to consider ROM software. No matter how many ROM programs exist and no matter how well the programs operate, you have to take what the manufacturer gives you. After you purchase a computer, however, try to keep abreast of the changes made to the ROM software and have your computer dealer replace ROMs with updated versions when possible.

With IBM compatibles, you need to consider only one question: Is the ROM BIOS compatible with the IBM's ROM BIOS? The *BIOS* (Basic Input/Output System) is software that handles communication between the microprocessor and components, such as disk drives and printers. Years ago, this question was important, but now the answer invariably is yes. Companies like Phoenix, Award, AMI, and DTK have been making IBM-compatible ROMs for many years and do a great job. You have to worry about a ROM problem only if you plan to buy an IBM compatible from a completely unknown manufacturer who uses an unknown ROM BIOS, or if you plan to buy an older (used) IBM compatible.

Checking the ROM BIOS for compatibility is difficult because problems, such as software not running properly, don't always show up right away. Most computer manufacturers provide specifications that tell you what company manufactured the ROM BIOS. If you don't see the information, ask about it.

RAM

RAM (random-access memory) is volatile memory. Anything stored in RAM—your latest budget figures, your sample chapter—is lost when you turn off power. Unless you have saved the information to a disk, the data is lost forever.

Because the price of a personal computer increases in proportion to the amount of RAM, you need to consider the memory requirements of the operating system, operating environment, and application software you intend to use. You can find this information by looking at the memory requirements listed on the software packages. Generally, the more RAM you have in your computer, the better.

Dynamic RAM is cheaper and slower than static RAM. In computers with high-performance microprocessors, you should look for some static RAM (many 80486 computers have 256K of static RAM). Static RAM is used as a memory cache. By holding frequently used data, a memory cache performs the equivalent of thinking ahead. When the microprocessor needs the data again, the static-RAM cache can supply the data much faster than main memory can. To take full advantage of the speed of the 80386, 80486, and 68030 microprocessors, you need a static-RAM memory cache. (Of all the Macintosh computers, only the top-of-the-line model has static RAM—32K).

When you purchase a computer, the system board has a certain amount of RAM. The chips used as RAM on the system board of a computer may be standard DIP (dual-in-line package) chips or SIMMs (single-in-line memory modules), shown in figures 2.7 and 2.8, respectively. To increase the memory in your computer, you must know what kind of chips your computer uses. Before you purchase a computer, you should ask about the type and capacity of RAM chips used and find out how you can get additional RAM if you want to expand the memory at a later date. A computer should enable you to increase the system memory to at least 8M of RAM on the system board. And the more RAM that fits on the system board, the better.

Fig. 2.7. *A standard dual-in-line-package (DIP) RAM chip.*

The following section describes RAM in IBM, IBM-compatible, and Apple Macintosh computer environments.

Fig. 2.8. A single-in-line memory module (SIMM).

Conventional, Extended, and Expanded Memory

Generally, in IBM and IBM-compatible computers that run under PC DOS and MS-DOS, memory is classified as conventional, extended, or expanded. *Conventional memory* is the first 1,024 kilobytes (1 megabyte) of memory and is made up of RAM and ROM. Computer specifications, such as "includes 640K RAM," refer to the first 640 kilobytes of conventional memory. This part of memory is where programs run (often referred to as the 640K DOS limit). The remainder of conventional memory is used by programs stored in ROM, data stored in video RAM, and in other ways. Typically, this area is not fully used.

Extended memory is RAM beyond one megabyte. Extended memory can be used only by certain computers (80286 through 80486) and by certain programs designed to use extended memory. A specification for 80286 through 80486 computers, such as "includes 1M RAM," means that you have 640K of RAM available for use as conventional memory and 384K of RAM available for use as extended memory. As the amount of RAM in the computer is increased, the amount of extended memory is increased.

Expanded memory is RAM that becomes part of conventional memory in the area above 640K. Large amounts of expanded memory can be made available to a program through a clever scheme that enables chunks of expanded memory to be swapped in and out of a small part of conventional memory. All IBM and IBM-compatible computers can use expanded memory, although not all programs can take advantage of expanded memory. Normally, you add expanded memory to an IBM or compatible computer by plugging a special expanded-memory board into an expansion slot. These boards should adhere to the Lotus-Intel-Microsoft Expanded Memory Specification Version 4.0 (LIM EMS 4.0).

Extended memory can be converted to expanded memory with an EMS emulation program. Usually, this software is provided when you purchase an IBM or compatible computer. If you don't know whether a computer manufacturer provides this software, ask about it.

The amount of RAM you need depends on the requirements of your operating system and application software. For example, an IBM-compatible computer running Lotus 1-2-3 Release 2.3 needs only 640K of conventional RAM. Certain versions of Lotus 1-2-3 and many other programs also can use expanded memory. An IBM-compatible computer running MS-DOS and software like Lotus 1-2-3 Release 3.1 needs a minimum of 1M of RAM. These programs may need even more memory if you create large spreadsheets. To run a graphical operating environment like Microsoft Windows 3.0 in Enhanced mode on computers with 80386SX, 80386, 80486SX or 80486 microprocessors, you need at least 2 megabytes of RAM.

Apple Macintosh computers don't suffer from the DOS 640K limit (these computers don't use MS-DOS). Therefore, you don't have to worry about conventional, extended, and expanded memory on these machines. You do need a general idea of how much RAM you need in the computer. For example, a Macintosh computer running System 6.0.2 and software like QuarkXPress 3.0 requires 2M of RAM.

The standard Apple Macintosh computers now come with at least 2M of RAM. The capability to have multiple applications open at one time requires that you have at least 2M of RAM, and 4M is preferable. System 7, Apple's latest operating system, requires at least 2M of RAM to run. A 2M System 7 machine operates like a 1M System 6.0 machine.

Expansion Slots and the Computer Bus

Unlike most other electronic products, personal computers are not limited to performing one kind of task. A personal computer can do many different kinds of tasks, depending on what software and hardware is added. To make sure that the PC you buy can do what you want a computer to do—now and in the future—you need to investigate the computer's expandability. Expandability depends on two factors: the number of expansion slots in the computer and the type of bus in the computer.

Expansion slots reside on the computer's system board. To expand a computer's capabilities, you insert an electronic board into an expansion slot. Generally, the smaller the computer, the fewer the expansion slots. When you shop for a computer, determine how many expansion slots you will need to provide the functionality you want. Some computers use expansion slots for serial ports, parallel ports, video monitor connection, and other functions. Other computers include these functions on the system board. A personal computer with only three expansion slots may be acceptable if many important functions are already built into the motherboard.

To get an idea of the number of expansion slots you need, consider some of the popular boards that can be inserted into these slots—FAX, MIDI (an interface to a musical instrument), modem, sound, joystick, scanner, memory, and high-performance graphics. Make a list of the applications that appeal to you; then compare your list with the number of expansion slots in the PC you are thinking of buying.

To help you with the list, table 2.6 includes some typical scenarios.

Table 2.6. Possible Expansion Equipment for Different Applications

Desktop Publisher	
Expansion 1:	Full-page monitor
Expansion 2:	Scanner
Expansion 3:	Modem
Expansion 4:	Fax
Expansion 5:	Memory
Small-Business User	
Expansion 1:	Modem
Expansion 2:	Fax
Expansion 3:	Memory
Expansion 4:	Bar Code Wand
Home User	
Expansion 1:	Sound board
Expansion 2:	Joystick
Expansion 3:	Modem
Expansion 4:	MIDI (for music)

A *bus* is the electronic roadway that connects the components of a computer system. Various bus designs are available for personal computers. The design of the bus affects the design of the expansion slots, which in turn affects the expandability of the computer.

When you purchase a computer, you should inquire about the type of bus the computer uses. Table 2.7 lists bus types for representative systems, expansion cards that can be used with them, and other information.

Table 2.7. Computer Buses

Bus Name	*Computers*	*Bus Width (bits)*	*Expansion Boards*
ISA (Industry Standard Architecture)	8088–80486 IBM AT compatibles	16	ISA
EISA (Extended Industry Standard Architecture)	80386, 80486SX, 80486	32	ISA, EISA
MCA (Micro Channel Architecture)	IBM PS/2 Model 50 and higher	16 or 32	MCA
NuBus	Macintosh II	32	NuBus
Processor Direct Slot	Mac SE/30, IIsi, LC	32	NuBus adapter bus SE/30 adapter

Many PC-compatible computers with 80386 and 80486 microprocessors have proprietary buses. A manufacturer designs a *proprietary bus* to give its computers features not found in the computers of its competitors. For example, the Hewlett-Packard Vectra 486 PC has a bus especially designed to improve the performance of graphics. A proprietary bus often coexists with a standard bus, such as ISA or EISA.

Proprietary buses have one major drawback. If a manufacturer decides to stop supporting the bus, you gain no further benefits from having it in your PC. If you are considering purchasing a certain computer model for the benefits associated with a proprietary bus, remember that you may become completely dependent on the manufacturer for new products and upgrades that support that bus.

The Macintosh computers generally expand differently from IBM-compatible computers. Although you can use expansion cards on some Macintosh models, most devices use the SCSI port. The SCSI port is designed so that you need only one port. You then can daisy chain one device to another.

Floppy Disk Drive

When you work with a PC, the information you type at the keyboard is stored temporarily in *short-term memory*, or RAM chips. As long as the computer's power switch is on, the RAM chips hold the information. When you turn off the power, however, the information is cleared from the RAM chips, and you lose it. You can also lose information accidentally if power is interrupted or cut off.

To avoid losing your information, you need to save your work before you turn off the computer. One way to save the information is to use a floppy disk drive and floppy disk. (The floppy disk drive also can send information back into the RAM chips.) Because you can send information to and retrieve information from a disk in a floppy disk drive, the drive is an *input/output device.*

Floppy disk drives for personal computers come in two popular sizes: 5 1/4 inches and 3 1/2 inches. These sizes reflect the size of the disks the drive uses. See figure 2.9 for a comparison of a 5 1/4-inch disk (a *minifloppy*) and a 3 1/2-inch disk (a *microfloppy*). A 5 1/4-inch disk has a flexible plastic jacket; a 3 1/2-inch disk has a hard plastic jacket. Disks of both sizes contain a round, flexible magnetic disk inside the plastic jacket.

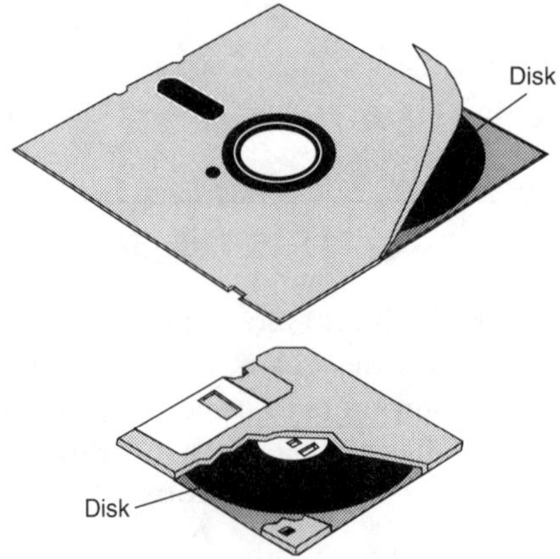

Fig. 2.9. *A 5 1/4-inch floppy disk and a 3 1/2-inch floppy disk.*

A floppy disk drive holds one disk at a time. Drives that hold the larger 5 1/4-inch floppy disks have a lever or latch that opens and closes the drive. You make sure that the latch or lever is in the open position, slide the disk into the drive, and then close the latch or lever. With the smaller 3 1/2-inch disks, you slide the disk all the way into the drive. To remove the disk, you push a button on the drive.

To use a floppy disk to save information that has been stored temporarily in RAM, you slide a floppy disk into the disk drive and issue a save command to your computer. The light on the drive goes on briefly, and you hear a whirring noise indicating that your information is being moved from RAM to the floppy disk. When the noise stops and the light goes off, you may start another task or remove the floppy disk from the disk drive.

To retrieve a file you have saved, you place the proper floppy disk into the disk drive and issue an open command to the computer. You hear the whirring noise again, and the light goes on. When the whirring stops and the light goes off, the information is resident again in your computer.

Floppy disk drives can be used to copy files from one floppy disk to another and between a floppy disk and the hard disk. Commercial software programs generally come on floppy disks and can be copied to a system's hard disk.

Floppy disk drives can be double (low) density or high density. A high-density drive can store more information on a floppy disk than a double-density drive can. High-density floppy disks are designed for high-density floppy drives and cannot be used in double-density drives. Double-density disks, however, can be used in double-density or high-density drives (with some exceptions, as explained later in this section).

For IBM and IBM-compatible computers, a 5 1/4-inch double-density disk can store 360K of information; a 5 1/4-inch high-density disk can store 1.2M of information; a 3 1/2-inch double-density disk can store 720K; and a 3 1/2-inch high-density disk can store 1.44M. (One kilobyte equals 1,024 bytes, or characters, of information; one megabyte equals 1,000 kilobytes.) The newest disk technology is the 3 1/2-inch extra-density disk, which can store up to 2.88M.

For Apple Macintosh computers, a 3 1/2-inch double-density disk stores 800K of information, and a 3 1/2-inch high-density disk stores 1.44M. Table 2.8 summarizes this information.

Table 2.8. Disk Storage Space

Floppy Disks	*Size (inches)*	*Double-Density Capacity (kilobytes)*	*High-Density Capacity (megabytes)*	*Extra-Density Capacity (megabytes)*
IBM &	5 1/4	360	1.2	
IBM Compatible	3 1/2	720	1.44	2.88
Apple Macintosh	3 1/2	800	1.44	

When you buy a box of disks, no matter what the capacity, you cannot use the disks until you have formatted them for your computer (unless you buy preformatted disks). On IBM and IBM-compatible computers, you format a disk by using a formatting command. The Apple Macintosh automatically detects an unformatted disk and asks you whether you want to format the disk.

Apple Macintosh computers use 3 1/2-inch floppy disk drives, as do IBM PS/1 and PS/2 computers and laptop computers. IBM-compatible computers use either 5 1/4-inch or 3 1/2-inch floppy drives. A 3 1/2-inch disk cannot be placed in a 5 1/4-inch floppy disk drive. Disk drive incompatibility, therefore, may prevent you from sharing data or programs with another computer user.

One solution to this problem is to install drives of both sizes in the system unit of a computer. Having two disk drives that can handle both double density and high density gives you four choices. Your choice of what type of floppy disk drive to put into an IBM-compatible computer depends on your needs. To share information or programs with an associate, you need a drive that matches the drive in your associate's computer.

Hard Disk Drive

A hard disk drive performs the same basic function as a floppy disk drive and works much the same way. The major difference between a hard disk drive and a floppy disk drive is that with a hard disk drive, you do not have to insert and remove disks. The disks, or platters, are sealed inside a metal case. The only way you see these platters is by looking at a photo or a figure such as figure 2.10.

Fig. 2.10. An internal view of a hard disk drive.

A hard disk drive is much faster than a floppy disk drive. Information that takes five seconds to save with a floppy disk drive may take less than a second to save with a hard disk drive. A hard disk drive has enormous storage capacity; a drive rated at 40M can store over 40 million characters. (Typical floppy disks store up to 1.4 million characters.)

> ***Note:*** Floppy disks are removable, so by accumulating piles of them you can actually store more information than you can store on the hard drive. You can also move a floppy disk from the disk drive on one computer to a drive on another computer. (Some hard disk drives have removable platters, but this type of drive is not common.)

Before you use a hard disk for the first time, you (or the dealer or manufacturer) must format and partition it. Information on these procedures can be found in the documentation that comes with the disk drive and with your computer's operating system software. If you don't have documentation or don't understand the manufacturer's instructions, you may want to consult one of Que's books, such as *Upgrading and Repairing PCs*, *Using MS-DOS 5*, or *Using Your Hard Disk*.

Most personal computer systems need a hard disk drive and a floppy disk drive. The hard disk drive gives the system speed and storage space, and the floppy disk drive gives the system flexibility.

Sometimes a computer manufacturer installs a hard drive as a standard feature of the computer, but usually you can specify the kind of hard disk drive you want. You need to look for several qualities in a hard drive. Among them are size, performance, and controller technology. The following sections explain these qualities.

Hard Disk Size

The size of a hard disk drive relates to two elements: the physical size of the drive and the amount of information the disk can hold. Hard disk drives come in three sizes: 5 1/4 inches, 3 1/2 inches, and 2 1/2 inches. Most hard drives are installed inside the system unit, but for a little more money, you can buy an external hard drive.

Physically, a 5 1/4-inch hard drive may be half-height or full-height. Height is measured in terms of the room the hard drive requires inside the system unit. A full-height drive occupies an entire disk drive bay in the system unit; a half-height drive occupies half as much space. If the computer is small and low, it probably accepts only 3 1/2-inch hard drives. Large system units normally accept only 5 1/4-inch hard drives. (To place a 3 1/2-inch hard drive into a large system unit, you must mount the hard drive on a 5 1/4-inch metal frame.) Some portable notebook computers use a 2 1/2-inch hard disk drive.

The storage capacity you choose for your hard drive depends on the programs you use and the amount of information you generate. You must consider the amount of space your programs use, the amount of space your information uses, and how long you want to keep your information on the hard drive.

As a rule of thumb, if you are purchasing the computer for home, a 40M hard disk probably will suit you. With this size hard disk, you can use a money management program, a small spreadsheet and word processing and database program, and a few games or educational programs. Especially if you select an integrated program such as Microsoft Works or Lotus Works, which combines several applications in one, a 40M hard disk will be enough. If you are planning to perform more sophisticated applications at home, such as bringing home work from the office, or to use graphics programs, a larger hard disk is better. Perhaps look at 80M hard disks.

For the office, again, the software you use will rule the size of hard disk you get. With spreadsheet, word processing, and database programs, an 80M hard disk probably will be adequate. If you plan to use desktop publishing or other higher power applications, you may need a 100M hard disk or greater. You are better off to buy too large a hard disk than have one that limits your work. But remember, the computer you select may enable adding a second hard disk for future expansion.

Hard Disk Performance

Hard disk performance is measured in terms of access speed and transfer rate. *Access speed* refers to the amount of time needed for the hard drive to find the information you need. *Transfer rate* refers to the amount of time needed to move that information from the hard drive to RAM or vice versa.

Access Speed

The fastest hard disk drives have an average access time of about 15 ms (milliseconds). A hard disk drive with an access time of more than 60 ms is adequate only if you use the drive in an IBM compatible with an 8088 or 8086 microprocessor. For all other personal computers, look for the fastest hard disk drive you can afford.

Sometimes a manufacturer claims that a particular hard disk has an access time lower than 15 ms. If you read the fine print, however, you will notice that this claim refers to an "effective" access time. This term means that a memory cache speeds the built-in action of the mechanical assembly of the hard disk. You can institute this feature yourself by purchasing disk caching software for your hard disk. (This software often is included in the purchase price of a computer system.)

Transfer Rate

How fast a hard drive moves information back and forth to RAM is called the transfer rate of a hard drive. The transfer rate depends partially on the type of hard drive controller, or interface. Macintosh computers use only one type of interface. IBM and IBM-compatible computers use several different kinds.

Advertisements for hard disk drives and controllers use the abbreviations MFM, RLL, ESDI, and SCSI. These terms indicate the data transfer rate you can expect with the drive-controller combination. If you want in-depth information on the different types of drives and controllers, refer to a Que book that covers this topic, *Upgrading and Repairing PCs*, for example. If you want to know how these items affect machine performance, see table 2.9.

Table 2.9. Hard Disk Technologies

Type	*Interface*	*Transfer Rate (bps)*	*Recommended For*	*Drive Capacity (megabytes)*
Modified Frequency Modulation (MFM)	S5-506/412	5M	8088 through 80286	20–80
Run Length Limited (RLL)	ST-506/412	7.5M	8088 through 80386SX	30–80
Integrated Drive Electronics (IDE)	ST-506/412 or other	5M to 10M	80286 through 80486	40–500
Enhance Small-Device Interface (ESDI)	ESDI	10M or faster	80386SX, 80386, and 80486	100 and over
Small Computer Systems Interface (SCSI)	ST-506/412 or other	10M or faster	80386SX, 80386, and 80486	100 and over

Hard Cards

A *hard card* is a circuit board with a hard drive attached. A hard card can be inserted into an expansion slot on an IBM-compatible computer. Hard cards are a convenient way of adding a hard drive to a personal computer, but they often are priced higher than conventional drives, and some hard cards offer no performance advantages. Hard cards can be useful for moving information from one computer to another, but any movement of the drive entails opening the system units of both computers, removing the drive from one computer, and inserting the drive into the other—not an elegant solution for moving data between two systems.

Although many manufacturers used to sell hard cards, they are not readily available today. If you need to upgrade an older PC and are interested in this type of hard disk drive, look for models sold by the Plus company. (These drives are not available for Macintosh computers.)

Removable Hard Disks

Some hard disk drives offer the same kind of convenience as a floppy disk drive—you can remove the disk from the drive. Naturally, individual removable hard disks are much more expensive than their floppy cousins. Removable hard disk drives are not widely used. However, users are finding the removable cartridge a good way to archive large files, such as database files or large desktop published documents. External removable cartridges, such as Syquest and Bernouilli, are becoming more and more popular. If you need quite a few cartridges, the cost per megabyte is low.

System Unit Case

Choosing the case that covers the system unit may seem trivial, but you probably will need to figure out what size and what style of case you prefer. Cases for IBM and IBM-compatible computers range in size from large floor-standing (tower) models to small desktop models. Some cases are regular height; some are slimline. The space a computer takes on a desk is called its *footprint*. The smallest desktop cases are just two inches high and can fit on a regular sheet of paper. Naturally, a system unit this size leaves little room for disk drives or expansion boards. A tower unit, on the other hand, can accommodate a variety of floppy and hard disk drives, tape drives, CD ROM drives, and expansion boards—all without taking up desk space.

If you want to purchase a computer with a small footprint, find out how the disk drives are positioned, how many expansion slots are available, and how the slots are oriented in the system unit. Very small computers sometimes have slots that hold expansion boards horizontally rather than vertically. You may not be thinking about expanding your system right away, but most people eventually add circuit boards to their computers. If you have a limited number of slots, or the orientation of the slots forces you to squeeze the boards into a small space, your plans for expansion may be squelched. Unless you have a real need for a computer with a small system unit footprint, a standard-size unit is better in the long run.

Monitor

A video monitor is the main device for displaying information to the user of a personal computer system. A video monitor is classified as an output device because it displays information that has been processed in the computer's system unit. Unless the components of the computer are in a single case, a cable from the video monitor connects to a video connector (such as the 9- or 15-pin connector shown in fig. 2.5) at the back of the system unit (see fig. 2.11). The Macintosh computer monitor cables have 15-pin connectors.

Video monitors differ in size, in resolution (a term defined later), in the colors displayed, and in the way information is displayed.

Most IBM-compatible personal computer systems use a video monitor with a 14-inch diagonal screen. The standard Macintosh monitor has a 13-inch screen, and the built-in Macintosh monitor has a 9-inch screen. The size of a video monitor can vary dramatically, however, from 5 inches diagonally to more than 20 inches diagonally. Small video monitors are built into compact computers, meant to be carried from place to place. Large video monitors are used for applications like desktop publishing, to display the entire page (or two pages) of a publication in readable form, and for group presentations. Unless you have a special application in mind, you should choose a standard 14-inch video monitor.

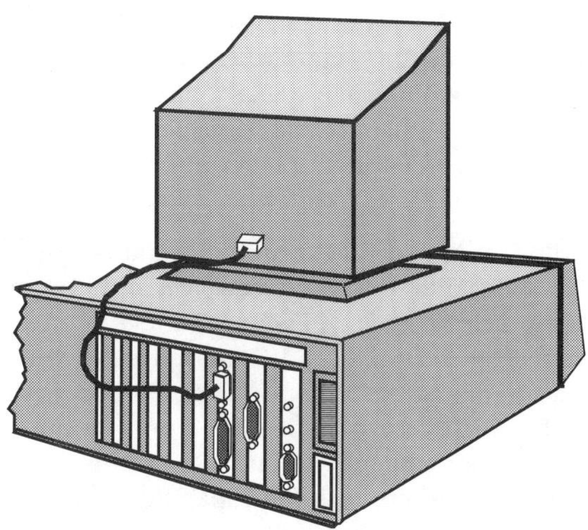

Fig. 2.11. The video monitor connects to the back of the system unit.

Video monitor *resolution* refers to the maximum number of individual dots (pixels) that can be placed on-screen. Resolution is given as a set of numbers, such as 640 × 480. The first number always refers to the horizontal resolution (the number of dots across the screen), and the second number specifies the vertical resolution (the number of dots up and down the screen). Generally, the higher the resolution, the sharper the display.

Computer video monitors are classified as monochrome or color. Monochrome video monitors usually have green and black, amber and black, or white and black displays. If you intend to use a monochrome monitor with an IBM-compatible computer that has no built-in video circuits, purchase a standard monochrome monitor and a Hercules (or compatible) monochrome graphics adapter, or purchase a VGA monochrome monitor and a VGA adapter (VGA is explained later in this section). The adapter fits into one of the expansion slots in the system unit and provides a 9-pin or 15-pin video connector for your monitor.

If you intend to use a monochrome monitor with an IBM PS/2 or PS/1 computer that has built-in VGA, all you need is a VGA monochrome monitor. If you want a Macintosh with a monochrome display, the logical choices are the Macintosh Classic and Macintosh SE/30; each comes with a built-in monochrome video monitor.

If you intend to purchase a color monitor for your system, you need to know something about color standards. IBM has set the standards for displaying color on IBM and IBM-compatible computers. Over the past decade, three IBM color display standards have emerged. The first of these display standards is CGA, which stands for Color Graphics Adapter. Typical CGA monitors are limited in the number of colors that can be displayed (16), and the number of dots (640 × 200).

Another IBM display standard is EGA, which stands for Enhanced Graphics Adapter. Monitors designed for this standard can display more colors (64) and have better resolution (640 × 350) than CGA monitors. A comparison of EGA and CGA displays shows that the alphanumeric characters on an EGA monitor are much sharper than the characters on a CGA monitor. This sharpness is a direct result of the increased resolution EGA offers.

The current standard for IBM and IBM-compatible computers is VGA, (Video Graphics Array). The major difference between VGA and EGA monitors is the way they display information electronically. EGA monitors use *digital*, or *discrete*, electronic signals to display information; VGA monitors use *analog*, or *continuous*, electronic signals to display information. A direct benefit of using analog signals is the number of colors that can be displayed on a monitor. An EGA monitor can display 64 different colors, but a VGA monitor can display an infinite number of colors. This difference translates into the capability to produce much more realistic images on the monitor. VGA monitors also have a higher resolution (640 × 480).

Super VGA is an enhancement of the VGA standard. Although not an IBM standard per se, super VGA is an accepted industry standard for IBM and IBM-compatible computers. Super VGA (800 × 600) has a higher resolution than VGA.

In 1990, IBM introduced a new video standard, XGA (Extended Graphics Array). The features of an XGA video adapter are described in Chapter 5.

If you are considering a color monitor for an IBM-compatible computer, you should narrow your selections to one of three possible monitor types: VGA, super VGA, or multiscanning. A VGA color monitor displays VGA only. A super VGA monitor normally is designed to display both VGA and super VGA. (This type of monitor is sometimes referred to as a multiple-frequency monitor.) A multiscanning monitor often works with any of the IBM display standards (although some multiscanning monitors cannot be connected to a CGA adapter) and with Apple Macintosh computers. Multiscan monitors display an infinite number of colors and typically have a maximum resolution of 800 × 600, but some of the better models go as high as 1,024 × 768. If you want flexibility and high resolution, a multiscan monitor is your best choice.

Some computers do not follow the IBM video-monitor standards. Apple Macintosh computers have built-in color circuitry or use color video adapters that provide 8-bit, 16-bit, or 24-bit color. (These numbers relate to the number of colors that can be displayed.) A typical 13-inch monitor for a Macintosh color computer has 640 × 480 resolution and can display from 256 to more than 16 million colors.

Further information about video monitors and video adapters is provided in Chapter 5.

The Keyboard and the Mouse

Although entering information into a PC usually is done with a keyboard, more and more people are using a mouse to supplement the keyboard. A keyboard is great for entering alphanumeric information, but a mouse excels at entering graphics into the computer. Both are input devices.

Keyboards vary according to the computer brand and model you buy. If you were to purchase a personal computer today, however, you would likely get a 101-key keyboard like the one shown in figure 2.12. When you buy a personal computer, you rarely get a chance to select the keyboard you want, except with certain Macintosh models. You may want to use the keyboard as the deciding factor between two similar computers. A few companies, however, such as Keytronics, specialize in replacement keyboards. If you want a particular computer but hate the keyboard that comes with it, you can purchase a keyboard from another source.

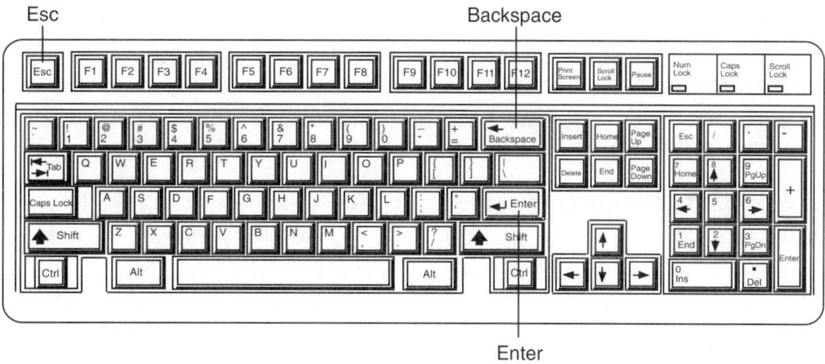

Fig. 2.12. *A high-tech 101-key personal computer keyboard.*

A mouse is a device with the look and feel of a bar of sculpted soap (see fig. 2.13). Set into the bottom of the mouse is a ball on which the mouse moves around. One or more buttons, located on the top of the mouse, enable you to do certain operations in an applications program. When you move the mouse on your desktop or mousepad, the cursor on the video display moves in a corresponding way. You use a mouse to perform operations that are difficult to do with a keyboard, such as drawing. In other applications, such as word processing, you can move the cursor more quickly with a mouse than with keyboard commands. A mouse is usually an optional accessory for IBM and IBM-compatible computers, but a mouse is standard fare for Macintosh computers.

The keyboard and mouse plug into connectors on the system unit. Keyboard connectors are various shapes and sizes, depending on the brand of computer, and may be located on the front or back of the system unit. You can attach the mouse to a mouse port or to a serial port. Some computers have labels or icons next to a connector to help you make the right connection.

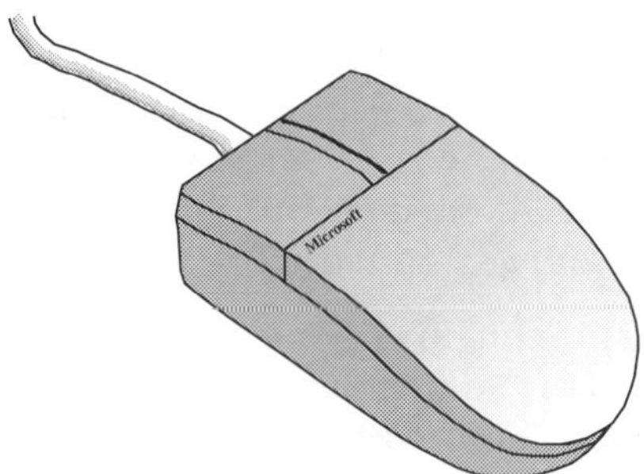

Fig. 2.13. A two-button mouse.

Because the keyboard and mouse are the primary ways to enter information into a computer, you should select these components carefully.

Keyboards differ in several ways: the number of keys, the feel of the keys, and the placement of the keys. The most popular keyboard is the 101-key keyboard. These keyboards offer more function keys and separate word processing keys, such as cursor-control keys, from the numeric keypad. Not all computers come equipped with this model, however. Some computers, such as laptops, just don't have room for 101 keys. If you have a choice, select the 101-key model.

Although keyboards may look the same, the feel of keyboards varies from one manufacturer to another. Some keyboards have a mushy keyboard action; some have a solid feel. Some click when you press the key; some are silent. Some keyboards have bumps on the F and J keys to remind your fingers where the home keys are. The feel of the keyboard is important. The only way to know how a keyboard feels is to try it.

Some keyboards have nonstandard key arrangements, especially for the backslash, Control, and Caps Lock keys. Remember that keyboards are replaceable items. You can buy a new keyboard from companies like Keytronics and Northgate. If you work on more than one computer, you should have keyboards that match—especially if you are a touch typist.

If you plan to use a graphics operating environment such as Microsoft Windows, a paint program, or any program with pull-down menus, you need a mouse. A mouse may seem to be an innocuous piece of equipment, but one model can differ from another in several ways: the number of buttons, the feel or shape, and the technology. Macintoshes use a one-button mouse; IBM and compatibles use a two- or three-button mouse. Choosing a two- or three-button mouse for a computer is a personal preference. The third button is used by only a few programs.

When considering the purchase of a mouse, place your hand on the mouse, roll it on the desktop or a mouse pad, and push the buttons to get an idea of how well the mouse reacts to your hand movements. Test a few different models before making your decision. Don't base your decision on other factors, such as price or software included with the mouse.

Although one mouse may look and feel different from another, most use a similar technology. An opto-mechanical mouse has a ball on the underside that rolls when you push the mouse. An alternative to this kind of mouse is an optical mouse, which has lights on the bottom and rolls over a special light-sensitive pad. You may want to use an optical mouse if you work at a small desk with limited space. Optical mice are not as popular as opto-mechanical mice.

Some computers, such as the Apple Macintosh, provide a mouse and a mouse port. Other computers, such as the IBM PS/2 series, do not come with a mouse but provide a port for the mouse. Most IBM-compatible computers don't provide a mouse port. For these computers, you must use a bus or serial mouse. A bus mouse comes with a circuit board that fits into one of the system board's expansion slots. A serial mouse connects to one of the serial ports at the back of the system unit. If you have a modem on your only serial port, buy a bus mouse. If you have no expansion slots but have an extra serial port, buy a serial mouse. If both a serial port and an expansion slot are available, the choice is up to you.

Instead of purchasing a mouse, you can purchase a keyboard that has a trackball set into it. Rolling the ball with your fingertips produces the same results as moving a mouse, with special keys acting as the mouse buttons. Another alternative to a mouse is a separate trackball, such as the one shown in figure 2.14. This device attaches to the computer the same way that the mouse does, but does not have to be moved. Instead, you roll the ball with your fingertips and press the buttons on either side.

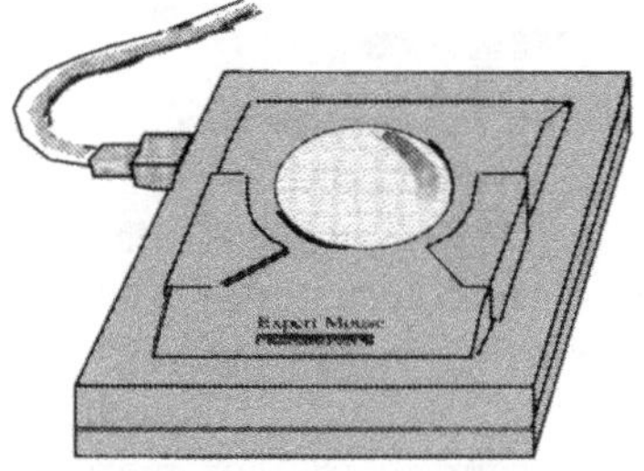

Fig. 2.14. *A trackball, sometimes used instead of a mouse.*

If you plan to purchase a laptop or notebook portable computer, you may want to consider a trackball that attaches to the side of the unit. The Microsoft Ballpoint Mouse is this kind of trackball. Keep in mind, though, that some portable computers have built-in pointing devices.

Understanding Personal Computer Software

Although the hardware components of a personal computer have the potential to do a great deal of work, nothing happens until you execute a program. A program is simply a series of instructions telling the microprocessor what to do with the characters typed on the keyboard or with information imported from the disk drives and what to display on the video monitor. Because a program is a series of instructions, programs are classified as software rather than hardware.

The following sections describe various kinds of software: ROM software, operating system software, and application software. Each type serves a purpose in making your computer run as smoothly and efficiently as possible. You need to understand what different manufacturers offer so that you can select the proper software for the tasks you want to do.

ROM Software

All personal computers have some programs stored in the ROM chips on the system board. ROM software is included with the computer. ROM programs start (or boot) the computer, perform diagnostic tests, send and receive information to and from the components connected to the computer, and do other technical tasks. These programs are a permanent fixture of the computer; they are not erased when you turn off the power.

In IBM and IBM-compatible computers, an important set of programs stored in ROM is the BIOS (basic input/output system—the instruction set that regulates all computer functions). If an IBM-compatible computer has a BIOS that duplicates the functions of the IBM BIOS, the compatible can run the same software that runs on an IBM personal computer.

Operating System Software

A personal computer's operating system software is a set of programs that perform essential computing tasks. Typical operating system tasks are to fetch information typed at the keyboard, to open and close data files, to terminate programs, to manage memory usage, to create files, to rename files, to delete files, and to format disks. The operating system—which is usually loaded into the computer from the disk drive but can be contained in ROM chips—acts as the interface between the computer and the person who uses the computer.

The MS-DOS disk operating system is clearly the most popular for IBM-compatible computers. (IBM models use PC DOS, an operating system almost identical to MS-DOS.) MS-DOS started with Version 1.0 but currently is up to Version 5. Using the latest version of an operating system is recommended but not imperative, although you definitely need to use a version of DOS more recent than 3.0. Digital Research (DR) DOS is a direct competitor of MS-DOS. DR DOS 5.0, the most recent version, offers some advanced features. For example, DR DOS 5.0 makes more memory available to run software programs, such as word processors and spreadsheets. DR DOS is compatible with MS-DOS. Other operating systems competing with MS-DOS are OS/2, UNIX, and XENIX.

With MS-DOS versions before V4, you have to memorize and type a command to perform a task. Although MS-DOS is easy to learn, it intimidates many beginners. With DOS 4, Microsoft included a Shell that enables you to perform several commands from menus. DOS 5 changed the Shell, making many more DOS commands available from menus and greatly increasing the user-friendliness of DOS.

Some computer software companies also have developed sophisticated graphical operating environments for MS-DOS. One of the most popular is Microsoft Windows. Microsoft Windows 3.0, the most recent version, uses small pictures (icons), pull-down menus, and on-screen windows to help people understand more easily how to perform particular computing tasks. With a mouse, you point to and click an icon to start a program or to indicate commands you want the program to execute. Figure 2.15 shows a typical Windows screen.

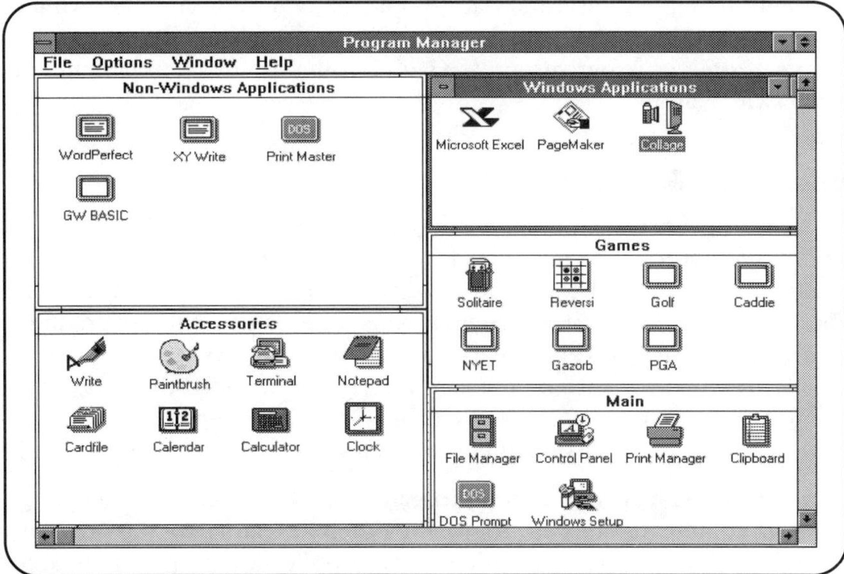

Fig. 2.15. *A Windows screen.*

Another operating environment similar to Windows is GEM. GEM is available for IBM systems but never gained popularity and is rarely used. Although Windows and GEM are the two best-known graphical user interfaces for IBM and IBM-compatible computers, some others are available. One is PC/GEOS. This interface currently works with a software program called GEO Works Ensemble. Another interface, ViewMax, is a graphical interface that works along with DR DOS 5.0. Not many software programs use the conventions of this interface. You lose consistency, therefore, as you switch from program to program. For example, you may have to work in one system with your word processor and in another system with your personal finance program.

The Apple Macintosh has always used a graphical operating environment. Judging by the success of the Macintosh, many people find this kind of interface preferable to a command-line interface like MS-DOS. The latest version of the Macintosh operating system software is System 7.0. This version includes the Sound Manager, a program that enhances the sound input capabilities of the Macintosh; true multitasking, the capability to run more than one program at a time; and other advanced features, such as on-line help from software manufacturers, TrueType fonts, and file sharing.

Of the many factors that go into purchasing a computer system, the user interface, which works closely with the operating system software, is one of the most important. If you feel more comfortable with a graphical user interface, any computer can supply one. Many of the most popular programs for IBM and IBM-compatible computers, including such favorites as Lotus 1-2-3 Release 2.3, do not use a common graphical user interface. Each program can use pull-down menus and supports a mouse. The structure of the menus from one program to the next is different, however. Programs written with a common user interface are much easier to switch among.

Application Software

Application software is a program or set of programs stored on disk and loaded into the computer to perform a specific task. Typical application programs are word processors, spreadsheets, paint programs, communications programs, and databases. Application software generally runs under a particular operating system, such as MS-DOS. You have to load the operating system first (done automatically when you turn on the computer) and then load the application program. A vast number of application programs that run under MS-DOS are available for IBM and IBM-compatible computers.

When you work with an application program, you must spend time learning how to give commands and how to use the different features of the program. Unfortunately, learning how to work with one application is no guarantee that you will understand how to work with another. For every application, especially those that run under MS-DOS, you have to repeat the learning process. Fortunately, more and more programs are providing pull-down menus, even in the DOS environment.

Operating environments like the one used by the Macintosh make learning to use a new application easier. Every Macintosh application presents a similar interface so that the user is comfortable performing basic tasks, such as saving and retrieving information. You still need to learn and understand specifics of the application, but many of the routine tasks of a Macintosh application are done the same way from program to program. Microsoft Windows attempts to provide this function for personal computers that use MS-DOS. Unfortunately, until all IBM-compatible computers run on the same operating system, you will find variations in program interfaces.

Application software programs come on floppy disks. If a computer has a hard-disk drive and a floppy-disk drive, the usual procedure is to copy the application software onto the hard disk drive so that the software is readily available for use. If you don't have a hard disk, using the application program can be difficult to impossible. Even if the program can be run from a floppy disk drive, you may have to switch disks many times to operate the program.

More information on application software and specific recommendations on what to buy are given in Chapter 11.

Chapter Summary

This chapter describes the components of a typical personal computer system—the system unit, monitor, keyboard, mouse, microprocessor, memory, floppy disk drive, and hard disk drive. The text explains the differences among microprocessors and tells how these differences affect computer performance. The chapter also points out differences among the other components—RAM, ROM, keyboard, mouse, monitor, hard drive, floppy disk, expansion slots, buses, and ports—and discusses the different kinds of software used in personal computers—ROM software, operating system software, and application software. The significance of these differences relates to the types of tasks you want to perform with a computer system. With the help of the information in this chapter, you can evaluate how what you want to do with a personal computer affects what you should buy.

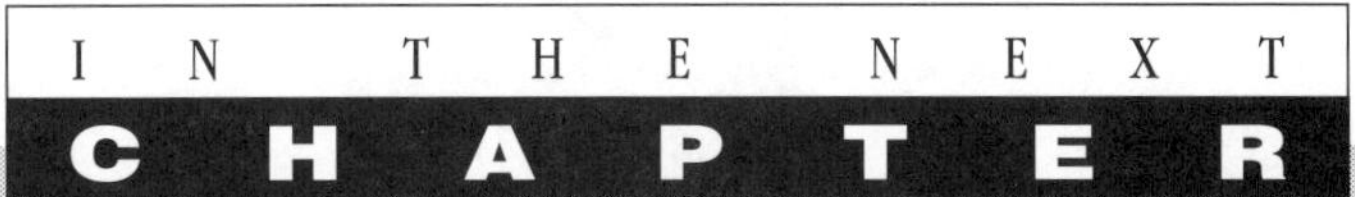

The next chapter offers guidelines for selecting a computer manufacturer. Chapter 3 explains the considerations when choosing a manufacturer—considerations such as available software, compatibility, performance, price, support, upgrades, warranties, and service.

PART II

Getting the Facts

Includes

Deciding What Type of Computer You Want

Listing of Computer Systems

Deciding What Type of Monitor You Need

Listing of Monitors

Reviewing Types of Printers

Deciding What Printer Model You Need

Listing of Printers

Deciding What Extras You Need

Determining What Software You Need

CHAPTER THREE

Deciding What Type of Computer You Want

IBM Corporation and Apple Computer, Inc., are well-known manufacturers of personal computers. If you have no limit on the amount of money you want to spend on a computer system, you can pick a top-of-the-line PC from one of these two companies and feel certain that you own a great system. This scenario, however, is not realistic for most people. You should consider products from a variety of manufacturers to find the computer that offers the best value for your money. In this chapter, you learn about different manufacturers. This information can help you choose the computer system that best suits your needs.

The criteria a buyer uses to pick a personal computer manufacturer vary from person to person. You may choose a company with a high level of support, or you may select a company with the lowest prices. You may want to purchase from a well-known manufacturer, although the computer costs hundreds of dollars more than a system from a comparable but less well-known company.

Issues of support, price, and name recognition are important, but you may want to consider other issues, too, such as how well an application works on a particular computer. For example, Apple Macintosh computers are best for desktop publishing.

This chapter presents computer-buying considerations, such as software availability, ease of use, performance, and price. Manufacturers are compared in these categories but not with the aim of choosing an overall winner. The goal of this chapter is not to recommend a specific manufacturer but rather to review the pros and cons of each so that you understand the manufacturer with whom you may be dealing.

Comparing Manufacturers

This book considers two personal computer types: IBM and compatibles and Apple Macintosh. Both personal computer types have their own software, operating systems, user groups, magazines, and so on. You need to pick one of these computer types. The type you choose plays a major part in determining what you can do with a personal computer and how well you perform your tasks.

This section is arranged to help you choose the best personal computer manufacturer for your needs. Consider the following categories before you decide on a computer type:

- Software availability
- Ease of use
- Performance
- Price

Try to decide which of these four categories is most important to you. Once you decide, you are well on the way to choosing a manufacturer that can satisfy your personal computer needs.

Software Availability

All computers mentioned in this book can run word processors, spreadsheets, databases, games, and so on. To run a particular software package, such as Lotus 1-2-3 Release 2.2 and 1-2-3 Release 2.3, however, you need to purchase a computer that can run that software—in this case, an IBM or a compatible computer. The software package you want to run often determines the type of computer you need to buy.

Some companies develop software that runs on more than one type of computer—for example, the spreadsheet application program Excel from Microsoft. One version of Excel runs on the Macintosh, and another version runs on IBM and compatible computers. Some of these applications (Microsoft Word and Excel, for instance) even enable you to transfer data between these two computer types. In such cases, other factors affect your decision about which computer type to buy.

Ease of Use

When you work with a personal computer, you give it commands—tell it what to do. Unfortunately, most personal computers are not designed to accept voice commands; instead, you must issue commands either by typing or by moving a device called a mouse and clicking its buttons. For the most part, when you type commands at the keyboard, you are working with a *command line interface*; when you issue commands by moving a mouse and clicking its buttons, you are working with a *graphical user interface*, or *GUI* (pronounced "gooey"). In general, the average person finds a GUI easier to learn and use than a command-line interface.

A GUI is easy to learn and use for a couple of reasons. First, it is consistent. Commands are always displayed along the top part of a screen or window. When you select one command, other commands appear in a pull-down menu, as shown in figure 3.1. You don't have to memorize commands, you just select them from the menus. When you start a program, the program appears in a window, as shown in figure 3.2. Notice the program commands along the top of the window. Other applications designed to work with the GUI exhibit the same degree of consistency. Therefore, you can learn quickly the basics of operating several different applications.

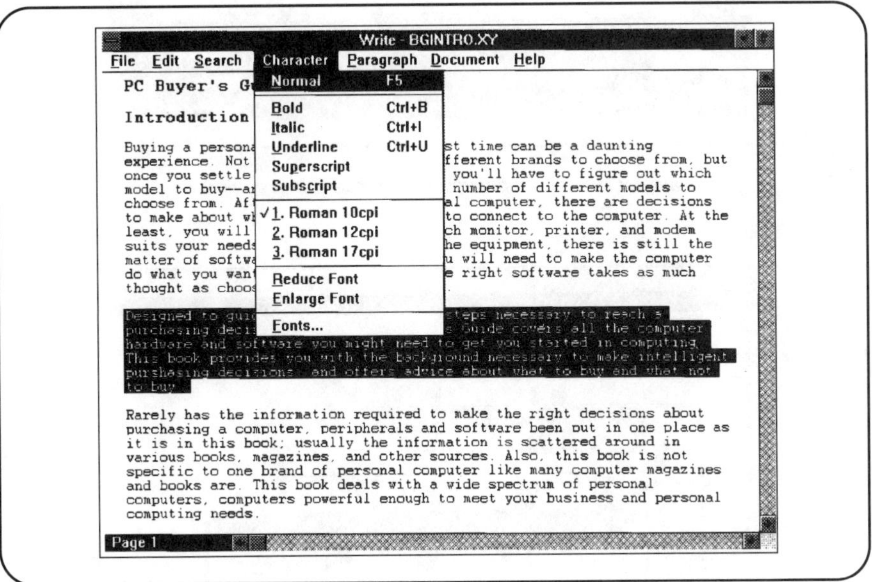

Fig. 3.1. *A pull-down menu of a graphical user interface.*

Besides being consistent, a GUI is intuitive. If you want to start a program, the screen usually contains a tiny picture (called an *icon*) of the program (see fig. 3.3). When you move the mouse, an arrow on the screen also moves. You point to the icon of the program, click the mouse button twice, and the program starts. In addition to using icons to represent programs, GUIs also use icons to represent many of the objects you normally find on and around your desk. (This practice is referred to as the *desktop metaphor*.) Depending on the GUI you use, you will see icons of file cabinets, file folders, trash cans, and other familiar objects on the screen. You certainly don't need a degree in computer science to figure out the meanings of these icons.

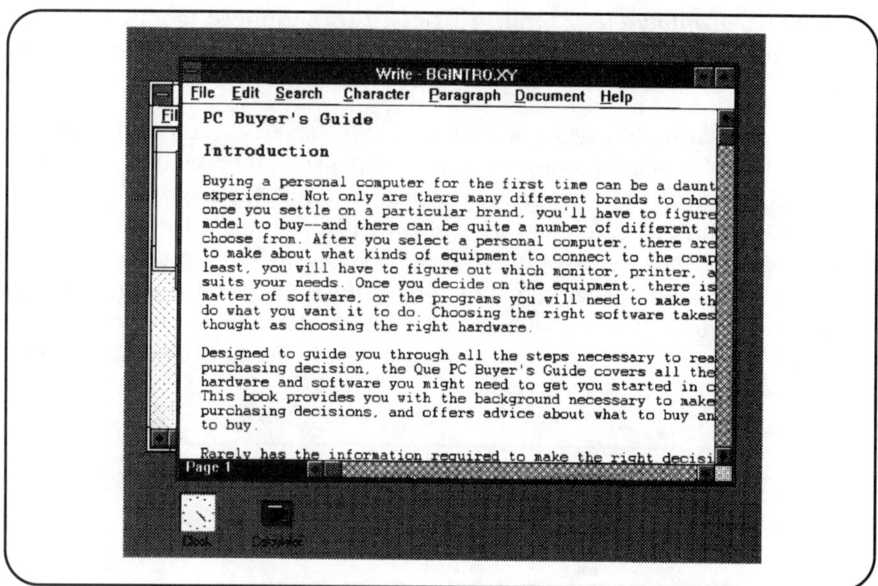

Fig. 3.2. A graphical user interface running a word processor in a window.

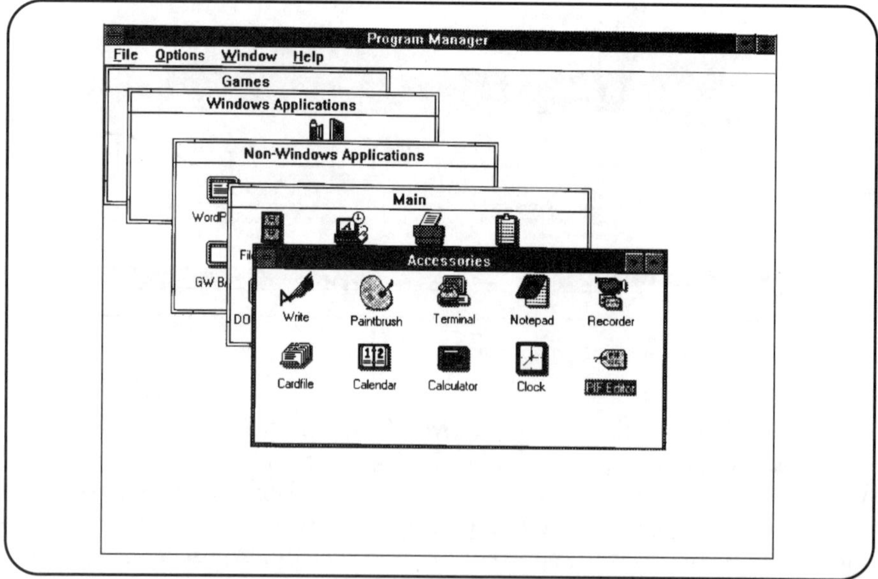

Fig. 3.3. A graphical user interface using icons to represent applications.

The Apple Macintosh comes standard with a graphical user interface. Most IBM and compatible computers do not include a GUI as a standard feature, but you can obtain one by purchasing a product like Microsoft Windows or Quarterdesk's DESQview.

Many of the most popular and more capable programs that run on IBM and compatible computers do not use a graphical user interface. The rules of operation vary tremendously from program to program. The way you operate Lotus 1-2-3, for example, has no relation to the way you work with WordPerfect. This operational difference makes transferring your skills from one program to another difficult. Soon, however, Lotus 1-2-3, WordPerfect, and most other major software packages will be Windows compatible.

If you plan to use your computer for only one job, such as word processing, an IBM or compatible without a GUI is as good a choice as any computer with a GUI. You can learn the rules of operation of that one program and not worry about other programs. If you plan to use several different kinds of software packages, however, consider purchasing a Macintosh or an IBM or compatible and a product like Windows.

Remember that the ease-of-use issue is highly subjective. Many people have mastered the IBM and compatible computers, learning the basics of its operating system, MS-DOS (or PC DOS), and the different rules of operation for all kinds of application programs. If you choose this path, you follow a well-traveled road.

Performance

Personal computer performance, as noted in Chapter 2, depends a great deal on the computer's CPU and its rated speed, which is measured in megahertz (MHz). Performance also depends on the speed of disk drives, video adapters, RAM, coprocessors, and all the other components that make up a personal computer system. Some companies cater to high-performance needs. Others do not. Most companies offer a line of computers with varying levels of performance.

If you are interested mainly in performance, compare the offerings of many different companies to see how much "bang you can get for your buck." If you make the decision to purchase a high-performance IBM compatible rather than an IBM PS/2 computer, you can save yourself hundreds or even thousands of dollars. The same statement holds true for components. Many companies make high-performance components for IBM, Apple Macintosh, and IBM-compatible computers. Often you can substitute lower-priced components for high-priced ones—without sacrificing performance. This flexibility can aid you in constructing a high-performance system at a reasonable price.

Performance is not just a hardware issue; performance is also a software issue. In other words, some word processors are faster than others; some spreadsheets are faster than others; some databases are faster than others; and so on. Before you purchase software, try to get an idea of how fast the software works. Software that is easy to use may not always work as fast as you would like. If you are considering a word processor, for example, watch a demonstration of how fast that program can do a job, such as replacing with exclamation points all the periods in a long body of text. If you need a database, find out how fast it can sort 1,000 names, 10,000 names, or any other job you expect of the software.

The performance of a computer system always should be uppermost in your mind as you try to sort out all the variables that go into making a purchase decision. A high-performance system will serve your needs better than one with lesser performance—no matter what the application may be. And by buying a "cutting edge" technology, you are protecting your investment from becoming prematurely obsolete. That is, buying a 16-bit 286-based machine knowing that most major software vendors are developing 32-bit applications means that your computer soon will be unable to run the newest programs.

Price

You have read about three suggested ways to compare manufacturers—by software availability, ease of use, and performance. Of the manufacturers considered in this book, just one makes a unique computer—Apple. The rest make computers that follow software and hardware standards established by IBM. If you use price to choose a manufacturer, compare the companies from this latter group. Purchasing a less expensive Apple computer because of its price doesn't make much sense if you really need IBM compatibility.

You definitely can use price as a guideline to choose among manufacturers of IBM-compatible computers. If you are in the market for an IBM-compatible computer, shop around for the best price. Buying an IBM instead of a compatible does not always mean that you receive a superior product, although IBMs may retain their resale value longer. Don't be afraid to choose a computer from one of IBM's competitors if that computer offers what you want.

Remember that other costs are associated with owning a personal computer. Although personal computers are reliable, you sometimes have to spend money on repairs and parts. Replacement parts for IBM-compatible computers usually are less expensive than parts for IBM or Apple computers. The costs are less because you can purchase the parts from many companies. The parts usually are interchangeable no matter what manufacturer originally sold you the computer.

Remember that price is most significant when you intend to purchase an IBM or compatible computer. Otherwise, the other factors play a greater role in your purchase decision. If you eventually decide to buy an Apple Macintosh, your thoughts about price should focus on what you can afford in the product line, rather than what a competitor may offer.

Reviewing Manufacturers

COMPARISON

This section covers most of the personal computer companies that have been around for a while and have established reputations. As each company is described, you will find that each one has strengths and weaknesses, and each company has unique objectives that it strives to achieve. Some firms excel at service and support; some offer money-back guarantees; and others concentrate on high performance. In the following sections, you can get a sense of what each company stands for so that you can decide whether a company's computer is appropriate for you.

IBM

IBM (International Business Machines) Corporation has been a standard setter in the microcomputer industry since the introduction of the IBM PC in 1981. IBM personal computers generally cost more than those from other companies, but in return, you get innovation, quality, and relative stability, although often not the highest performance.

IBM models fall into two categories: Micro Channel and non-Micro Channel (ISA) computers. A good reason to purchase an IBM computer is the Micro Channel architecture. (Micro Channel is an advanced circuit architecture that makes the computer easy to upgrade and also can enhance its performance.) Other good reasons to purchase an IBM are overall quality and the backing of a company that won't go out of business in the foreseeable future.

Some disadvantages of buying an IBM computer are the higher cost and lower level of performance when compared to the competition. A perceived disadvantage of buying an IBM computer is the price vs. performance issue. Some competitors offer computers that are equal to IBM in terms of performance but at a lower cost. IBM has recently addressed this issue with drastic price cuts. You can find more information about specific IBM models at the end of this chapter.

IBM computers are excellent general-purpose business computers. A huge number of software packages are designed to run on IBM computers. Many are industry standards, such as Lotus 1-2-3, WordPerfect, and Micro Channel dBASE.

You can buy IBM computers at authorized dealers, such as ComputerLand, Entre Computer Centers, and Sears Business Centers. IBM stopped selling its PC, XT, and AT computers several years ago and replaced them with the PS/2 and PS/1 computers the company sells today. IBM's entry-level computer, the PS/1 also is sold through department stores, such as Sears. IBM warrants its computer systems for one year from the date of purchase. In terms of service, IBM expects dealers to provide trained technicians and maintain a repair facility. The dealer also can provide on-site service.

Apple Computer

Apple Computer has sold personal computers since the late 1970s. Apple's initial success, the Apple II, gave birth to a line of computers that Apple still sells today (the II series is no longer Apple's major product line). But Apple is an innovative company, and in 1985, the company introduced the first reasonably priced personal computer with a graphical user interface—the Apple Macintosh. Today, Apple sells several different Macintosh models, which are described in more detail later in this chapter. Unlike IBM, Apple Computer has no direct competitors.

No computers are billed as Macintosh compatibles. To run Macintosh software and use circuit boards designed for Macintosh computers, you must purchase an Apple Macintosh or a product like the Outbound portable, which is licensed by Apple.

Because of its graphical user interface, the Macintosh is excellent for graphics applications like desktop publishing. As a high-performance business computer, the Macintosh is also a fine choice for word processing, spreadsheet, database, and many other applications.

You can purchase Apple computers from computer dealers, such as Connecting Point Computer Centers and The Computer Factory. Apple warrants its products for one year and offers an extended warranty program called Apple Care. Service and support are provided by Apple dealers.

IBM Compatibles

COMPARISON

Two categories of IBM compatibles are covered in this section: computers you can buy in retail stores and computers you can buy through mail order. IBM compatibles sold in retail stores are brands like Acer, AST, ALR, COMPAQ, EPSON, NEC, Tandy, and so on. Also, many stores often sell their own brands. Some IBM compatibles sold through mail order are Dell, Gateway, Northgate, Swan, ZEOS, and so on. Some companies that originally sold through mail order, CompuAdd, for example, now also sell through retail stores.

Separating one IBM-compatible computer manufacturer from another is a difficult assignment. To make this task a little easier, the following sections provide information on the goals, financial stability, and service policies of a number of companies that sell IBM compatibles. The sections also provide some general information about each company's product line.

Keep in mind that most companies whose products are sold through computer retail stores expect those dealers to provide service and support. Mail-order firms, on the other hand, handle service and support themselves or subcontract those services through third-party service agencies like Sorbus and Interlogic Trace.

Acer

Acer America (San Jose, CA) manufactures IBM-compatible computers that use ISA and EISA bus architectures. Acer maintains a low profile; you probably will have to call the company to find a dealer in your area.

Acer computers come with a four-month on-site warranty, which can be extended to twelve months or two years for an extra charge, and a one-year parts and labor warranty. Acer does not provide telephone support; you must depend on the dealer or a certified service center for support. If a customer brings in a computer for repair, the company follows up the dealer's service with a personal call. An Acer computer is a fine choice and certainly deserves careful consideration.

Acer was one of the first companies to announce a 486SX computer and has also introduced new lines of computers.

ALR

ALR, Advanced Logic Research (Irvine, CA), specializes in fast, high-performance PCs and sells them for less than most competing brands. You can upgrade many ALR computers, so you can switch from an 80386 to an 80486 CPU just by swapping a board. This feature enables you to purchase a computer for less money and later upgrade its performance.

If you are considering a high-performance computer from ALR, make sure that you purchase your computer from an authorized dealer who provides proper technical support. Computers on the cutting edge of technology tend to have more problems than older, more proven models. This situation occurs simply because it takes a little while to iron out all the "bugs," or errors, that occur in technologically advanced products. If problems occur, you need to have a reliable way to have the computer quickly repaired.

ALR is one of the few companies that offer an 80286 computer which is easy to upgrade to an 80386SX and then to an 80486 computer. If you don't want to buy a low-end 8088 model but cannot afford an 80386SX, an ALR Power Flex is a good compromise. ALR also was one of the first companies to announce 486SX support, and the company also offers ISA, EISA, and MCA computers.

You can buy an ALR computer through authorized dealers, such as Entre Computer Centers. To find an authorized dealer near you, you should call the company. ALR warrants its products for one year, and on-site service is available. Although ALR expects you to rely on a dealer for service and support, the company does provide a technical-support telephone number and a bulletin board on which you can find technical bulletins and other service updates.

AST

AST Research (Irvine, CA) made its fame with a circuit board called the Six Pack, which provided several expansion functions for the old IBM PC and XT computers. AST parlayed its success with this board into the manufacture of high-performance IBM-compatible personal computers. AST is an innovative company, with proprietary designs, such as the Cupid Architecture, that enable you to upgrade the CPU by swapping a board. Cupid Architecture is proprietary in that AST is the only company that makes Cupid adapter boards. Although priced lower than competing models from IBM and COMPAQ, AST still demands a higher price for its computers than most other compatibles cost.

You can purchase AST computers through authorized dealers. For customer support, AST uses authorized dealers, a nationwide network of authorized service centers, a 24-hour bulletin board system called AST On-Line!, and a toll-free technical-support line. AST offers a one-year warranty on parts and service.

Austin

Austin Computer Systems (Austin, TX) is a mail-order company that sells high-performance IBM-compatible desktop and portable computers at competitive prices. Austin offers both ISA and EISA computer systems. All Austin 80386 and 80486 models include Microsoft Windows 3.0 and a Microsoft mouse. Austin also offers ISA and EISA systems.

Austin offers toll-free technical support, a one-year warranty on parts and labor, and one year of free on-site service from GE. Consider a personal computer from Austin Computer Systems for a high-performance machine at an affordable price.

Club Computer Corporation

Club Computer Corporation (Fremont, CA) has been getting many good reviews in the press. Club was one of the first companies to offer an 80486SX computer when Intel announced the chip's release. Club's most notable system is its Falcon system. This computer is an upgradable CPU computer. Using this computer, you easily can upgrade from an 80386 25 MHz to an 80486 33MHz processor.

Club sells its computers directly. Club provides support for its systems and offers optional one-year on-site service agreements. You can contact Club through its toll-free phone number.

COMPAQ

COMPAQ Computer (Houston, TX) is one of the leaders of the personal computer industry. The company has accomplished several "firsts," such as building the first IBM-compatible portable computer and building the first personal computer with an 80386 CPU. COMPAQ also was a driving force behind the development of the EISA bus standard. COMPAQ specializes in high-performance desktop and portable computers that are well-designed and solidly built.

COMPAQ started a trend in high-performance computers for use as Local Area Network file servers when it introduced the SystemPro, a computer specifically designed to be a file server. The SystemPro can perform multiprocessing with two 386 computers, a 386 and 486, or two 486 computers. Many other companies have followed COMPAQ's lead.

Like IBM and some other major manufacturers, COMPAQ sells its computers at a premium price. COMPAQ computers are sold through authorized dealers, such as The Computer Factory, ComputerLand, and Sears Business Centers. COMPAQ trains and certifies authorized dealers, who offer customers support and service.

Consider COMPAQ if you want a state-of-the-art desktop or portable personal computer and can afford the premium prices.

CompuAdd

CompuAdd (Austin, TX) is a mail-order company that also sells products through its CompuAdd Superstores. CompuAdd sells, at competitive prices, a complete range of IBM-compatible and portable computers, including high-performance models. Because CompuAdd engineers and manufactures its personal computer systems, the company also can produce an innovative product, such as the 333T 80386 model.

CompuAdd has a toll-free technical-support number that provides service covering all the products the company sells. Additionally, the company has a 900 service number that provides PC information, advice, and technical help for non-CompuAdd products (free for the first minute, two dollars per minute thereafter). The company also has a program called Direct Effect, which enables you to call on a FAX phone and immediately receive specification sheets on any CompuAdd product.

CompuAdd products are backed with a no-risk, 30-day money-back guarantee. Products also have a 1-year warranty for parts and labor. If you have a problem with a CompuAdd PC, you can ship your computer to the company's Austin Service Center or take the computer to one of the Superstores. If any problem occurs in the first 90 days, CompuAdd will ship you a replacement part within 48 hours. If you purchase a CompuAdd 325, 333, 425, or 433 system, you get free on-site service during the 1-year warranty period, through Memorex/Telex.

Consider a CompuAdd computer if you want average to high performance at an affordable price. If a Superstore is in your area, you can drop in and check the system before you make a decision.

Dell

Dell Computer (Austin, TX) sells high-performance IBM-compatible desktop and portable computers primarily through mail order but also through value-added resellers. (A value-added reseller sells a complete hardware and software solution to a niche market, such as attorneys and doctors.) The company competes directly with other companies, such as COMPAQ Computer, by manufacturing similar products at significantly lower prices. Dell operates its own factory and maintains its own research and development staff.

Dell offers a 30-day, no-questions-asked money-back guarantee, a 1-year limited warranty on parts and labor, and toll-free technical support. Dell also offers one free year of next-day on-site service through Xerox.

Consider a Dell computer for high performance at a reasonable price and for the security of knowing that free on-site service is available.

DTK

DTK Computer (City of Industry, CA), a subdivision of Datatech Enterprises of Taiwan, was an early supplier of IBM-compatible motherboards and other components. In 1989, DTK started selling a complete personal computer through distributors. DTK has chosen smaller distributors to carry its product and refers you to distributors if you have problems. These smaller distributors do not necessarily sell through dealers. You will find DTK computers for sale in places like copy centers or business centers.

If you have a problem, you can call DTK directly, but you pay for the phone call. DTK also runs a 24-hour bulletin board service. For repairs, you take the DTK back to the distributor, who usually sends the problem computer to California for repair. Although the number of DTK personal computers sold is small, many other compatibles currently on the market are actually DTK computers on the inside. Consider a DTK if the price is right, but do not expect much in the way of service.

EPSON

EPSON America (Torrance, CA) is best known for its superb line of dot-matrix printers. EPSON personal computers, however, had a hard time getting off the ground. For a few years, EPSON tried to create its own unique computer—totally different from IBM, Apple, and other standards. Finally, EPSON gave up and started making IBM compatibles.

Today, EPSON trails only IBM, Apple, and COMPAQ in sales. EPSON computers are competitively priced, reliable, and easy to repair. Although EPSON does not normally try to compete on performance, some of its high-end models use the advanced EISA bus design. EPSON also manufactures a line of portable computers.

EPSON computers are sold through authorized dealers, such as ComputerLand, Entre Computer Centers, and MicroAge. The company also manufactures the Apex line of personal computers, which are sold exclusively in consumer electronics stores. EPSON depends on dealers for technical support and service—the company offers no telephone support. Consider an EPSON computer for average to high performance at a moderate price if you are sure that the dealer can support the product if problems arise.

Everex

Everex Systems (Torrance, CA) started out designing IBM-compatible boards and parts for other companies. Several years ago, however, the company decided to build its own brand of PCs. Today Everex is best known for its high-performance

STEP line of IBM-compatible computers and its new Tempo line of low- and medium-performance computers. All systems come with DOS, and 386SX and 386 systems come with Windows.

You can find Everex computers in computer retail stores, but the company sells its products mostly to value-added resellers. (A value-added reseller sells a complete hardware and software solution to a niche market, such as attorneys and doctors.)

Everex encourages end users to contact dealers or resellers for technical support and service. Everex also has a direct end-user support line. Everex has a one-year warranty on parts and labor and uses on-site service to make repairs during the warranty period.

Although finding a supplier may be difficult, consider an Everex computer for a competitively priced product that delivers average to high performance.

Gateway 2000

Gateway 2000 (N. Sioux City, SD) is a mail-order company that sells competitively priced IBM-compatible computers which use the ISA bus. The company includes a free copy of Microsoft Windows with all 386 and 486 systems.

Gateway uses high-quality components to make its systems. All 80386 systems come with a noninterlaced monitor that supports 1024 × 768 resolution. Gateway's systems also come with a mouse. The company recently introduced new cases for its computers and a new keyboard.

Gateway 2000 offers a 30-day money-back guarantee, a 1-year warranty on parts and labor, free on-site service from TRW, and toll-free technical support. The company also maintains a bulletin board for technical support. If you return a Gateway 2000 PC to the company for repairs, labor is free. Consider a Gateway 2000 if you want average performance at an affordable price.

Hewlett-Packard

Hewlett-Packard (Cupertino, CA) takes pride in manufacturing high-performance ISA and EISA personal computers. Hewlett-Packard is one of those companies that spent much effort during the 1980s trying to build computers that were technically superior but not completely compatible with the IBM standard. Like most of the other companies who used this strategy, Hewlett-Packard failed. It did, however, produce for IBM and compatible computers a laser printer that made Hewlett-Packard number one in that segment of the market.

Hewlett-Packard makes reliable personal computers, just as it makes reliable laser and inkjet printers. Hewlett-Packard also uses innovative design techniques to improve the performance of its personal computer systems. HP maintains a full line of PCs from SX desktop to 486 EISA Tower. Quality is second to none.

For this reliability and innovation, you pay a premium price. If you are interested in a personal computer from Hewlett-Packard, you should consult a dealer who can explain the high-performance features of these computers to you.

You can purchase Hewlett-Packard computers through authorized dealers, such as ComputerLand and MicroAge. Hewlett-Packard relies on dealers for end-user service and support. The company provides full training and certification to dealers and even travels to the dealer to service a PC if needed.

Leading Edge

Leading Edge (Westborough, MA), which is more of a marketing company than a manufacturer, successfully sold IBM compatibles in the mid-1980s. Early in 1989, Leading Edge reorganized under the protection of the Bankruptcy Court according to Chapter 11. The company now has merged with Daewoo, a huge Korean company. Leading Edge sells IBM compatibles at competitive prices. Its PCs use the ISA bus.

You can purchase Leading Edge computers at computer retail stores (call the company for a retailer in your area). Leading Edge offers a 20-month warranty on its desktop models and certifies dealers so that they can support end users. Consider Leading Edge if you are interested in average performance at a good price.

NEC

NEC Technologies (Boxborough, MA), an affiliate of Japan-based NEC, made its first major impact in the personal computer market with its line of multiscan monitors and remains a leader in this area. NEC also attempted to become a leader in the notebook portable market with its NEC Ultralite but was not as successful as the company was with monitors. Like several other large companies, NEC at first tried to buck the IBM standard by selling personal computers that were not completely compatible with IBM models. Now NEC's desktop models are ISA-based IBM compatibles that have a reputation for reliability.

NEC computers are sold through computer dealers, such as The Computer Factory. While the computer is under warranty, NEC service is excellent, but out-of-warranty service is expensive. NEC does most warranty service and repair directly through the mail. Consider a NEC computer if you want average performance and good reliability at a competitive price.

Northgate

Northgate Computer Systems (Eden Prairie, MN) is a large mail-order company that sells IBM-compatible ISA and EISA computers designed for above-average performance at affordable prices. Northgate manufactures its own computers and handles its own research and development.

Northgate offers a 60-day money-back guarantee, a 1-year warranty on parts and labor, free on-site service for 1 year through Bell-Atlantic, and 24-hour 7-day toll-free technical support. If a part fails, Northgate ships you a new one overnight at the company's expense. For an additional charge, Northgate warrants the keyboard for an additional five years.

Consider a Northgate computer if you are interested in a computer with high performance at an affordable price and if you want to take advantage of Northgate's special support deals, such as the five-year warranty on the keyboard and the technical-support hotline.

Packard Bell

Packard Bell (Chatsworth, CA) made radios in the 1920s and TV sets in the 1950s. Today, the company uses its reputation for dependability in order to sell personal computers, although this Packard Bell is actually a different company. Packard Bell sells IBM compatibles that use the ISA bus. These PCs compete in price with similar models from other companies.

Packard Bell computers are sold through computer retailers and consumer electronics stores (call the company for a retailer in your area). Packard Bell offers a one-year warranty on parts and labor and four months of free on-site service. For technical support, Packard Bell supplies a toll-free voice-automated hotline. Consider a Packard Bell if you're interested in a PC with average performance and if the model you want is competitively priced.

PC Brand

PC Brand (Chicago, IL) is a mail-order company that sells competitively priced IBM-compatible computers that use the ISA bus. The company offers a five-year warranty for all systems that it sells, free on-site service through TRW for its 80386SX, 80386, and 80486 systems, toll-free technical support, and a 30-day money-back guarantee. Consider a PC Brand computer for average performance at a competitive price, plus a warranty period that is five times longer than warranties from most other companies.

Swan

Swan Technologies (State College, PA), formerly called Tussey, is a mail-order company that sells competitively priced IBM-compatible computers which use the ISA bus. Swan offers a 30-day money-back guarantee, one year of free on-site service from TRW (an independent computer service company) for all systems except for XT models, a 12-hour toll-free help line, and a bulletin board. Replacement parts under warranty are shipped overnight without charge. Consider a Swan computer if you want average performance at a competitive price.

Tandon

A well-known and respected name in the computer industry, Tandon (Moorpark, CA) offers a full line of IBM-compatible computers that use the ISA and EISA bus architecture, as well as portable systems. Tandon's claim to fame is its disk drives. Many of the original IBM PCs were delivered with disk drives made by Tandon. Tandon has accumulated many patents on disk drive technology since its first patent in 1975.

Tandon sells its computers in one of three ways. First, you may contact the company through its 800 line to purchase direct. Second, national sales representatives are stationed throughout the country to service large customers. Finally, Tandon systems are available through value-added resellers (VAR) and value-added distributors (VAD). When purchasing a system through a VAR or VAD, you normally get a complete system, including application software. VARs and VADs normally are contacted when someone has specific needs.

Tandon's warranties are much like other manufacturers—one year parts and labor. Tandon does, however, offer on-site service in certain areas during the warranty period or under extended warranty contracts. If you are not in a Tandon service area, you must return your computer to a depot repair center, where the system will be repaired within three to five days.

Tandy

Tandy (Fort Worth, TX) sells its computers through a large chain of Radio Shack stores. Tandy was one of the first players in the personal computer market, with a PC called the TRS-80. Tandy did not compete successfully with IBM and Apple, however, and finally dropped the TRS-80 line. Tandy did have great success, though, with the Model 100 portable.

Trying to become more of a mainstream computer manufacturer, Tandy made the same mistake as many other large companies by selling computers that were not completely compatible with the IBM standard. Today, most of Tandy's desktop and portable computers are IBM compatible.

Tandy is one of the few manufacturers that sell a Micro Channel bus computer, but Tandy's line also includes IBM-compatible computers that use the ISA bus. These computers usually are priced higher than models from competing manufacturers, but Radio Shack stores often run sales that bring this computer's prices more in line with the competition.

Tandy is wooing the home market with its RL-1000 personal computer. This computer comes with DeskMate software, which uses a graphical user interface specific to Tandy computers. The RL-1000 is a typical Tandy offering—a computer that costs 30 to 40 percent more than its competitors. Unlike the high-priced low-end models, the Tandy Micro Channel computer is actually a lower cost alternative to a comparable IBM PS/2 model. Keep in mind, however, that your local Radio Shack store does not carry this model—it is sold at Radio Shack/ Tandy Computer Centers.

Tandy offers a one-year warranty on parts and labor. If a computer needs repair, you can return it to the store, which may provide on-site repair, or you can send the computer to a Tandy service center. Tandy also has a technical support line, but it is not toll free.

Texas Instruments (TI)

Shortly after IBM introduced the IBM PC, Texas Instruments (Austin, TX) released a similar model that was technically superior in some ways. TI's computer was not completely compatible with the IBM PC, however. The incompatibilities caused TI's first personal computer to be relatively short-lived. Today, TI's most successful computers are its notebook portables (see Chapter 12 for more information on notebook portables). You may purchase TI computers through established dealers. Warranty repair also is provided through the dealer. Call TI to find the dealer in your area.

Toshiba

Toshiba (Irvine, CA) offers a wide variety of laptop and notebook computers and color portables. Although Toshiba's T1000 Plus and T1000 models are the most popular laptops on the market, the company faces stiff competition in the laptop and notebook portable arena today.

Toshiba's computers are sold through mail-order suppliers as well as retail dealers. Service, including Toshiba's one-year warranty, also is provided through the dealer.

Wyse

Wyse Technology (San Jose, CA) has always been better known for its terminals than for its personal computer products. Wyse traditionally has built attractively designed IBM compatibles that use the ISA bus. The company was acquired in January 1990 by Channel International, a consortium of investors from Taiwan, and today Wyse is undergoing a period of transition. At the time of this writing, the company is preparing to announce several new products and changes in the way it supports end users.

Wyse sells its products to distributors who sell to end users or to computer dealers. Wyse dealers, however, can be difficult to locate. Consider a Wyse if you can find a dealer in your area and if you are interested in attractively designed computers with average performance.

Zenith

Zenith Data Systems (Mt. Prospect, IL) is a subsidiary of the French company, Groupe Bull. Zenith made its name in the portable computer market in the late 1980s but also sells high-performance desktop models. Zenith's desktop

80386SX and 80386 models include Microsoft Windows and the Microsoft mouse. Because Zenith doesn't compete on price, expect to pay more for its desktop models than you would pay for some competing brands. Zenith portables, on the other hand, offer excellent performance at competitive prices.

Zenith sells computers through authorized dealers (call the company for a dealer in your area). Zenith provides service and support through authorized dealers and offers a toll-free number and a bulletin board for technical support. Consider a Zenith desktop or portable system if you want a high-performance, brand-name personal computer.

ZEOS

ZEOS International (St. Paul, MN) is a large mail-order company that sells high-performance IBM compatibles at affordable prices. The company maintains a research and development staff and has its own manufacturing facilities. The company's attention to detail enhances the quality of its products. For example, if you order a monochrome system, it comes with a genuine Hercules adapter, not a compatible adapter card. In some systems, ZEOS adds a second cooling fan to improve system reliability.

ZEOS backs its computers with a no-questions-asked 30-day money-back guarantee, a 1-year warranty, and a 24-hour 7-days-a-week technical support line. The company also maintains the ZEOS bulletin board. Consider ZEOS if a high-performance computer at an affordable price interests you.

Other Manufacturers

Many more companies sell IBM-compatible computers than can be mentioned in this book. Some companies sell through dealers; others sell through mail order. All these companies sell basically the same kind of computer with little technical twists here and there. Finding distinctions among them is hard but not impossible. Always ask a company to explain what sets its computers apart from the crowd. The differences are found mainly in technical features, service, support, price, and financing methods. You also may find differences in the competence of the sales and support staffs. No matter what company you consider, you must evaluate your selection based on the criteria that are important to you.

Reviewing Your Choices

By now you should have an idea of the kind of computer you intend to buy. If not, this short review should help you crystallize your ideas. First, you need to settle on a manufacturer. You should choose IBM, Apple, or one of the many companies that sell IBM compatibles.

If you select an IBM or compatible computer maker, you need to decide what CPU and speed you want. The following list shows the choices available (at the time of this writing) for IBM and compatible computers:

CPU	*Speed (MHz)*
8088 (or V20)	4.77, 8, 10, or 12
8086 (or V30)	8, 10, or 12
80286	8, 10, 12.5, 16, or 20
80386SX	16 or 20
80386	16, 20, 25, 33, or 40
80486SX	20
80486	25, 33, or 50

If you choose Apple, you need to select the CPU and speed from a different CPU family. The following list shows what is available (at the time of this writing) for Apple computers:

CPU	*Speed (MHz)*
68000	8 or 16
68020	16
68030	20, 25, or 40

Keep in mind that the higher the CPU number and the faster the speed, the more expensive the computer and the better the performance. As for Apple computers, expect to see a System released based on the 68040 microprocessor.

Selecting a Video Adapter

Another important consideration is the video adapter. This circuit board generates the computer's video signals. For some computers, the video circuits are built into the system board, for example, the IBM PS/2 and PS/1 computers and some Macintosh computers. All portable computers also come with built-in video circuits. If you intend to purchase an IBM-compatible computer, you need to select the type of video adapter you want. The following list shows some of the choices:

Monochrome system

Hercules monochrome graphics adapter
Hercules compatible monochrome graphics adapter
Enhanced Graphics Adapter (EGA)
Video Graphics Array (VGA) adapter
Super VGA adapter
Extended Graphics Array (XGA) adapter

Color system

Color Graphics Adapter (CGA)
Enhanced Graphics Adapter (EGA)
Video Graphics Array (VGA) adapter
Super VGA adapter
Extended Graphics Array (XGA) adapter

Notice that an EGA, VGA, Super VGA, or XGA adapter can provide a monochrome and a color display. The VGA, Super VGA, and XGA adapters, however, require fewer changes of switches between a monochrome and color monitor than does the EGA adapter.

Your choice of video adapter can affect your choice of a monitor. Certain adapters work only with certain monitors. One exception is a multiscan monitor. These monitors often work with all the IBM video standards. If you don't choose a multiscan monitor, you have the following choices:

Video Adapter	*Video Monitor*
Hercules monochrome graphics	Digital monochrome monitor
Hercules compatible	Digital monochrome monitor monochrome graphics
CGA	CGA color monitor
EGA	EGA color monitor/digital monochrome monitor
VGA	VGA color or monochrome monitor
Super VGA	Super VGA color or monochrome or multiscanning monitor

Of the Macintosh models available at this writing, only the IIfx lacks built-in video. The IIfx requires that you select a video adapter to meet your needs. Even Macintoshes with built-in video do not have just one video option. Macintoshes that support multiple video modes adapt to the resolution of the monitor you attach to the computer. The following list outlines your Apple video options:

Monochrome

512 × 384 pixel resolution
640 × 480 pixel resolution
640 × 870 pixel resolution (portrait display)
1152 × 870 pixel resolution (two-page display)

Color

512 × 384 pixel resolution
640 × 480 pixel resolution

The Macintosh Classic and SE/30, with built-in 9-inch monitors, support only the 512 × 384 monochrome video mode. A major difference between these two models is the SE/30's internal expansion slot. This slot lets you add a video adapter that supports a large-screen external monitor. The LC, IIsi, and IIci support the 512 × 384 and 640 × 480 monochrome and color modes. In addition, the IIsi and IIci can support the 640 × 870 portrait display. The portrait display enables you to view an entire page—a nice feature for desktop publishing.

Apple also offers an 8/24-bit color adapter. You can use this adapter with any of the monitors listed previously. You get the most benefit from this video card with a portrait or a two-page display, however. A 24-bit adapter contains more memory than an 8-bit adapter, so the computer can show a larger array of colors and greater resolution. Apple's 8/24-bit video adapter can be used in the IIfx, IIsi, and IIci. Apple also offers a 24-bit video card, the 8/24 GC, with an accelerator built on it. This accelerator speeds the processing of the video image.

Of course, Apple is not the only manufacturer of video adapters. Before you select a Macintosh, determine your needs and then choose the video card that best meets your requirements.

Deciding How Much Memory

The next issue to consider is memory, or RAM. Most computers come with a sufficient amount of RAM to get you started. You should consider, however, the memory requirements of the applications and operating system at the time of purchase. After you use your computer for a while, you may find that you need more RAM—for example, if you are building a large spreadsheet and your computer informs you that you are out of memory. Be sure to ask, before you buy a computer, how to add RAM in case you want to do the job yourself.

Selecting a Hard Drive

To round out your computer system, you should consider a hard disk drive. In most cases, computer manufacturers offer a choice of sizes (from 20 megabytes to more than 600 megabytes). Some IBM-compatible computer manufacturers also offer a choice of hard disk drive type. The following are the choices:

MFM (Modified Frequency Modulation)

RLL (Run-Length Limited)

IDE (Integrated Device Electronics)

ESDI (Enhanced Small Device Interface)

SCSI (Small Computer Systems Interface)

ESDI and SCSI drives, which are used with 80386 and 80486 IBM and compatible computers, are usually high-performance, high-capacity drives. IDE drives are used in many IBM-compatible systems because of these drives' excellent performance and their affordable cost. SCSI drives are used with all Macintosh systems. Therefore, SCSI drives for the Macintosh are not necessarily the high-performance, high-capacity models used with IBM and compatible computers.

Selecting a Manufacturer

If you are interested in an IBM or compatible computer, you need to focus your attention on a particular CPU and speed as a starting point for comparison shopping. For example, to compare different manufacturers' 80386SX offerings is better than to compare one manufacturer's 80286 to another's 80386 model. For example, an IBM PS/2 Model 55SX should be compared with an AST 386SX Premium. After you compare, you can take into account the other factors: video adapter, video monitor, RAM, and disk drives.

Finally, ask about the *architecture*, or design, of the computer: ISA, Micro Channel, EISA, or proprietary. The architecture of a personal computer can affect its overall performance. Advanced architectures, such as Micro Channel and EISA, however, significantly increase the cost of a system.

After you narrow the selection to a few models, you are ready to consider several other factors. One factor is expandability. You can increase the functionality of your system by adding new circuit boards. If a system has only one or two expansion slots, expandability is limited; you may not be able to add capabilities to your system, such as a FAX or scanner, for example.

Another factor to consider is the documentation that comes with a system. Some manufacturers offer sparse documentation, and others offer well-written and thorough guides to help you to become proficient with your system. Finally, many manufacturers and dealers offer special deals. One company may bundle a top-quality software package, such as Lotus 1-2-3 Release 3.1, with a system. Another company may offer a rebate of several hundred dollars. These factors can sway your final purchase decision.

Selecting a Model

When you shop for a personal computer, not only do you need to compare models from different manufacturers, you also need to compare different models within a manufacturer's line. Because IBM and Apple personal computers are two of the top brands used in business, an examination of each firm's product lines can illuminate this comparison.

Regardless of the model you select, consider the following pairs of questions:

- Is the microprocessor the capacity and speed I need or will need as software advances? Or will the processor limit me?
- Does the computer let me add drives? Or is there no room to add another drive?
- Can I increase memory on the main system board? Or must I purchase an additional expansion board to add memory?

- Does the computer have enough expansion slots to add adapter cards I need or want? Or will I have to sacrifice expansion?
- Am I comfortable with the service offered for my model? Or does another model have a better service plan?
- Is this model a good dollar-for-performance investment? Or is the next model up more power for not much more money?

If you can answer yes to the first of each set of questions, the model you are considering is probably a good selection for you. If, however, you answer yes to the second question of each or most sets, select another model.

IBM Models

IBM no longer sells or produces its PC, XT, and AT computers. Today, the company markets two lines of computers: the PS/2 and PS/1.

COMPARISON

The IBM PS/2 product line is divided neatly into two categories, according to the design of the internal bus: industry standard architecture (ISA) or Micro Channel architecture. PS/2 computers with an ISA bus are the Model 25, Model 25-286, and Model 30-286. Models 25 and 25-286 differ from Model 30-286 in terms of size and expandability (two expansion slots versus three expansion slots); the Model 25 differs from the 25-286 and 30-286 in terms of CPU (8086 versus 80286). The built-in video for Model 25 is called MCGA (or MultiColor Graphics Array), which can be considered an enhanced version of the CGA standard.

IBM's PS/2 computers that have a Micro Channel bus are the Model 55SX, Models 70-386 and 70-486, Model 80-386, Model 90 XP 486SX, Model 90 XP 486, Model 95 XP 486, Model 35, Model 40, and Model 57. These models differ in CPU and speed, as well as other features. Some PS/2s are designed to sit on a desktop, and others are floor-standing (tower) models. Table 3.1 describes the features of the various IBM models.

IBM's newest Micro Channel computers (as of this writing) are three PS/2 Models: 90 XP 486 SX, 90 XP 486, and 95 XP 486. These computers incorporate a new graphics standard from IBM, called XGA. This standard offers higher resolution and more colors and works significantly faster than IBM's older graphics standard, VGA. (XGA also is available as an option for other Micro Channel computers.) The desktop PS/2 Model 90 XP 486SX and PS/2 Model 90 XP 486 and the floor-standing PS/2 Model 95 XP 486 are worth your consideration, but be advised that the suggested retail prices of these computers top $8,000, $12,000 and $14,000, respectively.

Table 3.1. IBM Personal Computer Product Line

CPU	*Bus*	*Speed*	*Video*		*Expansion Slots*	*Style*
Low-end models						
PS/1	80286	10 MHz	Proprietary	VGA	3	Desktop
PS/2 Model 25	8086	8 MHz	ISA	MCGA	2	Desktop
PS/2 Model 25-286	8086	10 MHz	ISA	VGA	2	Desktop
PS/2 Model 30-286	80286	10 MHz	ISA	VGA	3	Desktop
PS/2 Model 35	80386SX	20 MHz	ISA	VGA	3	Desktop
Mid-range models						
PS/2 Model 40SX	80386SX	20	ISA	VGA	3	Desktop
PS/2 Model 55SX	80386SX	16 MHz	Micro Channel	VGA	3	Desktop
PS/2 Model 57SX	80386SX	20 Mhz	Micro Channel	VGA	5	Desktop
PS/2 Model 70-386	80386	20/25 MHz	Micro Channel	VGA	3	Desktop
PS/2 Model 80-386	80386	20/25 MHz	Micro Channel	VGA	7	Floor standing
High-end models						
PS/2 Model 90 XP	486SX 80486SX	20 MHz	Micro Channel	XGA	3	Desktop
PS/2 Model 90 XP	486 80486	25/33 MHz	Micro Channel	XGA	3	Desktop
PS/2 Model 95 XP	486 80486	25/33 MHz	Micro Channel	XGA	6	Floor standing
Portable models						
PS/2 Model L40 SX	80386SX	20 MHz	Micro Channel	VGA	0	Laptop
PS/2 Model P70 386	80386	20 MHz	Micro Channel	VGA	2	Luggable
PS/2 Model P75 486	80486	33 MHz	Micro Channel	XGA	4	Luggable

You probably are aware that IBM also sells a computer targeted for the home user; this computer is the PS/1. IBM attempted to make the PS/1 as easy as possible to use by providing a mouse and a graphical user interface that divides the screen into four quadrants. Depending on which quadrant you click, you can connect to an on-line service such as Prodigy, load Microsoft Works (software included with the system), start IBM DOS, or launch any of your own software. IBM also provides a toll-free technical support line. IBM is seeking to take advantage of the connectability of personal computers by building a modem into the PS/1.

Besides Prodigy, PS/1 owners can connect to other on-line services, such as the PS/1 Users Club and an education and entertainment service called Promenade. Although these features seem like a boon to the novice, the computer has several nonstandard features, such as proprietary expansion slots and a power supply housed in the monitor. In addition to these variations, the price may cause you to stop and think before you buy a PS/1. If you are seriously interested in a personal computer that gives you the most for your money, you are better off choosing another IBM or a model from a competing manufacturer.

IBM-Compatible Models

IBM-compatible computers share many features: they use the Intel (or compatible) family of CPUs—8088 through 80486; most of the desktop models use the ISA bus; and some high-performance 80386 and 80486 models use the EISA or the Micro Channel bus. System units come in various styles: standard desktop, low-profile desktop, and floor-standing (often called tower) models.

You can upgrade many systems; that is, you can replace the current processor with a faster more powerful processor when you need better performance. This capability is good because you are assured that you can keep up with technology. However, see whether the manufacturer offers a trade-up policy. That is, will he give you a credit for your old processor when you purchase a new one?

All computers use chips that contain the Basic Input/Output System (BIOS). Make sure that the model you buy uses a BIOS from a well-known company. Some of these companies are AMI, Phoenix, and Award.

Ensure that all necessary components and software accompany the model: floppy drives, hard drive, video display and adapter, memory, keyboard, mouse, DOS or another operating system. Sometimes, especially in a magazine, you see an ad for a computer showing a display. However, in small print may be "Monitor not included."

There is no reason to avoid an IBM-compatible computer. You often can find a very good value. And many companies have as good a reputation as IBM itself.

Macintosh Models

COMPARISON

If you plan to purchase an Apple Macintosh computer, you should know about the features that distinguish one Macintosh from another. Apple sells three Macintosh models that come with built-in monochrome displays: the Macintosh Classic, the Macintosh SE/30, and the Macintosh Portable. The remaining Macintosh models have a separate system unit and use a separate monitor that connects to the unit; these models are the Macintosh LC, IIsi, IIci, and IIfx.

The low end of the line is the Classic, which uses a 68000 CPU, and the high end of the line is the IIfx, which uses a fast 68030 CPU. The LC, IIsi, and IIci have built-in color circuits. Of all the current Macintosh models, only the IIci and IIfx have more than one expansion slot. These computers also have an advanced bus design, called NuBus. If you plan to add more functionality to the computer, the availability of a NuBus expansion slot is an important consideration. (Most add-in circuit boards are designed to work with the NuBus.)

When you consider the Macintosh line of computers, you should weigh cost against other factors, such as speed, power, and expandability. Table 3.2 summarizes the features of the various Macintosh models.

Table 3.2. Apple Macintosh Product Line Features

	CPU	*Speed*	*Bus*	*Video*	*Expansion Slots*	*Style*
Low-end models						
Macintosh Classic	68000	8 MHz	Proprietary	Monochrome	0	Desktop*
Macintosh LC	68020	16 MHz	Proprietary	8-bit color	1	Desktop
Mid-range models						
Macintosh SE/30	68030	16 MHz	Proprietary	Monochrome	1	Desktop*
Macintosh IIsi	68030	20 MHz	NuBus	8-bit color	1	Desktop
High-end models						
Macintosh IIci	68030	25 MHz	NuBus	8-bit color	3	Desktop
Macintosh IIfx	68030	40 MHz	6 NuBus slots, 1 DOS slot	None	7	Desktop
Portable model						
Macintosh Portable	68000	16 MHz	Proprietary	Monochrome LCD	1	Luggable

*With built-in monitor.

Points To Remember

As you have learned in this chapter, when you are selecting a system, you need to consider many points. The following checklist may help you remember the key issues:

- Software availability for the model
- Adequate performance of the model
- Upgradability of the model
- Fair price for the model
- Good reputation of the model's manufacturer

Keep these issues in mind when you are selecting a model of computer. If the model you are considering doesn't satisfy all these points, select another model. When investing money in a computer, you will be more satisfied if you do not "settle" on a model but rather "select" a model.

Chapter Summary

This chapter reviews the rationale for purchasing a personal computer from one particular manufacturer compared to another manufacturer. The chapter gives you some criteria to help you decide on a manufacturer: software availability, ease of use, compatibility, performance, and price. The chapter presents short profiles of a selection of personal computer companies. The personal computer systems and service and support policies of each company are described. Finally, the chapter adds some specifics for the IBM and Apple product lines that you can use as a basis for comparison among manufacturers. Hopefully, this chapter has given you sufficient insight to help you decide whether you want an IBM, Apple, or IBM-compatible computer.

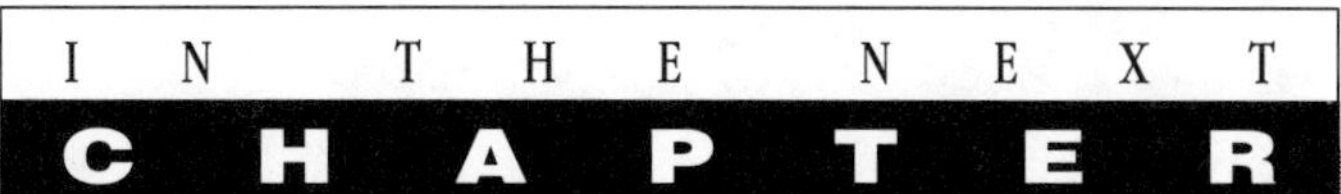

You have some ideas about the personal computer you want, and you know which company, or group of companies, you are considering. The next chapter provides a listing of computer systems. This listing will help you to make comparisons among various systems.

CHAPTER FOUR

Listing of Computers

Your life includes many important occasions—graduation from high school, graduation from college or technical school, your wedding day, the births of your children, and the purchase of your first house. Another important event is the purchase of your first computer. (Rank this event in order of importance with the others mentioned, as you see fit.) With each important event, you spend much time, give much thought, and do much planning before the event takes place. By your purchasing this book and reading it, you show that you are spending time for, giving thought to, and planning the purchase of a computer.

The tables in this chapter give you information essential for selecting a computer that best fits your needs. The tables have been divided by category of computer. In the IBM and compatible area, the tables have been split by microprocessor (8086, 80286, 80386SX, 80386, 80486SX, and 80486). Two additional tables are included—one for laptop computers and the other listing notebook computers. Two tables are Macintosh specific. One table lists desktop Macintosh computers; the other lists portable Macintosh computers.

All tables have been sorted in the same way. First, the tables have been sorted by the *CPU, SPEED, CACHE* column. The tables next are sorted by company and then by model. This kind of organization enables you to compare computers within a class of computer.

The Columns of the Tables

All ten tables in this chapter display the same type of information. This section explains what each of the 17 columns displays.

The first two columns display the manufacturer and model of a particular computer system. The next column gives the CPU that the computer uses, the speed of the CPU, and the presence of fast cache memory (if any). The *MIN, MAX RAM* column tells how much RAM memory comes with the system and how high the memory can be expanded.

UNIT SIZE tells you the approximate size of the computer. For desktop computers, full size means the size of an IBM AT computer. All other sizes are in comparison to that computer. Tower means that the CPU is meant to stand on the floor rather than sit on a desk top. Mac means that the Macintosh computer is the size of the standard Macintosh Classic. Laptop and notebook computers are rated according to weight.

The next column shows who manufactures the BIOS and what version the BIOS is. The eighth column gives the capacity and speed of the hard disk, if one accompanies the computer. Because most computers come with built-in adapters—to connect printers and modems, for example—the *ADAPTERS INCLUDED* column indicates adapters.

Because you need to know a computer's expansion capabilities, the *EXP SLOTS* column shows you how many expansion slots are available in the computer. In the case of IBM and compatible computers, each expansion slot is rated as to the width of the data bus of the expansion slot. The *BUS TYPE* lets you know what type of adapter cards the computer is compatible with. Many computers come with a video adapter and display. The *VIDEO ADAPTER, DISPLAY* column tells what each computer provides.

Before you can expand your computer with additional drives and adapters, the computer's power supply must be capable of handling the additional load. The *POWER SUPPLY* column shows the wattage of the power supply provided with each computer.

Service is an important factor when selecting a computer. The *WARRANTY* column gives you the length of each computer's warranty. If possible, the type of warranty has been included in this column—that is, whether you must carry (or send) the computer back to the vendor or on-site service is provided. On-site service means that a company service person will come to your location to repair your computer.

Often, software is bundled with a computer system. The *SOFTWARE INCLUDED* column lets you know what software you can expect to receive with a computer system. This software may change from time-to-time. Before purchasing a computer, verify from the vendor what software, if any, comes with the computer system.

The last two columns give the retail price of the computer and other information. Remember, prices change periodically, generally lowering. The *OTHER INFORMATION* column includes specific information that may help you with your decision.

Desktop Computer Listing

In this chapter, the term *desktop computer* is used as a generic term meaning that the computer is meant to stay in a given area, rather than be moved from place to place as a laptop or notebook computer can be moved. The desktop computers represented in the following tables may actually sit on a desk, or a computer may sit on the floor in a tower case. This section includes seven of the ten tables in this chapter. Table 4.1 lists Macintosh computers. Tables 4.2 through 4.7 list the different kinds of IBM-compatible computers.

Table 4.1. Macintosh Desktop Computers

COMPANY	MODEL	CPU, SPEED, CACHE	MIN, MAX RAM (M)	UNIT SIZE	BIOS, VER.	DISK DRIVES (M)	HARD DISK CAP, SPEED, TYPE	ADAPTERS INCLUDED	EXP SLOTS
Apple Computer	Macintosh Classic (1M) w/keybd	68000, 8MHz	1, 4	Mac	Apple	1.4		2 ser, 1 SCSI, 1 ADB, 1 ext 35' disk, 1 sound	
Apple Computer	Macintosh Classic 2/40 w/keybd	68000, 8MHz	2, 4	Mac	Apple	1.4	40M, SCSI	2 ser, 1 SCSI, 1 ADB, 1 ext 35' disk, 1 sound	
Apple Computer	Macintosh LC 2/40 512K VRAM	68020, 16MHz	2, 10	Small	Apple	1.4	40M, SCSI	2 ser, 1 SCSI, 1 ADB, 1 sound-in, 1 sound-out, 1 video	1-020 exp slot
Apple Computer	Macintosh LC 2/40 w/keybd	68020, 16MHz	2, 10	Small	Apple	1.4	80M, SCSI	2 ser, 1 SCSI, 1 ADB, 1 sound-in/out, 1 video	1-020 exp slot
Apple Computer	Macintosh IIsi 3/40	68030, 20MHz	3, 17	Small	Apple	1.4	40M, SCSI	2 ser, 2 ADB, 1 SCSI, 1 DB-15 video, 1 sound	1 NuBus or 030 Direct Slot
Apple Computer	Macintosh IIsi 5/80	68030, 20MHz	5, 17	Small	Apple	1.4	40M, SCSI	2 ser, 1 SCSI, 1 ADB, 1 sound-in/out, 1 video	1 NuBus or 030 Direct Slot
Apple Computer	Macintosh SE/30 2/40	68030, 16MHz	2, 8	Mac	Apple	1.4	40M, SCSI	2 ser, 1 SCSI, 1 disk, 2 ADB, 1 stereo sound	1 32- bit
Apple Computer	Macintosh SE/30 4/80	68030, 16MHz	4, 8	Mac	Apple	1.4	80M, SCSI	2 ser, 1 SCSI, 1 disk, 2 ADB, 1 stereo sound	1 32-bit
Apple Computer	Mac IIci 4/80 Parity	68030, 25MHz	4, 8	Small	Apple	1.4	80M, 25 ms, SCSI	2 ser, 2 ADB, 1 SCSI, 1 DB-15 video, 1 sound	3 NuBus
Apple Computer	Mac IIci 5/160	68030, 25MHz	5, 8	Small	Apple	1.4	160M, 25ms, SCSI	2 ser, 2 ADB, 1 SCSI, 1 DB-15 video, 1 sound	3 NuBus
Apple Computer	Mac IIci 5/80	68030, 25MHz	5, 8	Small	Apple	1.4	80M, 25 ms, SCSI	2 ser, 2 ADB, 1 SCSI, 1 DB-15 video, 1 sound	3 NuBus
Apple Computer	Macintosh IIci 5MB	68030, 25MHz	5, 8	Small	Apple	1.4		2 ser, 2 ADB, 1 SCSI, 1 DB-15 video, 1 sound	3 NuBus
Apple Computer	Macintosh IIfx	68030, 40MHz	4, 32	Desktop	Apple	1.4	80M, 25 ms, SCSI	2 ser, 2 ADB, 1 SCSI, 1 sound	6 NuBus, 1 PDS
Apple Computer	Macintosh IIfx	68030, 40MHz	4, 32	Desktop	Apple	1.4	160M, 25ms, SCSI	2 ser, 2 ADB, 1 SCSI, 1 sound	6 NuBus, 1 PDS

BUS TYPE	VIDEO ADAPTER, DISPLAY	POWER SUPPLY (watts)	WARRANTY (years)	SOFTWARE INCLUDED	RETAIL PRICE	OTHER INFORMATION
	Built-in 9" display, 512 x 342 monochrome	100	1, carry-in	Sys software, HyperCard, training	$999.00	Includes keyboard & display
	Built-in 9" display, 512 x 342 monochrome	100	1, carry-in	Sys software, HyperCard, training	$1,499.00	Includes keyboard & display
020 PDS	4-bit color	50 not including monitor power	1, carry-in	Sys software, HyperCard, training	$2,499.00	Keyboards & display sold separately
020 PDS	4-bit color	50 not including monitor power	1, carry-in	Sys software, HyperCard, training	$2,699.00	Includes keyboard, sound input, Apple IIe Card
NuBus, 030 PDS		100	1, carry-in	Sys software, HyperCard, training	$3,769.00	Keyboards & display sold separately
NuBus or 030 PDS		100	1, carry-in	Sys software, HyperCard, training	$4,569.00	Keyboards & display sold separately
030 PDS	Built-in 9" display, 512 x 342 monochrome	75	1, carry-in	Sys software, HyperCard, training	$3,369.00	Includes 68882 math coprocessor, keyboard not included
030 PDS	Built-in 9" display, 512 x 342 monochrome	75	1, carry-in	Sys software, HyperCard, training	$3,869.00	Includes 68882 math coprocessor, keyboard not included
NuBus		90	1, carry-in	Sys software, HyperCard, training	$6,369.00	Includes 68882 math coprocessor, keyboards & display sold separately
NuBus		90 not including monitor power	1, carry-in	Sys software, HyperCard, training	$6,569.00	Includes 68882 math coprocessor, keyboards & display sold separately
NuBus		90 not including monitor power	1, carry-in	Sys software, HyperCard, training	$5,969.00	Includes 68882 math coprocessor, keyboards & display sold separately
NuBus		90 not including monitor power	1, carry-in	Sys software, HyperCard, training	$5,269.00	Includes 68882 math coprocessor, keyboards & display sold separately
NuBus, 030 PDS		230	1, carry-in	Sys software, HyperCard, training	$8,069.00	Includes 68882 math coprocessor, keyboards & display sold separately
NuBus, 030 PDS		230	1, carry-in	Sys software, HyperCard, training	$8,669.00	Includes 68882 math coprocessor, keyboards & display sold separately

Table 4.2. IBM-Compatible 8086 Desktop Computers

COMPANY	MODEL	CPU, SPEED, CACHE	MIN, MAX RAM (K)	UNIT SIZE	BIOS, VER.	DISK DRIVES (K)	HARD DISK CAP, SPEED, TYPE	ADAPTERS INCLUDED	EXP SLOTS
IBM	8525-1	8086, 8MHz	512K, 640K	Small	IBM	720		1 ser, 1 par, 1 mouse	2 8-bit
Tandy	1000RL HD	8086, 9.54MHz	512K, 640K	Mid size		720	20M	1 ser, 1 par, 1 mouse, 2 game	1 8-bit
Tandy	1000RL HD w/mono monitor	8086, 9.54MHz	512K, 640K	Mid size		720	20M	1 ser, 1 par, 1 mouse, 2 game	1 8-bit
Tandy	1000RL w/color monitor	8086, 9.54MHz	512K, 640K	Mid size		720		1 ser, 1 par, 1 mouse, 2 game	1 8-bit
Tandy	1000RL w/monitor	8086, 9.54MHz	512K, 640K	Mid size		720		1 ser, 1 par, 1 mouse, 2 game	1 8-bit
CompuAdd	CompuAdd 810	NEC V-20, 10MHz	640K, 640K	Small	Phoenix XT	360	40M, 39ms, IDE		3 16-bit, 2 8-bit

BUS TYPE	VIDEO DISPLAY, ADAPTER	POWER SUPPLY (watts)	WARRANTY (years)	SOFTWARE INCLUDED	RETAIL PRICE	OTHER INFORMATION
ISA	Monochrome display, MCGA	200	1, carry-in; on-site avail		$1,350.00	Other opt avail
ISA	Color display, TCGA, CGA adapter		1, carry-in		$1,299.90	Includes 3-voice sound, 8-bit DAC digital sound, headphone & microphone jack, other opt avail
ISA	Monochrome display, TCGA, CGA		1, carry-in		$1,149.90	Includes 3-voice sound, 8-bit DAC digital sound, headphone & microphone jack, other opt avail
ISA	Color display, TCGA, CGA adapter		1, carry-in		$899.90	Includes 3-voice sound, 8-bit DAC digital sound, headphone & microphone jack, other opt avail
ISA	Monochrome display, TCGA, CGA		1, carry-in		$749.90	Includes 3-voice sound, 8-bit DAC digital sound, headphone & microphone jack, other opt avail
ISA	VGA (800 x 600)	145	1, send-back; carry-in		$1,225.00	Other opt avail

Table 4.3. IBM-Compatible 80286 Desktop Computers

COMPANY	MODEL	CPU, SPEED, CACHE	MIN, MAX RAM (M)	UNIT SIZE	BIOS, VER.	DISK DRIVES (M)	HARD DISK CAP, SPEED, TYPE	ADAPTERS INCLUDED	EXP. SLOTS
IBM	8525-6	80286, 10MHz	1, 16	Full size	IBM	1.44		1 ser, 1 par, 1 mouse	2 8-bit
IBM	8530-EP2	80286, 10MHz	1, 16	Mid size	IBM	1.44		1 ser, 1 par, 1 mouse	3 16-bit
Tandy	1000 RLX HD w/ color monitor	80286, 10MHz	1	Mid size		1.44	40M	1 ser, 1 par, 1 mouse, 2 game, headphone, mike	1 8-bit
Tandy	1000 RLX HD w/monochrome monitor	80286, 10MHz	1	Mid size		1.44	40M	1 ser, 1 par, 1 mouse, 2 game, headphone, mike	1 8-bit
Tandy	1000 TL/3	80286, 10MHz	640K, 768K	Mid size		720K			4 8-bit
Tandy	1000RLX w/ color monitor	80286, 10MHz	512K, 1	Mid size		1.44		1 ser, 1 par, 1 mouse, 2 game, headphone, mike	1 8-bit
Tandy	1000RLX w/ monochrome monitor	80286, 10MHz	512K, 1	Mid size		1.44		1 ser, 1 par, 1 mouse, 2 game, headphone, mike	1 8-bit
Acer America Corporation	915P (II)	80286, 12MHz	640K, 5	Small		1.2		2 ser, 1 par, 1 mouse, IDE interface	4 16-bit
Acer America Corporation	Acer Station II	80286, 12MHz	1, 5	3.3 x 14 x 16				2 ser, 1 par, IDE interface	2 16-bit
COMPAQ	COMPAQ DeskPro 286N Mdl 0	80286, 12MHz	1, 13	Mid size	COMPAQ			1 ser, 1 par, 1 mouse	2 8-bit or 16-bit/1 RAM
COMPAQ	COMPAQ DeskPro 286N Mdl 1	80286, 12MHz	1, 13	Mid size	COMPAQ	1.44		1 ser, 1 par, 1 mouse	2 8-bit or 16-bit/1 RAM
COMPAQ	COMPAQ DeskPro 286N Mdl 40	80286, 12MHz	1, 13	Mid size	COMPAQ	1.44	40M, 29ms	1 ser, 1 par, 1 mouse	2 8-bit or 16-bit/1 RAM
COMPAQ	COMPAQ Portable III Model 20	80286, 12MHz	640K, 6.6	Port	COMPAQ	1.44	20M, 29ms	1 ser, 1 par, 1 ext CGA	
COMPAQ	COMPAQ Portable III Model 40	80286, 12MHz	640K, 6.6	Port	COMPAQ	1.44	40M, 29ms	1 ser, 1 par, 1 ext CGA	
CompuAdd	CompuAdd 212	80286, 12MHz	512K, 4	Small	Phoenix 286AT	1.44 or 1.2	40M, 28ms, IDE		3 16-bit/2 8-bit
EPSON	Equity 286 Plus	80286, 12MHz	1, 16	Mid size	Seiko EPSON (proprietary)	1.2 or 1.44		1 ser, 1 par, 1 mouse	1 8-bit/3 16-bit
Hewlett-Packard	HP Vectra 286/12 PC D2460A	80286, 12MHz	1, 8	Mid size	Hewlett-Packard	1.2 or 1.44	20M or 42M	1 ser, 1 par	1 8-bit/4 16-bit/1 prop
Hyundai	Super-286E Plus	80286, 12MHz	1, 4	Mid size	Hewlett-Packard	1.2	40M, IDE	2 ser, 1 par, IDE	1 8-bit/4 16-bit
Hyundai	Super-286T	80286, 12MHz	640K, 1	Mid size	Hewlett-Packard	1.2	40M, IDE	1 ser, 1 par, IDE	1 8-bit/3 16-bit
Leading Edge	D2/Plus D2P2041	80286, 12MHz	1, 16	Mid size	Phoenix 3.10.02	1.2/1.44	44M, 28ms, IDE	1 25-pin ser, 1 9-pin ser, 1 par, 1 mouse	2 8-bit/4 16-bit

BUS TYPE	VIDEO ADAPTER, DISPLAY	POWER SUPPLY (watts)	WARRANTY (years)	SOFTWARE INCLUDED	RETAIL PRICE	OTHER INFORMATION
ISA	Color display, MCGA	200	1, carry-in; on-site avail		$2,135.00	Other opt avail
ISA	VGA	90	1, carry-in; on-site avail		$1,625.00	Other opt avail
ISA	VGA color display, VGA adapter		1, carry-in	DOS, DeskMate and applications	$1,599.90	Includes 3-voice sound, 8-bit DAC digital sound, headphone & microphone jack, mouse, other opt avail
ISA	VGA monochrome display, VGA adapter		1, carry-in	DOS, DeskMate and applications	$1,399.90	Includes 3-voice sound, 8-bit DAC digital sound, headphone & microphone jack, mouse, other opt avail
ISA	CGA, MDA, Hercules adapter	67	1, carry-in	DOS, DeskMate 3	$1,099.95	Other opt avail
ISA	Color display, VGA adapter		1, carry-in	DOS, DeskMate and applications	$1,199.90	Includes 3-voice sound, 8-bit DAC digital sound, headphone & microphone jack, mouse, other opt avail
ISA	Monochrome display, VGA adapter		1, carry-in	DOS, DeskMate and applications	$999.90	Includes 3-voice sound, 8-bit DAC digital sound, headphone & microphone jack, mouse, other opt avail
ISA	CGA, Hercules	100	2, carry-in	DOS	$995.00	Displays avail
ISA	VGA (800 x 600)	72	2, carry-in		$1,199.00	
ISA	VGA		1, carry-in		$1,299.00	Other opt avail, other OS avail
ISA	VGA		1, carry-in		$1,399.00	Other opt avail, other OS avail
ISA	VGA		1, carry-in		$1,799.00	Other opt avail, other OS avail
	Dual-mode plasma display, 640 x 400 text, 640 x 200 graphics	110V-220V AC	1, carry-in		$4,999.00	Other opt avail, other OS avail
	Dual-mode plasma display, 640 x 400 text, 640 x 200 graphics	110V-220V AC	1, carry-in		$5,799.00	Other opt avail, other OS avail
ISA	VGA	145	1, send-back; carry-in	DOS, Software Toolworks Office, Twist & Shout	$1,459.00	Other opt avail
ISA	VGA	145	1, carry-in	EPSON enhanced utils and diags	$1,099.00	Other opt avail
ISA	VGA (800 x 600)	260	1, on-site	Setup, LIM 40 util, speed-switch		Other opt avail
ISA		135	18 months; on-site avail	DOS	$795.00	Other opt avail
ISA		75	18 months; on-site avail	DOS	$745.00	Other opt avail
ISA	VGA (800 x 600)	100	20 months carry-in; 6 months on-site	DOS, Microsoft Works	$1,199.00	Other opt avail

continues

Table 4.3. Continued

COMPANY	MODEL	CPU, SPEED, CACHE	MIN, MAX RAM (M)	UNIT SIZE	BIOS, VER.	DISK DRIVES (M)	HARD DISK CAP, SPEED, TYPE	ADAPTERS INCLUDED	EXP. SLOTS
Microlab	212e	80286, 12MHz	1, 4	Mid size	AMI	1.2/1.44	44M, 28ms, IDE	2 ser, 1 par, 1 game	2 8-bit/6 16-bit
NEC	PowerMate Portable Plus	80286, 12MHz	1, 16	Port 19 lbs		1.2 or 1.44	42M, 28ms	1 ser, 1 par	3 8-bit or 16-bit
NEC	PowerMate 286/12	80286, 12MHz	1, 16	Small	Phoenix 3.10.84	1.2 or 1.44		1 ser, 1 par, 1 mouse	4 8-bit or 16-bit
Northgate	SlimLine 286/12 MHz	80286, 12MHz	2, 4	Mid size	AMI	1.2/1.44	40M, IDE	2 ser, 1 par, IDE	2 8-bit/3 16-bit
Packard Bell	Force 111	80286, 12MHz	1, 16	Small	Phoenix	1.2/1.44	40M, 28ms, IDE	2 ser, 1 par, 1 mouse, 2 game	3 16-bit
Samsung Information Systems	DeskMaster 286/12/ SD620	80286, 12MHz	1, 2	Small		1.44		1 ser, 1 par, 1 mouse, IDE	3 16-bit
Sun Moon Star	286/12 CD-ROM system	80286, 12MHz	1, 4	Mid size		1.2	40M	2 ser, 1 par	3 16-bit
Tri-Star Computer Corporation	Tri-Star TS 212i	80286, 12MHz	2, 8	Small	AMI	1.2 and 1.44	42M, 25ms, IDE		2 8-bit/5 16-bit
Wyse Technology	WY-2012	80286, 12MHz	1, 16	Small	Phoenix, Wyse	1.2 or 1.44	40M, 28ms	2 ser, 1 par, IDE	2 8-bit/5 16-bit
Zenith	Z-286 LP Plus Model 1	80286, 12MHz	1, 16	Full size		1.44			
Advanced Logic Research	PowerFlex 286 Model 1	80286, 12.5MHz	1, 16	Small	Phoenix	1.44		1 par, 1 ser, 1 mouse	5 16-bit/1 8-bit
Dell Computer Corporation	Dell System 210	80286, 12.5MHz	1, 16	Small	Phoenix, Dell	1.2 or 1.44	40M, 29ms, IDE	2 ser, 1 par	3 16-bit
Tandon	Option-Modular System	80286, 16MHz	2, 32	Mid size	Tandon	1.2 or 1.44	40M, IDE to 400M, IDE	2 ser, 1 par, IDE	1 8-bit/6 16-bit
Acer America Corporation	915V (II)	80286, 16MHz	1, 5	Small		1.2		2 ser, 1 par, 1 mouse, IDE interface	4 16-bit
AST Research	Bravo 286/16	80286, 16MHz	1, 16	Mid size	AST	1.2	40M	2 ser, 1 par, 1 PS, 2 comp mouse	5 16-bit
Austin Computer Systems	286/16	80286, 16MHz	1, 8	Small	Quadtel	1.2 or 1.44	40M, IDE		6 16-bit/1 8-bit
CompuAdd	CompuAdd 216	80286, 16MHz	512K, 4	Small	Phoenix 286AT	1.44 or 1.2	40M, 28ms, IDE		3 16-bit/2 8-bit
DTK Computer Inc.	TECH-1632	80286, 16MHz	0, 5	Mid size	27256 4.26V				3 8-bit/5 16-bit
DTK Computer Inc.	TECH-1663	80286, 16MHz	0, 5	Small	27256 4.26V				1 16-bit expandable
PC Brand, Inc.	286/16	80286, 16MHz	512K, 8	Full size		1.2 or 1.44		2 ser, 1 par	ISA

BUS TYPE	VIDEO ADAPTER, DISPLAY	POWER SUPPLY (watts)	WARRANTY (years)	SOFTWARE INCLUDED	RETAIL PRICE	OTHER INFORMATION
ISA	Diamond Speedstar VGA 1024 x 768, 512K	200	1, send-back; free shipping	DOS	$1,195.00	Free shipping, other opt avail
ISA	VGA LCD, 8 gray shades	115V, 230V Universal	1, carry-in	DOS, Windows 3.0	$4,199.00	Other opt avail
ISA	NEC Super VGA adapter	115V, 230V Universal	1, carry-in; on-site avail	DOS	$1,299.00	Other opt avail
ISA	12" VGA gray	150 watt	30 days money back; 1, on-site	DOS	$1,699.00	Includes OmniKey, 102 keyboard, lifetime 24-hr tech support, other opt avail
ISA	VGA (800 x 600)	60	1, on-site	DOS, Packard Bell Desktop, Lotus Works	$1,649.00	Includes mouse, other opt avail
ISA		100	1, carry-in	DOS	$999.00	Contact via 800#, BBS, fax, authorized service vendors, other opt avail
ISA	VGA display, VGA adapter	145	3, send-back; 1, on-site	DOS, PFS: First Choice, GEM and apps, Check It	$2,595.00	Includes mouse, CD ROM drive with extensive software bundle, discounts avail for educators, other opt avail
ISA	Matsushita Viewsonic 4 multisync display, Paradise 1024 x 768, 512K	200	30 days money back; 15 months send-back	DOS	$1,295.00	Includes lifetime toll-free tech support, other opt avail
ISA		200	1, carry-in	DOS, Wyse Setup, diagnostics	$999.00	Other opt avail
	VGA		1, carry-in		$1,399.00	CPU upgradable to 386SX, other opt avail
ISA		145	1, carry-in	ALR utilities	$795.00	CPU upg, other opt avail
ISA	VGA	85	1, on-site	Tutorial, diagnostics	$1,499.00	Includes unlimited toll-free tech support, other opt avail, other hard drive cap avail
	VGA monochrome display, VGA (800 x 600)					Upgr CPU, 80386SX, 20, 80486SX, 20, 80486DX, 33, 80486DX, 50 module, other opt avail
ISA	VGA (800 x 600)	100	2, carry-in	DOS	$1,295.00	Displays avail
ISA	VGA (800 x 600)	145, 110/220V AC	1, carry-in	DOS, disk cache, FASTRAM, Super Spool, LIM 40	$4,725.00	CPU upgradable, other opt avail
ISA	Samsung MA2565, Diamond Flower MG180 adapter	110/220V	1, GE on-site	DOS, Windows 3.0		Other opt avail
ISA	VGA	145	1, send-back; carry-in	DOS, Software Toolworks Office, Twist & Shout	$1,509.00	Other opt avail
ISA		200	1, carry-in		$375.00	Other opt avail
ISA		150	1, carry-in		$449.00	Other opt avail
ISA		200	1, send-back; 5, prorated		$619.00	Choice of Desktop or SlimLine Case, other opt avail

continues

Table 4.3. Concluded

COMPANY	MODEL	CPU, SPEED, CACHE	MIN, MAX RAM (M)	UNIT SIZE	BIOS, VER.	DISK DRIVES (M)	HARD DISK CAP, SPEED, TYPE	ADAPTERS INCLUDED	EXP. SLOTS
Swan Technologies	286/16	80286, 16MHz	512K, 8	Mid size	Quadtel C & T Neat	1.2 or 1.44	40M, 28ms, IDE	2 ser, 1 par	1 8-bit/6 16-bit
Tandy	2500 XL/2	80286, 16MHz	1, 16	Mid size		1.44			3 16-bit
Tri-Star Computer Corporation	Tri-Lan Workstation WS216i	80286, 16MHz	1, 8	Small	Award	Option			1 16-bit
Tri-Star Computer Corporation ·	Tri-Star TS 286/16	80286, 16MHz	2, 8	Small	AMI	1.2 and 1.44	42M, 25ms, IDE		2 8-bit/5 16-bit
Gateway 2000	286-16	80286, 16MHz, 32K	2, 16	Mid size	Quadtel	1.2/1.44	40M, 17ms, IDE	2 ser, 1 par, 1 PS, 2 mouse	5 16-bit

BUS TYPE	VIDEO ADAPTER, DISPLAY	POWER SUPPLY (watts)	WARRANTY (years)	SOFTWARE INCLUDED	RETAIL PRICE	OTHER INFORMATION
ISA	Swan 1024 x 768 display, optional adapters	200	2, on-site	Swan utils, LIM 40	$1,445.00	Lifetime toll-free tech support, other opt avail
ISA	VGA (1024 x 768)	70	1, carry-in	DOS, DeskMate 3	$1,499.00	Other opt avail
ISA	14" Septre monochrome display, MDA	250	30 days money back; 1, send-back		$695.00	Includes lifetime toll-free tech support, other opt avail
ISA	Matsushita Viewsonic 4 multisync display, Paradise 1024 x 768, 512K	200	30 days money back; 15 months send-back	DOS	$1,395.00	Includes lifetime toll-free tech support, other opt avail
ISA	14" Crystal Scan 1024 VGA color display, VGA 1024 x 768, 512K	200	30 days money back; 1, on-site	DOS	$1,395.00	Includes mouse, other opt avail

Table 4.4. IBM-Compatible 80386SX Desktop Computers

COMPANY	MODEL	CPU, SPEED, CACHE	MIN, MAX RAM (M)	UNIT SIZE	BIOS, VER.	DISK DRIVES (M)	HARD DISK CAP, SPEED, TYPE	ADAPTERS INCLUDED	EXP. SLOTS
DTK Computer Inc.	PEER-2030	80386SX	0, 16	Full size	27256, 4.26V				3 8-bit, 5 16-bit
Acer America Corporation	1116SX	80386SX, 16MHz	1, 8	Small		1.2		2 ser, 1 par, 1 mouse, IDE interface	4 16-bit
Advanced Logic Research	PowerFlex 386sx Mdl 1	80386SX, 16MHz	1, 16	Small	Phoenix	1.44		1 par, 1 ser, 1 mouse	5 16-bit, 1 8-bit
Austin Computer Systems	386/SX-16 Winstation	80386SX, 16MHz	2, 8	Small	Quadtel	1.2 or 1.44	40M, IDE		6 16-bit, 1 8-bit
Cardinal	386SX	80386SX, 16MHz	1, 16	Small		1.44		2 ser, 1 par, 1 PS, 2 mouse	3 16-bit
COMPAQ	COMPAQ DeskPro 386N Mdl 0	80386SX, 16MHz	1, 16	Mid size	COMPAQ			1 ser, 1 par, 1 mouse	2 8-bit or 16-bit, 1 RAM
COMPAQ	COMPAQ DeskPro 386N Mdl 1	80386SX, 16MHz	1, 16	Mid size	COMPAQ	1.44		1 ser, 1 par, 1 mouse	2 8-bit or 16-bit, 1 RAM
COMPAQ	COMPAQ DeskPro 386N Mdl 40	80386SX, 16MHz	1, 16	Mid size	COMPAQ	1.44	40M, 29ms	1 ser, 1 par, 1 mouse	2 8-bit or 16-bit, 1 RAM
COMPAQ	COMPAQ DeskPro 386s Mdl 1	80386SX, 16MHz	2, 13	Mid size	COMPAQ	1.44		1 ser, 1 par, 1 mouse	4 8-bit or 16-bit, 1 RAM
COMPAQ	COMPAQ DeskPro 386s Mdl 40	80386SX, 16MHz	2, 13	Mid size	COMPAQ	1.44	40M, 29ms	1 ser, 1 par, 1 mouse	4 8-bit or 16-bit, 1 RAM
COMPAQ	COMPAQ DeskPro 386s Mdl 84	80386SX, 16MHz	2, 13	Mid size	COMPAQ	1.44	84M, 25ms	1 ser, 1 par, 1 mouse	4 8-bit or 16-bit, 1 RAM
Dell Computer Corporation	Dell System 316 SX	80386SX, 16MHz	1, 16	Small	Phoenix, Dell	1.2 or 1.4	40M, 29ms, IDE	2 ser, 1 par	3 16-bit
DTK Computer Inc.	PEER-1630	80386SX, 16MHz	0, 16	Full size	27256, 4.26				5 16-bit, 3 8-bit
DTK Computer Inc.	PEER-166-	80386SX, 16MHz	0, 5	Small	27256, 4.26V				1 16-bit expandable
EPSON	Equity 386SX Plus	80386SX, 16MHz	2, 16	Small	Seiko EPSON (proprietary)	1.2 or 1.44		1 ser, 1 par, 1 mouse, IDE	1 8-bit, 3 16-bit
Ergo Computing	Brick	80386SX, 16MHz	2, 8	Brick	Ergo 1.07	1.44	44M, Connor, 28ms-13ms, IDE		1 8-bit, 1 16-bit
Hewlett-Packard	HP Vectra QS/16S PC	80386SX, 16MHz	2, 8	Mid size	Hewlett-Packard	1.2 or 1.44	40M, IDE or 80M, IDE	1 ser, 1 par, 1 mouse	1 8-bit, 6 16-bit
IBM	8555	80386SX, 16MHz	4, 16	Mid size	IBM	1.44	40M, 17ms, ESDI	1 ser, 1 par, 1 mouse	3 16-bit
Leading Edge	D3/SX D3S2041	80386SX, 16MHz	1, 16	Small	Phoenix 1.10.63	1.2/1.44	44M, 28ms, IDE	1 25-pin ser, 1 9-pin ser, 1 par, 1 mouse	2 8-bit, 4 16-bit
Microlab	316s	80386SX, 16MHz	4, 8	Mid size	AMI	1.2/1.44	44M, 28ms, IDE	2 ser, 1 par, 1 game	1 8-bit, 6 16-bit

BUS TYPE	VIDEO ADAPTER, DISPLAY	POWER SUPPLY (watts)	WARRANTY (years)	SOFTWARE INCLUDED	RETAIL PRICE	OTHER INFORMATION
ISA		200	1, carry-in		$725.00	Other opt avail
ISA	VGA (800 x 600)	145	2, carry-in	DOS	$1,395.00	Other hard disk sizes avail, displays avail
ISA		145	1, carry-in	ALR utils	$995.00	CPU upgr, other opt avail
		110/220V 50/60Hz	1, GE on-site	DOS, Windows 3.0		Other opt avail
ISA	VGA	135		DOS, Windows 3.0		80386SX, 20 avail, other opt avail
ISA	VGA		1, carry-in		$1,599.00	Other opt avail, other OS avail
ISA	VGA		1, carry-in		$1,699.00	Other opt avail, other OS avail
ISA	VGA		1, carry-in		$1,999.00	Other opt avail, other OS avail
ISA	VGA		1, carry-in		$2,099.00	Other opt avail, other OS avail
ISA	VGA		1, carry-in		$2,399.00	Other opt avail, other OS avail
ISA	VGA		1, carry-in		$2,799.00	Other opt avail, other OS avail
ISA	VGA	85	1, on-site	Tutorial, diags	$1,699.00	Includes unlimited toll-free tech support, other opt avail
ISA		200	1, carry-in		$625.00	Other opt avail
ISA		150	1, carry-in		$699.00	Other opt avail
ISA	VGA (800 x 600)	140	1, carry-in			Other opt avail
ISA		42	1, send-back	DOS, Windows 3.0, Adobe ATM, Logitech mouse	$1795.00-$4695.00	80386SX, 20 avail, DesqView 386, QEMM 386, Manifest, Tree 86 avail, Other opt avail
ISA	VGA (800 x 600)	456	1, on-site	Setup, LIM 4.0 util, Windows 3.0		Other opt avail
MCA	VGA	90	1, carry-in; on-site avail		$2,745.00	Other opt avail
ISA	ATI VGA (1024 x 768)	200	20 months carry-in; 6 months on-site	DOS, Microsoft Works	$1,399.00	Other opt avail
ISA	Diamond Speedstar VGA 1024 x 768, 512K	200	1, send-back; free shipping	DOS	$1,495.00	Free shipping, other opt avail

continues

Table 4.4. Continued

COMPANY	MODEL	CPU, SPEED, CACHE	MIN, MAX RAM (M)	UNIT SIZE	BIOS, VER.	DISK DRIVES (M)	HARD DISK CAP, SPEED, TYPE	ADAPTERS INCLUDED	EXP. SLOTS
NCR	NCR PC386SX	80386SX, 16MHz	1, 15	Mid size		1.44	40M or 100M	2 ser, 1 par	4 16-bit
NEC	PowerMate SX/16	80386SX, 16MHz	2, 16	Small	Phoenix 1.10.53	1.2/1.44		1 ser, 1 par, 1 mouse	5 16-bit
Packard Bell	Force SX 16	80386SX, 16MHz	1, 5	Mid size	Phoenix	1.2/1.44	40M, 28ms	1 ser, 1 par, 1 mouse, 1 game, 1 int modem	3 16-bit
PC Brand, Inc.	386SX/16	80386SX, 16MHz	512K, 8	Full size		1.2 or 1.44		2 ser, 1 par	ISA
Samsung Information Systems	DeskMaster 386S/16/ SD716	80386SX, 16MHz	2, 8	Small		1.44		1 ser, 1 par, 1 mouse, IDE	3 16-bit
Standard Computer	386SX/16	80386SX, 16MHz	2, 8	Small	Phoenix 1.01	1.2/1.44	40M, 28ms, IDE	2 ser, 1 par	4 16-bit
Standard Computer	386SX/20	80386SX, 16MHz	2, 8	Mid size	Phoenix 1.01	1.2/1.44	40M, 28ms, IDE	2 ser, 1 par	4 16-bit
Sun Moon Star	386/SX/16 CD ROM system	80386SX, 16MHz	2, 8	Mid size		1.2	40M	2 ser, 1 par	2 8-bit, 3 16-bit
Swan Technologies	386SX-16	80386SX, 16MHz	1, 8	Mid size	Quadtel Flex AT, VIA	1.2 or 1.44	50M, 17ms, IDE	2 ser, 1 par	1 8-bit, 6 16-bit
USA Flex	Flex 386sx	80386SX, 16MHz	2, 16	Mid size	AMI 4, 9, 90	1.2 and two 1.44	106.9M, 16ms, IDE		4 16-bit
Wyse Technology	Decision 386SX/16s	80386SX, 16MHz	1, 16	Small	Phoenix, Wyse	Optional 1.44	40M, 19ms	1 ser, 1 par, 1 mouse, IDE	2 16-bit
Wyse Technology	WY 3016SX	80386SX, 16MHz	1, 16	Small	Phoenix, Wyse	1.2 or 1.44	40M or 110M	2 ser, 1 par, IDE	2 8-bit, 5 16-bit
CompuAdd	CompuAdd 316s	80386SX, 16MHz, 32K	2, 4	Small	Phoenix 386AT Plus	1.44 or 1.2	40M, 28ms, IDE		3 16-bit, 2 8-bit
Zenith	Z-386 SX Mdl 40	80386SX, 16MHz, 4K	2, 16	Mid size		1.44	40M, 28ms	2 ser, 1 par	4 16-bit
Northgate	SlimLine 316SX	80386SX, 16MHz, 64K	1, 16	Mid size	AMI	1.2/1.44	40M, IDE	2 ser, 1 par, IDE	2 8-bit, 3 16-bit
Acer America Corporation	1120SX	80386SX, 20MHz	2, 8	Small		1.44		2 ser, 1 par, 1 mouse, IDE interface	4 16-bit
Advanced Logic Research	PowerFlex 20sx Mdl 1	80386SX, 20MHz	1, 16	Small	Phoenix	1.44		1 par, 1 ser, 1 mouse	5 16-bit, 1 8-bit
AST Research	Bravo 386SX/20	80386SX, 20MHz	2, 16	Mid size	AST	1.2	40M	2 ser, 1 par, 1 PS, 2 comp mouse	5 16-bit
Austin Computer Systems	386/SX-20 Winstation	80386SX, 20MHz	2, 8	Small	Quadtel	1.2 or 1.44	40M, IDE		6 16-bit, 1 8-bit
Falco Data Products, Inc.	INFINITY 386sx/20 DT40	80386SX, 20MHz	1, 8	Small	Falco	1.44	40M, 17ms, IDE		2 16-bit

BUS TYPE	VIDEO ADAPTER, DISPLAY	POWER SUPPLY (watts)	WARRANTY (years)	SOFTWARE INCLUDED	RETAIL PRICE	OTHER INFORMATION
ISA	VGA (800 x 600)	110/ 240VAC	1, carry-in			Other opt avail
ISA	NEC Super VGA Adapter	110, 115V/ 230V Universal	1, carry-in; on-site avail	DOS, Windows 3.0	$1,999.00	Other opt avail
ISA	VGA	60	1, on-site	DOS, Packard Bell Desktop, Lotus Works	$2,049.00	Includes mouse, 2400B int modem, Prodigy Service start-up kit, other opt avail
ISA		200	1, send-back; 5, prorated		$669.00	Choice of Desktop or SlimLine Case, other opt avail
ISA		100	1, carry-in	DOS, Windows 3.0, VGA utils	$1,439.00	Contact via 800#, BBS, fax, authorized service vendors, other opt avail
ISA	14" Viewsonic 4, VGA 1024 x 768, 512K	200	1, TRW on-site	DOS	$1,395.00	Other opt avail
ISA	14" Viewsonic 4, VGA 1024 x 768, 1M	200	1, TRW on-site	DOS	$1,495.00	Other opt avail
ISA	VGA display, VGA adapter	145	3, send-back; 1, on-site	DOS, PFS: First Choice, Windows 3.0, Check It	$2,995.00	Includes mouse, CD ROM drive with extensive software bundle, discounts avail for educators, other opt avail
ISA	Swan 1024 x 768 display, optional adapters	200	2, on-site	Swan utils, LIM 4.0	$1,695.00	Lifetime toll-free tech support, other opt avail
ISA	Samsung, Samtron, or CTX 1024 x 768 display, VGA 1024 x 768, 512K	100	1, on-site	DOS, Windows 3.0, Lotus Works 2.0		Includes mouse, other opt avail
ISA	VGA (800 x 600)	60	1, carry-in	Wyse Enhanced DOS, Wyse Setup & Test.	$1,599.00	Other opt avail
ISA		200	1, carry-in	DOS, Wyse Setup, Diagnostics	$1,699.00	Other opt avail
ISA	VGA (800 x 600)	145	1, send-back; carry-in	DOS	$2,005.00	Other opt avail
ISA	VGA	125, 110/220VAC 60/50Hz	1, carry-in	DOS, Windows 3.0	$2,599.00	Includes mouse, other opt avail
ISA	12" VGA gray display, VGA 1024 x 768, 512K	150 watt	30 days money back; 1, on-site	DOS, Windows 3.0	$1,999.00	Includes mouse, OmniKey, 102 keyboard, lifetime 24-hr tech support, other opt avail
ISA	VGA (800 x 600)	145	2, carry-in	DOS, Windows 3.0	$1,895.00	Other hard disk sizes avail, displays avail, mouse inc
ISA		145	1, carry-in	ALR utils	$1,195.00	CPU upgr, other opt avail
ISA	VGA (800 x 600)	145, 110V or 220V AC	1, carry-in	DOS, DiskCache, FASTRAM, Super Spool, LIM 4.0	$2,395.00	Other opt avail
		110/220V 50/60Hz	1, GE on-site	DOS, Windows 3.0		Other opt avail
ISA	VGA (1024 x 768) 1M	65	1, send-back	DOS	$1,635.00	Other opt avail

continues

Table 4.4. Continued

COMPANY	MODEL	CPU, SPEED, CACHE	MIN, MAX RAM (M)	UNIT SIZE	BIOS, VER.	DISK DRIVES (M)	HARD DISK CAP, SPEED, TYPE	ADAPTERS INCLUDED	EXP. SLOTS
IBM	8535	80386SX, 20MHz	2, 16	Mid size	IBM	1.44		1 ser, 1 par, 1 mouse	3 16-bit
IBM	8540	80386SX, 20MHz	2, 16	Mid size	IBM	1.44		1 ser, 1 par, 1 mouse	3 16-bit
IBM	8557	80386SX, 20MHz	4, 16	Mid size	IBM	2.88	80M, 17ms, SCSI	1 ser, 1 par, 1 mouse, 1 SCSI	1 16-bit, 2 32-bit
NCR	PC386SX20	80386SX, 20MHz	2,	Mid size		1.2 or 1.44	40M or 100M	2 ser, 1 par	4 16-bit
NEC	PowerMate SX/20	80386SX, 20MHz	2, 16	Small	Phoenix 1.40.07	1.2 or 1.44		1 ser, 1 par, 1 mouse	4 16-bit
Samsung Information Systems	DeskMaster 386S/20/ SD721	80386SX, 20MHz	2, 32	Small		1.44		1 ser, 1 par, 1 mouse, IDE	3 16-bit
Swan Technologies	386SX-20	80386SX, 20MHz	1, 8	Mid size	Quadtel Flex AT, VIA	1.2 or 1.44	50M, 17ms, IDE	2 ser, 1 par	1 8-bit, 6 16-bit
Tandy	4020 SX	80386SX, 20MHz	1, 16	Mid size		1.44			3 16-bit
Wyse Technology	Decision 386SX/20	80386SX, 20MHz	1, 16	Small	Phoenix, Wyse	1.2 or 1.44	40M or 110M	2 ser, 1 par, IDE	2 8-bit, 5 16-bit
Zeos International, Ltd.	386SX-20	80386SX, 20MHz	1, 16	Mid size	Award	1.2/1.44	42M, IDE	2 ser, 1 par, 1 game	1 8-bit, 7 16-bit
Zeos International, Ltd.	386SX-20	80386SX, 20MHz	2, 16	Mid size	Award	1.2/1.44	85M, IDE	2 ser, 1 par, 1 game	1 8-bit, 7 16-bit
Zeos International, Ltd.	386SX-20	80386SX, 20MHz	512K, 16	Mid size	Award	1.2 or 1.44	42M, IDE	2 ser, 1 par, 1 game	1 8-bit, 7 16-bit
Zeos International, Ltd.	386SX-20	80386SX, 20MHz	1, 16	Mid size	Award	1.2 or 1.44	42M, IDE	2 ser, 1 par, 1 game	1 8-bit, 7 16-bit
Zeos International, Ltd.	386SX-20	80386SX, 20MHz	4, 16	Mid size	Award	1.2/1.44	130M, IDE	2 ser, 1 par, 1 game	1 8-bit, 7 16-bit
COMPAQ	COMPAQ DeskPro 386s/20 1	80386SX, 20MHz, 4K	2, 16	Mid size	COMPAQ	1.44		1 ser, 1 par, 1 mouse	5 16-bit
COMPAQ	COMPAQ DeskPro 386s/20 120	80386SX, 20MHz, 4K	2, 16	Mid size	COMPAQ	1.44	120M, 19ms	1 ser, 1 par, 1 mouse	5 16-bit
COMPAQ	COMPAQ DeskPro 386s/20 60	80386SX, 20MHz, 4K	2, 16	Mid size	COMPAQ	1.44	60M, 19ms	1 ser, 1 par, 1 mouse	5 16-bit
Packard Bell	Force 820	80386SX, 20MHz, 16K	2, 16	Mid size	Phoenix	1.2/1.44	85M, 20ms, IDE	2 ser, 1 par, 1 mouse	1 8-bit, 3 16-bit
Hyundai	Super-386STc	80386SX, 20MHz, 16K	2, 16	Mid size	Hewlett-Packard	1.2	40M, IDE	2 ser, 1 par, IDE	1 8-bit, 4 16-bit
CompuAdd	CompuAdd 320sc	80386SX, 20MHz, 32K	2, 32	Small	Phoenix 386AT Plus	1.44 or 1.2	40M, 28ms, IDE		3 16-bit, 2 8-bit

BUS TYPE	VIDEO ADAPTER, DISPLAY	POWER SUPPLY (watts)	WARRANTY (years)	SOFTWARE INCLUDED	RETAIL PRICE	OTHER INFORMATION
ISA	VGA	118	1, carry-in; on-site avail		$1,995.00	Other opt avail
ISA	VGA	197	1, carry-in; on-site avail		$2,395.00	Other opt avail
MCA	VGA	197	1, carry-in; on-site avail		$3,625.00	Other opt avail
ISA	VGA (1024 x 768)	175	1, carry-in			NCR planar board technology, other opt avail
ISA	NEC VGA	110, 115V/ 230V Universal	1, carry-in	DOS, Windows 3.0	$2,149.00	Other opt avail
ISA		100	1, carry-in	DOS, Windows 3.0, VGA utils	$1,749.00	Contact via 800#, BBS, fax, authorized service vendors, other opt avail
ISA	Swan 1024 x 768 display, optional adapters	200	2, on-site	Swan utils, LIM 4.0	$1,845.00	Lifetime toll-free tech support, other opt avail
ISA	VGA (1024 x 768)	100	1, carry-in		$1,999.00	Other opt avail
ISA		200	1, carry-in	Wyse Enhanced DOS, Wyse Setup & Test	$1,799.00	Other opt avail
ISA	VGA color display, Diamond Speedstar Plus 1024 x 768, 1M	200	30 days money back; 1, on-site avail	DOS	$1,695.00	RS or F12 Case has 7-bay desktop, 2 fans, other opt avail
ISA	VGA color display, Diamond Speedstar Plus 1024 x 768, 1M	200	30 days money back; 1, on-site avail	DOS, Windows 3.0	$1,995.00	RS or F12 Case has 7-bay desktop, 2 fans, other opt avail
ISA	Monochrome display, Hercules Graphics Adapter	200	30 days money back; 1, on-site avail		$1,195.00	RS or F12 Case has 7-bay desktop, 2 fans, other opt avail
ISA	VGA monochrome disp Diamond Speedstar Plus 1024 x 768, 1M	200	30 days money back; 1, on-site avail	DOS	$1,395.00	RS or F12 Case has 7-bay desktop, 2 fans, other opt avail
ISA	VGA color display, Diamond Speedstar Plus 1024 x 768, 1M	200	30 days money back; 1, on-site avail	DOS, Windows 3.0	$2,295.00	RS or F12 Case has 7-bay desktop, 2 fans, other opt avail
ISA	VGA		1, carry-in		$2,299.00	Other opt avail, other OS avail
ISA	VGA		1, carry-in		$3,299.00	Other opt avail, other OS avail
ISA	VGA		1, carry-in		$2,899.00	Other opt avail, other OS avail
ISA	VGA (1024 x 768)	150	1, on-site	DOS, Packard Bell Desktop, Lotus Works	$2,995.00	CPU cache upgr to 32K, includes mouse, other opt avail
ISA		135	18 months; on-site avail	DOS, Windows 3.0	$1,595.00	100M, 200M, and 300M hard disks avail, other opt avail
ISA	VGA (800 x 600)	145	1, send-back; carry-in	DOS, Windows 3.0	$2,245.00	Other opt avail

continues

Table 4.4. Concluded

COMPANY	MODEL	CPU, SPEED, CACHE	MIN, MAX RAM (M)	UNIT SIZE	BIOS, VER.	DISK DRIVES (M)	HARD DISK CAP, SPEED, TYPE	ADAPTERS INCLUDED	EXP. SLOTS
Data World	DW-386-20SX	80386SX, 20MHz, 32K	4, 16	Full size	AMI	1.2/1.4	120M, 19ms, IDE		2 8-bit, 5 16-bit
EPSON	Equity 386SX/20 Plus	80386SX, 20MHz, 32K	2, 16	Small	Seiko EPSON (proprietary)	1.2 or 1.44		1 ser, 1 par, 1 mouse	1 8-bit, 3 16-bit
Gateway 2000	386SX-20C	80386SX, 20MHz, 32K	4, 16	Mid size	Quadtel	1.2/1.44	80M, 17ms, IDE	2 ser, 1 par, 1 PS, 2 mouse	5 16-bit
Microlab	320S	80386SX, 20MHz, 32K	4, 8	Mid size	AMI	1.2/1.44	44M, 28ms, IDE	2 ser, 1 par, 1 game	2 8-bit, 5 16-bit
Tangent Computer	Mdl 320s	80386SX, 20MHz, 32K	2, 16	Mid size	AMI	1.2 or 1.44	100M, 15ms, IDE	2 ser, 1 par	
Zenith	Z-386 SX/20 Mdl 40	80386SX, 20MHz, 32K	2, 16	Mid size		1.44	40M, 28ms	2 ser, 1 par	4 16-bit
Northgate	SlimLine 320SX	80386SX, 20MHz, 64K	1, 16	Mid size	AMI	1.2/1.44	40M, IDE	2 ser, 1 par, IDE	2 8-bit, 3 16-bit
Zeos International, Ltd.	386SX-20 with cache	80386SX, 20MHz, 64K	1, 16	Mid size	Award	1.2 or 1.44	42M, IDE	2 ser, 1 par, 1 game	1 8-bit, 7 16-bit
Zeos International, Ltd.	386SX-20 with cache	80386SX, 20MHz, 64K	1, 16	Mid size	Award	1.2/1.44	42M, IDE	2 ser, 1 par, 1 game	1 8-bit, 7 16-bit
Zeos International, Ltd.	386SX-20 with cache	80386SX, 20MHz, 64K	2, 16	Mid size	Award	1.2/1.44	85M, IDE	2 ser, 1 par, 1 game	1 8-bit, 7 16-bit
Zeos International, Ltd.	386SX-20 with cache	80386SX, 20MHz, 64K	4, 16	Mid size	Award	1.2/1.44	130M, IDE	2 ser, 1 par, 1 game	1 8-bit, 7 16-bit
Zeos International, Ltd.	386SX-20 with cache	80386SX, 20MHz, 64K	512K, 16	Mid size	Award	1.2 or 1.44	42M, IDE	2 ser, 1 par, 1 game	1 8-bit, 7 16-bit
PC Brand, Inc.	386SX/20 cache	80386SX, 20MHz, 64K	512K, 8	Full size		1.2 or 1.44		2 ser, 1 par	ISA
CompuAdd	CompuAdd 325	80386SX, 25MHz, 32K	4, 16	Full size	Phoenix 386AT Plus	1.44 or 1.2	40M, 28ms, IDE		6 16-bit, 1 8-bit

BUS TYPE	VIDEO ADAPTER, DISPLAY	POWER SUPPLY (watts)	WARRANTY (years)	SOFTWARE INCLUDED	RETAIL PRICE	OTHER INFORMATION
ISA	Viewsonic 5 SuperVGA display, Orchid Pro Designer IIs	200	1, on-site	DOS, Windows 3.0 with mouse	$2,795.00	Other opt avail
ISA	VGA (800 x 600) Edsun CEG	140	1, carry-in	Windows 3.0, Bitstream Facelift, diags	$2,199.00	Other opt avail
ISA	14" Crystal Scan 1024 VGA color display, VGA 1024 x 768, 512K	200	30 days money back; 1, on-site	DOS, Windows 3.0	$1,895.00	Includes mouse, other opt avail
ISA	Diamond Speedstar VGA 1024 x 768, 1M	200	1, send-back; free shipping	DOS	$1,595.00	Free shipping, other opt avail
ISA	14" NI display, Orchid Pro Designer IIs 1024 x 768 ni VESA	220	1, send-back	DOS	$1,995.00	Other opt avail
ISA	VGA	125, 110/220VA C 60/50Hz	1, carry-in	DOS, Windows 3.0	$2,599.00	Includes mouse, other opt avail
ISA	12" VGA gray display, VGA 1024 x 768, 512K	150 watt	30 days money back; 1, on-site	DOS, Windows 3.0	$2,199.00	Includes mouse, OmniKey, 102 keyboard, lifetime 24-hr tech support, other opt avail
ISA	Monochrome VGA display, Diamond Speedstar Plus, 1M	200	30 days money back; 1, on-site avail	DOS	$1,595.00	RS or F12 Case has 7-bay desktop, 2 fans, other opt avail
ISA	VGA color display, Diamond Speedstar Plus 1024 x 768, 1M	200	30 days money back; 1, on-site avail	DOS	$1,895.00	RS or F12 Case has 7-bay desktop, 2 fans, other opt avail
ISA	VGA color display, Diamond Speedstar Plus 1024 x 768, 1M	200	30 days money back; 1, on-site avail	DOS, Windows 3.0	$2,195.00	RS or F12 Case has 7-bay desktop, 2 fans, other opt avail
ISA	VGA color display, Diamond Speedstar Plus 1024 x 768, 1M	200	30 days money back; 1, on-site avail	DOS, Windows 3.0	$2,495.00	RS or F12 Case has 7-bay desktop, 2 fans, other opt avail
ISA	Monochrome display, Hercules Graphics Adapter	200	30 days money back; 1, on-site avail		$1,395.00	RS or F12 Case has 7-bay desktop, 2 fans, other opt avail
ISA		200	1, send-back; 5, prorated		$819.00	Choice of Desktop or SlimLine Case, other opt avail
ISA	VGA (800 x 600)	200	1, send-back; carry-in	DOS, Windows 3.0	$2,679.00	Other opt avail

Table 4.5. IBM-Compatible 80386 Desktop Computers

COMPANY	MODEL	CPU, SPEED, CACHE	MIN, MAX RAM (M)	UNIT SIZE	BIOS, VER.	DISK DRIVES (M)	HARD DISK CAP, SPEED, TYPE	ADAPTERS INCLUDED	EXP. SLOTS
Hyundai	Super-386SE	80386DX, 16MHz	2, 16	Mid size	Hewlett-Packard	1.2	40M, IDE	2 ser, 1 par, IDE	1 8-bit, 4 16-bit
Insight	Insight 386SX-16MHz	80386DX, 16MHz	4, 8	Mid size	Chips & Tech 1.2 1, 31, 91	1.2/1.44	52M, 25ms, IDE		6 16-bit, 1 8-bit
Tandy	4016	80386DX, 16MHz	1, 16	Mid size		1.44			6 16-bit, 2 32-bit
Tri-Star Computer Corporation	Tri-Star TS316i SX	80386DX, 16MHz	2, 8	Small	AMI	1.2 and 1.44	80M, 25ms, IDE		2 8-bit, 5 16-bit, 1 32-bit
Gateway 2000	386SX-16	80386DX, 16MHz, 32K	2, 16	Mid size	Quadtel	1.2/1.44	40M, 17ms, IDE	2 ser, 1 par, 1 PS, 2 mouse	5 16-bit
Acer America Corporation	1100/20	80386DX, 20MHz	2, 4	Full size		1.2		2 ser, 1 par	5 8-bit, 2 16-bit, 1 32-bit
COMPAQ	COMPAQ Portable 386 Model 110	80386DX, 20MHz	1, 10	Port 21 lbs	COMPAQ	1.2 or 1.44	110M, 25ms	1 ser, 1 par, 1 RGBI	
COMPAQ	COMPAQ Portable 386 Model 40	80386DX, 20MHz	1, 10	Port 21 lbs	COMPAQ	1.2 or 1.44	40M, 29ms	1 ser, 1 par, 1 RGB	
Hewlett-Packard	HP Vectra QS/20 PC Model 1	80386DX, 20MHz	1, 16	Mid size	Hewlett-Packard	1.2 or 1.44	42M or 84M	1 ser, 1 par, 1 mouse	1 8-bit, 6 16-bit
IBM	8570	80386DX, 20MHz	4, 16	Mid size	IBM	1.44	80M, 17ms, ESDI	1 ser, 1 par, 1 mouse, 1 SCSI	1 16-bit, 2 32-bit
IBM	8580	80386DX, 20MHz	4, 16	Full size	IBM	1.44	80M, 17ms, SCSI	1 ser, 1 par, 1 mouse, 1 SCSI	5 16-bit, 3 32-bit
Insight	Insight 386SX-20MHz	80386DX, 20MHz	4, 8	Mid size	Chips & Tech 1, 31, 91	1.2/1.44	80M, 17ms, IDE		6 16-bit, 1 8-bit
Northgate	Page Mode 320	80386DX, 20MHz	4, 16	Full size	AMI	1.2/1.44	40M, IDE	2 ser, 1 par	1 8-bit, 5 16-bit, 2 32-bit
Northgate	SlimLine 320	80386DX, 20MHz	4, 8	Mid size	AMI	1.2/1.44	40M, IDE	2 ser, 1 par, IDE	2 8-bit, 3 16-bit
Tri-Star Computer Corporation	Tri-Lan Workstation WS320i	80386DX, 20MHz	1, 8	Small	Award	Option			1 16-bit
Tri-Star Computer Corporation	Tri-Star TS320i SX	80386DX, 20MHz	2, 8	Small	AMI	1.2 and 1.44	80M, 25ms, IDE		2 8-bit, 5 16-bit, 1 32-bit
Zenith	Z-386/20 Model 40	80386DX, 20MHz, 16K	1, 20	Full size		1.44	40M, 23ms, ESDI	2 ser, 1 par	1 16-bit, 3 32-bit
COMPAQ	COMPAQ DeskPro 386/20e 1	80386DX, 20MHz, 32K	4, 16	Mid size	COMPAQ	1.44		1 ser, 1 par, 1 mouse	4 8-bit or 16-bit
COMPAQ	COMPAQ DeskPro 386/20e 110	80386DX, 20MHz, 32K	4, 16	Mid size	COMPAQ	1.44	110M, 25ms	1 ser, 1 par, 1 mouse	4 8-bit or 16-bit
COMPAQ	COMPAQ DeskPro 386/20e 40	80386DX, 20MHz, 32K	4, 16	Mid size	COMPAQ	1.44	40M, 29ms	1 ser, 1 par, 1 mouse	4 8-bit or 16-bit

BUS TYPE	VIDEO ADAPTER, DISPLAY	POWER SUPPLY (watts)	WARRANTY (years)	SOFTWARE INCLUDED	RETAIL PRICE	OTHER INFORMATION
ISA		135	18 months; on-site avail	DOS	$1,295.00	100M, 200M, and 300M hard drives available, other opt avail
ISA	Insight SuperVGA Display, Diamond Speed Star 1024 x 768, 1M	200	1, send-back	DOS	$1,495.00	Includes Microsoft-compatible mouse, toll-free tech support
ISA	VGA	200	1, carry-in		$2,299.00	Other opt avail
ISA	Matsushita Viewsonic 4 Multisync Display, Paradise 1024 x 768, 512K	220	30 days money back; 15 months send-back	DOS	$1,595.00	Includes lifetime toll-free tech support, other opt avail
ISA	14" Crystal Scan 1024 VGA Color Display, VGA 1024 x 768, 512K	200	30 days money back; 1, on-site	DOS, Windows 3.0	$1,495.00	Includes mouse, other opt avail
ISA		196	2, carry-in	DOS, Windows 3.0	$2,395.00	Other hard disk sizes avail, displays avail
	Dual-Mode Plasma Display, 640 x 400 text, 640 x 200 graphics	110V-220V AC	1, carry-in		$7,999.00	Other opt avail, other OS avail
	Dual-Mode Plasma Display, 640 x 400 text, 640 x 200 graphics	110V-220V AC	1, carry-in		$6,999.00	Other opt avail, other OS avail
ISA	VGA (800 x 600)	456	1, on-site	Setup, LIM 4.0 util, Windows 3.0		Other opt avail
MCA	VGA	132	1, carry-in; on-site avail		$4,095.00	Upgr CPU, other opt avail
MCA	VGA	225	1, carry-in; on-site avail		$4,595.00	Other opt avail
ISA	Insight SuperVGA Display, Diamond Speed Star 1024 x 768, 1M	200	1, send-back	DOS	$1,695.00	Includes Microsoft-compatible mouse, toll-free tech support
ISA	14" VGA Gray	200	30 days money back; 1, on-site	DOS, Windows 3.0	$2,999.00	Includes mouse, OmniKey, ULTRA keyboard, lifetime 24-hr tech support, other opt avail
ISA	12" VGA Gray Display, VGA 1024 x 768, 512K	150 watt	30 days money back; 1, on-site	DOS, Windows 3.0	$2,499.00	Includes mouse, OmniKey, 102 keyboard, lifetime 24-hr tech support, other opt avail
ISA	14" Septre Monochrome Display, MDA	250	30 days money back; 1, send-back		$995.00	Includes lifetime toll-free tech support, other opt avail
ISA	Matsushita Viewsonic 4 Multisync Display, Paradise 1024 x 768, 512K	220	30 days money back; 15 month send-back	DOS	$1,695.00	Includes lifetime toll-free tech support, other opt avail
ISA	VGA	200, 110/220 VAC	1, carry-in	DOS, Windows 3.0	$3,299.00	Includes mouse, other opt avail
ISA	VGA		1, carry-in		$2,799.00	Other opt avail, other OS avail
ISA	VGA		1, carry-in		$3,699.00	Other opt avail, other OS avail
ISA	VGA		1, carry-in		$3,199.00	Other opt avail, other OS avail

4

continues

Table 4.5. Continued

COMPANY	MODEL	CPU, SPEED, CACHE	MIN, MAX RAM (M)	UNIT SIZE	BIOS, VER.	DISK DRIVES (M)	HARD DISK CAP, SPEED, TYPE	ADAPTERS INCLUDED	EXP. SLOTS
Acer America Corporation	1100/25	80386DX, 25MHz	2, 8	Full size		1.2		2 ser, 1 par, IDE interface	6 8-bit, 1 16-bit, 1 32-bit
Austin Computer Systems	386/25 Winstation	80386DX, 25MHz	2, 8	Small	Quadtel	1.2 or 1.44	85M, IDE		6 16-bit, 1 8-bit
Data World	DW-386-25	80386DX, 25MHz	4, 16	Full size	Phoenix	1.2/1.4	120M, 19ms, IDE		8 16-bit
Dell Computer Corporation	Dell System 325P	80386DX, 25MHz	4, 16	Small	Phoenix, Dell	1.2 or 1.44	80M, 15ms, IDE	2 ser, 1 par, 1 mouse	3 16-bit
Insight	Insight 386SX-25MHz	80386DX, 25MHz	4, 16	Mid size	AMI 8, 30, 90	1.2/1.44	130M, 15ms, IDE		2 8-bit, 6 16-bit
Microlab	325d	80386DX, 25MHz	4, 8	Full size	AMI	1.2/1.44	130M, 19ms, IDE	2 ser, 1 par, 1 game	1 8-bit, 6 16-bit
NEC	Business Mate 386/25	80386DX, 25MHz	4, 16	Full size	Phoenix			2 ser, 1 par	2 8-bit, 5 8-bit or 16-bit, 1 32-bit
Packard Bell	Force 386/25	80386DX, 25MHz	2, 32	Full size	Phoenix	1.2/1.44	130M, 20ms, IDE	2 ser, 1 par	2 8-bit, 5 16-bit
PC Brand, Inc.	386/25	80386DX, 25MHz	1, 16	Full size		1.2 or 1.44		2 ser, 1 par	ISA
Swan Technologies	386/25	80386DX, 25MHz	1, 16	Mid size	AMI C & T 8230	1.2 or 1.44	50M, 17ms, IDE	2 ser, 1 par	2 8-bit, 5 16-bit, 1 32-bit
Tandon	386/25	80386DX, 25MHz	2, 8	Full size	Tandon	1.2 or 1.44	110M, 25ms, IDE		
Tri-Star Computer Corporation	Tri-Star TS325i DX	80386DX, 25MHz	2, 8	Small	AMI	1.2 and 1.44	80M, 25ms, IDE		2 8-bit, 5 16-bit, 1 32-bit
USA Flex	Flex 386 25 Non Cache	80386DX, 25MHz	2, 16	Full size	Phoenix 1.10.01	1.2 and 1.44	89.1M, 19ms, IDE		2 8-bit, 5 16-bit, 1 32-bit
Zeos International, Ltd.	386-25 Upgradable systems	80386DX, 25MHz	4, 32	Mid size	Award	1.2/1.44	130M, IDE	2 ser, 1 par, 1 game	1 8-bit, 7 16-bit
Zeos International, Ltd.	386-25 Upgradable systems	80386DX, 25MHz	1, 32	Mid size	Award	1.2 or 1.44	42M, IDE	2 ser, 1 par, 1 game	1 8-bit, 7 16-bit
Zeos International, Ltd.	386-25 Upgradable systems	80386DX, 25MHz	8, 32	Mid size	Award	1.2/1.44	210M, IDE	2 ser, 1 par, 1 game	1 8-bit, 7 16-bit
DTK Computer Inc.	KEEN-2530	80386DX, 25MHz	0, 16	Full size	27256, 4.26				2 8-bit, 5 16-bit, 1 32-bit
Zeos International, Ltd.	386-25 Upgradable systems	80386DX, 25MHz	2, 32	Mid size	Award	1.2/1.44	85M, IDE	2 ser, 1 par, 1 game	1 8-bit, 7 16-bit
Zenith	Z-386/25 Model 70	80386DX, 25MHz, 16K	4, 20	Full size		1.44	70M, 18ms, ESDI	2 ser, 1 par	1 16-bit, 3 32-bit
COMPAQ	COMPAQ DeskPro 386/25e 1	80386DX, 25MHz, 32K	4, 16	Mid size	COMPAQ	1.44		1 ser, 1 par, 1 mouse	4 8-bit or 16-bit

BUS TYPE	VIDEO ADAPTER, DISPLAY	POWER SUPPLY (watts)	WARRANTY (years)	SOFTWARE INCLUDED	RETAIL PRICE	OTHER INFORMATION
ISA		230	2, carry-in	DOS, Windows 3.0	$2,995.00	Other hard disk sizes avail, displays avail
		110/220V 50/60Hz	1, GE on-site	DOS, Windows 3.0		Other opt avail
ISA	Viewsonic 5 SuperVGA Display, Orchid Pro Designer IIs	200	1, on-site	DOS, Windows 3.0 with mouse	$2,945.00	Other opt avail
ISA	VGA	85	1, on-site	Tutorial, diags	$2,899.00	Includes unlimited toll-free tech support, optional 32K CPU cache, other opt avail
ISA	Insight SuperVGA Display, Diamond Speed Star 1024 x 768, 1M	200	1, send-back	DOS	$1,895.00	Includes Microsoft-compatible mouse, toll-free tech support
ISA	Diamond Speedstar VGA 1024 x 768, 1M	200	1, send-back; free shipping	DOS	$1,995.00	Free shipping, other opt avail
ISA		115V/ 230V Universal	1, carry-in		$5,299.00	Other opt avail
ISA	VGA (1024 x 768)	150	1, on-site	DOS, Packard Bell Desktop, Lotus Works	$4,195.00	Includes mouse, 2400B int modem, Prodigy Service start-up kit, other opt avail
ISA		200	1, send-back; 5, prorated		$1,049.00	Choice of Desktop or SlimLine Case, other opt avail
ISA	Swan 1024 x 768 Display, Optional Adapters	200	2, on-site	Swan utils, LIM 4.0	$2,095.00	Lifetime toll-free tech support, other opt avail
	14" VGA Monochrome Display, VGA	190	1, on-site	DOS, Windows 3.0	$3,099.00	Other opt avail
ISA	Matsushita Viewsonic 4 Multisync Display, Paradise 1024 x 768, 512K	220	30 days money back; 15 months send-back	DOS	$1,895.00	Includes lifetime toll-free tech support, other opt avail
ISA	Samsung, Samtron, or CTX 1024 x 768 Display, VGA 1024 x 768, 512K	200	1, on-site	DOS, Windows 3.0		Includes mouse, other opt avail
ISA	VGA Color Display, Diamond Speedstar Plus 1024 x 768, 1M	300	30 days money back; 1, on-site avail	DOS, Windows 3.0	$2,495.00	RS or F12 Case has 7-bay desktop, 2 fans, other opt avail
ISA	Monochrome Display, Hercules Graphics Adapter	300	30 days money back; 1, on-site avail		$1,395.00	RS or F12 Case has 7-bay desktop, 2 fans, other opt avail
ISA	VGA Color Display, Diamond Speedstar Plus 1024 x 768, 1M	300	30 days money back; 1, on-site avail	DOS, Windows 3.0	$2,995.00	RS or F12 Case has 7-bay desktop, 2 fans, other opt avail
ISA		200	1, carry-in		$925.00	Other opt avail
ISA	VGA Monochrome Disp, Diamond Speedstar Plus 1024 x 768, 1M	300	30 days money back; 1, on-site avail	DOS, Windows 3.0	$1,995.00	RS or F12 Case has 7-bay desktop, 2 fans, other opt avail
ISA	VGA	200, 110/220 VAC	1, carry-in	DOS, Windows 3.0	$4,499.00	Includes mouse, other opt avail
ISA	VGA		1, carry-in		$3,999.00	Other opt avail, other OS avail

continues

Table 4.5. Continued

COMPANY	MODEL	CPU, SPEED, CACHE	MIN, MAX RAM (M)	UNIT SIZE	BIOS, VER.	DISK DRIVES (M)	HARD DISK CAP, SPEED, TYPE	ADAPTERS INCLUDED	EXP. SLOTS
COMPAQ	COMPAQ DeskPro 386/25e 120	80386DX, 25MHz, 32K	4, 16	Mid size	COMPAQ	1.44	120M, 19ms	1 ser, 1 par, 1 mouse	4 8-bit or 16-bit
COMPAQ	COMPAQ DeskPro 386/25e 60	80386DX, 25MHz, 32K	4, 16	Mid size	COMPAQ	1.44	60M, 19ms	1 ser, 1 par, 1 mouse	4 8-bit or 16-bit
Dell Computer Corporation	Dell System 325D	80386DX, 25MHz, 32K	1, 16	Mid size	Phoenix, Dell	1.44	80M, 15ms, IDE	2 ser, 1 par, 1 mouse	1 8-bit, 5 16-bit
EPSON	Equity 386/25 Plus	80386DX, 25MHz, 32K	4, 16	Small	Seiko EPSON (proprietary)	1.2 or 1.44		1 ser, 1 par, 1 mouse	1 8-bit, 3 16-bit
Gateway 2000	386-25	80386DX, 25MHz, 32K	4, 8	Full size	Phoenix	1.2/1.44	80M, 17ms, IDE	2 ser, 1 par	7 16-bit, 1 32-bit
Hewlett-Packard	HP Vectra RS/25C PC	80386DX, 25MHz, 32K	4, 16	Full tower	Hewlett-Packard	1.2 or 1.44	168M or 330M, EDSI	1 ser, 1 par, 1 mouse	2 8-bit, 6 16-bit
Hyundai	Super-386N	80386DX, 25MHz, 32K	2, 16	Full size	Hewlett-Packard	1.2	40M, IDE	1 ser, 1 par	1 8-bit, 1 8-bit or 32-bit, 6 16-bit
NEC	PowerMate 386/25	80386DX, 25MHz, 32K	2, 16	Full size	Phoenix 1.10.78	1.2/1.44/ 360K		2 ser, 1 par	2 8-bit, 5 8-bit or 16-bit, 1 32-bit
NEC	PowerMate 386/25S	80386DX, 25MHz, 32K	4, 16	Small	Phoenix 1.40.21	1.2/1.44		1 ser, 1 par, 1 mouse	4 8-bit or 16-bit, 1 32-bit
PC Brand, Inc.	15.44	80386DX, 25MHz, 32K	1, 16	Full size		1.2 or 1.44		2 ser, 1 par	ISA
Tandy	4025 LX	80386DX, 25MHz, 32K	1, 16	Mid size		1.44			6 16-bit, 2 32-bit
Club Computer Corporation	Falcon	80386DX, 25MHz, 64K	4, 64	Mid size	AMI	1.2 or 1.44	200M, 15ms, IDE		1 32-bit, 7 8-bit or 16-bit
Insight	Insight 386-25MHz w/64K cache	80386DX, 25MHz, 64K	4, 16	Full size	AMI 8, 30, 90	1.2/1.44	130M, 15ms, IDE		2 8-bit, 6 16-bit
MIS Computer Systems	386/25	80386DX, 25MHz, 64K	2, 16	Mini tower	Phoenix	1.2/1.44	80M, IDE	2 ser, 1 par, 1 game	7 16-bit, 1 16-bit or 32-bit
Northgate	Elegance 325	80386DX, 25MHz, 64K	4, 16	Full size	AMI	1.2/1.44	40M, IDE	2 ser, 1 par	1 8-bit, 6 16-bit, 1 32-bit
Northgate	SlimLine 325	80386DX, 25MHz, 64K	4, 16	Mid size	AMI	1.2/1.44	40M, IDE	2 ser, 1 par, IDE	2 8-bit, 3 16-bit
Samsung Information Systems	Power-Master 386/25/ SD820	80386DX, 25MHz, 64K	4, 8	Full size		1.2/1.44		2 ser, 1 par	1 8-bit, 5 16-bit, 2 32-bit
Standard Computer	386/25	80386DX, 25MHz, 64K	2, 16	Mid size	Phoenix 1.01	1.2/1.44	80M, 19ms, IDE	2 ser, 1 par	6 16-bit
Tangent Computer	Model 325	80386DX, 25MHz, 64K	2, 64	Mid size	AMI 5, 9, 91	1.2 or 1.44	100M, 15ms, IDE	2 ser, 1 par	7 16-bit, 18-bit or 32-bit
USA Flex	Flex 386/25 Cache	80386DX, 25MHz, 64K	2, 16	Full size	AMI 4, 9, 90	1.2 and 1.44	106.9M, 16ms, IDE		1 8-bit, 6 16-bit, 1 32-bit

BUS TYPE	VIDEO ADAPTER, DISPLAY	POWER SUPPLY (watts)	WARRANTY (years)	SOFTWARE INCLUDED	RETAIL PRICE	OTHER INFORMATION
ISA	VGA		1, carry-in		$4,899.00	Other opt avail, other OS avail
ISA	VGA		1, carry-in		$4,499.00	Other opt avail, other OS avail
ISA	VGA	177	1, on-site	Tutorial, diags	$3,199.00	Includes unlimited toll-free tech support, other opt avail
ISA	VGA (1024 x 768)	140	1, carry-in	Windows 3.0, Bitstream Facelift, diags	$3,099.00	Other opt avail
ISA	14" Crystal Scan 1024 VGA, Diamond Speedstar VGA 1024 x 768 1M	200 desktop, 220 twr	30 days money back; 1, on-site	DOS, Windows 3.0	$2,095.00	Includes mouse, other opt avail
ISA	VGA (800 x 600)	460	1, on-site	Setup, LIM 4.0 util, Windows 3.0		Other opt avail
ISA		200	18 months; on-site avail	DOS	$2,295.00	100M, 200M, and 300M hard drives available, other opt avail
ISA		115V/ 230V Universal	1, carry-in; on-site avail	DOS, Windows 3.0	$4,999.00	Other opt avail
ISA		115V/ 230V Universal	1, carry-in	DOS, Windows 3.0	$3,599.00	Other opt avail
ISA		200	1, send-back; 5, prorated		$1,149.00	Choice of Desktop or SlimLine Case, other opt avail
ISA	VGA	200	1, carry-in		$3,299.00	Other opt avail
ISA		200	1, send-back; GE on-site avail	DOS, Windows 3.0		Shadow RAM, BIOS Caching, CPU upgr 386, 486SX, 486, Club Rainbow SuperVGA adapter avail
ISA	Insight SuperVGA Display, Diamond Speed Star 1024 x 768, 1M	200	1, send-back	DOS	$1,995.00	Includes Microsoft-compatible mouse, toll-free tech support
ISA	CTX 14" Display, Trident VGA 1024 x 768, 1M	200-250 switching	1, send-back	DOS	$2,062.00	Other opt avail
ISA	14" VGA Gray	200	30 days money back; 1, on-site	DOS, Windows 3.0	$2,999.00	Includes mouse, OmniKey, ULTRA keyboard, lifetime 24-hr tech support, other opt avail
ISA	12" VGA Gray Display, VGA 1024 x 768, 512K, Edsun CEG	150	30 days money back; 1, on-site	DOS, Windows 3.0	$2,699.00	Includes mouse, OmniKey, 102 keyboard, lifetime 24-hr tech support, other opt avail
ISA		250	1, carry-in	DOS, Windows 3.0	$3,199.00	Contact via 800#, BBS, fax, authorized service vendors, other opt avail
ISA	14" Viewsonic 4, VGA 1024 x 768, 512K	200	1, TRW on-site	DOS	$1,995.00	Other opt avail
ISA	14" NI Display, Orchid Pro Designer IIs 1024 x 768 ni VESA	220	1, send-back	DOS	$2,195.00	Other opt avail
ISA	Samsung, Samtron, or CTX 1024 x 768 Display, VGA 1024 x 768, 512K	200	1, on-site	DOS, Windows 3.0, Lotus Works 2.0		Includes mouse, other opt avail

continues

Table 4.5. Continued

COMPANY	MODEL	CPU, SPEED, CACHE	MIN, MAX RAM (M)	UNIT SIZE	BIOS, VER.	DISK DRIVES (M)	HARD DISK CAP, SPEED, TYPE	ADAPTERS INCLUDED	EXP. SLOTS
Wyse Technology	Decision 386/25	80386DX, 25MHz, 64K	2, 32	Small		1.2 or 1.44	40M or 110M	2 ser, 1 par, IDE	2 8-bit, 6 16-bit
Zeos International, Ltd.	386-25C Upgradable systems	80386DX, 25MHz, 128K	1, 32	Mid size	Award	1.2/1.44	42M, IDE	2 ser, 1 par, 1 game	1 8-bit, 7 16-bit
Zeos International, Ltd.	386-25C Upgradable systems	80386DX, 25MHz, 128K	2, 32	Mid size	Award	1.2/1.44	85M, IDE	2 ser, 1 par, 1 game	1 8-bit, 7 16-bit
Zeos International, Ltd.	386-25C Upgradable systems	80386DX, 25MHz, 128K	4, 32	Mid size	Award	1.2/1.44	130M, IDE	2 ser, 1 par, 1 game	1 8-bit, 7 16-bit
Zeos International, Ltd.	386-25C Upgradable systems	80386DX, 25MHz, 128K	8, 32	Mid size	Award	1.2/1.44	210M, IDE	2 ser, 1 par, 1 game	1 8-bit, 7 16-bit
Acer America Corporation	1100/33	80386DX, 33MHz	4, 24	Full size		1.2		2 ser, 1 par, IDE interface	6 8-bit, 1 16-bit, 1 32-bit
Advanced Logic Research	Business STATION 386/33 80	80386DX, 33MHz	1, 33	Slim line	Phoenix 10.01.10	1.44	80M, 15ms, IDE	2 ser, 1 par, 1 proprietary	4 32-bit, 1 16-bit
Advanced Logic Research	Business VEISA 386/33	80386DX, 33MHz	1, 49	Small	Phoenix	1.2		1 ser, 1 par, 1 mouse	4 32-bit, 2 16-bit
Advanced Logic Research	MPS 386/33 101	80386DX, 33MHz	1, 17	Mid size	Phoenix	1.44		1 ser, 1 par, 1 PS, 2 mouse, IDE	4 16-bit, 2 32-bit, 2 prop
Austin Computer Systems	386/33 Winstation	80386DX, 33MHz	4, 8	Small	Quadtel	1.2 or 1.44	125M, IDE		6 16-bit, 1 8-bit
Dell Computer Corporation	Dell System 333P	80386DX, 33MHz	4, 16	Small	Phoenix, Dell	1.2 or 1.44	80M, 15ms, IDE	2 ser, 1 par, 1 mouse	3 16-bit
Insight	Insight 386-33MHz w/ 64K cache	80386DX, 33MHz	4, 16	Full tower	AMI 8, 30, 90	1.2/1.44	130M, 15ms, IDE		2 8-bit, 6 16-bit
NEC	PowerMate 386/33E	80386DX, 33MHz	4, 32	Full size	Phoenix 0.10.33 EISA	1.2 or 1.44		2 ser, 1 par, 1 PS, 2 mouse	1 8-/16-bit, 1 32-bit, 5 16-/32-bit
Packard Bell	Force 386/33	80386DX, 33MHz	2, 40	Full size	Phoenix	1.2/1.44		2 ser, 1 par	1 8-bit, 5 16-bit, 2 32-bit
Tandon	386/33	80386DX, 33MHz	1, 16	Full size	Tandon	1.2 or 1.44	110M, 25ms, IDE		
Zeos International, Ltd.	386-33 Upgradable systems	80386DX, 33MHz	8, 32	Mid size	Award	1.2/1.44	210M, IDE	2 ser, 1 par, 1 game	1 8-bit, 7 16-bit
Zeos International, Ltd.	386-33 Upgradable systems	80386DX, 33MHz	4, 32	Mid size	Award	1.2/1.44	130M, IDE	2 ser, 1 par, 1 game	1 8-bit, 7 16-bit
Zeos International, Ltd.	386-33 Upgradable systems	80386DX, 33MHz	1, 32	Mid size	Award	1.2 or 1.44	42M, IDE	2 ser, 1 par, 1 game	1 8-bit, 7 16-bit
Zeos International, Ltd.	386-33 Upgradable systems	80386DX, 33MHz	2, 32	Mid size	Award	1.2/1.44	85M, IDE	2 ser, 1 par, 1 game	1 8-bit, 7 16-bit
Leading Edge	MT33	80386DX, 33MHz, 16K	2, 64	Mini tower		1.2	89M, 19ms, IDE	1 25-pin ser, 1 9-pin ser, 1 par, 1 mouse	1 32-bit, 6 16-bit

BUS TYPE	VIDEO ADAPTER, DISPLAY	POWER SUPPLY (watts)	WARRANTY (years)	SOFTWARE INCLUDED	RETAIL PRICE	OTHER INFORMATION
ISA		200	1, carry-in	Wyse Enhanced DOS, Wyse Setup & Test	$2,599.00	CPU cache exp to 128K, other opt avail
ISA	Monochrome Display, Hercules Graphics Adapter	300	30 days money back; 1, on-site avail		$1,595.00	RS or F12 Case has 7-bay desktop, 2 fans, other opt avail
ISA	VGA Monochrome Disp, Diamond Speedstar Plus 1024 x 768, 1M	300	30 days money back; 1, on-site avail	DOS, Windows 3.0	$2,195.00	RS or F12 Case has 7-bay desktop, 2 fans, other opt avail
ISA	VGA Color Display, Diamond Speedstar Plus 1024 x 768, 1M	300	30 days money back; 1, on-site avail	DOS, Windows 3.0	$2,695.00	RS or F12 Case has 7-bay desktop, 2 fans, other opt avail
ISA	VGA Color Display, Diamond Speedstar Plus 1024 x 768, 1M	300	30 days money back; 1, on-site avail	DOS, Windows 3.0	$3,195.00	RS or F12 Case has 7-bay desktop, 2 fans, other opt avail
ISA		230	2, carry-in	DOS, Windows 3.0	$3,995.00	Other hard disk sizes avail, displays avail
EISA, Prop	VGA	150	1, carry-in	EISA config util & lib, EISA sys util	$3,795.00	CPU upgrade, other opt avail
EISA		145	1, carry-in	Utils & lib (ISA) & User Setup	$1,995.00	CPU upgr, opt 64K CPU cache, other opt avail
MCA, Prop	VGA (1024 x 768)	145	1, carry-in	ALR Micro Channel utils	$1,995.00	CPU upgrade, other opt avail
		110/ 220V 50/60Hz	1, GE on-site	DOS, Windows 3.0		Other opt avail
ISA	VGA	85	1, on-site	Tutorial, diags	$3,299.00	Opt 32K CPU cache, includes unlimited toll-free tech support, other opt avail
ISA	Insight SuperVGA Display, Diamond Speed Star 1024 x 768, 1M	250	1, send-back	DOS	$2,195.00	Includes Microsoft-compatible mouse, toll-free tech support
ISA, EISA		115V/ 230V Universal	1, carry-in	DOS, Windows 3.0	$5,999.00	Other opt avail
ISA		230	1, on-site	DOS, Packard Bell Desktop, Lotus Works	$4,399.00	Includes mouse, 2400B int modem, Prodigy Service start-up kit, other opt avail
	14" VGA Monochrome Display, VGA	190	1, on-site	DOS, Windows 3.0	$3,119.00	Other opt avail
ISA	VGA Color Display, Diamond Speedstar Plus 1024 x 768, 1M	300	30 days money back; 1, on-site avail	DOS, Windows 3.0	$3,095.00	RS or F12 Case has 7-bay desktop, 2 fans, other opt avail
ISA	VGA Color Display, Diamond Speedstar Plus 1024 x 768, 1M	300	30 days money back; 1, on-site avail	DOS, Windows 3.0	$2,595.00	RS or F12 Case has 7-bay desktop, 2 fans, other opt avail
ISA	Monochrome Display, Hercules Graphics Adapter	300	30 days money back; 1, on-site avail		$1,495.00	RS or F12 Case has 7-bay desktop, 2 fans, other opt avail
ISA	VGA Monochrome Disp, Diamond Speedstar Plus 1024 x 768, 1M	300	30 days money back; 1, on-site avail	DOS, Windows 3.0	$2,095.00	RS or F12 Case has 7-bay desktop, 2 fans, other opt avail
ISA	ATI VGA (1024 x 768)	200	20 months carry-in; 6 months on-site	DOS, Windows 3.0	$2,499.00	130M and 210M hard drives avail, other opt avail

continues

Table 4.5. Continued

COMPANY	MODEL	CPU, SPEED, CACHE	MIN, MAX RAM (M)	UNIT SIZE	BIOS, VER.	DISK DRIVES (M)	HARD DISK CAP, SPEED, TYPE	ADAPTERS INCLUDED	EXP. SLOTS
Zenith	Z-386/33E Model 150	80386DX, 33MHz, 16K	4, 20	Full size		1.44	150M, 18ms, ESDI	2 ser, 1 par	1 16-bit, 3 32-bit
Tandy	4033 LX	80386DX, 33MHz, 32K	1, 16	Mid size		1.44			6 16-bit, 2 32-bit
Advanced Logic Research	PowerProVM 386/33	80386DX, 33MHz, 64K	5, 49	Full tower	Phoenix	1.2		2 ser, 1 par, 1 mouse	8 32-bit, 2 16-bit
Altec	Altec 386/33 Cache	80386DX, 33MHz, 64K	4, 32	Mid size	ATI	1.2/1.44	130M, 15ms, IDE	1 par, 2 ser, mouse, 1 game	2 8-bit, 6 16-bit
Club Computer Corporation	Falcon	80386DX, 33MHz, 64K	4, 64	Mid size	AMI	1.2 or 1.44	200M, 15ms, IDE		1 32-bit, 7 8-bit or 16-bit
COMPAQ	COMPAQ DeskPro 386/33L 120	80386DX, 33MHz, 64K	4, 100	Full size	COMPAQ	1.44	120M, 19ms	2 ser, 1 par, 1 mouse	7 8-bit or 16-bit or 32-bit
COMPAQ	COMPAQ DeskPro 386/33L 320	80386DX, 33MHz, 64K	4, 100	Full size	COMPAQ	1.44	320M, 18ms	2 ser, 1 par, 1 mouse	7 8-bit or 16-bit or 32-bit
COMPAQ	COMPAQ DeskPro 386/33L 650	80386DX, 33MHz, 64K	4, 100	Full size	COMPAQ	1.44	650M, 18ms	2 ser, 1 par, 1 mouse	7 8-bit or 16-bit or 32-bit
COMPAQ	COMPAQ SystemPro Mdl 386-240	80386DX, 33MHz, 64K	8, 256	Full tower	COMPAQ	1.44	240M, 19ms	2 ser, 1 par, 1 mouse	6 8-, 16-, or 32-bit, 2 RAM
COMPAQ	COMPAQ SystemPro Mdl 386-420	80386DX, 33MHz, 64K	8, 256	Full tower	COMPAQ	1.44	420M, 18ms	2 ser, 1 par, 1 mouse	6 8-, 16-, or 32-bit, 2 RAM
COMPAQ	COMPAQ SystemPro Mdl 386-840	80386DX, 33MHz, 64K	8, 256	Full tower	COMPAQ	1.44	840M, 18ms	2 ser, 1 par, 1 mouse	6 8-, 16-, or 32-bit, 2 RAM
Data World	DW-386-33I	80386DX, 33MHz, 64K	4, 32	Full size	Phoenix	1.2/1.4	120M, 19ms, IDE		1 8-bit, 5 16-bit, 2 32-bit
Dell Computer Corporation	Dell System 333D	80386DX, 33MHz, 64K	1, 16	Mid size	Phoenix, Dell	1.44	80M, 15ms, IDE	2 ser, 1 par, 1 mouse	1 8-bit, 5 16-bit
DTK Computer Inc.	KEEN-3304	80386DX, 33MHz, 64K	0, 16	Full tower	27256, 4.26				6 16-bit, 1 8-bit, 1 32-bit
Gateway 2000	386-33 Cache	80386DX, 33MHz, 64K	4, 16	Full size	Phoenix	1.2/1.44	200M, 15ms, IDE	2 ser, 1 par	7 16-bit, 1 32-bit
Hyundai	Super-386D	80386DX, 33MHz, 64K	4, 16	Mid size	Hewlett-Packard	1.2	40M, IDE	2 ser, 1 par, IDE	1 8-bit, 1 8-bit or 32-bit, 6 16-bit
Leading Edge	D3/33 D3DT2081	80386DX, 33MHz, 64K	2, 16	Full size	Phoenix	1.2/1.44	89M, 19ms, IDE	1 25-pin ser, 1 9-pin ser, 1 par, 1 mouse	2 8-bit, 6 16-bit
Microlab	333c	80386DX, 33MHz, 64K	4, 32	Mini tower	AMI	1.2/1.44	130M, 19ms, IDE	2 ser, 1 par, 1 game	8 16-bit
NEC	Business Mate 386/33E	80386DX, 33MHz, 64K	4, 16	Full tower				1 ser, 1 par	5 8-bit or 16-bit, 2-EISA, 1 prop
Northgate	Elegance 333	80386DX, 33MHz, 64K	4, 16	Full size	AMI	1.2/1.44	40M, IDE	2 ser, 1 par	1 8-bit, 6 16-bit, 1 32-bit

BUS TYPE	VIDEO ADAPTER, DISPLAY	POWER SUPPLY (watts)	WARRANTY (years)	SOFTWARE INCLUDED	RETAIL PRICE	OTHER INFORMATION
EISA	VGA	198, 110/220 VAC	1, carry-in	DOS, Windows 3.0	$6,699.00	Includes mouse, other opt avail
ISA	VGA	200	1, carry-in		$3,799.00	Other opt avail
EISA		300	1, carry-in	EISA config utils & lib, ALR & EISA sys util	$4,995.00	Other opt avail
ISA	View Sonic 5 SuperVGA Monitor, Orchid Pro-Designer II	200	2, 1 TRW on-site	DOS, Windows 3.0	$2,495.00	Opt 256K CPU cache, may sub Diamond Speedstar Plus for Orchid Pro-Designer II, other opt avail
ISA		200	1, send-back; GE on-site avail	DOS, Windows 3.0		Shadow RAM, BIOS Caching, CPU upgr 386, 486sx, 486, Club Rainbow SuperVGA adapter available
EISA	VGA		1, carry-in		$6,199.00	Other opt avail, other OS avail
EISA	VGA		1, carry-in		$7,899.00	Other opt avail, other OS avail
EISA	VGA		1, carry-in		$8,899.00	Other opt avail, other OS avail
EISA	VGA		1, carry-in		$11,999.00	Accepts multiple CPU cards, other opt avail
EISA	VGA		1, carry-in		$13,999.00	Accepts multiple CPU cards, other opt avail
EISA	VGA		1, carry-in		$17,999.00	Accepts multiple CPU cards, other opt avail
ISA	Viewsonic 5 SuperVGA Display, Orchid Pro Designer IIs	200	1, on-site	DOS, Windows 3.0 with mouse	$3,245.00	Other opt avail
ISA	VGA	177	1, on-site	Tutorial, diags	$3,599.00	Includes unlimited toll-free tech support, other opt avail
ISA		220	1, carry-in		$1,299.00	Other opt avail
ISA	14" Crystal Scan 1024 VGA, Diamond Speedstar VGA 1024 x 768 1M	200 desktop, 220 twr	30 days money back; 1, on-site	DOS, Windows 3.0	$2,795.00	Includes mouse, non-interlaced display, other opt avail
ISA	VGA (800 x 600)	200	18 months; on-site avail	DOS	$2,845.00	100M, 200M, and 300M hard drives available, other opt avail
ISA	ATI VGA (1024 x 768)	200	20 months carry-in; 6 months on-site	DOS, Windows 3.0	$2,799.00	Other opt avail
ISA	Diamond Speedstar VGA 1024 x 768, 1M	200	1, send-back; free shipping	DOS	$2,195.00	Free shipping, other opt avail
ISA, EISA		115V/ 230V Universal	1, carry-in		$6,899.00	Other opt avail
ISA	14" VGA Gray	200	30 days money back; 1, on-site	DOS, Windows 3.0	$3,299.00	Includes mouse, OmniKey, ULTRA keyboard, lifetime 24-hr tech support, other opt avail

continues

Table 4.5. Continued

COMPANY	MODEL	CPU, SPEED, CACHE	MIN, MAX RAM (M)	UNIT SIZE	BIOS, VER.	DISK DRIVES (M)	HARD DISK CAP, SPEED, TYPE	ADAPTERS INCLUDED	EXP. SLOTS
Northgate	SlimLine 333	80386DX, 33MHz, 64K	4, 16	Mid size	AMI	1.2/1.44	40M, IDE	2 ser, 1 par, IDE	2 8-bit, 3 16-bit
PC Brand, Inc.	386/33 Cache	80386DX, 33MHz, 64K	1, 16	Full size		1.2 or 1.44		2 ser, 1 par	ISA
Samsung Information Systems	386A3 File Server	80386DX, 33MHz, 64K	4, 8	Full size	Samsung Advanced LAN	1.2		2 ser, 1 par	1 8-bit, 6 16-bit, 1 32-bit
Samsung Information Systems	System-Master 386/33T	80386DX, 33MHz, 64K	4, 24	Full tower		1.2/1.44		2 ser, 1 par, 1 PS, 2 mouse	2 8-bit, 6 8-bit or 16-bit
Standard Computer	386/33	80386DX, 33MHz, 64K	4, 16	Mid size	Phoenix 1.01	1.2/1.44	120M, 19ms, IDE	2 ser, 1 par	6 16-bit
Swan Technologies	386/33 Desk	80386DX, 33MHz, 64K	4, 16	Full size	Phoenix, MCI 386	1.2/1.44	100M, 17ms, IDE	2 ser, 1 par	7 16-bit, 1 16-bit or 32-bit
Tangent Computer	Model 333	80386DX, 33MHz, 64K	4, 64	Mid size	AMI 5, 9, 91	1.2 or 1.44	100M, 15ms, IDE	2 ser, 1 par	7 16-bit, 1 8-bit or 32-bit
Tangent Computer	Window-Station 333	80386DX, 33MHz, 64K	4, 64	Mini tower	AMI 5, 9, 91	1.2 or 1.44	207M, 15ms, IDE	2 ser, 1 par	7 16-bit, 1 8-bit or 32-bit
Tri-Star Computer Corporation	Flash Cache FC333i	80386DX, 33MHz, 64K	4, 16	Full tower	AMI	1.2 and 1.44	125M, 19ms, IDE		2 8-bit, 6 16-bit
Tri-Star Computer Corporation	Tri-Cad Advanced TC333i	80386DX, 33MHz, 64K	4, 16	Full tower	AMI	1.2 and 1.44	125M, 15ms, IDE		2 8-bit, 6 16-bit
Tri-Star Computer Corporation	Tri-Lan TL333i ISA	80386DX, 33MHz, 64K	4, 16	Full tower	Award	1.2 and 1.44	330M, 19ms, SCSI		2 16-bit, 6 32-bit
Tri-Star Computer Corporation	Tri-Star TS333i	80386DX, 33MHz, 64K	2, 8	Small	AMI	1.2 and 1.44	80M, 25ms, IDE		2 8-bit, 5 16-bit, 1 32-bit
Zeos International, Ltd.	386-33C Upgradable systems	80386DX, 33MHz, 128K	4, 32	Mid size	Award	1.2/1.44	130M, IDE	2 ser, 1 par, 1 game	1 8-bit, 7 16-bit
Zeos International, Ltd.	386-33C Upgradable systems	80386DX, 33MHz, 128K	2, 32	Mid size	Award	1.2/1.44	85M, IDE	2 ser, 1 par, 1 game	1 8-bit, 7 16-bit
Zeos International, Ltd.	386-33C Upgradable systems	80386DX, 33MHz, 128K	8, 32	Mid size	Award	1.2/1.44	210M, IDE	2 ser, 1 par, 1 game	1 8-bit, 7 16-bit
Zeos International, Ltd.	386-33C Upgradable systems	80386DX, 33MHz, 128K	1, 32	Mid size	Award	1.2 or 1.44	42M, IDE	2 ser, 1 par, 1 game	1 8-bit, 7 16-bit
Tri-Star Computer Corporation	Tri-Lan TL333i EISA	80386DX, 33MHz, 256K	4, 64	Full tower	Award	1.2 and 1.44	330M, 19ms, SCSI		2 16-bit, 6 32-bit
CompuAdd	CompuAdd 333	80386DX, 33MHz, 640K	4, 16	Full size	Phoenix 386AT Plus	1.44/1.2	150M, 18ms, ESDI		6 16-bit, 1 8-bit
CompuAdd	CompuAdd 333T	80386DX, 33MHz, 640K	4, 16	Full tower	Phoenix 386AT Plus	1.44/1.2	150M, 18ms, ESDI		6 16-bit, 1 8-bit
CompuAdd	CompuAdd 333T	80386DX, 33MHz, 640K	4, 16	Full tower	Phoenix 386AT Plus	1.44/1.2	150M, 18ms, ESDI		6 16-bit, 1 8-bit

BUS TYPE	VIDEO ADAPTER, DISPLAY	POWER SUPPLY (watts)	WARRANTY (years)	SOFTWARE INCLUDED	RETAIL PRICE	OTHER INFORMATION
ISA	12" VGA Gray Display, VGA 1024 x 768, 512K, Edsun CEG	150	30 days money back; 1, on-site	DOS, Windows 3.0	$2,899.00	Includes mouse, OmniKey, 102 keyboard, lifetime 24-hr tech support, other opt avail
ISA		200	1, send-back; 5, prorated		$1,299.00	Choice of Desktop or SlimLine Case, other opt avail
ISA		375	1, carry-in		$4,299.00	CPU cache exp to 256K, contact via 800#, BBS, fax, authorized service vendors, other opt avail
ISA		275	1, carry-in	DOS, Windows 3.0	$3,999.00	CPU cache exp to 128K, contact via 800#, BBS, fax, authorized service vendors, other opt avail
ISA	14" Viewsonic 4, VGA 1024 x 768, 512K	200	1, TRW on-site	DOS, Windows 3.0	$2,395.00	Includes mouse, other opt avail
ISA	Swan 1024 x 768 Display, Optional Adapters	200	2, on-site	DOS, Swan utils, LIM 4.0	$2,795.00	Lifetime toll-free tech support, other opt avail
ISA	14" NI Display, Orchid Pro Designer IIs 1024 x 768 ni VESA	220	1, send-back	DOS	$2,495.00	Other opt avail
ISA	14" NI Display, ATI 8514, Ultra 1024 x 768ni VESA	200	1, send-back	DOS, Windows 3.0	$3,995.00	CPU cache exp to 256K, other opt avail
ISA	Mag Computronics 1024 x 768 NI, Diamond Speedstar 1024 x 768, 1M	220	60 days money back; 2, send-back	DOS, Windows 3.0	$2,395.00	CPU cache exp to 256K, includes lifetime toll-free tech support, mouse, other opt avail
ISA	17" IDEK MF-5117 Display, Diamond Speedstar 1024 x 768, 1M	220	60 days money back; 2, send-back	DOS, Fast Cad 2-D Version 2.6	$3,995.00	Lifetime toll-free tech support, Calcomp Drawingboard II 12 x 12, Digitizer, Intel Math Co-Processor, other opt avail
ISA	14" Septre Monochrome Display, MDA	250	60 days money back; 2, send-back	DOS	$3,195.00	Includes lifetime toll-free tech support, other opt avail
ISA	Matsushita Viewsonic 4 Multisync Display, Paradise 1024 x 768, 512K	220	30 days money back; 15 months send-back	DOS	$2,055.00	CPU cache exp to 256K, includes lifetime toll-free tech support, other opt avail
ISA	VGA Color Display, Diamond Speedstar Plus 1024 x 768, 1M	300	30 days money back; 1, on-site avail	DOS, Windows 3.0	$2,795.00	RS or F12 Case has 7-bay desktop, 2 fans, other opt avail
ISA	VGA Monochrome Display, Diamond Speedstar Plus 1024 x 768, 1M	300	30 days money back; 1, on-site avail	DOS, Windows 3.0	$2,295.00	RS or F12 Case has 7-bay desktop, 2 fans, other opt avail
ISA	VGA Color Display, Diamond Speedstar Plus 1024 x 768, 1M	300	30 days money back; 1, on-site avail	DOS, Windows 3.0	$3,295.00	RS or F12 Case has 7-bay desktop, 2 fans, other opt avail
ISA	Monochrome Display, Hercules Graphics Adapter	300	30 days money back; 1, on-site avail		$1,695.00	RS or F12 Case has 7-bay desktop, 2 fans, other opt avail
ISA	14" Septre Monochrome Display, MDA	250	60 days money back; 2, send-back	DOS	$3,695.00	Includes lifetime toll-free tech support, other opt avail
ISA	VGA (800 x 600)	300	1, on-site	DOS, Windows 3.0	$5,195.00	Other opt avail
ISA	VGA (800 x 600)	300	1, on-site	DOS, Windows 3.0	$5,375.00	Other opt avail
ISA	VGA (800 x 600)	300	1, on-site	DOS, Windows 3.0	$5,375.00	Other opt avail

continues

Table 4.5. Concluded

COMPANY	MODEL	CPU, SPEED, CACHE	MIN, MAX RAM (M)	UNIT SIZE	BIOS, VER.	DISK DRIVES (M)	HARD DISK CAP, SPEED, TYPE	ADAPTERS INCLUDED	EXP. SLOTS
USA Flex	Flex 386/33MHz	AMD386, 33MHz, 64K	4, 16	Full tower	Phoenix 1.10.01	1.2 and 1.44	130.7M, 19ms, IDE		1 8-bit, 6 16-bit, 1 32-bit
Data World	DW-386-40	AMD386, 40MHz	4, 64	Full size	AMI	1.2/1.4	120M, 19ms, IDE		8 16-bit
Club Computer Corporation	Falcon	AMD386, 40MHz, 64K	4, 64	Mid size	AMI	1.2 or 1.44	200M, 15ms, IDE		1 32-bit, 7 8-bit or 16-bit
Microlab	340c	AMD386, 40MHz, 64K	4, 32	Mini tower	AMI	1.2/1.44	130M, 19ms, IDE	2 ser, 1 par, 1 game	8 16-bit
Tangent Computer	340	AMD386, 40MHz, 64K	4, 64	Mid size	AMI 5, 9, 91	1.2 or 1.44	100M, 15ms, IDE	2 ser, 1 par	7 16-bit, 1 16-bit or 32-bit

BUS TYPE	VIDEO ADAPTER, DISPLAY	POWER SUPPLY (watts)	WARRANTY (years)	SOFTWARE INCLUDED	RETAIL PRICE	OTHER INFORMATION
ISA	Samsung, Samtron or CTX 1024 x 768 Display, VGA 1024 x 768, 512K	200	1, on-site	DOS, Windows 3.0		Includes mouse, other opt avail
ISA	Viewsonic 5 SuperVGA Display, Orchid Pro Designer IIs	200	1, on-site	DOS, Windows 3.0 with mouse	$3,195.00	Other opt avail
ISA		200	1, send-back; GE on-site avail	DOS, Windows 3.0		Shadow RAM, BIOS Caching, CPU upgr 386, 486sx, 486, Club Rainbow SuperVGA adapter available
ISA	Diamond Speedstar VGA 1024 x 768, 1M	200	1, send-back; free shipping	DOS	$2,395.00	Free shipping, other opt avail
ISA	14" NI Display, Orchid Pro Designer IIs 1024 x 768 ni VESA	220	1, send-back	DOS	$2,795.00	CPU is the AMD386DXL, other opt avail

Table 4.6. IBM-Compatible 80486SX Desktop Computers

COMPANY	MODEL	CPU, SPEED, CACHE	MIN, MAX RAM (M)	UNIT SIZE	BIOS, VER.	DISK DRIVES (M)	HARD DISK CAP, SPEED, TYPE	ADAPTERS INCLUDED	EXP SLOTS
Acer America Corporation	AcerPower 486SX	80486SX, 20MHz, 8K	2, 98	Small		1.44			4 16-bit
Advanced Logic Research	Business STATION 486ASX 80	80486SX, 20MHz, 8K	1, 33	Slim line	Phoenix 10.01.10	1.44	80M, 20ms, IDE	2 ser, 1 par, 1 proprietary	4 32-bit, 1 16-bit
Advanced Logic Research	Business VEISA 486ASX 101	80486SX, 20MHz, 8K	1, 49	Small	Phoenix	1.2		1 ser, 1 par, 1 mouse	4 32-bit, 2 16-bit
Advanced Logic Research	MPS 486ASX 101	80486SX, 20MHz, 8K	1, 17	Mid size	Phoenix	1.44		1 ser, 1 par, 1 PS, 2 mouse, IDE	4 16-bit, 2 32-bit, 2 prop
Advanced Logic Research	PowerFlex 486ASX Model 1	80486SX, 20MHz, 8K	1, 16	Small	Phoenix	1.44		1 par, 1 ser, 1 mouse	5 16-bit, 1 8-bit
Dell Computer Corporation	Dell Powerline 420DE	80486SX, 20MHz, 8K	4, 48	Full size	Phoenix, Dell	1.2 or 1.4	80M, 25ms, IDE	2 ser, 1 par, 1 mouse, 1 keybd, 1 ext VGA	6 32-bit
Ergo Computing	Moby Brick	80486SX, 20MHz, 8K	4, 32	Brick	Ergo 2.04	1.44	44M-510M, 28ms-13ms, IDE		1 8-bit, 1 16-bit.
IBM	8590	80486SX, 20MHz, 8K	4, 32	Mid size	IBM	1.44	80M, 17ms, SCSI	1 ser, 1 par, 1 mouse, 1 SCSI	3 32-bit
IBM	8595-0G9	80486SX, 20MHz, 8K	4, 32	Full tower	IBM	1.44	160M, 17ms, SCSI	1 ser, 1 par, 1 mouse	6 32-bit
Zeos International, Ltd	486SX-20 upgradable systems	80486SX, 20MHz, 8K	1, 32	Mid size	Award	1.2 or 1.44	42M, IDE	2 ser, 1 par, 1 game	1 8-bit, 7 16-bit
Zeos International, Ltd.	486SX-20 upgradable systems	80486SX, 20MHz, 8K	4, 32	Mid size	Award	1.2, 1.44	130M, IDE	2 ser, 1 par, 1 game	1 8-bit, 7 16-bit
Zeos International, Ltd	486SX-20 upgradable systems	80486SX, 20MHz, 8K	2, 32	Mid size	Award	1.2, 1.44	85M, IDE	2 ser, 1 par, 1 game	1 8-bit, 7 16-bit
Zeos International, Ltd.	486SX-20 upgradable systems	80486SX, 20MHz, 8K	8, 32	Mid size	Award	1.2, 1.44	210M, IDE	2 ser, 1 par, 1 game	1 8-bit, 7 16-bit
Dell Computer Corporation	Dell Powerline 420SE	80486SX, 20MHz, 8K	4, 128	Full size	Phoenix, Dell	1.2 or 1.4	80M, 25ms, IDE	2 ser, 1 par, 1 mouse, 1 keybd, 1 ext VGA	8 32-bit, 2 prop
Club Computer Corporation	Falcon	80486SX, 20MHz, 64K	4, 64	Mid size	AMI	1.2 or 1.44	200M, 15ms, IDE		1 32-bit, 7 8-bit or 16-bit
Advanced Logic Research	PowerProVM 486/25	80486SX, 20MHz, 64K	5, 49	Full tower	Phoenix	1.2		2 ser, 1 par, 1 mouse	8 32-bit, 2 16-bit
Advanced Logic Research	PowerProVM 486/35	80486SX, 20MHz, 64K	5, 49	Full tower	Phoenix	1.2		2 ser, 1 par, 1 mouse	8 32-bit, 2 16-bit
Advanced Logic Research	PowerProVM 486ASX	80486SX, 20MHz, 64K	5, 49	Full tower	Phoenix	1.2		2 ser, 1 par, 1 mouse	8 32-bit, 2 16-bit
Tangent Computer	420s	80486SX, 20MHz, 64K	4, 64	Mini tower	AMI 5, 9, 91	1.2 or 1.44	207M, 15ms, IDE	2 ser, 1 par	7 16-bit, 1 16-bit or 32-bit
Zeos International, Ltd.	486SX-20C	80486SX, 20MHz, 128K	8, 32	Mid size	Award	1.2, 1.44	210M, IDE	2 ser, 1 par, 1 game	1 8-bit, 7 16-bit

BUS TYPE	VIDEO ADAPTER, DISPLAY	POWER SUPPLY (watts)	WARRANTY (years)	SOFTWARE INCLUDED	RETAIL PRICE	OTHER INFORMATION
ISA		145	2 carry-in	DOS, Windows 3.0	$2,745.00	Other hard disk sizes avail, displays avail, mouse inc
EISA, prop	VGA	150	1, carry-in	EISA config util & lib, EISA sys util	$3,995.00	CPU upgr, other opt avail
EISA		145	1, carry-in	Utils & lib. (ISA) & User Setup	$2,795.00	CPU upgr, other opt avail
MCA/Prop.	VGA (1024 x 768)	145	1, carry-in	ALR Micro Channel utils	$2,995.00	CPU upgr, other opt avail
ISA		145	1, carry-in	ALR utils	$1,995.00	CPU upgr, other opt avail
EISA	VGA Color Plus display, VGA 1024 x 768, 1M	220	1, on-site		$4,099.00	Includes unlimited toll-free tech support, other opt avail
ISA		42	1, send-back	DOS, Windows 3.0, Adobe ATM, Logitech mouse	$3,395.00 $9,095.00	80486DX/25 and 80486DX/33 avail, DesqView 386, QEMM 386, Manifest, Tree 86 avail, other opt avail
MCA	XGA	194	1, carry-in; on-site avail		$8,345.00	Upgr to 50MHz
MCA	XGA	329	1, carry-in; on-site avail		$9,995.00	Upgr to 50MHz
ISA	Monochrome display, Hercules Graphics Adapter	300	30 day money back; 1, on-site avail		$1,595.00	RS or F12 Case has 7-bay desktop, 2 fans, other opt avail
ISA	VGA color display, Diamond Speedstar Plus 1024 x 768, 1M	300	30 day money back; 1, on-site avail	DOS, Windows 3.0	$2,695.00	RS or F12 Case has 7-bay desktop, 2 fans, other opt avail
ISA	VGA monochrome disp, Diamond Speedstar Plus 1024 x 768, 1M	300	30 day money back; 1, on-site avail	DOS, Windows 3.0	$2,195.00	RS or F12 Case has 7-bay desktop, 2 fans, other opt avail
ISA	VGA color display, Diamond Speedstar Plus 1024 x 768, 1M	300	30 day money back; 1, on-site avail	DOS, Windows 3.0	$3,195.00	RS or F12 Case has 7-bay desktop, 2 fans, other opt avail
EISA	VGA Color Plus Display, VGA 1024 x 768, 512K	300	1, on-site		$5,399.00	Includes unlimited toll-free tech support, other opt avail
ISA		200	1, send back; GE on-site aval	DOS, Windows 3.0		Shadow RAM, BIOS Caching, CPU upgr 386, 486sx, 486, Club Rainbow SuperVGA adapter available
EISA		300	1, carry-in	EISA config utils & lib, ALR & EISA sys util	$6,495.00	Other opt avail
EISA		300	1, carry-in	EISA config utils & lib, ALR & EISA sys util	$7,495.00	Other opt avail
EISA		300	1, carry-in	EISA config utils & lib, ALR & EISA sys util	$5,795.00	Other opt avail
ISA	14" NI display, Orchid Pro Designer IIs 1024 x 768 ni VESA	300	1, send-back	DOS	$3,295.00	Other opt avail
ISA	VGA color display, Diamond Speedstar Plus 1024 x 768, 1M	300	30 day money back; 1, on-site avail	DOS, Windows 3.0	$3,395.00	RS or F12 Case has 7-bay desktop, 2 fans, other opt avail

continues

Table 4.6. Concluded

COMPANY	MODEL	CPU, SPEED, CACHE	MIN, MAX RAM (M)	UNIT SIZE	BIOS, VER.	DISK DRIVES (M)	HARD DISK CAP, SPEED, TYPE	ADAPTERS INCLUDED	EXP SLOTS
Zeos International, Ltd.	486SX-20C	80486SX, 20MHz, 128K	4, 32	Mid size	Award	1.2, 1.44	130M, IDE	2 ser, 1 par, 1 game	1 8-bit, 7 16-bit
Zeos International, Ltd.	486SX-20C	80486SX, 20MHz, 128K	1, 32	Mid size	Award	1.2 or 1.44	42M, IDE	2 ser, 1 par, 1 game	1 8-bit, 7 16-bit
Zeos International, Ltd.	486SX-20C	80486SX, 20MHz, 128K	2, 32	Mid size	Award	1.2, 1.44	85M, IDE	2 ser, 1 par, 1 game	1 8-bit, 7 16-bit

BUS TYPE	VIDEO ADAPTER, DISPLAY	POWER SUPPLY (watts)	WARRANTY (years)	SOFTWARE INCLUDED	RETAIL PRICE	OTHER INFORMATION
ISA	VGA color display, Diamond Speedstar Plus 1024 x 768, 1M	300	30 day money back; 1, on-site avail	DOS, Windows 3.0	$2,895.00	RS or F12 Case has 7-bay desktop, 2 fans, other opt avail
ISA	Monochrome display, Hercules Graphics Adapter	300	30 day money back; 1, on-site avail		$1,795.00	RS or F12 Case has 7-bay desktop, 2 fans, other opt avail
ISA	VGA monochrome disp, Diamond Speedstar Plus 1024 x 768, 1M	300	30 day money back; 1, on-site avail	DOS, Windows 3.0	$2,395.00	RS or F12 Case has 7-bay desktop, 2 fans, other opt avail

Table 4.7. IBM-Compatible 80486 Desktop Computers

COMPANY	MODEL	CPU, SPEED, CACHE	MIN, MAX RAM (M)	UNIT SIZE	BIOS, VER.	DISK DRIVES (M)	HARD DISK CAP, SPEED, TYPE	ADAPTERS INCLUDED	EXP SLOTS
Acer America Corporation	1170	80486DX, 25MHz, 8K	4, 64	Small		1.44		2 ser, 1 par, 1 mouse, IDE interface	4 16-bit
Advanced Logic Research	Business STATION 486/25 80	80486DX, 25MHz, 8K	1, 33	Slim line	Phoenix 10.01.10	1.44	80M, 20ms, IDE	2 ser, 1 par, 1 proprietary	4 32-bit, 1 16-bit
Advanced Logic Research	Business STATION 486/33 80	80486DX, 25MHz, 8K	1, 33	Slim line	Phoenix 10.01.10	1.44	80M, 20ms, IDE	2 ser, 1 par, 1 proprietary	4 32-bit, 1 16-bit
Advanced Logic Research	Business VEISA 486/25 101	80486DX, 25MHz, 8K	1, 49	Small	Phoenix	1.2		1 ser, 1 par, 1 mouse	4 32-bit, 2 16-bit
Advanced Logic Research	MPS 486/25 101	80486DX, 25MHz, 8K	1, 17	Mid size	Phoenix	1.44		1 ser, 1 par, 1 PS, 2 mouse, IDE	4 16-bit, 2 32-bit, 2 prop
Advanced Logic Research	MultiAccess Series 3000 Model 10	80486DX, 25MHz, 8K	8, 64	Tower	Phoenix 1.10.24	1.2	330M, 16ms, SCSI	9 ser, 1 par	3 CBUS, 10 CBUS-ISA
AST Research	Bravo 486/25	80486DX, 25MHz, 8K	2, 16	Mid size	AST	1.2	80M	2 ser, 1 par, 1 PS, 2 comp mouse	5 16-bit
Austin Computer Systems	486/25 Winstation	80486DX, 25MHz, 8K	4, 64	Full size	AMI	1.2 or 1.44	125M, IDE		8 32-bit
Data World	DW-486-25	80486DX, 25MHz, 8K	4, 16	Full size	AMI	1.2, 1.4	120M, 19ms, IDE		1 8-bit, 6 16-bit, 1 32-bit
Hewlett-Packard	HP Vectra 486/25T PC	80486DX, 25MHz, 8K	4, 64	Full tower	Hewlett-Packard	1.2 or 1.44	170M, IDE	2 ser, 1 par, 1 mouse	9 32-bit
IBM	8095-0J9	80486DX, 25MHz, 8K	4, 32	Full tower	IBM	1.44	160M, 17ms, SCSI	1 ser, 1 par, 1 mouse	6 32-bit
IBM	8590-OJ5	80486DX, 25MHz, 8K	4, 32	Mid size	IBM	1.44	80M, 17ms, SCSI	2 ser, 1 par, 1 mouse	3 32-bit
NEC	Business Mate 486/25E	80486DX, 25MHz, 8K	4, 64	Full tower				2 ser, 1 par, 1 PS, 2 mouse	2 8-bit or 16-bit, 5 8/16/32-bit
NEC	PowerMate 486/25E	80486DX, 25MHz, 8K	4,	Small	Phoenix 0.10.19 EISA	1.2 or 1.44		2 ser, 1 par, 1 PS, 2 mouse	2 8-bit or 16-bit, 1 32-bit
Northgate	OmniSystem 425	80486DX, 25MHz, 8K	8, 128	Full tower	Phoenix	1.2		2 ser, 1 par	8 32-bit
PC Brand, Inc.	486/25	80486DX, 25MHz, 8K	1, 16	Full size		1.2 or 1.44		2 ser, 1 par	ISA
Zenith	Z-486/25E Model 170	80486DX, 25MHz, 8K	4, 64	Mid size		1.44	170M, 15ms, IDE	2 ser, 1 par	3 32-bit
Zenith	Z-486/25E Model 80	80486DX, 25MHz, 8K	4, 64	Mid size		1.44	80M, 19ms, IDE	2 ser, 1 par	3 32-bit
Club Computer Corporation	Falcon	80486DX, 25MHz, 64K	4, 64	Mid size	AMI	1.2 or 1.44	200M, 15ms, IDE		1 32-bit, 7 8-bit or 16-bit
DTK Computer Inc.	FEAT-2502	80486DX, 25MHz, 64K	0, 16	Full tower	27256; 4.26				1 8-bit, 6 16-bit, 1 32-bit

BUS TYPE	VIDEO ADAPTER, DISPLAY	POWER SUPPLY (watts)	WARRANTY (years)	SOFTWARE INCLUDED	RETAIL PRICE	OTHER INFORMATION
ISA		145	2, carry-in	DOS, Windows 3.0	$3,795.00	Other hard disk sizes avail, displays avail, mouse included
EISA, prop	VGA	150	1, carry-in	EISA config util & lib, EISA sys util	$4,895.00	CPU upgr, other opt avail
EISA, prop	VGA	150	1, carry-in	EISA config util & lib, EISA sys util	$5,195.00	CPU upgr, other opt avail
EISA		145	1, carry-in	Utils & lib (ISA) & User Setup	$3,695.00	CPU upgr, other opt avail
MCA, prop	VGA (1024 x 768)	145	1, carry-in	ALR Micro Channel utils	$3,795.00	CPU upgr, other opt avail
ISA, CBUS		300	1, carry-in		$15,999.00	CPU upgr, other opt avail
ISA	VGA (800 x 600)	145, 110V or 220V AC	1, carry-in	DOS, Caching Software, FASTRAM util,	$4,725.00	Other opt avail
		230	1, GE on-site	DOS, Windows 3.0		Other opt avail
ISA	Viewsonic 5 SuperVGA Display, Orchid Pro Designer IIs	200	1, on-site	DOS, Windows 3.0 with mouse	$3,545.00	Other opt avail
EISA		408	1, on-site	Setup, LIM 40 util, Windows 3.0		440M or 1000M SCSI-2 hard disks avail, other opt avail
MCA	XGA	329	1, carry-in; on-site avail		$12,545.00	Upgr to 50MHz, 256K cache option, other opt avail
MCA	XGA	194	1, carry-in; on-site avail		$10,845.00	Upgr to 50MHz, 256K cache option
ISA, EISA		115V/ 230V Universal	1, carry-in		$8,899.00	Other opt avail
ISA		115V/ 230V Universal	1, carry-in	DOS, Windows 3.0	$7,999.00	Other opt avail
EISA	Hercules comp adapter	500	30 days money back; 1, on-site			Dual 80486 CPU support, dual-channel Intelligent Disk Subsystem with on-board 80386 CPU, other opt avail
ISA		200	1, send-back; 5, prorated		$1,599.00	Choice of Desktop or SlimLine Case, other opt avail
EISA	TIGA, VGA card w/ 32-bit 60MHz 304010 video processor	150, 110/220 VAC	1, carry-in	DOS, Windows 3.0	$8,699.00	Includes mouse, other opt avail
EISA	VGA	150, 110/220 VAC	1, carry-in	DOS, Windows 3.0	$7,499.00	Includes mouse, other opt avail
ISA		200	1, send-back; GE on-site avail	DOS, Windows 3.0		Shadow RAM, BIOS Caching, CPU upgr 386, 486sx, 486, Club Rainbow SuperVGA adapter available
ISA		250	1, carry-in		$2,399.00	Other opt avail

continues

Table 4.7. Continued

COMPANY	MODEL	CPU, SPEED, CACHE	MIN, MAX RAM (M)	UNIT SIZE	BIOS, VER.	DISK DRIVES (M)	HARD DISK CAP, SPEED, TYPE	ADAPTERS INCLUDED	EXP SLOTS
Gateway 2000	486-25 Cache	80486DX, 25MHz, 64K	4, 16	Full size	Phoenix	1.2, 1.44	200M, 15ms, IDE	2 ser, 1 par	8 16-bit
Insight	Insight 486-25MHz w/ 64K cache	80486DX, 25MHz, 64K	4, 64	Full tower	Phoenix 4, 9, 90	1.2, 1.44	130M, 15ms, IDE		7 16-bit, 1 8-bit or 32-bit
MIS Computer Systems	486/25 ISA	80486DX, 25MHz, 64K	1, 16	Tower	Phoenix	1.2, 1.44	120M, IDE	2 ser, 1 par, 1 game	5 16-bit
Northgate	Elegance 425i	80486DX, 25MHz, 64K	4, 16	Full size	AMI	1.2, 1.44	40M, IDE	2 ser, 1 par	1 8-bit, 6 16-bit, 1 32-bit
Swan Technologies	486/25 Desk	80486DX, 25MHz, 64K	4, 16	Full size	Phoenix, MCI 486	1.2, 1.44	100M, 17ms, IDE	2 ser, 1 par	8 16-bit
Tangent Computer	425i	80486DX, 25MHz, 64K	4, 64	Mini tower	AMI 5, 9, 91	1.2 or 1.44	207M, 15ms, IDE	2 ser, 1 par	7 16-bit, 1 16-bit or 32-bit
Tri-Star Computer Corporation	Flash Cache FC425i	80486DX, 25MHz, 64K	8, 16	Full tower	AMI	1.2 and 1.44	210M, 15ms, IDE		2 8-bit, 6 16-bit
Tri-Star Computer Corporation	Tri-Cad Ultra TC425i	80486DX, 25MHz, 64K	4, 16	Full tower	AMI	1.2 and 1.44	210M, 15ms, IDE		2 8-bit, 6 16-bit
Tri-Star Computer Corporation	Tri-Lan TL425i ISA	80486DX, 25MHz, 64K	4, 16	Full tower	Award	1.2 and 1.44	330M, 19ms, SCSI		2 16-bit, 6 32-bit
USA Flex	Flex 486 25	80486DX, 25MHz, 64K	4, 16	Full tower	Phoenix 1.10.01	1.2 and 1.44	210.7M, 19ms, IDE		1 8-bit, 6 16-bit, 1 32-bit
Acer America Corporation	1200	80486DX, 25MHz, 128K	4, 64	Tower		1.2		2 ser, 1 par, 1 mouse, IDE interface	8 32-bit
COMPAQ	COMPAQ DeskPro 486/25 120	80486DX, 25MHz, 128K	4, 100	Full size	COMPAQ	1.44	120M, 19ms	1 ser, 1 par, 1 mouse	8 32-bit
COMPAQ	COMPAQ DeskPro 486/25 320	80486DX, 25MHz, 128K	4, 100	Full size	COMPAQ	1.44	320M, 18ms	1 ser, 1 par, 1 mouse	8 32-bit
COMPAQ	COMPAQ DeskPro 486/25 650	80486DX, 25MHz, 128K	4, 100	Full size	COMPAQ	1.44	650M, 18ms	1 ser, 1 par, 1 mouse	8 32-bit
Microlab	425i	80486DX, 25MHz, 128K	4, 32	Full tower	AMI	1.2, 1.44	211M, 15ms, IDE	2 ser, 1 par, 1 game	8 16-bit
NCR	NCR 3340	80486DX, 25MHz, 128K	2, 16	Mid size		1.44	100M, SCSI	1 ser, 1 par, 1 mouse, 1 ext SCSI-I	1 16-bit, 2 32-bit, 1 video
Northgate	Elegance 425e	80486DX, 25MHz, 128K	4, 32	Full tower	Northgate	1.2, 1.44	40M, IDE	1 ser, 1 par, 1 mouse, IDE	8 32-bit EISA
Packard Bell	Force 486/25	80486DX, 25MHz, 128K	4, 16	Full size	Phoenix	1.2, 1.44	130M, 20ms	2 ser, 1 par	2 8-bit, 5 16-bit, 1 32-bit
Samsung Information Systems	System Master 486/25TE	80486DX, 25MHz, 128K	4, 32	Full tower		1.2, 1.44		2 ser, 1 par, IDE	8 32-bit
Standard Computer	486/25	80486DX, 25MHz, 128K	4, 16	Mid size	AMI	1.2, 1.44	210M, 15ms, IDE	2 ser, 1 par, 1 game	1 8-bit, 6 16-bit, 1 32-bit

BUS TYPE	VIDEO ADAPTER, DISPLAY	POWER SUPPLY (watts)	WARRANTY (years)	SOFTWARE INCLUDED	RETAIL PRICE	OTHER INFORMATION
ISA	14" Crystal Scan 1024 VGA, Diamond Speedstar VGA 1024 x 768 1M	200, 220	30 days money back; 1, on-site	DOS, Windows 3.0	$2,995.00	Includes mouse, non-interlaced display, other opt avail
ISA	Insight SuperVGA display, Diamond Speed Star 1024 x 768, 1M	250	1, send-back	DOS	$2,795.00	Includes Microsoft-compatible mouse, toll-free tech support
ISA	Optiquest 14" NI, Trident VGA 1024 x 768, 1M	200-250 switching	1, send-back	DOS	$2,735.00	Other opt avail
EISA	14" VGA gray	200	30 days money back; 1, on-site	DOS, Windows 3.0	$4,349.00	Includes mouse, OmniKey, ULTRA keyboard, lifetime 24-hr tech support, other opt avail
ISA	Swan 1024 x 768 display, optional adapters	200	2, on-site	DOS, Swan utils, LIM 40	$3,695.00	Lifetime toll-free tech support, other opt avail
ISA	14" NI display, Orchid Pro Designer IIs 1024 x 768 ni VESA	300	1, send-back	DOS	$3,595.00	Other opt avail
ISA	Mag Computronics 1024 x 768 NI, Diamond Speedstar 1024 x 768, 1M	220	60 days money back; 2, send-back	DOS, Windows 3.0	$3,195.00	Includes lifetime toll-free tech support, mouse, other opt avail
ISA	17" IDEK MF-5117 display, Diamond Speedstar 1024 x 768, 1M	220	60 days money back; 2, send-back	DOS, Fast Cad 2-D Version 26	$4,395.00	Lifetime toll-free tech support, Calcomp Drawingboard II 12x12, Digitizer, Intel Math Co-Processor, other opt avail
ISA	14" Septre monochrome display, MDA	250	60 days money back; 2, send-back	DOS	$3,995.00	Includes lifetime toll-free tech support, other opt avail
ISA	Samsung, Samtron, or CTX 1024 x 768 display, VGA 1024 x 768, 512K	200	1, on-site	DOS, Windows 3.0		Includes mouse, other opt avail
EISA		230	2, carry-in	DOS, Windows 3.0	$6,495.00	Other hard disk sizes avail, displays avail, mouse included
EISA	VGA		1, carry-in		$12,499.00	Other opt avail, other OS avail
EISA	VGA		1, carry-in		$14,999.00	Other opt avail, other OS avail
EISA	VGA		1, carry-in		$17,999.00	Other opt avail, other OS avail
ISA	Diamond Speedstar VGA 1024 x 768, 1M	230	1, send-back; free shipping	DOS	$2,995.00	Free shipping, other opt avail
MCA	VGA (800 x 600)	110-250VAC	1, carry-in			200M SCSI hard drive avail, other opt avail
EISA	14" VGA gray display, VGA, 512K	300	30 days money back; 1, on-site	DOS	$5,999.00	Includes mouse, OmniKey, ULTRA keyboard, lifetime 24-hr tech support, other opt avail
ISA	VGA (1024 x 768)	230	1, on-site	DOS, Packard Bell Desktop, Lotus Works	$5,995.00	Includes mouse, 2400B int modem, Prodigy Service start-up kit, other opt avail
EISA		300	1, carry-in	DOS, Windows 3.0	$6,999.00	Contact via 800#, BBS,ffax, authorized service vendors, other opt avail
ISA	14" Viewsonic 5 NI display, Trident 1024 x 768, 1M	200	1, TRW on-site	DOS, Windows 3.0	$3,295.00	Includes mouse, other opt avail

continues

Table 4.7. continued

COMPANY	MODEL	CPU, SPEED, CACHE	MIN, MAX RAM (M)	UNIT SIZE	BIOS, VER.	DISK DRIVES (M)	HARD DISK CAP, SPEED, TYPE	ADAPTERS INCLUDED	EXP SLOTS
Tangent Computer	425e	80486DX, 25MHz, 128K	4, 32	Full tower	Mylex 6.04	1.2 or 1.44	207M, 15ms, SCSI	2 ser, 1 par	8 32-bit
Wyse Technology	Decision 486/25	80486DX, 25MHz, 128K	2, 16	Small	Phoenix, Wyse	1.2 or 1.44	110M	2 ser, 1 par, IDE	2 8-bit, 6 16-bit
Zeos International, Ltd.	486-25E systems	80486DX, 25MHz, 128K	4, 32	Mid size	Mylex	1.2, 1.44	85M, IDE	2 ser, 1 par, 1 game	8 32-bit
Zeos International, Ltd.	486-25E systems	80486DX, 25MHz, 128K	1, 32	Mid size	Mylex	1.2 or 1.44	85M, IDE	2 ser, 1 par, 1 game	8 32-bit
Zeos International, Ltd.	486-25E systems	80486DX, 25MHz, 128K	4, 32	Mid size	Mylex	1.2, 1.44	330M, SCSI	2 ser, 1 par, 1 game	8 32-bit
Tri-Star Computer Corporation	Flash Cache FC425i EISA	80486DX, 25MHz, 256K	8, 16	Full tower	Award	1.2 and 1.44	210M, 15ms, IDE		2 16-bit, 6 32-bit
Tri-Star Computer Corporation	Tri-Lan TL425i EISA	80486DX, 25MHz, 256K	4, 64	Full tower	Award	1.2 and 1.44	330M, 19ms, SCSI		2 16-bit, 6 32-bit
Advanced Logic Research	Business VEISA 486/33 101	80486DX, 33MHz, 8K	1, 49	Small	Phoenix	1.2		1 ser, 1 par, 1 mouse	4 32-bit, 2 16-bit
Advanced Logic Research	MPS 486/33 101	80486DX, 33MHz, 8K	1, 17	Mid size	Phoenix	1.44		1 ser, 1 par, 1 PS, 2 mouse, IDE	4 16-bit, 2 32-bit, 2 prop
Advanced Logic Research	PowerPro Array SMP 512/1360	80486DX, 33MHz, 8K	17, 49	Full tower	Phoenix 1.00.10A, 1.00.09A	1.2	340M, 15ms, IDE (four)	2 ser, 1 par, 1 mouse	2 8-bit or 16-bit, 10 32-bit
Advanced Logic Research	PowerPro Array SMP 512/420	80486DX, 33MHz, 8K	17, 49	Full tower	Phoenix 1.00.10A, 1.00.09A	1.2	210M, 15ms, IDE (two)	2 ser, 1 par, 1 mouse	2 8-bit or 16-bit, 10 32-bit
Advanced Logic Research	PowerPro Array SMP 512/680	80486DX, 33MHz, 8K	17, 49	Full tower	Phoenix 1.00.10A, 1.00.09A	1.2	340M, 15ms, IDE (two)	2 ser, 1 par, 1 mouse	2 8-bit or 16-bit, 10 32-bit
Advanced Logic Research	PowerPro Array SMP 512/840	80486DX, 33MHz, 8K	17, 49	Full tower	Phoenix 1.00.10A, 1.00.09A	1.2	210M, 15ms, IDE (four)	2 ser, 1 par, 1 mouse	2 8-bit or 16-bit, 10 32-bit
Advanced Logic Research	PowerPro SMP 128/1	80486DX, 33MHz, 8K	17, 49	Full tower	Phoenix 1.00.10A, 1.00.09A	1.2		2 ser, 1 par, 1 mouse	2 8-bit or 16-bit, 10 32-bit
Austin Computer Systems	486/33 EISA WinTower	80486DX, 33MHz, 8K	8, 64	Tower	Phoenix	1.2 or 1.44	330M, SCSI		8 32-bit
Dell Computer Corporation	Dell System 433P	80486DX, 33MHz, 8K	4, 16	Small	Phoenix, Dell	1.2 or 1.44	80M, 15ms, IDE	2 ser, 1 par, 1 mouse	3 16-bit
Hewlett-Packard	HP Vectra 486/33T PC	80486DX, 33MHz, 8K	4, 64	Full tower	Hewlett-Packard	1.2 or 1.44	170M, IDE	2 ser, 1 par, 1 mouse	8 32-bit
NCR	NCR 3345	80486DX, 33MHz, 8K	4, 64	Mid size	ABIOS	1.44	100M	1 ser, 1 par, 1 mouse	1 16-bit, 3 32-bit, 1video
Zenith	Z-486/33ET LAN Server Model 0	80486DX, 33MHz, 8K	8, 64	Full size		1.44	338M, 16ms, SCSI	2 ser, 2 par, 1 SCSI, 1 mouse	10 32-bit
Zeos International, Ltd.	486-33 Upgradable systems	80486DX, 33MHz, 8K	2, 32	Mid size	Award	1.2, 1.44	85M, IDE	2 ser, 1 par, 1 game	1 8-bit, 7 16-bit

BUS TYPE	VIDEO ADAPTER, DISPLAY	POWER SUPPLY (watts)	WARRANTY (years)	SOFTWARE INCLUDED	RETAIL PRICE	OTHER INFORMATION
EISA	14" NI display, Orchid Pro Designer IIs 1024 x 768 ni VESA	300	1, send-back	DOS	$5,995.00	Other opt avail
ISA		200, 110-240 VAC	1, carry-in	Wyse Enhanced DOS, Wyse Setup & Test	$4,399.00	200M or 300M hard disk avail, other opt avail
EISA	VGA color display, Diamond Speedstar Plus 1024 x 768, 1M	300	30 days money back; 1, on-site avail	DOS, Windows 3.0	$4,495.00	RS or F12 Case has 8-bay vertical case, other opt avail
EISA	Monochrome display, Hercules Graphics Adapter	300	30 days money back; 1, on-site avail		$3,495.00	RS or F12 Case has 7-bay desktop, 2 fans, other opt avail
EISA	VGA monochrome dis, Diamond Speedstar Plus 1024 x 768, 1M	300	30 days money back; 1, on-site avail	DOS, Windows 3.0	$6,495.00	RS or F12 Case has 8-bay vertical case, other opt avail
ISA	Mag Computronics 1024 x 768 NI, Diamond Speedstar 1024 x 768, 1M	220	60 days money back; 2, send-back	DOS, Windows 3.0	$3,795.00	Includes lifetime toll-free tech support, mouse, other opt avail
ISA	14" Septre monochrome display, MDA	250	60 days money back; 2, send-back	DOS	$4,595.00	Includes lifetime toll-free tech support, other opt avail
EISA		145	1, carry-in	Utils & lib (ISA) & User Setup	$3,995.00	CPU upgr, other opt avail
MCA, prop	VGA (1024 x 768)	145	1, carry-in	ALR Micro Channel utils	$4,995.00	CPU upgr, other opt avail
ISA, EISA		300	1, carry-in	EISA config util & lib, EISA sys util, adv array drvs	$22,995.00	CPU upgr, accepts a second CPU card
ISA, EISA		300	1, carry-in	EISA config util & lib, EISA sys util, adv array drvs	$16,995.00	CPU upgr, accepts a second CPU card
ISA, EISA		300	1, carry-in	EISA config util & lib, EISA sys util, adv array drvs	$18,995.00	CPU upgr, accepts a second CPU card
ISA, EISA		300	1, carry-in	EISA config util & lib, EISA sys util, adv array drvs	$20,995.00	CPU upgr, accepts a second CPU card
ISA, EISA		300	1, carry-in	EISA config util & lib, EISA sys util	$10,495.00	Other opt avail
ISA, EISA		300	1, GE on-site	DOS, Windows 3.0		Other opt avail
ISA	VGA	85	1, on-site	Tutorial, diags	$4,199.00	Includes unlimited toll-free tech support, other opt avail
EISA		408	1, on-site	Setup, LIM 40 util, Windows 3.0		440M or 1000M SCSI-2 hard disks avail, other opt avail
MCA	VGA (800 x 600)	110-240VAC	1, carry-in			200M or 340M hard disk avail, other opt avail
EISA	VGA	395, 110-240 VAC	1, carry-in	DOS	$14,999.00	Includes mouse, RAID 5 disk array option, other opt avail
ISA	VGA monochrome disp, Diamond Speedstar Plus 1024 x 768, 1M	300	30 days money back; 1, on-site avail	DOS, Windows 3.0	$2,395.00	RS or F12 Case has 7-bay desktop, 2 fans, other opt avail

continues

Table 4.7. Continued

COMPANY	MODEL	CPU, SPEED, CACHE	MIN, MAX RAM (M)	UNIT SIZE	BIOS, VER.	DISK DRIVES (M)	HARD DISK CAP, SPEED, TYPE	ADAPTERS INCLUDED	EXP SLOTS
Zeos International, Ltd.	486-33 Upgradable systems	80486DX, 33MHz, 8K	4, 32	Mid size	Award	1.2, 1.44	130M, IDE	2 ser, 1 par, 1 game	1 8-bit, 7 16-bit
Zeos International, Ltd.	486-33 Upgradable systems	80486DX, 33MHz, 8K	8, 32	Mid size	Award	1.2, 1.44	210M, IDE	2 ser, 1 par, 1 game	1 8-bit, 7 16-bit
Zeos International, Ltd.	486-33 Upgradable systems	80486DX, 33MHz, 8K	1, 32	Mid size	Award	1.2 or 1.44	42M, IDE	2 ser, 1 par, 1 game	1 8-bit, 7 16-bit
Advanced Logic Research	PowerPro DMP 256/330S	80486DX, 33MHz, 8K	17, 49	Full tower	Phoenix 1.00.10A, 1.00.09A	1.2	330M, 16ms, SCSI	2 ser, 1 par, 1 mouse	2 8-bit or 16-bit, 10 32-bit
Club Computer Corporation	Falcon	80486DX, 33MHz, 64K	4, 64	Mid size	AMI	1.2 or 1.44	200M, 15ms, IDE		1 32-bit, 7 8-bit or 16-bit
DTK Computer Inc.	FEAT-3300	80486DX, 33MHz, 64K	0, 16	Full tower	27256; 4.26V.				1 8-bit, 6 16-bit, 1 32-bit
Gateway 2000	486-33 Cache	80486DX, 33MHz, 64K	8, 64	Full size	Phoenix	1.2, 1.44	200M, 15ms, IDE	2 ser, 1 par	8 16-bit
Hyundai	Super 486/33I	80486DX, 33MHz, 64K	4, 16	Full tower	Hewlett-Packard	1.44	100M, IDE	2 ser, 1 par, IDE	1 8-bit, 6 16-bit, 1 32-bit
Insight	Insight 486-33MHz EISA w/ 64K cache	80486DX, 33MHz, 64K	8, 64	Full tower	Award EISA 486, H	1.2, 1.44	105M, 14ms, SCSI		8 16-bit
Insight	Insight 486-33MHz ISA cache	80486DX, 33MHz, 64K	4, 64	Full tower	AMI	1.2, 1.44	130M, 15ms, IDE		6 16-bit, 1 8-bit, 1 32-bit
MIS Computer Systems	486/25 EISA	80486DX, 33MHz, 64K	1, 64	Tower	Phoenix	1.2, 1.44	120M, IDE	2 ser, 1 par, 1 game	7 32-bit EISA, 1 16-bit
MIS Computer Systems	486/33 EISA	80486DX, 33MHz, 64K	1, 64	Tower	Phoenix	1.2, 1.44	120M, IDE	2 ser, 1 par, 1 game	7 32-bit EISA, 1 16-bit
MIS Computer Systems	486/33 ISA	80486DX, 33MHz, 64K	1, 16	Tower	Phoenix	1.2, 1.44	120M, IDE	2 ser, 1 par, 1 game	5 16-bit
Northgate	Elegance 433i	80486DX, 33MHz, 64K	4, 16	Full size	AMI	1.2, 1.44	40M, IDE	2 ser, 1 par	1 8-bit, 6 16-bit, 1 32-bit
Swan Technologies	486/33 Desk	80486DX, 33MHz, 64K	4, 64	Full size	Phoenix, MCI 486	1.2, 1.44	100M, 17ms, IDE	2 ser, 1 par	8 16-bit
Tangent Computer	433i	80486DX, 33MHz, 64K	4, 64	Mini tower	AMI 5, 9, 91	1.2 or 1.44	207M, 15ms, IDE	2 ser, 1 par	7 16-bit, 1 16-bit or 32-bit
Tri-Star Computer Corporation	Flash Cache FC433i	80486DX, 33MHz, 64K	8, 16	Full tower	AMI	1.2 and 1.44	210M, 15ms, IDE		2 8-bit, 6 16-bit
Tri-Star Computer Corporation	Tri-Cad Ultra TC433i	80486DX, 33MHz, 64K	4, 16	Full tower	AMI	1.2 and 1.44	210M, 15ms, IDE		2 8-bit, 6 16-bit
Tri-Star Computer Corporation	Tri-Lan TL433i ISA	80486DX, 33MHz, 64K	4, 16	Full tower	Award	1.2 and 1.44	330M, 19ms, SCSI		2 16-bit, 6 32-bit
Acer America Corporation	AcerFrame 3000SP 33	80486DX, 33MHz, 128K	8, 64	Twin tower		1.2		2 ser, 1 par	8 32-bit

BUS TYPE	VIDEO ADAPTER, DISPLAY	POWER SUPPLY (watts)	WARRANTY (years)	SOFTWARE INCLUDED	RETAIL PRICE	OTHER INFORMATION
ISA	VGA color display, Diamond Speedstar Plus 1024 x 768, 1M	300	30 days money back; 1, on-site avail	DOS, Windows 3.0	$2,895.00	RS or F12 Case has 7-bay desktop, 2 fans, other opt avail
ISA	VGA color display, Diamond Speedstar Plus 1024 x 768, 1M	300	30 days money back; 1, on-site avail	DOS, Windows 3.0	$3,395.00	RS or F12 Case has 7-bay desktop, 2 fans, other opt avail
ISA	Monochrome display, Hercules Graphics Adapter	300	30 days money back; 1, on-site avail		$1,795.00	RS or F12 Case has 7-bay desktop, 2 fans, other opt avail
ISA, EISA		300	1, carry-in	EISA config util & lib, EISA sys util	$18,495.00	Dual CPUs, Intelligent EISA SCSI Host Adptr prov Bus Master DMA data xfers up to 33M/sec
ISA		200	1, send-back; GE on-site avail	DOS, Windows 3.0	$3,395.00	Shadow RAM, BIOS Caching, CPU upgr 386, 486sx, 486, Club Rainbow SuperVGA adapter available
ISA		250	1, carry-in		$3,199.00	Other opt avail
ISA	14" Crystal Scan 1024 VGA, Diamond Speedstar VGA 1024 x 768 1M	200, 220	30 days money back; 1, on-site	DOS, Windows 3.0	$3,395.00	Includes mouse, non-interlaced display, other opt avail
ISA		300	18 mos on-site avail	DOS, Windows 3.0	$5,595.00	200M or 300M hard disks avail, other opt avail
EISA	Insight SuperVGA display, Diamond Speed Star 1024 x 768, 1M	375	1, send-back	DOS	$9,995.00	Includes Microsoft-compatible mouse, toll-free tech support
ISA	Insight SuperVGA display, Diamond Speed Star 1024 x 768, 1M	250	1, send-back	DOS	$2,995.00	Includes Microsoft-compatible mouse, toll-free tech support, may subst Orchid ProDesigner II for Diamond Speed Star
ISA, EISA	Optiquest 2000 15" NI, Trident VGA 1024 x 768, 1M	200-250 switching	1, send-back	DOS	$3,410.00	Other opt avail
ISA, EISA	Optiquest 2000 15" NI, Trident VGA 1024 x 768, 1M	200-250 switching	1, send-back	DOS	$3,645.00	Other opt avail
ISA	Optiquest 14" NI, Trident VGA 1024 x 768, 1M	200-250 switching	1, send-back	DOS	$3,030.00	Other opt avail
ISA	14" VGA gray	200	30 days money back; 1, on-site	DOS, Windows 3.0	$5,249.00	Includes mouse, OmniKey, ULTRA keyboard, lifetime 24-hr tech support, other opt avail
ISA	Swan 1024 x 768 display, optional adapters	200	2, on-site	DOS, Swan utils, LIM 40	$3,795.00	Lifetime toll-free tech support, other opt avail
ISA	14" NI display, Orchid Pro Designer IIs 1024 x 768 ni VESA	300	1, send-back	DOS	$3,995.00	Other opt avail
ISA	Mag Computronics 1024 x 768 NI , Diamond Speedstar 1024 x 768, 1M	220	60 days money back; 2, send-back	DOS, Windows 3.0	$3,495.00	Includes lifetime toll-free tech support, mouse, other opt avail
ISA	17" IDEK MF-5117 display, Diamond Speedstar 1024 x 768, 1M	220	60 days money back; 2, send-back	DOS, Fast Cad 2-D Version 26	$4,695.00	Lifetime toll-free tech support, Calcomp Drawingboard II 12 x 12, Digitizer, Intel Math Co-Processor, other opt avail
ISA	14" Septre monochrome display, MDA	250	60 days money back; 2, send-back	DOS	$4,295.00	Includes lifetime toll-free tech support, other opt avail
EISA	VGA (800 x 600)	430	2, carry-in	DOS, EMM 4.0, EISA utils	$11,995.00	Other hard disk sizes avail, displays avail

continues

Table 4.7. Continued

COMPANY	MODEL	CPU, SPEED, CACHE	MIN, MAX RAM (M)	UNIT SIZE	BIOS, VER.	DISK DRIVES (M)	HARD DISK CAP, SPEED, TYPE	ADAPTERS INCLUDED	EXP SLOTS
COMPAQ	COMPAQ DeskPro 486/33L 120	80486DX, 33MHz, 128K	4, 100	Full size	COMPAQ	1.44	120M, 19ms	2 ser, 1 par, 1 mouse	7 8-/16- or 32-bit, 1 RAM
COMPAQ	COMPAQ DeskPro 486/33L 320	80486DX, 33MHz, 128K	4, 100	Full size	COMPAQ	1.44	320M, 18ms	2 ser, 1 par, 1 mouse	7 8-/16- or 32-bit, 1 RAM
COMPAQ	COMPAQ DeskPro 486/33L 650	80486DX, 33MHz, 128K	4, 100	Full size	COMPAQ	1.44	650M, 18ms	2 ser, 1 par, 1 mouse	7 8-/16- or 32-bit, 1 RAM
Dell Computer Corporation	Dell Powerline 433DE	80486DX, 33MHz, 128K	4, 48	Full size	Phoenix, Dell	1.2 or 1.4	80M, 25ms, IDE	2 ser, 1 par, 1 mouse, 1 keybd, 1 ext VGA	6 32-bit
Dell Computer Corporation	Dell Powerline 433SE	80486DX, 33MHz, 128K	4, 128	Full size	Phoenix, Dell	1.2 or 1.4	80M, 25ms, IDE	2 ser, 1 par, 1 mouse, 1 keybd, 1 ext VGA	8 32-bit, 2 prop
Northgate	Elegance 433e	80486DX, 33MHz, 128K	4, 32	Full tower	Northgate	1.2, 1.44	40M, IDE	1 ser, 1 par, 1 mouse, IDE	8 32-bit EISA
PC Brand, Inc.	486/33	80486DX, 33MHz, 128K	1, 16	Full size		1.2 or 1.44		2 ser, 1 par	EISA
PC Brand, Inc.	486/33	80486DX, 33MHz, 128K	1, 16	Full size		1.2 or 1.44		2 ser, 1 par	ISA
Samsung Information Systems	System Master 486/33 TE	80486DX, 33MHz, 128K	4, 32	Full tower		1.2, 1.44		2 ser, 1 par, IDE	8 32-bit
Standard Computer	486/33	80486DX, 33MHz, 128K	4, 16	Mid size	AMI	1.2, 1.44	210M, 15ms, IDE	2 ser, 1 par, 1 game	1 8-bit, 6 16-bit, 1 32-bit
Tangent Computer	433e	80486DX, 33MHz, 128K	4, 32	Full tower	Mylex 6.04	1.2 or 1.44	207M, 15ms, SCSI	2 ser, 1 par	8 32-bit
Wyse Technology	Decision 486 33 E	80486DX, 33MHz, 128K	2, 192	Full tower	Phoenix, Wyse	1.2 or 1.44	300M or 660 M	1 ser, 1 par, 1 mouse, IDE	9 32-bit
Wyse Technology	Decision 486 33 T	80486DX, 33MHz, 128K	4, 16	Full tower	Phoenix, Wyse	1.2 or 1.44	110M, IDE	2 ser, 1 par, IDE	2 8-bit, 6 16-bit
Zeos International, Ltd.	486-33C Upgradable systems	80486DX, 33MHz, 128K	1, 32	Mid size	Award	1.2 or 1.44	42M, IDE	2 ser, 1 par, 1 game	1 8-bit, 7 16-bit
Zeos International, Ltd.	486-33C Upgradable systems	80486DX, 33MHz, 128K	2, 32	Mid size	Award	1.2, 1.44	85M, IDE	2 ser, 1 par, 1 game	1 8-bit, 7 16-bit
Zeos International, Ltd.	486-33C Upgradable systems	80486DX, 33MHz, 128K	8, 32	Mid size	Award	1.2, 1.44	210M, IDE	2 ser, 1 par, 1 game	1 8-bit, 7 16-bit
Zeos International, Ltd.	486-33C Upgradable systems	80486DX, 33MHz, 128K	4, 32	Mid size	Award	1.2, 1.44	130M, IDE	2 ser, 1 par, 1 game	1 8-bit, 7 16-bit
Zeos International, Ltd.	486-33E systems	80486DX, 33MHz, 128K	4, 32	Mid size	Mylex	1.2, 1.44	85M, IDE	2 ser, 1 par, 1 game	8 32-bit
Zeos International, Ltd.	486-33E systems	80486DX, 33MHz, 128K	1, 32	Mid size	Mylex	1.2 or 1.44	85M, IDE	2 ser, 1 par, 1 game	8 32-bit
Zeos International, Ltd.	486-33E systems	80486DX, 33MHz, 128K	4, 32	Mid size	Mylex	1.2, 1.44	330M, SCSI	2 ser, 1 par, 1 game	8 32-bit

BUS TYPE	VIDEO ADAPTER, DISPLAY	POWER SUPPLY (watts)	WARRANTY (years)	SOFTWARE INCLUDED	RETAIL PRICE	OTHER INFORMATION
EISA	VGA		1, carry-in		$10,099.00	Other opt avail, other OS avail
EISA	VGA		1, carry-in		$11,799.00	Other opt avail, other OS avail
EISA	VGA		1, carry-in		$12,799.00	Other opt avail, other OS avail
EISA	VGA Color Plus display, VGA 1024 x 768, 1M	220	1, on-site		$6,099.00	Includes unlimited toll-free tech support, other opt avail
EISA	VGA Color Plus display, VGA 1024 x 768, 512K	300	1, on-site		$7,399.00	Includes unlimited toll-free tech support, other opt avail
EISA	14" VGA Gray display, VGA, 512K	450	30 days money back; 1, on-site	DOS	$6,999.00	Includes mouse, OmniKey, ULTRA keyboard, lifetime 24-hr tech support, other opt avail
EISA		200	1, send-back; 5, prorated		$3,999.00	Choice of Desktop or SlimLine Case, other opt avail
ISA		200	1, send-back; 5, prorated		$1,899.00	Choice of Desktop or SlimLine Case, other opt avail
EISA		300	1, carry-in	DOS, Windows 3.0	$7,699.00	Contact via 800#, BBS, fax, authorized service vendors, other opt avail
ISA	14" Viewsonic 5 NI display, Trident 1024 x 768, 1M	200	1, TRW on-site	DOS, Windows 3.0	$3,595.00	Includes mouse, other opt avail
EISA	14" NI display, Orchid Pro Designer IIs 1024 x 768 ni VESA	300	1, send-back	DOS	$6,495.00	Other opt avail
EISA		325, auto sensing	1, carry-in	Wyse Enhanced DOS, Wyse Setup & Test	$8,999.00	Other opt avail
ISA		325	1, carry-in	Wyse Enhanced DOS, Wyse Setup & Test	$5,999.00	300M ESDI or 420M SCSI hard disks avail, other opt avail
ISA	Monochrome display, Hercules Graphics Adapter	300	30 days money back; 1, on-site avail		$1,995.00	RS or F12 Case has 7-bay desktop, 2 fans, other opt avail
ISA	VGA monochrome disp, Diamond Speedstar Plus 1024 x 768, 1M	300	30 days money back; 1, on-site avail	DOS, Windows 3.0	$2,595.00	RS or F12 Case has 7-bay desktop, 2 fans, other opt avail
ISA	VGA color display, Diamond Speedstar Plus 1024 x 768, 1M	300	30 days money back; 1, on-site avail	DOS, Windows 3.0	$3,595.00	RS or F12 Case has 7-bay desktop, 2 fans, other opt avail
ISA	VGA color display, Diamond Speedstar Plus 1024 x 768, 1M	300	30 days money back; 1, on-site avail	DOS, Windows 3.0	$3,095.00	RS or F12 Case has 7-bay desktop, 2 fans, other opt avail
EISA	VGA color display, Diamond Speedstar Plus 1024 x 768, 1M.	450	30 days money back; 1, on-site avail	DOS, Windows 3.0	$5,495.00	RS or F12 Case has 8-bay vertical case, other opt avail
EISA	Moncohrome display, Hercules Graphics Adapter	300	30 days money back; 1, on-site avail		$4,495.00	RS or F12 Case has 7-bay desktop, 2 fans, other opt avail
EISA	VGA monochrome disp, Diamond Speedstar Plus 1024 x 768, 1M	450	30 days money back; 1, on-site avail	DOS, Windows 3.0	$7,495.00	RS or F12 Case has 8-bay vertical case, other opt avail

continues

Table 4.7. Concluded

COMPANY	MODEL	CPU, SPEED, CACHE	MIN, MAX RAM (M)	UNIT SIZE	BIOS, VER.	DISK DRIVES (M)	HARD DISK CAP, SPEED, TYPE	ADAPTERS INCLUDED	EXP SLOTS
Microlab	433i	80486DX, 33MHz, 256K	4, 32	Full tower	AMI	1.2, 1.44	211M, 15ms, IDE	2 ser, 1 par, 1 game	8 16-bit
Tri-Star Computer Corporation	Flash Cache FC333i EISA	80486DX, 33MHz, 256K	4, 16	Full tower	Award	1.2 and 1.44	120M, 19ms, IDE		2 16-bit, 6 32-bit
Tri-Star Computer Corporation	Flash Cache FC433i EISA	80486DX, 33MHz, 256K	8, 16	Full tower	Award	1.2 and 1.44	210M, 15ms, IDE		2 16-bit, 6 32-bit
Tri-Star Computer Corporation	Tri-Lan TL433i EISA	80486DX, 33MHz, 256K	4, 64	Full tower	Award	1.2 and 1.44	330M, 19ms, SCSI		2 16-bit, 6 32-bit
COMPAQ	COMPAQ SystemPro 486-240	80486DX, 33MHz, 512K	8, 256	Full tower	COMPAQ	1.44	240M, 19ms	2 ser, 1 par, 1 mouse	6 8-/16- or 32-bit, 2 RAM
COMPAQ	COMPAQ SystemPro 486-420	80486DX, 33MHz, 512K	8, 256	Full tower	COMPAQ	1.44	420M, 18ms	2 ser, 1 par, 1 mouse	6 8-/16- or 32-bit, 2 RAM
COMPAQ	COMPAQ SystemPro 486-840	80486DX, 33MHz, 512K	8, 256	Full tower	COMPAQ	1.44	840M, 18ms	2 ser, 1 par, 1 mouse	6 8-/16- or 32-bit, 2 RAM
Falco Data Products, Inc.	FALCO GT486/40	80486DX, 40MHz, 256K	4, 32	Small	Falco .	2.88			3 16-bit
Dell Computer Corporation	Dell Powerline 433SE	80486DX, 50MHz, 128K	4, 128	Full size	Phoenix, Dell	1.2 or 1.4	80M, 25ms, IDE	2 ser, 1 par, 1 mouse, 1 keybd, 1 ext VGA	8 32-bit, 2 prop
Dell Computer Corporation	Dell Powerline 450DE	80486DX, 50MHz, 128K	4, 48	Full size	Phoenix, Dell	1.2 or 1.4	80M, 25ms, IDE	2 ser, 1 par, 1 mouse, 1 keybd, 1 ext VGA	6 32-bit
Advanced Logic Research	MultiAccess Series 3000 Model 30	Dual 80486DX, 25MHz, 8K	8, 64	Full size	Phoenix 1.10.24	1.2	330M, 16ms, SCSI	9 ser, 1 par	3 CBUS, 10 CBUS-ISA

BUS TYPE	VIDEO ADAPTER, DISPLAY	POWER SUPPLY (watts)	WARRANTY (years)	SOFTWARE INCLUDED	RETAIL PRICE	OTHER INFORMATION
ISA	Diamond Speedstar VGA 1024 x 768, 1M	230	1, send-back; free shipping	DOS	$3,495.00	Free shipping, other opt avail
ISA	Mag Computronics 1024 x 768 NI, Diamond Speedstar 1024 x 768, 1M	220	60 days money back; 2, send-back	DOS, Windows 3.0	$2,995.00	Includes lifetime toll-free tech support, mouse, other opt avail
ISA	Mag Computronics 1024 x 768 NI, Diamond Speedstar 1024 x 768, 1M	220	60 days money back; 2, send-back	DOS, Windows 3.0	$4,095.00	Includes lifetime toll-free tech support, mouse, other opt avail
ISA	14" Septre monochrome display, MDA	250	60 days money back; 2, send-back	DOS	$4,895.00	Includes lifetime toll-free tech support, other opt avail
EISA	VGA		1, carry-in		$16,999.00	Accepts multiple CPU cards, other opt avail
EISA	VGA		1, carry-in		$18,999.00	Accepts multiple CPU cards, other opt avail
EISA	VGA		1, carry-in		$22,999.00	Accepts multiple CPU cards, other opt avail
ISA			1, send-back		$5,990.00	Other opt avail
EISA	VGA Color Plus display, VGA 1024 x 768, 512K	300	1, on-site		$9,399.00	Includes unlimited toll-free tech support, other opt avail
EISA	VGA Color Plus display, VGA 1024 x 768, 1M	220	1, on-site		$8,099.00	Includes unlimited toll-free tech support, other opt avail
ISA, CBUS		300	1, carry-in		$23,999.00	CPU upgr, other opt avail

Laptop and Notebook Computer Listing

We eat on the go. We use the telephone while on the go. The capability to compute on the go is gaining in popularity. The three tables in this section list portable, laptop, and notebook computers.

Table 4.8. Macintosh Portable Computers

COMPANY	MODEL	CPU, SPEED, CACHE	MIN, MAX RAM (M)	UNIT SIZE (lbs)	BIOS, VER.	DISK DRIVES (M)	HARD DISK CAP, SPEED, TYPE	ADAPTERS INCLUDED	EXP SLOTS
Apple Computer	Macintosh Portable 2/40 Laptop	CMOS 68000, 16MHz	2, 9	15.75	Apple	1.4	40M	1 SCSI, 1 ADB, 1 printer, 1 ser, 1 audio, 1 video	4 prop
Apple Computer	Macintosh Portable 4/40 Laptop	CMOS 68000, 16MHz	4, 9	15.75	Apple	1.4	40M	1 SCSI, 1 ADB, 1 printer, 1 ser, 1 audio, 1 video	4 prop
Outbound Systems	Notebook System 2000	68000, 20MHz	2, 4	6.25		1.44	20M		
Outbound Systems	Notebook System 2030	MC68ECO 30, 30MHz	2, 4	6.25		1.44	40M		
Outbound Systems	Notebook System 2030s	MC68ECO 30, 30MHz	4, 4	6.25		1.44	40M		

BUS TYPE	VIDEO ADAPTER, DISPLAY	POWER SUPPLY (watts)	WARRANTY (years)	SOFTWARE INCLUDED	RETAIL PRICE	OTHER INFORMATION
020 PDS	Built-in 10" backlit, 640 x 400 monochrome	15	1, carry-in	Sys software, HyperCard, training	$4,199.00	Includes battery, trackball, carrying case
020 PDS	Built-in 10" backlit, 640 x 400 monochrome	15	1, carry-in	Sys software, HyperCard, training	$4,699.00	Includes battery, trackball, carrying case
	10" VGA Sidelit LCD		1, send-back			
	10" VGA Sidelit LCD		1, send-back			
	10" VGA Sidelit LCD		1, send-back			

Table 4.9. IBM-Compatible Laptop Computers

COMPANY	MODEL	CPU, SPEED, CACHE	MIN, MAX RAM (M)	UNIT SIZE (lbs)	BIOS, VER.	DISK DRIVES (M)	HARD DISK CAP, SPEED, TYPE	ADAPTERS INCLUDED	EXP SLOTS
COMPAQ	COMPAQ SLT/286 Model 20	80C286, 12MHz	640K, 12.6	14	COMPAQ	1.44	20M, 29ms	1 ser, 1 par, 1 ext disp, ext keybd, ext opt	Opt
COMPAQ	COMPAQ SLT/286 Model 40	80C286, 12MHz	640K, 12.6	14	COMPAQ	1.44	40M, 29ms	1 ser, 1 par, 1 ext disp, ext keybd, ext opt	Opt
EPSON	Equity LT-286e	80C286, 12MHz	1, 2	17	Seiko EPSON (proprietary)	1.44	20M, 27ms	1 ser, 1 par, 1 ext disk, 1 keybd, 1 EGA disp	3 prop
Zenith	SupersPort 286e Model 40	80C286, 12MHz	1, 5	15.6		1.44	40M		
Altima	Altima NSX 20 M	80386SX, 16MHz	2, 8	9.3	Award	1.44	20M, 25ms	1 ser, 1 par, VGA ext	Opt exp unit
Altima	Altima Three/80 M Laptop	80386SX, 16MHz	1, 5	15	Phoenix	1.44	80M, 25ms, IDE	1 ser, 1 par	1 16-bit
Dell Computer Corporation	Dell System 316LT	80386SX, 16MHz	1, 8	15	Phoenix, Dell	1.44	20M, 27ms, IDE	VGA disp, keybd, keypad, disk, par & ser	1 8-bit, 1 prop fax, modem slot
EPSON	Equity LT-386SX	80386SX, 16MHz	2, 4	17	Seiko EPSON (proprietary)	1.44	20M, 27ms	1 ser, 1 par, 1 ext disk, 1 keybd, 1 VGA disp	3 prop
Leading Edge	D/LT386P-100 Laptop	80386SX, 16MHz	2, 2		Phoenix 1.55.02	1.44	10M, 19ms	1 ser, 1 par, ext VGA, ext disk	1 prop
Leading Edge	D/LT386P-40 Laptop	80386SX, 16MHz	2, 2		Phoenix 1.55.02	1.44	40M, 19ms	1 ser, 1 par, ext VGA, ext disk	1 prop
NEC	PowerMate Portable	80386SX, 16MHz	2, 16	21		1.44	42M, 28ms	1 ser, 1 par	3 8-bit or 16-bit
Zenith	SupersPort SX Model 120	80386SX, 16MHz	1, 8	16.8		1.44	120M		
Zenith	SupersPort SX Model 40	80386SX, 16MHz	1, 8	16.8		1.44	40M		
Altima	Altima LSX 40MB	80386SX, 20MHz	1, 5		Phoenix	1.44	40M, 23ms	1 ser, 1 par, VGA ext	
CompuAdd	CompuAdd 320SL Laptop	80386SX, 20MHz	2, 6		AMI	1.44	40M, 28ms, IDE		1 prop
Dell Computer Corporation	Dell System 320LT	80386SX, 20MHz	1, 8	15	Phoenix, Dell	1.44	20M, 27ms, IDE	VGA disp, keybd, keypad, disk, par & ser	1 8-bit, 1 prop fax, modem slot
COMPAQ	COMPAQ SLT 386s/20 Model 120	80386SX, 20MHz, 4K	2, 14	14	COMPAQ	1.44	120M, 19ms	1 ser, 1 par, 1 ext disp, ext keybd, ext opt	
COMPAQ	COMPAQ SLT 386s/20 Model 60	80386SX, 20MHz, 4K	2, 14	14	COMPAQ	1.44	60M, 19ms	1 ser, 1 par, 1 ext disp, ext keybd, ext opt	
IBM	8573-031 Laptop	80386DX, 20MHz	4, 16		IBM	1.44	120M, 17ms, ESDI	1 ser, 1 par, 1 mouse	1 16-bit, 1 32-bit
IBM	IBM P70-121/8573-121 Portable	80386DX, 20MHz	4, 16	19.4	IBM	1.44	120M, 23ms, ESDI		1 16-bit, 1 32-bit

BUS TYPE	VIDEO DISPLAY, ADAPTER	POWER SUPPLY	WARRANTY (years)	SOFTWARE INCLUDED	RETAIL PRICE	OTHER INFORMATION
	10" COMPAQ VGA backlit display, VGA	NiCad batt pack 120V to 220/240V AC adptr	1, carry-in		$3,999.00	Detachable keyboard, detachable docking-station, other opt avail
	10" COMPAQ VGA backlit display, VGA	NiCad batt pack 120V to 220/240V AC adptr	1, carry-in		$4,499.00	Detachable keyboard, detachable docking-station, other opt avail
ISA, prop	EGA white LCD	100 to 240V auto adjusting, 50/60Hz	1, carry-in			Other opt avail
	VGA fluorescent-backlit LCD		1, carry-in	DOS	$3,199.00	Other opt avail
	VGA backlit LCD, 32 gray shd	NiCad batt, AC adptr	1, Dow Jones carry-in	DOS, SQUISH, Fax software	$3,499.00	Inc 2400B modem with Send Fax, carry case, user manual, modem cable, opt 5.25" drive
ISA	VGA backlit LCD, 32 gray shd		1, Dow Jones carry-in	DOS, Fax software	$3,699.00	Exp slot, inc 2400B modem w/ Send Fax cap, carry case, user manual, modem cable, opt 5.25" drive
ISA, prop	Adj, det VGA backlit supertwist LCD, 16 gray shd	Removable, rechg NiCad, AC adptr/ charger	1, on-site	Tutorial, diags	$2,499.00	Includes unlimited toll-free tech support, other opt avail
ISA, prop	VGA white LCD	100 to 240V auto adjusting, 50/60Hz	1, carry-in			Other opt avail
Modem slot	VGA	38 watts	1, carry-in	DOS, Windows 3.0	$2,599.00	Other opt avail
Modem slot	VGA	38 watts	1, carry-in	DOS, Windows 3.0	$2,199.00	Other opt avail
ISA	VGA gas plasma display	115V/230V universal	1, carry-in	DOS, Windows 3.0	$5,499.00	Other opt avail
	VGA fluorescent-backlit LCD		1, carry-in	DOS	$5,199.00	Other opt avail
	VGA fluorescent-backlit LCD		1, carry-in	DOS	$4,399.00	Other opt avail
	VGA backlit LCD, 32 gray shd	Batt AC adptr/ charger for 110/220V, 50/60Hz	1, Dow Jones carry-in	DOS	$2,999.00	Incl carry case, user manual, software bundle, opt 5.25" drive
Modem slot	VGA LCD	Batt pack	1, send-back; carry-in	DOS, Laplink II with cable	$2,895.00	Includes carry case
ISA, prop	Adj, det VGA backlit supertwist LCD, 16 gray shd	Removable, rechg NiCad, AC adptr/charger	1, on-site	Tutorial, diags	$2,999.00	Includes unlimited toll-free tech support, other opt avail
	10" COMPAQ VGA backlit display, VGA	NiCad batt pack 120V to 220/240V AC adptr	1, carry-in		$5,699.00	Detachable keyboard, detachable docking-station, other opt avail
	10" COMPAQ VGA backlit display, VGA	NiCad batt pack 120V to 220/240V AC adptr	1, carry-in		$5,199.00	Detachable keyboard, detachable docking-station, other opt avail
MCA	IBM gas panel display, VGA	85 watts	1, carry-in; on-site avail		$5,995.00	Other opt avail
MCA	IBM gas panel display, VGA	85 watts	1, carry-in; on-site avail		$8,295.00	Other opt avail

continues

Table 4.9. Concluded

COMPANY	MODEL	CPU, SPEED, CACHE	MIN, MAX RAM (M)	UNIT SIZE (lbs)	BIOS, VER.	DISK DRIVES (M)	HARD DISK CAP, SPEED, TYPE	ADAPTERS INCLUDED	EXP SLOTS
Zenith	SupersPort 486sx	80486SX, 20MHz	4, 16	15	Flash	1.44, 720K	120M, 19ms, IDE	1 ser, 1 par, 1 ext video, 1 mouse, 1 ext keybd, 1 ext disk	2 int, 1 ext 8-bit or 16-bit
Zenith	SupersPort 486	80486DX, 25MHz	4, 16	15	Flash	1.44, 720K	120M, 19ms, IDE	1 ser, 1 par, 1 ext video, 1 mouse, 1 ext keybd, 1 ext disk	2 int, 1 ext 8-bit or 16-bit
IBM	8573-161 laptop	80486DX, 33MHz	8, 16		IBM	1.44	160M, 16ms, SCSI	1 ser, 1 par, 1 mouse	2 16-bit, 2 32-bit

BUS TYPE	VIDEO DISPLAY, ADAPTER	POWER SUPPLY	WARRANTY (years)	SOFTWARE INCLUDED	RETAIL PRICE	OTHER INFORMATION
Modem, Exp	10.7" VGA edgelit LCD, 64 gray shd	110/220VAC, 60/50Hz	1, carry-in	DOS, Windows 3.0	$7,499.00	Includes ISOPOINT mouse function, other opt avail
Modem, Exp	10.7" VGA edgelit LCD, 64 gray shd	110/220VAC, 60/50Hz	1, carry-in	DOS, Windows 3.0	$8,899.00	Includes ISOPOINT mouse function, other opt avail
MCA	IBM gas panel display, VGA	120 watts	1, carry-in; on-site avail		$15,990.00	Other opt avail

Table 4.10. IBM-Compatible Notebook Computers

COMPANY	MODEL	CPU, SPEED, CACHE	MIN, MAX RAM (M)	UNIT SIZE (lbs)	BIOS, VER	DISK DRIVES (M)	HARD DISK CAP, SPD, TYPE	ADAPTERS INCLUDED	EXP SLOTS
COMPAQ	COMPAQ LTE Model 20 Notebook	80C86, 9.54MHz	640K, 1	6.9	COMPAQ	1.44	20M, 29ms	1 ser, 1 par	
Zenith	MinisPort HD Notebook	80C88, 10MHz	1, 1	5.5		1.44	20M		
Tandy	1500 HD Notebook	NECV-20, 10MHz	640K, 1.64	6		1.44	20M, 23ms		
Tandy	1100FD Laptop-Notebook	NECV-20, 8MHz	640K, 640K	6.2		720K		1 ser, 1 par	
Dell Computer Corporation	Dell System 212N Notebook	80286, 12MHz	1, 5		Phoenix, Dell	1.44	20M, 23ms, IDE	1 ser, 1 par, 1 VGA, 1 keybd, 1 keypad, 1 mouse	3 prop
Tandon	286SX/N Notebook	80286, 12MHz	1, 8		Tandon				
Texas Instruments	TravelMate 3000 Notebook PC	80286, 12MHz	2, 6	4.4	Phoenix 3.10 Jan 1988	Optional removable 1.44	21M, 23 ms, IDE	1 ser, 1 par, 1 mouse, 1 keypad, 1 exp bus	1 8-bit, 1 16-bit
Tandy	2810 HD Notebook	80286, 16MHz	1, 5	6.7		1.44	20M, 23ms	1 ser, 1 par, 1 ext RGB, 1 ext keybd, 1 modem	
COMPAQ	COMPAQ LTE/286 Model 20	80C286, 12MHz	640K, 4.6	6.9	COMPAQ	1.44	20M, 29ms	1 ser, 1 par, 1 ext CGA, ext storage module	
COMPAQ	COMPAQ LTE/286 Model 40	80C286, 12MHz	640K, 4.6	6.9	COMPAQ	1.44	40M, 29ms	1 ser, 1 par, 1 ext disp, ext options	
Packard Bell	PB 286NB Notebook	80C286, 12MHz	1, 8		Phoenix	1.44	20M, 23ms	1 ser, 1 par, 1 ext video, 1 mouse, 1 ext disk	
Zenith	MastersSport 286 Notebook	80C286, 12MHz	1, 2	6.6		1.44, 720K	30M, 19ms, IDE	1 ser, 1 par, 1 ext video	2 prop
Zenith	SlimsPort 286 Model 40	80C286, 16MHz	1, 5	9.25		1.44	40M		
Zenith	SlimsPort 286 Model 20	80C286, 16MHz	1, 5	9.25		1.44	20M		
NCR	NCR Model 3125 Notepad	80386SL, 20MHz, 16KB	4, 20	4				1 ser, 1 par	Opt exp unit
Advanced Logic Research	Venture/16 Model 20	80386SX, 16MHz	1, 5	7	AMI	1.44	20M, 23ms, IDE	2 ser, 1 par, 1 ext VGA, 1 ISA exp	
Advanced Logic Research	Venture/16 Model 40	80386SX, 16MHz	1, 5	7	AMI	1.44	40M, 23ms, IDE	2 ser, 1 par, 1 ext VGA, 1 ISA exp	
CompuAdd	CompuAdd 316nx Notebook	80386SX, 16MHz	1, 5		Chips & Technology	1.44	30M, 23ms, IDE		
EPSON	NB3s Notebook	80386SX, 16MHz	1, 5	5.8	AMI	1.44	20M, 23ms, IDE	1 ser, 1 par, 1 video, 1 keybd	1 + opt exp unit
Leading Edge	N3/SX DNE162SX Notebook	80386SX, 16MHz	1, 5	6.9	Phoenix: 1.10.03	1.44	20M, 23ms	1 ser, 1 par, 1 ext VGA, 1 ext keybd	1 prop

BUS TYPE	VIDEO ADAPTER, DISPLAY	POWER SUPPLY	WARRANTY (years)	SOFTWARE INCLUDED	RETAIL PRICE	OTHER INFORMATION
	9" COMPAQ EL Backlit, CGA (640 x 200)	NiCad battery pack 120V to 220/240V AC adapter	1, carry-in		$1,999.00	Other opt avail, other OS avail
	CGA LCD		1, carry-in	DOS, FastLynx LX	$1,599.00	Other opt avail
	CGA Backlit LCD	9.5VDC, 110VAC	1, carry-in	DOS, DeskMate 3		Other opt avail
	8 7, 8" Reflective LCD	AC adapter 9.5VDC 1.7A. battery: 6 V, 1.8 Ah	1, carry-in	DOS, DeskMate, DeskMate apps		Other opt avail
Prop	Built-in VGA Edgelit LCD, 16 gray shd	Removable, rechrg NiCad, AC charger/adapter	1, on-site	Tutorial, diags	$2,399.00	Includes unlimited toll-free tech support, other opt avail
	VGA monochrome	50 watts	1, on-site			Other opt avail
ISA	VGA Triple Supertwist Sidelit LCD	27 watts	1, carry-in	DOS, Laplink, Battery Watch, Laptop File Mgr	$2,369.00	Other opt avail
	VGA Backlit LCD, 16 or 32 gray shades	16VDC, 110VAC	1, carry-in	DOS, DeskMate 3		Other opt avail
	9" COMPAQ EL Backlit, CGA (640 x 200)	NiCad battery pack 120V to 220/240V AC adapter	1, carry-in		$2,499.00	Other opt avail, other OS avail
	9" COMPAQ EL Backlit, CGA (640 x 200)	NiCad battery pack 120V to 220/240V AC adapter	1, carry-in		$2,799.00	Other opt avail, other OS avail
	VGA backlit LCD	AC, NiCad battery	1, send-back	DOS, Packard Bell Desktop, Lotus Works		Other opt avail
Prop	8.85" VGA Edgelit LCD, 16 gray shd	110/220 VAC, 60/50Hz	1, carry-in	DOS, Windows 3.0	$2,699.00	Other opt avail
	VGA fluorescent-backlit LCD		1, carry-in	DOS	$2,899.00	Other opt avail
	VGA fluorescent-backlit LCD		1, carry-in	DOS	$2,599.00	Other opt avail
ISA	VGA LCD, 16 gray shd (external VGA 800 x 600)	120VAC to 240VA	1, carry-in			A pen-like stylus writes on a digitized LCD screen
ISA	VGA backlit LCD, 32 gray shade	90-240V auto-sensing	1, carry-in	DR-DOS, ALR utils	$2,395.00	Other opt avail
ISA	VGA backlit LCD, 32 gray shades	90-240V auto-sensing	1, carry-in	DR-DOS, ALR utils	$2,495.00	Other opt avail
	VGA LCD		1, send-back; carry-in	DOS	$2,495.00	Other opt avail
Modem, exp	VGA white LCD, 16 gray shades	35.6 watts	1, carry-in	DOS, LCD, HD pwr-sav utils, EPSON diags	$3,999.00	Includes 2 rechargeable NiCad battery units, slip case, AC adapter, owner's manual
Modem slot	VGA LCD	25 watts	1, carry-in	DOS	$2,599.00	Other opt avail

continues

Table 4.10. Continued

COMPANY	MODEL	CPU, SPEED, CACHE	MIN, MAX RAM (M)	UNIT SIZE (lbs)	BIOS, VER	DISK DRIVES (M)	HARD DISK CAP, SPD, TYPE	ADAPTERS INCLUDED	EXP SLOTS
Packard Bell	386MB2 Notebook	80386SX, 16MHz	2, 5		Phoenix	1.44	40M, 27ms	1 ser, 1 par, 1 mouse, 1 ext VGA video, 1 ext disk	
PC Brand, Inc.	386SX/16 Notebook System	80386SX, 16MHz	2, 16	7.2		1.44	20M, 19ms, IDE	2 ser, 1 par, 1 ext exp	Opt exp unit
Samsung Information Systems	Notemaster 386S/16/20MB/ S3710	80386SX, 16MHz	1, 5			1.44	20M, 23ms, IDE	1 ser, 1 par, 1 mouse, 1 num keypad, 1 VGA	
Tandon	386SX/N Notebook	80386SX, 16MHz	1, 8		Tandon				
Zeos International, Ltd.	Zeos Notebook 386	80386SX, 16MHz	1, 5	7	Phoenix 80386 ROM Plus V. 3.10	1.44	20M, IDE	1 ser, 1 par, 1 ext video	
Zeos International, Ltd.	Zeos Notebook 386	80386SX, 16MHz	3, 5	7	Phoenix 80386 ROM Plus V. 3.10	1.44	20M, IDE	1 ser, 1 par, 1 ext video	
Zeos International, Ltd.	Zeos Notebook 386	80386SX, 16MHz	5, 5	7	Phoenix 80386 ROM Plus V. 3.10	1.44	20M, IDE	1 ser, 1 par, 1 ext video	
CompuAdd	CompuAdd Companion SX Notebook	80386SX, 20MHz	2, 6		Phoenix	1.44	20M, 23ms, IDE		1 prop
Data World	NB-320SX Notebook	80386SX, 20MHz	4, 16	6.5		1.44	40M	2 ser, 1 par, 1 keybd, 1 ext VGA	
Dell Computer Corporation	Dell System 320N Notebook	80386SX, 20MHz	1, 5		Phoenix, Dell	1.44	40M, 23ms, IDE	1 ser, 1 par, 1 VGA, keybd, keypad, mouse	3 prop
Hyundai	Super-NB386SC Notebook	80386SX, 20MHz	1, 4		Hewlett-Packard	1.44	20M, IDE	2 ser, 1 par, 1 ext disk, 1 ext keybd, 1 VGA	1 prop
IBM	IBM L40sx/8543-044 Laptop	80386SX, 20MHz	2, 18	7.7	IBM	1.44	60M, 19ms		
Leading Edge	N3/SX20 Notebook	80386SX, 20MHz	1, 5	6.9	Phoenix: 1.10.03	1.44	40M	1 ser, 1 par, 1 ext VGA, 1 ext keybd	1 prop
NCR	NCR Model 3120 Notebook	80386SX, 20MHz	1, 5	5.7		1.44	30M, 19ms	1 ser, 1 par, 1 PS, 2 mouse	1 prop
Northgate	SlimLite 386SX/20	80386SX, 20MHz	3, 5	6.1	Quadtel	1.44	20M	1 ser, 1 par, ext keybd, 1 ext VGA	
PC Brand, Inc.	386SX/20 Notebook System	80386SX, 20MHz	2, 16	7.2		1.44	20M, 19ms, IDE	2 ser, 1 par, 1 ext exp	Opt exp unit
Standard Computer	386SX/20 Notebook	80386SX, 20MHz	1, 5	7	AMI	1.44		1 ser, 1 par, 1 fax/modem, 1 scanner, 1 VGA	
Tandy	3819HD Notebook	80386SX, 20MHz	1, 5	7		1.44	60M, 19ms	1 ser, 1 par, 1 ext keybd, 1 disp, 1 ext disk	2 prop
Tangent Computer	Model 320N Notebook	80386SX, 20MHz	1, 5		AMI 8, 15, 90	1.44	20M, 25ms, IDE	2 ser, 1 par, 1 ext keybd, 1 ext VGA	
Texas Instruments	TravelMate 3000 Notebook PC	80386SX, 20MHz	2, 6	5.7	Phoenix 386SX A.1.30.1.1	1.44	20M, 23 ms, IDE	1 ser, 1 par, 1 PS, 2 mouse, 1 exp bus	1 8-bit, 1 16-bit

BUS TYPE	VIDEO ADAPTER, DISPLAY	POWER SUPPLY	WARRANTY (years)	SOFTWARE INCLUDED	RETAIL PRICE	OTHER INFORMATION
	VGA backlit LCD, 32 gray shades	NiCad battery, AC Adapter	1, send-back	DOS		Other opt avail
	9" VGA LCD, 32 gray shades	NiCad battery, AC adapter	1, send-back; 5, prorated		$2,195.00	Intelligent system with 3 levels: suspend, doze, sleep, Cordura (nylon) carrying case avail, other opt
ISA	VGA Sidelit	NiCad battery, AC adapter	1, carry-in	DOS, Windows 3.0, LapLink III	$2,799.00	Scalable Smart Sleep int power mgt, other opt avail
	VGA monochrome	50 watts	1, on-site		$1,199.00	Other opt avail
	VGA Backlit LCD, 32 gray shades	NiCad battery, AC adapter	30 days money back; 1, on-site avail		$2,295.00	Other opt avail
	VGA Backlit LCD, 32 gray shades	NiCad battery, AC adapter	30 days money back; 1, on-site avail	DOS	$2,795.00	Includes carrying case, battery charging stand & extra battery and software, other opt avail
	VGA Backlit LCD, 32 gray shades	NiCad battery, AC adapter	30 days money back; 1, on-site avail	DOS	$3,195.00	Includes custom carry case, battery chg stand, int 2400-baud MNP 5 Modem, extra battery, software,
Modem slot	VGA LCD	Battery pack	1, send-back; carry-in	DOS	$2,999.00	Includes carrying case
	VGA LCD	40 watts, 90-270V	1, send-back	DOS, FASTLYNX. with cables	$3,150.00	Other opt avail
Prop	Built-in VGA Edgelit LCD, 16 gray shd	Removable, rechrg NiCad, AC adapter/charger	1, on-site	Tutorial, diags	$3,399.00	Includes unlimited toll-free tech support, other opt avail
Prop	VGA Backlit LCD, 16 gray shades	30 watts, AC adapter	18 mos; on-site avail	DOS, FastLynx	$2,895.00	Includes carrying case, power management functions, other opt avail
	10" VGA LCD	Battery	1, carry-in; Int'l		$5,995.00	Inlcudes 2nd serial adapter internal DATA, FAX Modem, Trackpoint
Modem slot	VGA LCD	25 watts	1, carry-in	DOS		Other opt avail
Prop	VGA LCD, 16 gray shades	NiCad battery, AC adapter	1, carry-in			Includes 2400-baud modem, power mgt, 60M hard disk avail, other opt avail
	9" VGA LCD, 32 gray shades	NiCad battery, AC adapter	1, on-site	DOS	$3,199.00	Includes lifetime 24-hr tech support, other opt avail
	9" VGA LCD, 32 gray shades	NiCad battery, AC adapter	1, send-back; 5 prorated		$2,995.00	Intelligent system with 3 levels: suspend, doze, sleep, Cordura (nylon) carrying case avail, other opt
	VGA	NiCad battery, AC adapter	1, send back	DOS	$1,995.00	Other opt avail
Modem, RAM	VGA Backlit LCD, 32 gray scales	NiCad batteries, AC adapter	1, carry-in	DOS, DeskMate 3	$3,299.00	Includes power mgt standby & resume modes, other opt avail
	VGA Supertwist Backlit LCD,16 gray shades	NiCad batteries, AC adapter	1, send-back	DOS	$2,095.00	Other opt avail
ISA	VGA Sidelit LCD	30 watts	1, carry-in	DOS, Laplink, Batt Watch, Laptop File Mgr	$3,199.00	Other opt avail

continues

Table 4.10. concluded

COMPANY	MODEL	CPU, SPEED, CACHE	MIN, MAX RAM (M)	UNIT SIZE (lbs)	BIOS, VER	DISK DRIVES (M)	HARD DISK CAP, SPD, TYPE	ADAPTERS INCLUDED	EXP SLOTS
Zenith	MastersSport 386sx Notebook	80386SX, 20MHz	2, 4	6.6		1.44, 720K	60M, 19ms, IDE	1 ser, 1 par, 1 ext video	2 prop
COMPAQ	COMPAQ LTE 386s/20 30M HD	80386SX, 20MHz, 4K	2, 10	7.5	COMPAQ	1.44	30M, 19ms	1 ser, 1 par, 1 ext monitor	Opt
COMPAQ	COMPAQ LTE 386s/20 60M HD	80386SX, 20MHz, 4K	2, 10	7.5	COMPAQ	1.44	60M, 19ms	1 ser, 1 par, 1 ext monitor	Opt
Zenith	MasterSport 386SL Notebook	80386SX, 20MHz, 64K	2, 8	6.8	Flash	1.44	60M, 19ms	1 ser, 1 par, 1 ext video, 1 mouse, 1 ext keybd, 1 ext	4 prop
Packard Bell	386 Notebook	80C386SX, 16MHz	1, 5		Phoenix	1.44	40M, 27ms	1 ser, 1 par, 1 mouse, 1 ext VGA, 1 ext disk	
Insight	Insight 386SX-20MHz	80386DX, 20MHz	2, 5	7.05	AMI	1.44	21.4M, 25ms		
Tri-Star Computer Corporation	Notebook MB320i 20M HD	80386DX, 20MHz	2, 5		AMI	1.44	20M, 25ms, IDE		
Tri-Star Computer Corporation	Notebook NB320i 40M HD	80386DX, 20MHz	2, 5		AMI	1.44	20M, 25ms, IDE		

BUS TYPE	VIDEO ADAPTER, DISPLAY	POWER SUPPLY	WARRANTY (years)	SOFTWARE INCLUDED	RETAIL PRICE	OTHER INFORMATION
Prop	8.85" VGA Edgelit LCD, 16 gray shades	110/220V AC, 60/50Hz	1, carry-in	DOS, Windows 3.0	$3,999.00	Other opt avail
	9" COMPAQ VGA Edgelit LCD, VGA	NiCad battery pack 120V to 220/240V AC adapter	1, carry-in		$4,399.00	Other opt avail, other OS avail
	9" COMPAQ VGA Edgelit LCD, VGA	NiCad battery pack 120V to 220/240V AC adapter	1, carry-in		$4,799.00	Other opt avail, other OS avail
Modem, RAM	8.85" VGA Backlit LCD, 32 gray shd	110/22 V AC, 60/50 Hz	1, carry-in	DOS, Windows 3.0	$4,999.00	Other opt avail
	VGA Backlit LCD, 32 gray shades	NiCad battery, AC adapter	1, send-back	DOS		Other opt avail
	10" VGA LCD, 16 gray shades	16.5V dc, 1.8A (AC input)	1, send-back	DOS	$1,995.00	Includes Microsoft-compatible mouse, toll-free tech support
	VGA	NiCad battery, AC adapter	30 days cash back; 15 mos send-back		$2,155.00	Includes lifetime toll-free tech support, other opt avail
	VGA	NiCad battery, AC adapter	30 days cash back; 15 mos send-back		$2,355.00	Includes lifetime toll-free tech support, other opt avail

4

CHAPTER FIVE

Deciding What Type of Monitor You Need

If, as you are shopping for a personal computer, you have the opportunity to visit a retailer with a variety of systems on display, you probably will be drawn to the one with the most compelling color images on-screen. For a moment, you may be entranced by multicolored geometric designs or amazed at the fine detail of an architectural drawing. Soon, however, you must get down to the business of deciding which type of display will best meet your needs. This chapter can help you make that decision.

Understanding the Display

In the not-too-distant past, choosing a monitor for an IBM-compatible computer was relatively easy: You chose monochrome or color. If you were buying a Macintosh, the choice was even easier: You used the monitor built into the computer.

More recently, however, video display technology has experienced vast growth in entry-level and high-end products. The computer buyer must give more than passing consideration to the purchase of a monitor because the number and types of monitors available have increased dramatically.

As an added twist, many IBM-compatible computer manufacturers are now integrating the display adapter into the computer's main logic board and, at least to some degree, dictating what type of display must be purchased with the system. Most Macintosh computers come with built-in video as a standard feature, which in many cases can be expanded by adding video memory or installing a different adapter. Keeping these factors and others, including cost, in mind, how do you make an informed decision as to what type of monitor to buy?

The Video Adapter

Before you can make a decision about what type of monitor you should purchase, you need to understand the two components that make up the video display portion of the personal computer system. The first of these components is the *video adapter* (or *interface*) to which the monitor connects at the system unit. The second component, the monitor, is discussed in the section "The Video Display."

The video adapter translates the video data produced by the CPU into electronic signals that are "painted" to individual dots on the monitor. The physical design of the video interface can vary greatly from one computer system to the next. Some of these adapters are *cards* that are installed in an expansion slot, but other adapters are integrated into the main logic board of the computer. Both types of adapters, however, perform the same function: acting as a channel of communication between the computer and the monitor.

Besides the physical differences, display adapters can have functional differences. Although rare today, early video adapters for IBM-compatible computers supported only text and often doubled as the parallel printer interface. Even though these interfaces were slow by today's standards and did not have a graphics display, most users got along nicely. The Macintosh, however, dazzled everyone with its wonderful graphics display. The problem with these Macintoshes was that you were limited to a built-in black-and-white display only nine inches in diagonal measurement.

With any monitor, the quality of the image displayed depends on the resolution of the video adapter. As resolution technology advances, monitor video quality improves. Resolution is discussed in more detail in the section "The Video Display."

Today's video adapter is likely to support high-resolution text and color graphics and to be dedicated solely to the video interface function. If the interface is built into the main logic board, you need only connect the display to the proper port on the system unit. If, however, the computer has no integrated video support, a video adapter must be installed in an expansion slot before you connect a monitor.

Video Adapter Memory

A video adapter must have built-in memory to "remember" how the image onscreen looks. The greater the complexity of the image you display, the more memory required.

Original video adapters for the IBM Personal Computer, which displayed text, contained only 16K of memory. This amount of memory can contain multiple screens full of text but is not enough to store complex graphics and colors.

The basic graphics adapter today contains 256K of memory. Not only does image resolution require more memory to store the image, but the number of colors requires additional memory. Higher-resolution adapters that display more than the usual 16 colors require even more memory, such as 512K to 1,024K (1M) of memory, or even more.

The video adapter is classified as conforming to one of the many video display standards described later in this chapter. Being able to recognize the type of display adapter and its function is invaluable to anyone preparing to buy a computer.

The Video Display

The second component of the video system on your personal computer is the display, or monitor. This device evolved from the cathode ray tube (CRT) technology commonly used in televisions. Fortunately, display technology has more than kept pace with the evolution of personal computers, giving the user a degree of latitude in determining what type of display will work best for a specific application program.

Computer displays vary in size from 9 to 21 inches or larger. The smallest displays usually are found in computers that, because of portability considerations, require the small screen. The very largest displays often are used with highly technical programs or in desktop publishing, where high resolution or the capability to display more than one page on a single screen is necessary. The most popular monitor size measures 14 inches diagonally.

Features common to most video display units include a tilt-swivel base that enables the user to adjust the viewing angle and a screen that is either etched or coated to reduce glare. A 9- or 15-pin data cable connects to the video adapter at the rear of the CPU. Power for the monitor comes from either the power supply on the system unit or alternating current from the surge protector. Controls on the display usually include a power switch and adjustments for brightness, contrast, horizontal and vertical size, and horizontal and vertical positioning. Controls for adjusting the horizontal and vertical size and position of the picture are especially important because the picture may need to be centered or increased in size when you switch from text to graphics or from one resolution to another.

Video displays come in one of two general types—monochrome or color. Monochrome means one color, generally white, green, or amber, with a black background. Various intensities of this one color mixed with black give the appearance of shades on the monitor. Color, on the other hand, enables you to display at least 16 colors on the screen. Various intensities of colors and mixtures of colors enable you to display even more than 16 colors on-screen—from more than two hundred into the millions.

Video Display Resolution

A video display also is measured in terms of *resolution*. A picture is made up of tiny dots, called *pixels*. The number of pixels on the video display is called its resolution. A common resolution is 640 × 480. The first number is the number of pixels across the screen horizontally, and the second number refers to the number of pixels down the screen vertically. The total number of dots at that resolution is 307,200. High resolution means a crisp picture.

Video Display Dot Pitch

Another unit of measurement is the size of the pixel, which is called *dot pitch*. A pixel is measured in millimeters. You may see advertised a video display with a dot pitch of 0.52, or you may see another advertisement for a video display with a dot pitch of 0.28. These numbers may seem small, but you would see a world of difference between their respective monitors. For the sharpest quality, select the smallest dot pitch. Remember, however, that a smaller dot pitch comes with a higher price. You have to weigh the two factors and come up with the best solution for your needs. For most purposes, however, select a video display that has a dot pitch no greater than 0.31. The following are dot pitch recommendations for different purposes:

- For VGA text resolution of 640 × 480, use a dot pitch of 0.31.
- For Super VGA graphics resolutions of 800 × 600 or 1024 × 768, use a dot pitch of 0.28.
- For precise resolutions of 1024 × 768 or greater, use a dot pitch of 0.26.

Scanning Rate

A more technical specification of a video display is the *scanning rate*. Scanning is done to *update*, or *refresh*, the video display, which means changing the image on-screen as you make changes, such as typing new text in your document. Each line on the screen is scanned and refreshed, from top to bottom. For example, if your video display has 480 lines (640 × 480 resolution), each of the 480 lines is scanned. This scanning must take place quickly. And as resolution is increased, the scanning rate must increase. As you might have expected, the price of the monitor increases as its scanning rate increases.

In order to cut the cost, some high-resolution video displays are manufactured using a method called *interlaced* scanning. This term means that every other line is scanned on one complete pass. On the second pass, the lines that were missed are updated. This technology works, but interlaced scanning also causes a flickering effect. Some people are sensitive to the flickering, and others do not really notice it or are not bothered by it. You can bypass this flickering by purchasing a more expensive *noninterlaced* monitor. On a noninterlaced monitor, scanning is very fast, and the screen is updated in the usual scanning manner.

Some video displays are called *multiscanning* monitors. These monitors generally support video display adapters of many different resolution ratings. As the resolution of the adapter increases, the scanning rate required increases. A multiscanning monitor can detect when a scanning rate changes and adjusts the rate at which each line is scanned in order to be compatible with the resolution required. A multiscanning monitor is more of a multipurpose monitor because of its capability to accommodate multiple scanning rates. As usual, the price reflects this extra capability.

Understanding Display Technology

Just as video adapters must conform to one of many standards, so must monitors. Since IBM first introduced the Personal Computer in 1981, no fewer than six distinct video standards have been established as "PC compatible." The Macintosh has not had quite as drastic a change in display differences, because the Macintosh could display graphics very well from its beginning.

Because of the many technologies that are available, the first-time buyer has an increasingly difficult choice to make. You must be sure that the monitor you are contemplating is indeed the one that will best suit your needs.

IBM-Compatible Monitors

Of the many classifications of IBM-compatible video displays, some apply specifically to monochrome, others only to color. These standards generally refer to the resolution and the number of colors that a given interface and monitor can produce. *Resolution* is defined as the maximum number of rows and columns of dots (*pixels*) that can be displayed on a given monitor. Color is specified in terms of the *palette*, which indicates the total number of colors that can be displayed on the screen at one time. The most common monochrome standards are MDA, Hercules, and VGA. Color standards include CGA, EGA, MCGA, VGA, and XGA.

MDA, CGA, and EGA

The MDA (Monochrome Display Adapter) standard was developed by IBM for the first generation IBM PC. An MDA adapter can generate text resolutions of up to 720 × 350, with each character cell being 9 × 14 dots in size. This adapter, however, does not support graphics, which severely limits its capability to function with many of today's software packages. Because of these shortcomings, about the only way that you currently can get an MDA is by special order or as a used item.

Shortly after IBM introduced the PC, a third-party manufacturer, Hercules Computer, recognized the shortcomings of the MDA and developed an improved monochrome adapter that supported high-resolution graphics (720 × 348) as well as text. The adapter, known as the Hercules Graphics Card, soon became the monochrome standard. Although still available today, the Hercules standard has been superseded by monochrome VGA. As a result, the Hercules adapter is rapidly declining in popularity.

Color standards have evolved even more rapidly than monochrome standards. CGA (Color Graphics Adapter) was the first color standard developed by IBM for the PC. CGA supports 80 columns and up to 8 colors in text mode. The graphics mode can display 4 colors simultaneously from a palette of 16 at a resolution of 320 × 200. Although CGA is still available, many improvements have been made since CGA was introduced, and CGA is not recommended.

EGA (Enhanced Graphics Adapter) was the second generation color standard developed for the PC. In text mode, EGA supports 80 columns and up to 16 colors simultaneously. The graphics mode is capable of displaying up to 16 colors simultaneously from a palette of 64 at a maximum resolution of 640 × 350. EGA is also downwardly compatible, so EGA supports software written for CGA and MDA. Just as the demand for CGA has declined, EGA also has rapidly fallen out of favor with PC buyers.

MCGA, VGA, and XGA

Another color standard, MCGA (Multi Color Graphics Array), was developed by IBM for the entry-level PS/2 systems. MCGA draws features from both CGA and EGA, supporting software drivers for both and switching automatically to the one in use with your system. In CGA mode, MCGA can display 64 shades of gray or up to 256 colors at a resolution of 320 × 200. MCGA also can provide EGA graphics performance, displaying at a resolution of 640 × 350 in 16 colors. The downside to purchasing a PC with the MCGA adapter is that you must (at least in the case of IBM) purchase a VGA monitor without realizing the benefits of the VGA standard.

VGA (Video Graphics Array) is a video standard originally developed by IBM for the PS/2. VGA has been improved on many times by other manufacturers. The entry-level VGA interface supports graphics in 16 colors at a resolution of 640 × 480. The text mode improves on EGA by offering a resolution of 720 × 400.

VGA has been enhanced by a number of companies. A standard, Super VGA, has resulted from these expansions. Super VGA can display images at two resolutions greater than standard VGA: 800 × 600 and 1024 × 768. Although most software supports only VGA resolution, the Super VGA graphics adapter comes with software that enables programs to support the higher-resolution mode.

Super VGA adapter and monitor packages offer more colors and better resolution than the standard VGA. The Super VGA adapters have additional RAM (512K or more), which enables you to display up to 256 colors at once. Table 5.1 lists the modes that usually are supported by VGA and Super VGA cards with different amounts of memory. (In the table, "640 × 480/16" means that the resolution is 640 × 480, with 16 colors supported.)

5

Table 5.1. Resolutions and Colors Supported by VGA and Super VGA Cards with Varying Amounts of Memory

Resolution/Color	*VGA 256K*	*Super VGA 512K*	*Super VGA 1,024K*
640 × 480/16	✓	✓	✓
640 × 480/256	✓	✓	✓
800 × 600/16	✓	✓	✓
800 × 600/256	—	✓	✓
1024 × 768/16	—	✓	✓
1024 × 768/256	—	—	✓

In order for companies to remain compatible with the original VGA standard, *chip sets* have been developed. A chip set is a custom set of integrated circuit chips that emulates a standard; in this case, VGA. Many companies make video adapters, but fewer manufacturers make chip sets. You may find, therefore, that the same chip set is used on several manufacturers' boards. Often, different adapters using the same chip set have similar performance.

To display VGA, you must have either a VGA or a multiscanning monitor. As the resolution of the adapter increases, the scanning rate, or frequency at which the image is processed by the display, must be increased. Standard VGA monitors scan at a slower rate than Super VGA monitors. When using the Super VGA 1024 × 768 mode, a noninterlaced monitor scans more quickly than an interlaced monitor.

Multiscanning monitors, also called *multisynchronous monitors*, such as the NEC Multisync line of monitors, can scan at various rates, so these monitors can display higher resolutions than the standard 640 × 480. The proper Super VGA adapter and monitor combination can achieve resolutions of 800 × 600, 1024 × 768, and higher. The advantage of the multisynchronous monitor is apparent when switching from one resolution to another, because the monitor automatically switches to the correct scanning rate. Otherwise, you would have to reset your video display each time you switch resolutions.

Obviously, additional costs are involved when you buy these products, but for the architect or graphic designer who relies on the accuracy of a computer display, the money is well spent. A modest investment of less than $500, however, can get the average user a VGA package that more than meets basic requirements.

IBM's latest generation of PS/2 has brought still another video standard to the industry. XGA (Extended Graphics Array) is an extension of VGA that enables a computer to display photographic-quality images. With up to 3M of video memory, resolutions can be driven to 1280 × 1024. What is even more impressive is XGA's capability to display as many as 32,768 colors on-screen at once. As always, the third-party video board manufacturers were quick to follow IBM's lead with their own 15-bit adapter called HiColor. These modestly priced adapters use newly developed video chip sets from companies such as Tseng Labs and a HiColor digital-to-analog converter chip from Sierra. The XGA and HiColor adapters are downwardly compatible with lower resolution monitors. Although the potential of these adapters is very bright, currently the number of software packages that can take advantage of their capabilities is limited.

Macintosh-Compatible Video Displays

Macintosh video standards are defined in terms different from those used for DOS machines. Instead of referring to IBM standards such as CGA or VGA, Macintosh video is classified by how many colors can be displayed. The original Macintosh had built-in adapter circuitry and a 9-inch monochrome monitor. This monitor is still standard on the Macintosh Classic and SE/30 computers. The rest of the Macintosh line, however, is modular in design, meaning that the monitor is separate from the computer. These computers can support different types of video displays, including monochrome, gray-scale, and 4-, 8-, 16-, and 24-bit color (explained in the following section).

Macintosh Video Adapters

Just as the video adapter on a DOS-based personal computer addresses pixels on a monitor, so does the Macintosh video adapter. The Macintosh has the capability to turn these dots on or off as a different shade of gray or as a color. If you have a monochrome monitor, the pixels can be toggled between black or white. With gray-scale monitors, each pixel can be addressed as one of either four or eight shades of gray, depending on the monitor and the installed video card. The capability to display shades of gray "simulates" color in the sense that the gray shades give you the illusion of more depth in your display.

A Macintosh color monitor can display each pixel in any color that exists on the active palette. With a 4-bit video adapter, you have access to 16 different colors (figured as follows: 2^4 or $2 \times 2 \times 2 \times 2 = 16$). With an 8-bit video adapter, your color palette increases to 256 colors (2^8). A 24-bit video card increases the number to 16.7 million colors (2^{24}), which is more colors than the human eye can differentiate. You also can operate a 24-bit card in 16-bit mode, which yields approximately 65,000 colors (2^{16}). The recent release of Apple's 32-bit QuickDraw program interface opens the door for a 32-bit color mode, which, when available, will support a palette of more than 4 billion colors. (Because the human eye cannot distinguish all the colors produced by even a 24-bit card, however, a 32-bit card may be overkill.) Currently, Apple provides 8-bit support on those Macintoshes with built-in video.

Macintosh computers with built-in monitors offer only the 9-inch monochrome monitor. Macintoshes with separate monitors have built-in 8-bit video adapters (the Macintosh LC, IIsi, and IIci models). The Macintosh FX doesn't have a standard adapter, so you must install the adapter in a NuBus slot before connecting a monitor. Alternative 24-bit adapters are available from Apple and many third-party manufacturers, such as RasterOps. These adapters are still a bit pricey for the home user, but as manufacturing costs decrease they should become more affordable.

The following list describes the type of video adapter Apple supplies as standard for each Macintosh model:

- **Classic:** Built-in video circuitry, 9-inch monochrome monitor
- **SE/30:** Built-in video circuitry, 9-inch monochrome monitor (upgradeable with third-party internal adapters)
- **Portable:** Active-matrix LCD monochrome monitor (in active-matrix LCD monitors, each screen element is turned off and on by a transistor, resulting in a sharp screen without the usual LCD ghost image)
- **LC:** Built-in 8-bit video support for the Apple 12-inch monitor (upgradeable to 16-bit video with additional video RAM) and built-in 4-bit video support for the Apple 13-inch monitor (upgradeable to 8-bit video with additional video RAM)
- **IIsi:** Built-in 8-bit video support (upgradeable to 24-bit video with an additional video board)
- **IIci:** Built-in 8-bit video support (upgradeable to 24-bit video with an additional video board)
- **IIfx:** No on-board video support; can use either 8- or 24-bit video cards

Macintosh Monitors

Of the dozens of different displays available for the Macintosh computer, most fall into one of four basic categories: built-in, standard, full-page, and two-page. The resolution for the Macintosh 13-inch high-resolution monitor is 640 × 480. The 12-inch color monitor has a resolution of 512 × 384. The built-in monochrome display is rated at 512 × 352.

The built-in classification refers to the 9-inch monitor that is part of the Macintosh Classic and SE/30 models. This monitor is essentially the same black-and-white monitor that came standard on the first Macintosh. The 9-inch monitor works, but its size gives it limitations; you cannot see the full width or length of a page. Fortunately, the SE/30 can support an external display. Note, however, that if you plan to work with graphics, as in desktop publishing, you will not be happy with the 9-inch monochrome screen. For typical home use and some business use, you may find the screen adequate.

Standard displays can be monochrome or color and are 12 to 14 inches in diagonal measurement. The color monitor should support 8-bit color and have resolution of at least 512 × 384. This category includes the displays that Apple manufactures as well as the third-party multiscanning displays that can be connected to the Macintosh. Although not always ideal, these multiscanning monitors are considered very practical and in most cases are affordable.

Monitors such as the Radius Pivot are classified as page displays because of their capability to display a full page of text on an 8 1/2-by-11-inch screen. Although designed specifically for desktop publishing and word processing, these monitors are practical for most uses and actually can enhance productivity by reducing the amount of scrolling that is necessary within a document. The capability to display a full page at once also aids in determining page composition.

Two-page video displays usually measure at least 19 inches diagonally and are capable of displaying two full-size pages of text on-screen simultaneously. This feature is especially beneficial when laying out facing pages for a publication using a desktop publishing program. The increased size of the screen also enhances the user's ability to *pixel-edit* detailed graphic images. (Because a picture is made up of dots, you can make fine changes to the picture by manually selecting which dots in the picture should be on or off. Selecting and deselecting these dots is called pixel editing.) Two-page displays also eliminate much of the scrolling that is necessary with smaller displays, thus increasing the user's speed and accuracy.

Low-Emission Monitors

As you may know, reports have indicated possible health risks linked to certain types of electromagnetic radiation emitted by computer monitors. Although no firm scientific conclusions have been reached, some studies indicate that prolonged exposure to ELF (extremely low frequency) and VLF (very low frequency) radiation can increase the risk of cancer and miscarriage. Although the average personal computer user is unlikely to be exposed to life-threatening doses of this radiation, special "low-emission" monitors now are being marketed. Priced slightly higher than a standard display, the low-emission models have special magnetic coils that effectively cancel the offending radiation. Other than reduced emissions, these video displays function the same as any others. Low-emission monitors are available for both IBM-compatible and Macintosh computers.

Finding the Right Monitor for You

When attempting to determine which monitor is right for you, you should start by evaluating your software needs. After you have selected the software, match the hardware components to the program requirements to achieve the maximum performance that your budget allows.

Selecting the proper monitor for the task can increase productivity greatly and enhance the perceived value of owning a computer. The following sections offer information about various types of software to help you see which factors you need to consider for each software type.

Spreadsheet Programs

Spreadsheet programs such as Lotus 1-2-3 and Microsoft Excel are some of the most popular and powerful programs available today. Besides the practical aspect of enabling the user to manipulate rows and columns of numbers, these programs offer the flexibility to integrate text, tables, and charts within a spreadsheet. As a result of this flexibility, your monitor needs to be capable of displaying not only text but also graphics.

The minimum display requirement for an IBM-compatible computer to take advantage of these capabilities is a monochrome display with a Hercules Graphics Card. Most spreadsheet software, however, does support a color monitor and printing, which makes a color monitor-and-adapter combination a better choice for most users. Although CGA and EGA solutions are available and could address most basic spreadsheet display needs, VGA offers better performance and is becoming quite affordable.

If you do not require color, you can select a VGA adapter with a monochrome VGA monitor. Select a VGA color monitor if color is required or preferred. Because of the higher resolution of Super VGA, some Super VGA adapters come with special software for 1-2-3 and Excel. This special software turns on the higher resolution mode, enabling you to view more of the worksheet on the screen at one time. If you will be creating large spreadsheets, Super VGA might be a better alternative than standard VGA.

For a Macintosh, any of the displays will work adequately with a spreadsheet program. If you will be creating large worksheets, however, you may want to select a larger monitor so that you can view more of the worksheet at once.

Database Programs

Most database programs, due to the nature of the task, do not provide extensive graphics support. Notable exceptions are Paradox (from Borland) for IBM compatibles, which integrates the graphics engine (the built-in graphics program) from the spreadsheet program Quattro Pro, and FileMaker Pro for the Macintosh, which provides several tools used to create basic graphics. Selecting a video display for a database program, therefore, is highly dependent on which program you are using or planning to use.

If a database is the only program on your IBM computer, then you may find that a text-only display is adequate, as well as inexpensive. Because you are unlikely to have only a database program on your system, however, monochrome VGA is the minimum recommended solution. If your preference is for color, then select a color VGA monitor with your VGA adapter.

For a Macintosh system, the built-in video works fine. If you find, however, that you create databases containing many records, you may want to purchase a larger monitor to display more information at a time.

Word Processing Programs

By far the most common use for the personal computer is word processing. The capability to edit a document on the monitor before printing a hard copy can save time and money compared to performing the same task on a typewriter. And most word processing packages offer optional typefaces that can be used to dress up an otherwise plain-looking document. Some word processors also provide a WYSIWYG ("*W*hat *Y*ou *S*ee *I*s *W*hat *Y*ou *G*et"—pronounced "wizzywig") user interface that enables the user to display fonts on the monitor as they will appear on the printed page. The monitor's capability to provide an accurate portrayal of the selected font can be critical to the user concerned with a document's design elements. Many software packages also enable the user to import graphic images into a document from other programs, making the capability to display more than just text an even greater issue.

As word processing software has continued to evolve, the days of the simple text-based monitor clearly have become a thing of the past. Only very basic packages can be used effectively with lower resolution displays. More advanced word processing software is moving even further beyond the standard and enabling color graphics to be displayed and printed within a document. Word processing software today is performing many of the tasks that you previously had to perform on a desktop publishing system.

If you purchase an IBM-compatible computer, you should select a VGA adapter. Whether you select a monochrome or color VGA monitor is a matter of choice. If you plan to buy a WYSIWYG word processor, you should consider a Super VGA adapter and monitor. Using Super VGA, you can display more information on the screen, decreasing the amount of scrolling you must perform when editing a document. Make sure that the Super VGA adapter includes special software that supports the word processing program you intend to use. This software comes in the form of a drivers disk, which must be loaded onto your computer.

Word processing on the Macintosh can be accomplished adequately with the built-in video adapter of the Macintosh. Selecting color is simply a preference. You may want to select a large display to view more of the text on the screen at a time, which increases your productivity by minimizing the amount of scrolling you must do when editing a document.

If you will be using your Macintosh or IBM compatible for word processing only, consider a full-page or two-page video display. Using these monitors, you can view at least one page on the screen at a time. With this convenience, however, comes additional cost. Make sure that special software is provided by the manufacturer of the full-page or two-page monitor for the word processing software that you select.

Desktop Publishing Programs

Desktop publishing programs enable the computer user to create high-quality output that is ready to send to a typesetter or high-quality printer. The major benefit of desktop publishing is the capability to retrieve text and graphic images from other programs and merge them into a format suitable for publication. These programs also are WYSIWYG, so the user can see the page design before printing it. Choosing a monitor for use with desktop publishing can be more interesting than for other application software, because the capability to view the entire page at once can be a critical feature. Resolution and color capabilities are issues for these monitors as well. Purchasing a full-page or even a two-page display becomes much more feasible when the capability to view your work as a whole, rather than scrolling through parts of it, becomes desirable.

When using an IBM-compatible computer, a standard VGA monitor and adapter are certainly adequate for desktop publishing. The selection of monochrome or color is a matter of choice. A better choice than the standard VGA combination, however, is a Super VGA monitor and adapter. Using Super VGA, you can display more of your current document on-screen at a time. Because the most popular desktop publishing programs operate with Microsoft Windows 3, most Super VGA adapters come with special software to enable Windows to take advantage of the higher resolution. If the majority of your computing time will be spent laying out pages, consider one of the full-page or two-page displays.

Any of the built-in video circuitry of the Macintosh can be used for desktop publishing, including a basic Macintosh with the built-in 9-inch monochrome monitor. You may find, however, that a larger display, full-page display, or two-page display is more practical if you will be doing much desktop publishing.

Graphics and Drawing Programs

Graphics and drawing programs are used to design objects electronically, ranging from stick figures to highly detailed engineering drawings. Types of drawing packages vary from the very simple, such as MacDraw, to the ultra-sophisticated (and more costly) computer-aided design (CAD) programs, such as AutoCAD. A CAD program uses vector graphics, enabling the user to isolate and manipulate individual parts of the drawing.

To take full advantage of the capabilities of drawing programs, you should have a display combination that fully supports the specific program you are using. In most cases, resolution is the key to displaying the detail necessary to use the program effectively. If you plan to use drawing and graphics programs with an IBM-compatible computer, the recommended solution is a VGA or Super VGA display package. For a Macintosh computer, you may want to select a large display.

Graphical User Interfaces

A graphical user interface (GUI) uses pictures, or icons, rather than typed characters to represent specific computer commands. Popular GUIs today include the Macintosh operating system, OS/2 Presentation Manager, Microsoft Windows, Hewlett-Packard's New Wave, GeoWorks, and several others. The purpose of a GUI is to emulate the top of a desk—you have access to files, you can place one file on another, and you can put unneeded files in the trash. You may hear a GUI referred to as a desktop. Because of the graphic nature of the interface, your video display package must have the capability to display the desktop effectively.

Because the Macintosh computer was designed with a GUI as the operating system, all Macintosh monitors support the desktop. Selecting a larger monitor enables you to view more of the desktop, making the desktop appear less cluttered.

On IBM-compatible computers, GUIs can be configured to operate under CGA and EGA modes, but VGA resolution is the widely accepted video standard. Many GUIs support Super VGA, and special software often is provided by the manufacturer of the video adapter to support the GUI. If you will be using a GUI, give consideration to the Super VGA display and adapter, but make sure that you ask the manufacturer of the video adapter whether the adapter you're considering supports the GUI you will be using.

Chapter Summary

This chapter describes the various video standards available for both IBM-compatible and Macintosh computers. Additionally, the chapter discusses what video displays work best within specific software environments.

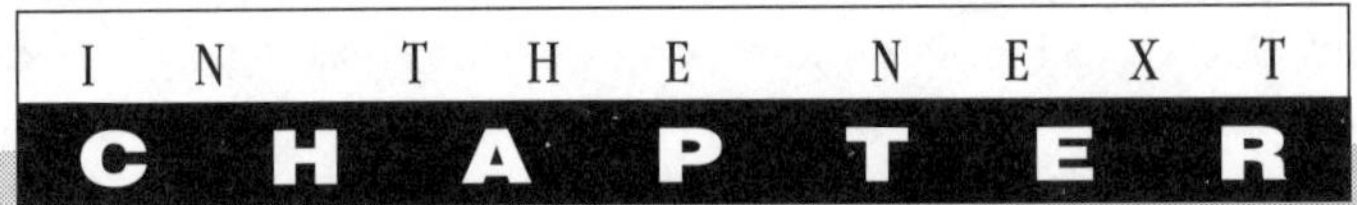

The next chapter contains a table that lists the available display types and compares their features and functions.

CHAPTER SIX

Listing of Monitors

Which do you prefer—viewing a beautiful sunrise on a clear day or peering through fog where you can barely make out the car in front of you? Do you enjoy a clear night with many stars in the sky and the moon shining brightly to light your way, or a dark, gloomy night when you can barely see your hand in front of your face? No doubt the majority of you will choose the clear day and night. In the same way, having a clear video display is important because—next to the keyboard—the display is the one part of your computer you will interact with most often.

Selecting an appropriate display and adapter to meet your needs is very important. And there are many displays and adapters from which to choose. Whether you are entering text in a word processor or spreadsheet, laying out pages with a desktop publishing application, or designing houses using a computer-aided design program, you can find a display and adapter to fit your application. The tables in this chapter list displays, adapters, and combinations of displays and adapters. Each table is organized so that you can easily find the appropriate display equipment for your computer system.

Video Display Listing

Many different video displays are available; you make your selection based on size, resolution, and other features. Table 6.1 lists more than 90 different displays. These displays range in screen size from 12 inches to 21 inches. The table lists displays that are compatible with IBM and compatible video adapters and Macintosh video adapters.

In table 6.1, the information is sorted first by screen size, then by display type, and finally by company. The first two columns show the company that manufactures the display and the display model name. Next is the display type, such as VGA or Mac. Next is the maximum horizontal and vertical resolution that the display can handle. The dot pitch is given so that you can tell the quality of the picture, with the smaller dot pitch giving the finest picture. The diagonal screen size comes next and then the entire size of the display. The two Yes and No columns tell you whether the display comes with a tilt and swivel stand and whether the screen is nonglare. The last three columns show you the warranty, retail price, and other information that may help you to select the best display for your system.

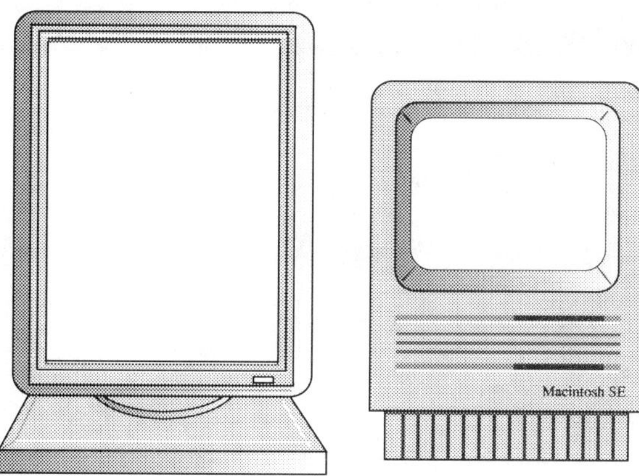

Fig. 6.1. Two kinds of screen displays.

Table 6.1. Video Displays Sorted by Screen Size, Display Type, and Company

COMPANY	MODEL	DISPLAY TYPE	MAX RES (horiz x vert)	DOT PITCH (mm)	SCREEN SIZE (inches)	DISPLAY SIZE (inches)
Hyundai	HMM-1200	Amber MDA, HGC	720 x 350		12	12 x 12.3 x 10.5
Hyundai	HMM-1201A	Amber MDA, HGC	720 x 350		12	12 x 12.3 x 10.5
Apple Computer	Macintosh 12" Monochrome Display	Mac Monochrome	640 x 480, 76 dpi		12	12.2 x 14.4 x 10.2
Apple Computer	Macintosh 12" RGB Display	Mac Color	512 x 384, 64 dpi	0.28	12	12.2 x 14.4 x 10
PC Brand, Inc.	Mono-Graphics adapter/12" amber display	MDA, HGC Monochrome			12	
PC Brand, Inc	Amber Display	MDA, HGC			12	
AST Research	VGA Monochrome	VGA Monochrome	720 x 480		12	12.6 x 11.4 x 11.9
Hyundai	HMM-202	VGA Paper white	640 x 480		12	12 x 12.3 x 10.5
IBM	8504	VGA, white monochrome	640 x 480		12	12 x 12.1 x 11.5
Seiko Instruments	CM 1445	Mac	640 x 480	0.25	13	
Apple Computer	AppleColor High-Resolution RGB Monitor	Mac Color	630 x 480, 69 dpi	0.26	13	11 x 13.5 x 15.2
IBM	8513	VGA	640 x 480	0.28	13	12.6 x 14.5 x 12.3
Zenith	ZCM-1492 (Flat Technology Monitor)	VGA	720 x 480	0.28	13	12.25 x 14.75 x 14.95
Zenith	ZCM-1390-Z	VGA	640 x 480	0.31	13	
AST Research	Super VGA Color	VGA, SVGA	1024 x 768i	0.28	13	14.1 x 12.2 x 14.2
Hyundai	HMM-1401A	Amber MDA, HGC	720 x 350		14	13 x 12.8 x 11.6
Samsung Information Systems	CGA Color Monitor CK4656	CGA	640 x 200	0.52	14	13.46 x 13.62 x 14.8
NEC	MacSync HC JC-1405HMA(HC)	Mac	640 x 480	0.29	14	14 x 14.3 x 16
NEC	MacSync JC-1405HMA	Mac	640 x 480	0.29	14	14 x 14.3 x 16
Acer America Corp.	Acer 7003	Monochrome MDA, HGC comp	720 x 348		14	13.6 x 12.6 x 12.8

TILT, SWIVEL STAND	NON-GLARE SCREEN	WARRANTY (years)	RETAIL PRICE	OTHER INFORMATION
Yes	Yes	18 mos, opt on-site	$125.00	Video input signal TTL level positive, vertical scanning frequency 50Hz
Yes	Yes	18 mos, opt on-site	$139.00	Video input signal TTL level positive, vertical scanning frequency 50Hz
No	Yes	Limited	$299.00	Card opt for LC, IIsi, IIci, NEC Equip inc, 256 gray shades with approp adpt, 16 shades with LC
No	No	Limited	$599.00	Card opt for LC, IIsi, IIci, NEC Equip inc, 256 gray shades with approp adpt, 16 shades with LC
			$109.00	
			$109.00	
Yes	Yes	1		315Hz horiz and 50-70Hz vert scan freq 64 gray shades, video band width 30MHz
Yes	Yes	18 mos, opt on-site	$169.00	Analog interface, 64 gray scale, vertical scanning frequency 50/60/70Hz
Yes	Yes	1, carry-in	$342.00	Viewable area 210mm x 1575mm, FST (Flatter Squares Tube) technology
Yes	No	1	$899.00	Specifications subject to change without notice
No	No	Limited	$999.00	Card optional with Macintosh LC, IIsi, IIci, 20-minute warm-up time to meet specs, NEC Equip included
Yes	Yes	1, carry-in	$772.00	
Yes	Yes	1	$869.00	
	Yes	1	$519.00	
Yes	Yes	1		315 -355KHz horiz, 56-87Hz vert scan freq, 262,144 colors, video band width 45MHz
Yes	Yes	18 mos, opt on-site	$160.00	Video input signal TTL level positive, vertical scanning frequency 50Hz
Yes	No	1	$319.00	16 bright colors or a crisp green text mode, controls on front and rear
Yes	High contrast	2		Screen is high contrast, dark tinted
Yes	Yes	2		Best used with Mac II family, general business, presentation and business graphics, imaging
Yes	Yes	2		

continues

Table 6.1. Continued

COMPANY	MODEL	DISPLAY TYPE	MAX RES (horiz x vert)	DOT PITCH (mm)	SCREEN SIZE (inches)	DISPLAY SIZE (inches)
Acer America Corp.	Acer 7004P	Monochrome VGA	640 x 480		14	12 x 12.8 x 11.8
Zenith	ZMM-149-P	Monochrome VGA	640 x 480		14	
Acer America Corp.	AcerView 31	VGA	640 x 480	0.28	14	13.4 x 14.1 x 15
Acer America Corp.	Acer 7013	VGA	640 x 480	0.31	14	14.6 x 14.2 x 13.6
Acer America Corp.	AcerView 11	VGA	640 x 480	0.39	14	14 x 13.4 x 15
Hyundai	HCM-402C	VGA	640 x 480	0.31	14	14 x 16.3 x 13.2
Hyundai	HCM-402B	VGA	640 x 480	0.39	14	14 x 16.3 x 13.2
Hyundai	HCM-402T	VGA	640 x 480	0.41	14	14 x 16.3 x 13.2
Hyundai	HCM-402S	VGA	640 x 480	0.52	14	14 x 16.3 x 13.2
IBM	8512	VGA	640 x 480	0.41	14	14 x 15.5 x 12
Leading Edge	CMON .31	VGA	640 x 480	0.31	14	13 x 13.5 x 16" (with stand)
Leading Edge	VMON VGA Monochrome Monitor	VGA	640 x 480	0.31	14	12.5 x 12.5 x 12"
Mirror Technologies	14" High-Resolution Color Display	VGA	640 x 480	0.31	14	14.1 x 14 x 14.8
Packard Bell	PB8509VG	VGA	640 x 480	0.28	14	14.25 x 14.5 x 15
Packard Bell	PB8529V6	VGA	640 x 480	0.31	14	14.75 x 14.33 x 15.75
Packard Bell	PB8551VG	VGA	640 x 480	0.51	14	14.75 x 14.33 x 15.75
PC Brand, Inc	VGA Display	VGA	640 x 480	0.39	14	
Samsung Information Systems	VGA Color Monitor CJ-4681	VGA	640 x 480	0.31	14	14.5 x 14.06 x 15.13
Samsung Information Systems	VGA Color Monitor CJ-4685	VGA	640 x 480	0.41	14	14.5 x 14.06 x 15.13
Samsung Information Systems	VGA Color Monitor CJ-4686	VGA	640 x 480	0.52	14	14.5 x 14.06 x 15.13

6

TILT, SWIVEL STAND	NON-GLARE SCREEN	WARRANTY (years)	RETAIL PRICE	OTHER INFORMATION
Yes	Yes	2		
	Yes	1	$234.00	
Yes	Yes	2	$595.00	
Yes	Yes	2	$610.00	
Yes	Yes	2	$445.00	
Yes		18 mos, opt on-site	$470.00	Vertical scanning frequency 50/60/70Hz
Yes		18 mos, opt on-site	$390.00	Vertical scanning frequency 50/60/70Hz
Yes		18 mos, opt on-site	$370.00	Vertical scanning frequency 50/60/70Hz
Yes		18 mos, opt on-site	$330.00	Vertical scanning frequency 50/60/70Hz
Opt	No	1, carry-in	$675.00	
Yes	Yes	20 mos send-back; 6 mos on-site	$579.00	
Yes	Yes	20 mos send-back; 6 mos on-site	$219.00	
Yes	Yes	1; 30 days money back		For Macintosh, color depth up to maximum bit depth of card
Yes	Yes	1	$729.00	
Yes	Yes	1	$699.00	
Yes	No	1	$469.00	
		1	$379.00	
Yes	Yes	1	$539.00	Analog input compatible with popular video stds, IBM PS/2, unlimited colors
Yes	Yes	1	$429.00	Analog input compatible with popular video stds, IBM PS/2, unlimited colors
Yes	Yes	1	$379.00	Analog input compatible with popular video stds, IBM PS/2, unlimited colors

continues

Table 6.1. Continued

COMPANY	MODEL	DISPLAY TYPE	MAX RES (horiz x vert)	DOT PITCH (mm)	SCREEN SIZE (inches)	DISPLAY SIZE (inches)
Swan Technologies	Swan VGA Monitor/SW584	VGA	640 x 480	0.41	14	
Tandy	VGM-200	VGA	720 x 480	0.42	14	
Tandy	VGM-220	VGA	640 x 480	0.52	14	
Hyundai	HMM-413	VGA Paper white	640 x 480		14	12 x 12.3 x 10.5
IBM	8515	VGA, 8514/A	1024 x 768i	0.31	14	14.0 x 15.5 x 13.6
IBM	8516	VGA, 8514/A, Touch Display	1024 x 768i	0.31	14	14.0 x 15.3 x 13.6
Microtek	MCD-14-4	VGA, PGA, SVGA, 8514/A, XGA, Mac II	1280 x 1024ni	0.28	14	14.1 x 14 x 16.3
Acer America Corp.	Acer 7015	VGA, SVGA	800 x 600	0.28	14	17.3 x 18 x 18
CTX	CVP-5468	VGA, SVGA	1024 x 768i	0.28	14	366 x 360 x 376mm
CTX	CVP-5468LR	VGA, SVGA	1024 x 768i	0.28	14	366 x 360 x 376mm
CTX	CVP-5468NI	VGA, SVGA	1024 x 768ni	0.28	14	418 x 434 x 415mm
EPSON	VGA Monitor	VGA, SVGA	1024 x 768i	0.28	14	13.9 x 14.02 x 14.76
Gateway 2000	Crystal Scan 1024 VGA Display	VGA, SVGA	1024 x 768i	0.28	14	14.25 x 13.25 x 14.85
Gateway 2000	Crystal Scan 1024NI VGA Display	VGA, SVGA	1024 x 768ni	0.28	14	14.25 x 13.25 x 14.85
Hyundai	HCM-421 E Super VGA	VGA, SVGA	1024 x 768i	0.28	14	14 x 16.3 x 13.2
Hyundai	HCM-423 E Super VGA	VGA, SVGA	1024 x 768i	0.28	14	14 x 16.3 x 13.2
NEC	MultiSync 2A JC-1403HMA	VGA, SVGA	800 x 600	0.31	14	14 x 14.3 x 15.9
Packard Bell	PB8538SVG	VGA, SVGA	1024 x 768i	0.39	14	14.75 x 14.33 x 15.75
Packard Bell	PB8539VG	VGA, SVGA	1024 x 768ni	0.39	14	14.75 x 14.33 x 15.75
Seiko Instruments	CM 1440	VGA, SVGA	1024 x 768i	0.25	14	

6

TILT, SWIVEL STAND	NON-GLARE SCREEN	WARRANTY (years)	RETAIL PRICE	OTHER INFORMATION
	Yes	2; 30 days money back	$299.00	
No	Yes	1	$499.95	
No	Yes	1	$399.95	
Yes	Yes	18 mos, opt on-site	$178.00	Analog interface, 64 gray scale, vertical scanning frequency 50/60/70Hz
Yes	Yes	1, carry-in	$950.00	
Yes	Yes	1, carry-in	$1695.00	Pressure level sensing, 255 pressure levels
Yes	Yes	1	$999.00	
Yes	Yes	2	$655.00	
Yes	Yes	1	$599.00	Anti-static screen coating
Yes	Yes	1	$699.00	Anti-static screen coating
Yes	Yes	1	$799.00	
Yes	Yes		$689.00	Compatible with IBM PS/2
Yes	Yes	1, on-site; 30 days money back		Standard with 286 and 386SX systems
Yes	Yes	1, on-site; 30 days money back		Standard with 286 and 386SX systems
Yes		18 mos, opt on-site	$500.00	Vertical scanning frequency 50/60/70Hz
Yes		18 mos, opt on-site		Vertical scanning frequency 50/60/70/86 Hz
Yes	Yes	2		Best uses, general business, presentation and business graphics
Yes	No	1	$759.00	
Yes	Yes	1	$599.00	
Yes	Yes	1	$849.00	Specifications subject to change without notice

continues

Table 6.1. Continued

COMPANY	MODEL	DISPLAY TYPE	MAX RES (horiz x vert)	DOT PITCH (mm)	SCREEN SIZE (inches)	DISPLAY SIZE (inches)
Seiko Instruments	CM1450	VGA, SVGA	1024 x 768 Non-interlaced	0.25	14	
Swan Technologies	Non-Interlaced 1024 VGA Monitor/SW59c	VGA, SVGA	1024 x 768ni	0.28	14	
Swan Technologies	Swan 1024 VGA Monitor/SW587	VGA, SVGA	1024 x 768i	0.28	14	13.9 x 13.3 x 15
Tandy	VGM-440	VGA, SVGA	1024 x 768ni	0.28	14	
Taxan America Inc.	MultiVision 795	VGA, SVGA	1024 x 768ni	0.25	14	13V
Samsung Information Systems	SyncMaster 3E/CVB4997	VGA, SVGA, 8514/A	1024 x 768i	0.28	14	14.17 x 13.07 x 14.80
Samsung Information Systems	SyncMaster 2E/CVB4993	VGA, SVGA, 8514/A	1024 x 768i	0.39	14	14.17 x 13.07 x 14.80
NEC	MultiSync 3DS	VGA, SVGA, 8514/A, XGA, EGA, Mac	1024 x 768i	0.28	14	14 x 14.3 x 15.9
CTX	CMS-3436	VGA, SVGA, Mac	1024 x 768i	0.28	14	368 x 378 x 387mm
CTX	CMS-3436	VGA, SVGA, Mac	1024 x 768i	0.28	14	368 x 378 x 387mm
Acer America Corp.	AcerView 35	VGA, SVGA, Mac II	1024 x 768ni	0.26	14	13.4 x 14 x 16.1
Acer America Corp.	AcerView 33	VGA, SVGA, Mac II, 8514/A	1024 x 768i	0.28	14	
NEC	MultiSync GS2A JC-1408HMA	VGA, SVGA, Mac, Monochrome	800 x 600		14	14.1 x 13.4 x 14.8
Apple Computer	Apple Macintosh Portrait Display	Mac Monochrome	640 x 870, 80 dpi		15	13.1 x 11.5 x 14.9
Sigma Designs	PageView GS	Mac full page	640 x 870		15	15.25 x 11.15 x 14.5
Swan Technologies	Swan VGA 15" Monitor/SW615	VGA, SVGA	1024 x 768ni	0.28	15	405 x 370 x 383mm
E-Machines	ColorPage E16	Mac	640 x 480, 832 x 624	0.26	16	16.4 x 16.6 x 16.5
E-Machines	ColorPage T16	Mac	832 x 624	0.26	16	15.9 x 14.9 x 18.7
E-Machines	E-Machines TX	Mac	1024 x 808ni	0.26	16	15.9 x 14.9 x 18.7
IBM	8514	VGA, 8514/A	1024 x 768i	0.31	16	15.7 x 16.3 x 14.2

6

TILT, SWIVEL STAND	NON-GLARE SCREEN	WARRANTY (years)	RETAIL PRICE	OTHER INFORMATION
Yes	Yes	1	$999.00	Specifications subject to change without notice
Yes	Yes	2; 30 days money back	$499.00	
Yes	Yes	2; 30 days money back	$399.00	
Yes	Yes	1	$649.00	
Yes	Yes	2	$1095.00	
Yes	Yes	1	$579.00	Unlimited colors, supports all popular video stds, multiscan, controls on side and rear
Yes	Yes	1	$499.00	Unlimited colors, supports all popular video stds, multiscan, controls on side and rear
Yes	Yes	2, parts; 1, labor	$1099.00	Reduced magnetic field protection built-in
Yes	Yes	1	$799.00	
Yes	Yes	1	$799.00	Anti-static screen coating
Yes	Yes	2	$995.00	
Yes	Yes	2	$695.00	
Yes	Yes	2		Best uses, general business, presentation and business graphics, affordable DTP
No	No	Limited	$1099.00	For IIcx, IIsi, IIci, IIfx, req NuBus card for IIsi, flat screen, Analog 1-/2-/4-/8-bit pixel depth for true shading
Yes	Opt	1		Includes all NEC Equip and disks, low emissions, plugs into video port of IIci, IIsi, no video card required
Yes	Yes	2; 30 days money back	$599.00	
Yes	Yes	1	$1595.00	
Yes	Yes	1	$2500.00	
Yes	Yes	1	$2500.00	
Yes		1, carry-in	$1665.00	

continues

Table 6.1. Concluded

COMPANY	MODEL	DISPLAY TYPE	MAX RES (horiz x vert)	DOT PITCH (mm)	SCREEN SIZE (inches)	DISPLAY SIZE (inches)
NEC	MultiSync 4DS	VGA, SVGA, 8514/A, XGA, EGA, Mac	1024 x 768ni	0.28	16	15.4 x 15.2 x 18.7
CTX	CPS-1780	Mac	1600 x 1280ni	0.26	17	418 x 434 x 415mm
Taxan America Inc.	Multivision 875	VGA, SVGA	1024 x 768i	0.26	17	15.75V
Samsung Information Systems	SyncMaster 4/CSA7571	VGA, SVGA, 8514/A, Mac	1024 x 768ni	0.31	17	21.3 x 22.8 x 22.4
CTX	CPS-1760	VGA, SVGA, Mac	1024 x 768ni	0.26	17	418 x 434 x 415mm
IBM	8506	VGA, white monochrome	848 x 1200i		17	13.15 x 14.61 x 18.5
E-Machines	E-Machines T19	Mac	1024 x 808ni	0.26	19	18.7 x 18.8 x 21.0
IBM	8507	VGA, white monochrome	1024 x 768i	0.35	19	18.75 x 17 x 17.75
IBM	8508	VGA, white monochrome	1360 x 1024ni, 1600 x 1200i		19	18.75 x 17.0 x 17.75
Taxan America Inc.	UltraVision 1000	VGA, SVGA, 8514/A	1280 x 1024i	0.31	20	19V
Taxan America Inc.	UltraVision 1095	VGA, SVGA, 8514/A, Mac	1600 x 1200i	0.31	20	19V
NEC	MultiSync 5D JC-2002VMA-1	VGA, SVGA, 8514/A, XGA, EGA, Mac	1280 X 1024ni	0.29	20	14.0 x 14.3 x 16.0
Samsung Information Systems	DesignMaster/ CC9511	VGA, SVGA, 8514/A, XGA, Mac	1280 x 1024ni	0.31	20	19.1 x 20.7 x 18.9
Apple Computer	Apple 2-page Monochrome Monitor	Mac Monochrome	1,152 x 870, 77 dpi		21	18.9 x 19.5 x 17.4
Taxan America Inc.	UltraVision 1150	VGA, SVGA, 8514/A, Mac	1600 x 1200i	0.31	21	20V

TILT, SWIVEL STAND	NON-GLARE SCREEN	WARRANTY (years)	RETAIL PRICE	OTHER INFORMATION
Yes	Yes	2, parts; 1, labor	$1499.00	Reduced Magnetic field protection built-in, dynamic beam focus, degauss switch
Yes	Yes	1	$1999.00	
Yes	Yes	2	$1978.00	
Yes	Yes	1	$1499.00	Multiscan, horiz freq auto adjust from 20KHz to 50KHz, unlimited colors, front panel controls, flat scrn
Yes	Yes	1	$1499.00	
Yes	Yes	1, carry-in	$1345.00	Requires IBM PS/2 Image adapter/A
Yes	Yes	1	$4200.00	
Yes	Yes	1, carry-in	$899.00	Requires 8514/A adptr with mem exp kit for max resolution, viewable area 356mm x 267mm
Yes	Yes	1, carry-in	$1345.00	
Yes	Yes	1	$3495.00	
Yes	Yes	1	$3999.00	
Yes	Yes	2		Best used with CAD, CAM, CIM, eng, pres and bus graphics, desktop publishing, imaging
Yes	Yes	1	$2995.00	100MHz bandwidth to provide optimum compatability and flicker-free images, unlimited colors
Yes	Yes	Limited	$2149.00	For IIcx, IIsi, IIci, IIfx, req NuBus card for IIsi, flat screen, Analog 1-/2-/4-/8-bit pixel depth for true shading
Yes	Yes	1	$4095.00	

6

Video Adapter Listing

If you select a display, you may want to match a video adapter to the display. Table 6.2 lists video adapters. This table is sorted by adapter type, maximum resolution, and then company. The first two columns of the table give the company and model of the adapter. The third and fourth columns show the adapter type and the maximum resolution the adapter supports. The *VIDEO RAM* column tells you how many megabytes of memory come on the adapter. Some adapters have special accompanying software, so the *SOFTWARE INCLUDED* column lists special software for each adapter. The *CHIP SET* column shows what set of chips the adapter has so that you will know compatibility. The last three columns provide warranty, retail price, and other information about the display adapter.

Table 6.2. Video Adapters Sorted by Adapter Type, Maximum Resolution, and Company

COMPANY	MODEL	ADAPTER TYPE	MAX RESOLUTION	VIDEO RAM (M)	SOFTWARE INCLUDED	CHIP SET	WARRANTY (years)	RETAIL PRICE	OTHER INFORMATION
IBM	PS/2 Image Adapter/A 1MB	Image	1600 x 1200i	1				$1,695.00	3M version available for $2650.00
Supermac	Color Card/24 Mac Nubus	Mac		1.5 VRAM					
Supermac	Mac Spectrum/8	Mac	1152 x 870, 1024 x 768						Spectrum/8 is for Mac NuBus, si, LC
PC Brand, Inc.	Mono-Graphics	MDA, HGC			HGC Utilities		1	$49.00	
PC Brand, Inc.	VGA 16-bit	VGA	640 x 480	256K	Software drivers		1	$129.00	
Swan Technologies	Video Card Swan Spectrum VGA	VGA	640 x 480i	256K	No	Cirrus Logic	2; 30 days money back		
Swan Technologies	Video Card Swan VGA Palette Plus	VGA, SVGA	800 x 600	256K	Drivers for Windows 3.0, 1-2-3, others	Tseng Labs, Sierra HiColor DAC	2; 30 days money back		
Swan Technologies	Video Card Swan VGA Palette Plus	VGA, SVGA	1024 x 768ni	512K	Drivers for Windows 3.0, 1-2-3, others	Tseng Labs, Sierra HiColor DAC	2; 30 days money back		
Swan Technologies	Video Card Swan VGA Palette Plus	VGA, SVGA	1024 x 768ni	512K	Drivers for Windows 3.0, 1-2-3, others	Tseng Labs, Sierra HiColor DAC	2; 30 days money back		
PC Brand, Inc.	SVGA 16-bit	VGA, SVGA	1024 x 768	1	Software drivers		1	$179.00	
PC Brand, Inc.	SVGA Premium 16-bit	VGA, SVGA	1024 x 768ni	1	Software drivers		1	$299.00	
USA Flex	UL16/32	VGA, SVGA	1024 x 768ni	1	Software drivers, utilities	Tseng Labs ET4000	1		
IBM	XGA Display Adapter	VGA, XGA	1024 x 768ni	512K				$1,095.00	Add'l 512K $350.00

Video Display and Adapter Listing

More often than not, when you purchase a display and adapter for your computer, you will purchase them together. Let's face it, an adapter is not much good without a monitor, and the monitor is pretty boring unless it shows a picture produced by the video adapter. Table 6.3, which begins on the following page, lists video displays and adapters that work nicely together. For your convenience, the table is sorted by screen size, display type, and then company.

The first two columns of table 6.3 display the company that manufactures the display and adapter and the display model name. Next is the display type, such as VGA or Mac. The next column lists the maximum horizontal and vertical resolution that the display can handle. The dot pitch of the display is given next so that you can tell the quality of the picture, with the smaller dot pitch giving the finest picture. The diagonal screen size is followed by the entire size of the display. Two Yes and No columns tell you whether the display comes with a tilt and swivel stand and whether the screen is nonglare. Two more columns show you the warranty of the display and the retail price of the combo display and adapter.

The next six columns give you specific information about the display adapter. These columns show the adapter type and maximum resolution the adapter supports. The *VIDEO RAM* column shows you how much memory comes on the adapter and to how many megabytes you can expand memory. Some adapters have special software accompanying the adapter, so the *SOFTWARE INCLUDED* column lists special software for the adapter. The *CHIP SET* column shows what set of chips the adapter has so that you will know compatibility. The final two columns are the adapter warranty and other information that may help you select the correct display and adapter combination for your system.

Table 6.3. Video Display and Adapters Sorted by Screen Size, Display Type, and Company

COMPANY	MODEL	DISPLAY TYPE	MAX RES (horiz x vert)	DOT PITCH (mm)	SCREEN SIZE (inches)	DISPLAY SIZE (inches)	TILT, SWIVEL STAND	NON-GLARE SCREEN	DISPLAY WARRANTY (years)
CompuAdd	CompuAdd VGA Monitor	VGA	640 x 480	0.31	14		No	No	1
Packard Bell	PB8508V6	VGA	640 x 480	0.41	14	14.5 x 14.5 x 15.5	Yes	Yes	1
Packard Bell	PB8542VG	VGA	640 x 480	0.41	14	14 x 14 x 14.5	Yes	Yes	1
PC Brand, Inc.	Monochrome VGA Display	VGA	640 x 480	0.28	14				1
Wyse Technology	WY-655	VGA	640 x 480	0.28	14		Yes	Yes	1
Wyse Technology	WY-550	VGA Monochrome	640 x 480		14		Yes	Yes	1
Altec	View Sonic 5	VGA, SVGA	1024 x 768ni	0.25	14	14	Yes	Yes	1
CompuAdd	CompuAdd High Res VGA Monitor	VGA, SVGA	1024 x 768i	0.25	14		Yes	No	1
Data World	VGA Video Display	VGA, SVGA	1024 x 768ni	0.25	14		Yes	No	1
Everex	Viewpoint Premium Adapter	VGA, SVGA	1024 x 768i	0.28	14		Yes	No	2
Everex	Vision VGA HC Adapter	VGA, SVGA	1024 x 768i	0.28	14		Yes	No	2
Everex	Viewpoint Premium Adapter	VGA, SVGA	1024 x 768i	0.28	14		Yes	No	2
Everex	Vision VGA HC Adapter	VGA, SVGA	1024 x 768i	0.28	14		Yes	No	2
Falco Data Products, Inc.	FVP	VGA, SVGA	1024 x 768ni	0.28	14		Yes	Yes	1, send-back
MIS Computer Systems	CTX	VGA, SVGA	1024 x 768i	0.28	14	376 x 366 x 360mm	Yes	Yes	1
MIS Computer Systems	Optiquest 1000	VGA, SVGA	1024 x 768ni	0.28	14	15.3 x 14.6 x 16.5	Yes	Yes	1
Packard Bell	PB8528SVG	VGA, SVGA	1024 x 768i	0.28	14	14.75 x 14.33 x 15.75	Yes	Yes	1
PC Brand, Inc.	SVGA Display	VGA, SVGA	1024 x 768i	0.28	14				1
Wyse Technology	WY-670	VGA, SVGA	1024 x 768i	0.28	14		Yes	Yes	1
Zenith	ZCM-1650 TIGA monitor	VGA, TIGA	1024 x 768ni	0.28	14	15.67 x 15.74 x 17.48	Yes	Yes	1

RETAIL PRICE	ADAPTER TYPE	MAX RESOLUTION	VIDEO RAM (M)	SOFTWARE INCLUDED	CHIP SET	ADAPTER WARRANTY (years)	OTHER INFORMATION
$359.00	VGA, SVGA	800 x 600	256K	None	Tseng Labs	1	
$539.00	VGA, SVGA	800 x 600	256K	VGA utilities		90 days	
$539.00	VGA, SVGA	800 x 600	256K	VGA utilities		90 days	
$209.00	VGA	640 x 480	256K			1	
$599.00	VGA, SVGA, WY-455	800 x 600	256K, 512K	WY-455 driver	Tseng Labs ET4000	1	
$209.00	VGA, SVGA, WY-455	800 x 600	256K, 512K	WY-455 driver	Tseng Labs ET4000	1	
$525.00	VGA, SVGA	1024 x 768ni	1	Most Popular software driver	Tseng Labs, Orchid	3	
$409.00	VGA, SVGA	1024 x 768i	512K, 1	None	Tseng Labs	1	
	VGA, SVGA	1024 x 768ni	1	Software drivers	Tseng Labs	1	
$339.00 for 1M version	VGA, SVGA	1280 x 1024i, 1024 x 768ni	1		Tseng Labs ET4000	2	
$715.00 for 1M version	VGA, SVGA	1280 x 1024i, 1024 x 768ni	1		Tseng Labs ET4000	2	
$299.00 for 512K version	VGA, SVGA	1280 x 1024i, 1024 x 768ni	512K		Tseng Labs ET4000	2	
$675.00 for 512K version	VGA, SVGA	1280 x 1024i, 1024 x 768ni	512K		Tseng Labs ET4000	2	
$380.00	VGA, SVGA	1024 x 768ni	512K	Software drivers	WD Paradise	1, send-back	Adapter is shipped as std with Falco Infinity Desktop
$335.00	VGA, SVGA	1024 x 768i	1		Trident	1	Resolution: 1024 x 768i, 800 x 600, 640 x 480 45MHz video bandwidth analog input signal, infinite display colors
$424.00	VGA, SVGA	1024 x 768ni	1		Trident	1	Infinite palette of colors, 72Hz refresh rate, VESA avail, video band width-65MHz, RGB analog, sync: TTL sep
$899.00	VGA, SVGA	1024 x 768i	512K	VGA utilities		90 days	
$449.00	VGA, SVGA	1024 x 768i	1	Software drivers		1	
$739.00	VGA, SVGA, WY-470	1024 x 768i	512K, 1	WY-470 driver	Tseng Labs ET4000	1	
$1699.00	VGA, SVGA, TIGA	1024 x 768ni					Based on TI 34010 architecture, integrates a 60MHz video processor, supports VGA

continues

Table 6.3. Continued

COMPANY	MODEL	DISPLAY TYPE	MAX RES (horiz x vert)	DOT PITCH (mm)	SCREEN SIZE (inches)	DISPLAY SIZE (inches)	TILT, SWIVEL STAND	NON-GLARE SCREEN	DISPLAY WARRANTY (years)
Mirror Technologies	Pixel View I Full-page Monochrome	Full-page monochrome	640 x 870	80 dpi	15	16.54 x 12.68 x 13.7	Yes	Yes	1; 30 days money back
Sigma Designs	Page View	High-Resolution IBM comp	768 x 1024ni, 96 dpi		15	15.25 x 11.25 x 14.50	Yes	Yes	1
Sigma Designs	PageView Multi-Mode	High-Resolution Mac comp	88dpi		15	15.25 x 11.15 x 14.5	Yes	Opt	1
Ehman Inc.	Ehman 15" FPD Monochrome Monitor	Mac	640 x 480, 80 DPI		15	8.5 x 10.5	Yes	Yes	1; 30 days money back
Radius & Pantone, Inc.	Radius Full Page Display	Mac	640 x 870		15	8.15 x 11	Opt	Yes	1
Radius & Pantone, Inc.	Radius Color Pivot Display	Mac	640 x 870	0.26	15	7.8 x 10.6	Yes	Yes	1
Radius & Pantone, Inc.	Radius Pivot Display	Mac	640 x 870		15	8.15 x 11	Yes	Opt	1
Falco Data Products, Inc.	FALCO FV15	VGA, SVGA	1024 x 768ni	0.28	15	16 x 14.5 x 15	Yes	Yes	1, send-back
Sigma Designs	L-view	High-Resolution IBM comp	1664 x 1200ni, 118 dpi		19	18 x 19 x 17	Yes	Yes	1
Sigma Designs	L-View GSP	High-Resolution IBM comp	1664 x 1200ni, 118 dpi		19	18 x 19 x 17	Yes	Yes	1
Taxan America Inc.	CrystalView 1901 Display Sys. for IBM	High-Resolution IBM comp	1280 x 960ni	96 dpi	19	19	Yes	Yes	1
Sigma Designs	L-View Multi-Mode	High-Resolution Mac comp	1664 x 1200ni, 120 dpi		19	18 x 19 x 17	Yes	Yes	1
Taxan America Inc.	CrystalView 1901 for Mac II, SE & SE/30	High-Resolution Mac comp	1024 x 768ni	72 dpi	19	19	Yes	Yes	1
Ehman Inc.	Ehman 19" DPD Gray Scale Monitor	Mac	1024 x 768ni, 72 DPI		19		Yes		1; 30 days money back
Ehman Inc.	Ehman 19" DPD Monochrome Monitor	Mac	1024 x 768ni, 72 DPI		19		Yes	No	1; 30 days money back
Radius & Pantone, Inc.	Radius Two Page Display/19	Mac	1152 x 882ni		19	14 x 10.75	Yes	Opt	1
Supermac	19" SuperMatch STD9782	Mac	1024 x 768	72 dpi	19		Yes	Yes	
Supermac	19" Dual Mode Trinitron STD9750	Mac	1024 x 768, 1152 x 870	72 dpi, 82 dpi	19		Yes	Yes	
Wyse Technology	WY-790N	VGA Monochrome	1280 x 1024ni		19		Yes	Yes	1
Mirror Technologies	ProView 24	24-bit Trinitron 2 page monitor & card	1024 x 768	72 dpi	20	19.25 x 18.9 x 20.71	Yes	Yes	1; 30 days money back

6

RETAIL PRICE	ADAPTER TYPE	MAX RESOLUTION	VIDEO RAM (M)	SOFTWARE INCLUDED	CHIP SET	ADAPTER WARRANTY (years)	OTHER INFORMATION
	Mac	1024 x 768				1; 30 days money-back	Monitor, card, software inc, models available for entire Mac family, lifetime tech support
	Custom Adapter board	768 x 1024ni		Software drivers		1	Comes with all NEC Equip and disks, meets MPR II for low emissions
	Custom Adapter board	704 x 940	128K	Software drivers		1	Comes with all NEC Equip and disks, low emission display
$495.00	Mac	1024 x 768ni		Init for SE, Classic, MAC Plus		1	
$895.00	Mac	640 x 870ni	1 VRAM	Radius Ware		1	Comp with IIsi, IIci built-in video, color pivot interfaces for SE/30, LC, IIsi, and II family , copro avail
$1995.00	Mac LC, SE/30, IIsi, II	640 x 870ni, 564 x 760ni	2 VRAM	RadiusWare, Soft Pivot		1	Comp with IIsi, IIci built-in video, color pivot interfaces for SE/30, LC, IIsi, and II family , copro avail
$1095.00	Mac LC, SE/30, IIsi, II	640 x 870ni	2 VRAM	RadiusWare, Soft Pivot		1	Comp with IIsi, IIci built-in video color pivot interfaces for SE/30, LC, IIsi, and II family
$595.00	VGA, SVGA	1024 x 768ni	2	Software drivers	Tseng Labs	. 1, send-back	
	Triple 8-bit DAC Video	1664 x 1200ni	512K, 4	Software drivers			Comes with all NEC Equip and disks, meets MPR II for low emissions
	Custom Adapter board	1664 x 1200ni		Software drivers		1	Comes with all NEC Equip and disks, meets MPR II for low emissions
$2195.00	HGC	1280 x 960ni	512K	Drivers for Windows 3.0, 1-2-3, others		1	The adapter comes with the CrystalView 1901 high resolution monochrome monitor
	Custom Adapter board	1664 x 1200ni		Software drivers			Comes with all NEC Equip and disks, low emission display
$1695.00	Mac II, SE, SE/30	1024 x 768ni	Mac II, 512K, SE, 256K, SE/30, 512K	Init for Mac SE		1	Adapter comes with 19" high resolution monochrome monitor
$1495.00	Mac	1024 x 768ni		FPU Pseudo Init for Mac IIsi		1	
$895.00	Mac	1024 x 768ni		Init for SE, Stepping Out II SE/30, Mac II		1	
$1395.00	Mac LC, SE/30, IIsi, II	1152 x 882ni	1 VRAM	Radiusware		1	TPD interfaces for the SE, SE/30, IIsi, and II family, gray scale/color interface for II family
$2800.00	Mac. Spectrum/ 24 series 3	1024 x 768	3 VRAM				
$4200.00	Mac. Spectrum/ 8.24 PDQ		3 VRAM				The Spectrum/824 PDQ is for Mac NuBus and si
$1149.00	VGA, SVGA, WY 7500	1280 x 1024ni, 1024 x 768ni	1	WY 7500 driver	Tseng Labs ET4000	1	
	Mac	1024 x 768				1; 30 days money-back	Monitor, card, software inc, models available for entire Mac family, lifetime tech support

continues

Table 6.3. Concluded

COMPANY	MODEL	DISPLAY TYPE	MAX RES (horiz x vert)	DOT PITCH (mm)	SCREEN SIZE (inches)	DISPLAY SIZE (inches)	TILT, SWIVEL STAND	NON-GLARE SCREEN	DISPLAY WARRANTY (years)
Mirror Technologies	ProView 8	8-bit Trinitron 2 page monitor & card	1024 x 768	72 dpi	20	19.25 x 18.9 x 20.71	Yes	Yes	1, parts & labor; 30 days money back
Ehman Inc.	Ehman 20" DPD 24-bit Color Monitor	Mac	1024 x 768ni, 72 DPI		20			No	1; 30 days money back
Ehman Inc.	Ehman 20" DPD 8-bit Color Monitor	Mac	1024 x 768ni, 72 DPI		20		Yes	No	1; 30 days money back
Seiko Instruments	CM 2050 Bundle	VGA, SVGA	1024 x 768ni	0.31	20		Yes	Yes	1
Sigma Designs	SilverView	High-Resolution IBM comp	1152 x 870i, 72 dpi		21	17.5 x 19 x 18	Yes	Opt	1
Sigma Designs	SilverView GS	High-Resolution IBM comp	1152 x 870ni, 72 dpi		21	17.5 x 19 x 18	Yes	Yes	1
Sigma Designs	SilverView	High-Resolution Mac comp	1152 x 870i, 72 dpi		21	17.7 x 19 x 18	Yes	Opt	1
Sigma Designs	SilverView Portrait	High-Resolution Mac comp	1152 x 870ni, 72 dpi		21	17.7 x 19 x 18	Yes	Yes	1
Radius & Pantone, Inc.	Radius Two Page Display/21	Mac	1152 x 882ni		21	15.5 x 11.8	Yes	Opt	1
Supermac	21" SuperMatch STD9771	Mac	1152 x 870	77 dpi	21	18.4 x 19.2 x 20.4	Yes	Yes	
MIS Computer Systems	Optiquest 2000	VGA, SVGA		0.28	15	16 x 14 x 15.75	Yes	Yes	1

RETAIL PRICE	ADAPTER TYPE	MAX RESOLUTION	VIDEO RAM (M)	SOFTWARE INCLUDED	CHIP SET	ADAPTER WARRANTY (years)	OTHER INFORMATION
	Mac	1024 x 768				1; 30 days money-back	Monitor, card, software inc, models available for entire Mac family, lifetime tech support
$3945.00	Mac	1024 x 768ni	3 VRAM	System 6.0.3 and 32-bit QuickDraw		1; 30 days money back	
$2895.00	Mac	1024 x 768ni				1	
$2999.00	VGA, SVGA	1024 x 768ni	512K	Drivers for Windows 3.0, 1-2-3, others	Tseng Labs ET4000	4	Specifications subject to change without notice
	Custom Adapter board	1152 x 870		Software drivers		1	Comes with all NEC Equip and disks, ISA or MCA bus, low emission monitor design
	Triple 8-bit DAC	ni	512K, 4	Software drivers		1	Comes with all NEC Equip and disks, adapter is 60MHz TI 34010 copro, 512K or 2MB std TI 34010 memory
	Custom Adapter board	1152 x 870	1	Software drivers			Comes with all NEC Equip and disks, low emission display, emulate VGA, HGC, MDA
	Custom NuBus	1152 x 870ni	1	Software drivers		1	Comes with all NEC Equip and disks, low emission monitor
$1795.00	Mac LC, SE/30, IIsi, II	1152 x 882ni	1 VRAM	Radiusware		1	TPD interfaces for the SE, SE/30, IIsi, and II family, gray scale/color interface for II family
$4400.00	Mac NuBus Spectrum/24 PDQ		3 VRAM	SuperMatch software.			
$571.00	VGA, SVGA	1024 x 768ni	1		Trident	1	40-70Hz vertical scanning input signal: RGB anaolog video, infinite palette of colors

CHAPTER SEVEN

Reviewing Types of Printers

When you work with an application program, such as a word processor, spreadsheet, database, or desktop publisher, you need to print the results of your efforts. For example, if you type a letter with a word processor, you need to print the letter before you can send it to someone. Without a printer, your computing power is severely limited. You should plan to buy a printer at the same time as or soon after you buy the other components of your system. This chapter asks questions about your printing needs and explains the kinds of printer technologies, features, and manufacturers to look for when purchasing a printer.

Kinds of Printing Tasks

Before you decide what printer to connect to your personal computer, you should consider the kinds of printing you want to do. Ask yourself these questions:

- What do I want to print—text, graphics, or both?
- What quality of output do I need?

  Does the appearance of the printed characters or images matter? Compare the type quality of the text samples in figure 7.1 as an example.
- What typefaces do I need? Do I need a variety of typefaces and fonts? (The term *typeface* is defined later in the chapter.)
- Do I want to print in black and white or in color?
- Am I concerned with printing speed?
- How much money can I spend?

A veteran applications analyst in start-up companies, even Ms. Lahey was unprepared for what she saw. "Never in my life have I seen such a promising start for a company still being run out of a garage," she	A veteran applications analyst in start-up companies, even Ms. Lahey was unprepared for what she saw. "Never in my life have I seen such a promising start for a comapny still being run out of a garage," she

Fig. 7.1. *The difference between Times Roman print (left) and draft print (right).*

Your answers to these questions can help you decide which kind of printer is best for you. In many cases, your answer to the final question determines the answers to the others.

Printer Technology

The major difference among printers lies in the way they form characters on the page. Some printers form characters by striking an inked ribbon with pins; others by spraying ink on paper; others by depositing a black powder, called toner, on the paper. Different printing methods affect the print quality and the speed of a printer. To help you understand the various kinds of printers available, the following sections describe the different printer technologies.

Dot-Matrix Printers

Dot-matrix printers produce alphanumeric characters and graphic images by striking an inked ribbon with tiny metal rods called *pins*. The pins are located in a *print head*, which moves back and forth to create one line of text or graphics (see fig. 7.2). Dot-matrix printers usually use 9 or 24 pins to produce a series of dots on the page but may use 18 pins or some other number. Because dot-matrix printers use an impact technology, they are noisy and relatively slow. If your application requires continuous-form or multipart paper, a dot-matrix printer may be the perfect solution.

Inkjet and Thermal Printers

Inkjet and thermal printers differ from standard dot-matrix printers in the way they form characters on the page. An inkjet printer has a mechanism that squirts dots of ink onto the page to form characters. A thermal printer uses heat to transfer dots from the ribbon to the page. Both kinds are quiet and have good type quality. You cannot use these printers for tasks like printing on multiple part forms because inkjet and thermal technologies do not use an impact method to create characters. You can, however, expect high-quality output at a reasonable price.

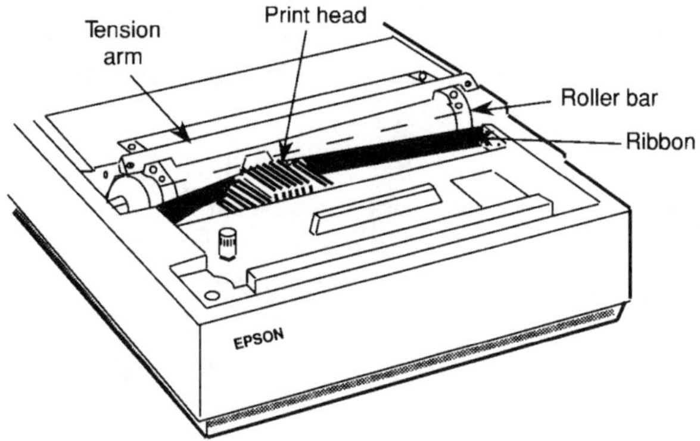

Fig. 7.2. A dot-matrix printer.

Daisywheel Printers

Daisywheel printers use a simple printing technology. A wheel of characters rotates, and a hammer mechanism pushes one piece of the wheel against the ribbon to form a character on the page (see fig. 7.3). These printers print with the same high quality as expensive typewriters.

Years ago, the daisywheel printer was the only kind of printer that could produce the sharp, clear characters necessary for business correspondence. Nowadays, daisywheel printers are the dinosaurs of the personal computer age. Too slow to compete with lasers and unable to print graphics, these printers fell into disfavor several years ago. Most stores do not carry daisywheel printers anymore, but you sometimes can find them in close-out catalogs at very low prices.

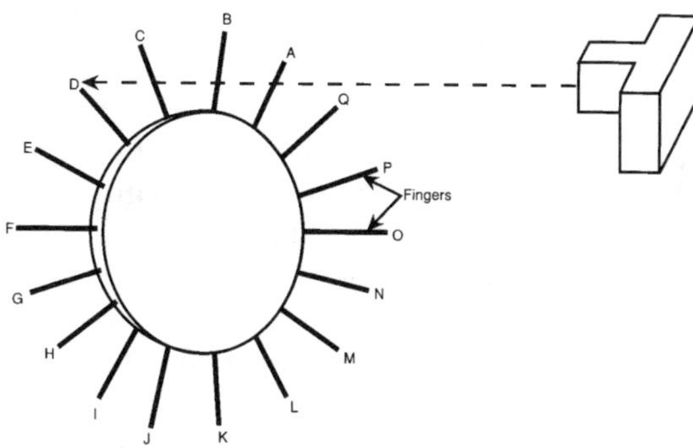

Fig. 7.3. The print wheel from a daisywheel printer.

Laser Printers

Laser printers form characters in a fairly complex way. A laser beam is pointed at a rotating hexagonal mirror. The light is reflected off the mirror onto a rotating cylinder called a drum. This reflection creates an electronic image on the drum. The image on the drum attracts a fine black powder, which adheres to the drum. When paper passes under the drum, the toner is attracted to the paper, forming the image. Finally, the image is fused to the paper by a combination of heat and pressure.

Many laser printers are actually high-powered computers. These printers contain high-performance microprocessors and several megabytes of memory. When you compare laser printers, you should ask about these technological differences. Ask about the type of microprocessor and its speed. Find out the amount of memory that comes with the printer and ask how much the memory can be expanded. Some very high-performance laser printers support external disks so that fonts can be loaded directly from the printer rather than be sent from the computer to the printer.

Page-Description Languages in Laser Printers

A major difference among laser printers is the page-description language built into the printer. The two prominent languages used in laser printers are Hewlett-Packard's Printer Control Language (PCL) and Adobe PostScript. Most laser printers use one of these languages or a language compatible with PCL or PostScript. Adobe PostScript is the more powerful language. With PostScript, you can print many kinds of alphanumeric characters, scale the characters to almost any size, and add special effects.

Hewlett-Packard's PCL is much more limited. The new Hewlett-Packard LaserJet III series, however, expands the capabilities of PCL with an improved version of the language called PCL 5. The LaserJet III series printers can do some of the tasks a PostScript printer can do, such as scale fonts and add special effects to type. A printout from a LaserJet III shows how the printer can add special effects to type (see fig. 7.4). Normally, you need a laser printer with the PostScript language to produce this kind of effect. Because Hewlett-Packard sets the standards for PCL laser printers, you can expect many other printers to use this improved version of PCL in the future.

Most PostScript printers contain the Level 1 PostScript language, but Level 2 is expected sometime during 1991. Data Products has introduced a Level 2 PostScript printer. The advantages of Level 2 over Level 1 are better memory management, improved handling of forms, pattern caching, and the capability to manipulate color. These features result in faster printing of documents. Apple recently has deviated from its long-standing relationship with Adobe and introduced TrueType, a new scheme for scalable type. TrueType gives you features of Level 1 PostScript and enables you to print scalable fonts on different printers.

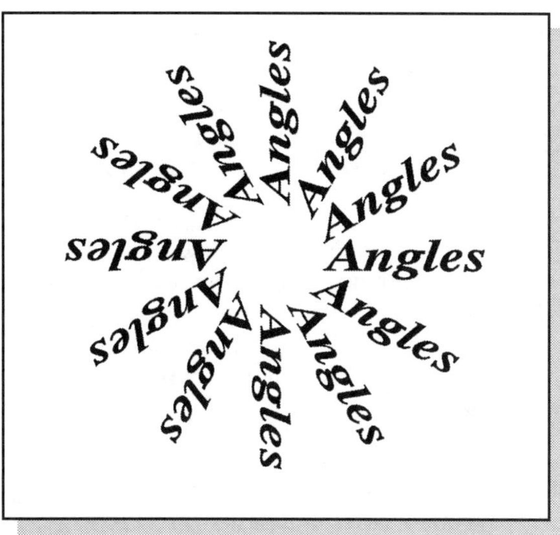

Fig. 7.4. *Special effects produced by a Hewlett-Packard LaserJet III printer.*

LCS and LED Printers

Sometimes a laser printer is not what it seems. Some printers that look like laser printers have basic technological differences. A laser printer can be more broadly classified as a *page printer*. Other kinds of page printers are *liquid-crystal shutter (LCS) printers* and *light-emitting diode (LED) array printers*. These printers look and act like laser printers but do not use a laser beam as part of their operation. The differences among the print outputs of LCS printers, LED printers, and laser printers are slight. Sometimes, you can tell the difference by printing a straight line across the width of the paper. A laser printer bends the line ever so slightly at the edges. This curve is usually not a problem unless your application demands perfectly straight lines. You may be equally pleased with the outputs of the laser, LCS, and LED printers.

Printer Purchase Considerations

Besides differences in printing technology, printers usually differ in the kinds of features they offer. These features can relate to print quality, ports, memory, resolution, speed, paper size and handling, controls, color, portability, purchase cost, and operating costs. Before you buy a printer, you need to consider the subjects discussed in the following sections.

Print Quality

Before a discussion of print quality, a few definitions are in order. When you print a document, the characters that appear on the page have a particular design, called the *typeface*. The typeface has a name, such as Courier, Helvetica, or Times Roman. Thousands of typefaces exist, and a single printer may have one, two, or several.

All typefaces contain letters, numbers, and symbols in a variety of sizes, from the fine print you see in advertisements to the large print used for headlines, banners, and signs. The collection of all characters of a particular size (measured in points) and weight (light, medium, bold) is called a *font*. For instance, in the Times Roman typeface, one of the fonts is 10-point Times Roman (if a weight is not given, it is medium).

All printers have one or more resident (built-in) fonts. Do not purchase a printer unless you can see a print sample that includes all the resident fonts. If you plan to use the printer for business correspondence, be sure to inspect the quality of the font.

If you do not like the printer's standard fonts, ask whether you can purchase optional font cartridges for the printer. A *font cartridge* gives you additional fonts and typefaces, a useful option if you are interested in spicing up the look of business correspondence and reports.

If a printer does not accept font cartridges, inquire whether the manufacturer offers downloadable fonts. (*Downloadable fonts*, which are supplied on a disk, are fonts the computer loads into the printer's memory.) Ask for sample printouts so that you can check the quality and variety of the fonts.

An alternative to font cartridges is the use of programs that offer scalable fonts. *Scalable fonts* give you any character size for a particular typeface. Special programs like Publisher's Powerpak from Atech Software add scalable fonts to such programs as WordPerfect and Microsoft Word. If you use Microsoft Windows 3.0 with an IBM or compatible computer, you can get programs like Adobe Type Manager, Powerpak for Windows, and FaceLift from Bitstream. These programs add scalable screen and printer fonts for any Windows application. The programs often slow printers considerably, so you may want a demonstration before deciding to purchase. Before purchasing a program, you also should make sure that the program works with the printer you are considering.

A new entry into the scalable font world is TrueType, Apple's new scheme of producing scalable typefaces. Apple's new operating system, System 7, incorporates TrueType, and Microsoft reportedly will include TrueType in its next version of Windows.

Ports

You can connect a printer to a computer in several ways. Most printers used with IBM and compatible computers have a Centronics parallel port. To connect the printer to the computer, you need a parallel port on the computer. A parallel port may be built into the computer or added to it by a card inserted into an expansion slot.

Printers intended for use with Macintosh computers have serial (also called RS-232C or RS-422), AppleTalk, or SCSI ports. All Macintosh computers have these ports built in.

Make sure that the personal computer you own or are buying and the printer you are considering have the same ports. Otherwise, the personal computer cannot send data to the printer.

Some laser printers have two serial ports, an AppleTalk port, and a parallel port. You can connect each of the four ports to a different personal computer. Laser printers with automatic port selection scan all the ports, select the first port that has a print job, and hold the other jobs in the queue until the first computer's print job is finished. If you will share your printer with other computers in your home or office, this capability may be a feature worth considering.

Memory

Memory, or RAM, is not only an element of a personal computer system but also an important element of a printer. RAM is most important for laser printers because an entire page is composed and stored in the printer's memory before the page is printed on paper. RAM in a laser printer is also used to store fonts. You should consider RAM when you evaluate other types of printers, too. Dot-matrix printers use RAM as a buffer. Because most dot-matrix printers print more slowly than the computer sends the information to be printed, the buffer enables the computer to continue sending data to be printed rather than have to wait on the printer. The computer is free for other use while the printer is still printing.

Resolution

Resolution is a measurement of the number of dots a printer can print on a page. The measurement is given in dots per inch (dpi). The higher the resolution, the better the quality of alphanumeric characters and graphics.

A printer prints dots horizontally and vertically. When discussing dpi, you normally are concerned with graphics. Look for a printer that has equal horizontal and vertical resolutions, for example, 300 by 300 dpi. If the vertical and horizontal resolutions are different, a graphic's aspect may be off. For instance, a circle may look like an oval when printed.

Speed

The speed of a printer means how fast it can print a page of text. Factors that influence printer speed are the speed at which the printer advances or ejects a page and the speed at which the printer can print graphics. Graphics printing is considerably slower than text printing. Dot-matrix printer speeds are given in characters per second (cps), and laser printers are rated in pages per minute (ppm).

When comparing print speeds for dot-matrix printers, make sure that the characters being printed are the same size, for example, 10 characters per inch. A dot-matrix printer generally has a faster speed when printing at 12 cpi than at 10 cpi. The page per minute rating of a laser printer is based on 10 cpi text. A 6 ppm printer prints 6 *text* pages per minute, not 6 graphics pages. Compare a laser printer's graphics pages per minute rating when purchasing a laser printer.

Paper Size and Handling

The standard paper size for business correspondence in the United States is 8 1/2 by 11 inches; legal-size paper is 8 1/2 by 14 inches. When working with printers, you should take into account these and other sizes of paper and labels on which you may want to print your work.

Some wide dot-matrix printers print on 14-by-11-inch paper, which is used for many business reports. Generally, a laser printer requires a different paper tray to print on legal paper. The paper tray that comes with a laser printer handles 8 1/2-by-11-inch paper automatically but can handle only one piece of legal paper at a time. If you plan to use legal paper, make sure that the manufacturer of the printer sells a legal-size paper tray. You cannot print on 14-by-11-inch paper, as you can on a dot-matrix printer.

Paper handling refers to the way a printer handles different kinds of paper, such as single sheets of standard and legal-size paper, continuous-forms paper, multiple-part forms paper, envelopes, and labels. Depending on the job you want to do, you may want to choose a printer based solely on its paper-handling capabilities.

Printer Controls

Every printer has some kind of control panel to govern different aspects of printing. Some control panels, however, are much more elaborate than others. Some printers use a small LCD screen that shows alphanumeric character codes, and others use simple LED indicators (on/off lights) to display information to the user. Even among printers that use LED indicators, some printers have much more complex control panels than others.

Color

You can print in color with dot-matrix, inkjet, and thermal printers. Currently, laser printers do not offer this feature. When you select a color printer, you consider the same features you consider in choosing any other printer. Remember, however, that you must have the correct software to use color.

Portability

A selling point of some inkjet printers is portability. Models like the BJ-10e Bubble Jet from Canon and the Diconix 150 Plus from Kodak weigh less than five pounds and easily can be carried in a briefcase. These printers are ideal for anyone who uses an IBM or compatible laptop or notebook computer and needs a portable printer. In addition to portability, both printers provide good quality output. Dot-matrix and laser printers are not designed for portability.

If you are looking for portability in a Macintosh-compatible printer, consider the Diconix 150M or Apple's StyleWriter. These printers are designed to work specifically with the Macintosh, and the StyleWriter supports TrueType. The primary advantage of the Diconix is its capability to operate on battery power, whereas the StyleWriter requires AC current.

Purchase and Operating Costs

Costs of printers range from less than $200 for an inexpensive dot-matrix model to more than $5,000 for a PostScript laser printer. Some color printers, namely thermal printers, can cost more than $10,000.

The cost of a printer includes more than just the purchase price, however. You need to consider the following additional expenses that affect the operating costs of your printer:

- Paper
- Consumables: toner, ribbons, and ink
- Repair of parts: drums, print heads, and so on

Prices of these items vary depending on your source of supply. Be sure to price these items, especially the cost of repairs, if you are undecided about which kind of printer to buy.

Printer Technology Considerations

As explained earlier in this chapter, the printer technology is a major purchasing consideration. The following sections consider the different technologies and tell you points to consider when you are deciding the type of printer you want.

Dot-Matrix Printers

The dot-matrix printer has been the printer of choice because of its flexibility in printing text and graphics, and its relatively affordable cost. As manufacturers try to keep up with printing technology advances, more printer features are available. The next few sections explore considerations for purchasing a dot-matrix printer. You look at speed, resolution, paper handling, and printing in color.

Print Quality

All dot-matrix printers can produce draft characters (again see fig. 7.1). Draft characters are formed with a minimum number of dots, so the printer can produce these characters quickly. Most dot-matrix printers also can produce *letter-quality* or *near-letter-quality* characters. In essence, these descriptions mean that the dot-matrix printer's font looks nearly or exactly like that of a good typewriter. If you believe the manufacturer's claims without question, however, you may be sorely disappointed when you print a letter or a report.

Look at the samples of near-letter-quality and letter-quality type from different dot-matrix printer manufacturers shown in figures 7.5 and 7.6. Notice the differences in the quality and sharpness of the images.

```
I went to the woods because I          I went to the woods because I
wished to live deliberately,           wished to live deliberately,
to front only the essential            to front only the essential
facts of life. - H. D. Thoreau         facts of life. - H. D. Thoreau
```

Fig. 7.5. Samples of near-letter-quality print from two different dot-matrix printers.

```
I went to the woods because I          I went to the woods because I
wished to live deliberately,           wished to live deliberately,
to front only the essential            to front only the essential
facts of life. - H. D. Thoreau         facts of life. - H. D. Thoreau
```

Fig. 7.6. Samples of letter-quality print from two different dot-matrix printers.

A high-quality dot-matrix printer may be capable of producing letter-quality print in a variety of typefaces and fonts. Sometimes, this feature is standard for a printer. For example, the EPSON LQ 1010 printer (a 24-pin printer) has three typefaces—Draft, Roman, and Sans Serif. Mixing and matching these typefaces with different characteristics makes different fonts. For example, you may print a boldface Roman character or an italicized Sans Serif character.

Some dot-matrix printers support additional font cartridges, enabling the printer to print in more than just the default fonts. For example, the EPSON LQ 1010 supports a font cartridge that contains multiple fonts; one cartridge contains Courier, Prestige, Script, OCR-B, OCR-A, Orator, and Orator-S. You need not be concerned about the manufacturer of the cartridges because no one cartridge font is standard.

Generally, dot-matrix printers create 12-point characters (in height). Some dot-matrix printers can create double-high characters, equivalent to 24 points.

In width, dot-matrix characters are measured in characters per inch (cpi). The normal mode for a dot-matrix printer is 10 cpi, called Pica. Most printers also print characters at different cpi settings. Other cpi settings are 12 cpi (Elite), 15 cpi (condensed), and 17 cpi (Elite condensed). Some dot-matrix printers also may print larger characters, called elongated characters. These cpi ratings may be 8 cpi, 6 cpi, and 5 cpi. No matter how wide the character is printed, from a wide 5 cpi to a narrow 17 cpi, the character is the same height—12 points.

The reason for the cpi rating is that dot-matrix printers often use monospaced characters, in which each character takes the same amount of space. The space allocated for the letter *l* is the same as the space allocated for the letter *m*. Some printers support proportional characters, where each character takes only as much space on the line as the character requires. Proportional characters cannot be measured in cpi, because the number of proportional *l*'s in one inch varies from the number of proportional *m*'s.

Nearly all dot-matrix printers can print graphics. Some dot-matrix printers may even print high-resolution graphics. Generally, 24-pin printers produce higher-resolution graphics than 9-pin printers produce.

Although graphics printed by a 24-pin printer may be of high resolution, they also may be less than desirable. Generally, a graphic printed by a dot-matrix printer looks striped. The print head may have to make many passes over a piece of paper to print the graphic. Each pass makes a stripe on the page. These stripes are most noticeable when you print a great deal of black on the paper. If you print only lines, as in a chart or graph, the stripes may be hardly noticeable.

Memory

Dot-matrix printers use memory as a print buffer; information sent to the printer goes into RAM first and then is printed. If the printer has enough RAM to accept all the information you want to print, waiting time is eliminated. You can continue working on your computer while your printer is printing. If two dot-matrix models are otherwise similar in features and price, choose the printer with the most RAM.

Resolution

The resolution of a dot-matrix printer depends on the number of wires, or pins, in the printhead. The typical resolution of a 24-pin printer is 360 by 360; the typical resolution of a 9-pin printer is 240 by 216. These numbers refer to the horizontal resolution and vertical resolution in dots per inch. Notice that dot-matrix printers can have different horizontal and vertical resolutions.

When considering a dot-matrix printer, ask about the resolution—especially if you are worried about type and graphics quality. Compare printouts from different printers to see how variations in resolution affect the print quality.

Speed

With dot-matrix printers, speed is sometimes more important than print quality. To create a large mailing list and print thousands of labels, you need a fast printer. Speed ratings for dot-matrix printers are in characters per second (cps). A printer normally has one rating for draft mode and another rating for letter-quality mode. Draft print can be generated much faster than letter-quality print. For example, the speed of draft print may be 200 cps, whereas letter-quality speed may be 50 cps.

To get a realistic assessment of a printer's speed, do not rely on a manufacturer's claims. You should witness a printing demonstration of the kind of material you intend to print. Examples of print jobs that require speed rather than fine appearance are mailing labels, checks, financial statements, and database reports.

Size

Dot-matrix printers come in two standard sizes: narrow carriage and wide carriage. The narrow-carriage printer accepts standard 8 1/2-by-11-inch paper. The wide-carriage printer accepts 8 1/2-by-14-inch paper.

You may find that the narrow-carriage printer is adequate for most printing. You can print as many as 80 characters per line using the standard (10 cpi) font on a narrow-carriage printer. Using a condensed font (17 cpi), you can print up to 144 characters per line.

If you print financial reports, you may find the wide-carriage printer more useful. On 14-inch paper, with a 10 cpi font, you can print 140 characters, and with a 17 cpi font, you can print as many as 238 characters per line. Using the condensed mode on wide paper enables you to print large amounts of information on one page.

Paper Handling

An important paper-handling feature of dot-matrix printers is a tractor-feed mechanism. This mechanism keeps continuous-form paper straight when you are printing long documents or labels. If you want to print labels, make sure that the tractor-feed mechanism can be adjusted to accommodate them.

Dot-matrix printers are especially adept at printing on multipart forms. If you need a printer for this kind of work, you can find 9-pin dot-matrix printers that feed forms from the bottom of the printer (to keep the forms straight) and that enable you to tear off the form exactly where you want (to avoid waste).

Paper parking is another convenient feature. With some printers, you can insert single sheets of paper or envelopes into the printer while you still have your normal continuous-form paper in the machine. Paper parking is one of the best paper-handling features a printer can offer.

If you regularly print on letterhead, be sure to ask whether you can purchase a cut-sheet feeder for the dot-matrix printer you are considering. With a cut-sheet feeder, you load 100 or more sheets of paper into a tray, and the printer usually has two trays so that you can load letterhead paper into one tray and plain paper into another tray. When printing your document, the printer feeds the first letterhead page into the printer. Subsequent pages will be fed from the plain paper tray. You can purchase cut-sheet feeders that feed the first page (letterhead), subsequent pages, and envelopes.

Control

Many dot-matrix printers have a control panel that enables you to switch easily between print modes, such as normal and condensed print. If the printer lacks a control panel, you have to rely on its internal switches or on your application program to switch between modes. You can find out how easily you can use the printer's mode controls by visiting a store that sells dot-matrix printers and testing a few different models. Look for buttons on the front panel. Try to switch from draft to letter-quality print and from normal to condensed print. If the printer does not have buttons to make these changes or if the procedure is confusing, you should ask for a demonstration of this feature.

Color

The dot-matrix printer is popular because it can print graphics and text. The capability to create graphics is used not only in homes and offices for printing banners and signs but also is used in business for creating presentation graphics. Graphs and charts help visually describe numbers. Although a graph helps you express, for example, the profitability of your business, the graph looks plain in black and white. Color spruces up an otherwise plain graph. Color dot-matrix printers offer an affordable way to create color graphs, charts, and pictures besides printing text in color.

Dot-matrix printers that offer color printing typically are more expensive than printers without this option. To print in color, you need a color ribbon. Be sure that your printer is compatible with a popular color printing standard, such as EPSON. If not, you may find that your application programs, such as a paint programs, do not support the printer. If you are operating the printer with a color ribbon, you can still print in black only, because one of the colors of the ribbon is black. The most important requisite is having software that supports color printing.

Costs

If your budget is limited, you can purchase for less than $300 a 24-pin dot-matrix printer that provides a type quality good enough for business correspondence. A dot-matrix printer also is inexpensive to operate. If you intend to use a dot-matrix printer for heavy-duty work, however, don't make the mistake of buying an inexpensive model. You could burn out the unit soon. Instead, try to match your workload to the capability of the printer. If you plan to use a dot-matrix printer to print several thousand pages per week, you need to purchase a more expensive printer that can handle the workload.

The cost of operating a dot-matrix printer is minimal. Typically, the only recurring expense during the lifetime of the printer is replacing the ribbon, which can cost less than $10. Printheads do wear out, but only with constant use.

Inkjet and Thermal Printers

Inkjet and thermal printers offer good quality printing at an affordable price. These printers (also called thermal transfer printers) are quiet, which is an important quality when you are in the office or if you need to print a report at home early in the morning while your family is still asleep. An inkjet printer often gives you nearly the capability of a laser printer for not much more money than a dot-matrix printer and less money than most laser printers cost. The next few sections discuss considerations to take into account when looking for an inkjet or thermal printer.

Print Quality

Inkjet and thermal printers offer a variety of fonts, usually all high quality. The standard fonts that inkjet and thermal printers produce are similar to the fonts produced by dot-matrix printers. You can select among monospaced characters of generally the same point size. Because of the high-resolution of some inkjet printers, however, these printers can print high-quality proportional fonts. A printer like the Hewlett-Packard DeskJet 500 also accepts optional font cartridges to expand the selection of fonts.

You can run into a problem with an inkjet printer when you print graphics. Because an inkjet printer sprays ink onto the page, large black areas of a graphic are wet with ink as the page comes out of the printer, and the page may curl or wrinkle as it dries.

Another problem may occur if the ink used by the printer is water soluble. If a page printed with water-soluble ink gets wet, the printing smears on the paper. To combat this problem, manufacturers also sell water-resistant ink for inkjet printers. These inks are solvent-based rather than water-based so that the print does not smear if it gets wet.

Inkjet and thermal printers generally are slower than laser printers and do not support PostScript. At resolutions of 300 by 300 dpi and greater, however, these printers compare favorably with some laser printers and cost much less

Paper Size and Handling

Inkjet printers generally use only 8 1/2-inch paper. But you can use either standard or legal-size paper (14 inches long). Some inkjet printers enable you to rotate the printed output. This rotation of print, called landscape mode, makes the printer treat the length of the paper as the width and the width of the paper as the length. Landscape mode works on letter- or legal-size paper. Although you may be able to select landscape mode from a front-panel button on your printer, most often you choose landscape mode through your software. Because these printers have nonimpact technologies, you cannot use them to print multipart forms, that is, forms that have carbon paper between the pages to make multiple copies.

Color

Many applications enable you to print in color. For example, Lotus 1-2-3 Releases 2.3 and 3.1+ and Excel 3.0 for the IBM and Mac enable you to print color documents and color graphs and charts. To take advantage of these features, you must have a color printer.

COMPARISON

Inkjet printers that print in color use four different colors of ink to do the job. Color inkjet printers are somewhat more expensive than black-only inkjet prints. For example, the color Hewlett-Packard PaintJet has a suggested list price of $995; whereas the price of a DeskJet 500 (single color only) is $729.

Color thermal printers work by melting different colors of wax onto the page. The quality is far superior to the output of either dot-matrix or inkjet printers but much more costly, too. A color thermal printer costs anywhere from $5,000 to $15,000. These printers enable you to print high quality documents from, for example, a desktop publishing package. Business may find these printers useful for giving impressive demonstrations or presentations, or for producing proofs of brochures before sending the brochure for publication.

Costs

Inkjet and thermal printers offer high-quality printing at prices that are more affordable than the prices laser printers offer. Because inkjet and thermal printers support many of the typefaces that laser printers support, a thermal or inkjet printer may fit your printing needs nicely. With prices starting at less than $400, these printers are welcome alternatives to higher-priced laser printers. In fact, their cost is not much more than the cost of some dot-matrix printers.

Laser Printers

Laser printers print more quickly than the other printers discussed so far. Added to the speed is the capability to create sharp, presentation-quality documents, which you used to get only from a commercial printer. As with other printers, however, you need to consider many features when you are purchasing a laser printer. The following sections tell you what to consider.

Print Quality

Laser printers are a great improvement over dot-matrix, inkjet, and thermal printers. Laser printers are relatively quiet and produce better-looking text and graphics. Some laser printers also have a large selection of typefaces and fonts. Many laser printers can scale fonts; that is, the printer can produce fonts of virtually any size.

If you are buying a laser printer, be careful to check the kind of font cartridges the printer accepts. The Hewlett-Packard Series II printers are an industry standard, and many third-party companies make font cartridges for these printers. If you purchase a printer that uses a different kind of cartridge, you have to depend on that printer's manufacturer to provide the fonts you want.

Memory

Laser printer memory is used mainly to store image data. To print a page, the laser printer must have enough memory to store all the information about the page, including text and formatting codes. A laser printer cannot print part of a page, receive more information, and then print the rest of the page. If a laser printer runs out of RAM, the printer prints half the page, ejects the paper, and then prints the other half of the page on another sheet of paper. The more white space on the page, the smaller the amount of memory required.

COMPARISON

The standard amount of printer memory varies with the manufacturer. For example, the standard Hewlett-Packard LaserJet III printer has one megabyte of RAM; whereas the standard EPSON EPL-7000 has one-half megabyte (512 kilobytes) of memory. If you choose the minimum amount of memory for a laser printer, you may find that it cannot print pages which contain both text and graphics. Make sure that the printer can print the kinds of documents you want. If not, you will have to order additional memory.

Adding RAM to a laser printer is not a prepurchase-only option. At any time, you can add RAM in amounts up to the printer's maximum capacity. Generally, adding RAM is not a difficult procedure. For example, the Hewlett-Packard LaserJet III contains a slot on the side of the printer where a memory-expansion board slides into the printer.

Some laser printers can be expanded without memory boards. For example, the Apple LaserWriter family supports SIMMs (Single In-line Memory Module) for RAM expansion. SIMMs are memory modules often used in computers. Expanding with SIMMs is much less expensive than purchasing a memory board for RAM expansion.

Whatever amount of added RAM you decide to purchase for a laser printer, be sure to shop around for the best prices. Typical prices of RAM for a Hewlett-Packard laser printer are $175 for 1M, $225 for 2M, and $350 for 4M. If you buy RAM from the printer manufacturer rather from a third party, you may find that you spend twice as much for the same amount of RAM.

Resolution

Laser printers typically have a resolution of 300 dpi both vertically and horizontally. The Hewlett-Packard III series of laser printers have a special feature called *resolution enhancement technology*, which varies the dot size so that smaller dots can be placed in areas where the normal-sized dots do not fit. This feature can sharpen the appearance of letters even though the resolution of the printer, 300 dpi, is the same as the resolution of many other laser printers.

Laser printers with resolutions higher than 300 dpi often cost considerably more than models with 300 dpi resolution. Unless you need increased resolution for producing camera-ready art, stick with 300 dpi.

Speed

For laser printers, speed ratings are in pages per minute (ppm). Several factors determine the speed of a laser printer. Some laser-printer engines are rated at 8 ppm and higher, but others have ratings as low as 4 ppm. Memory is another factor influencing speed. The rated speed reflects print time for a page with characters only—not graphics. The more memory a PostScript printer has, the faster the printer can process data. Yet another factor is the laser printer's microprocessor (such as the Motorola 68000 or 68020). Some microprocessors are faster than others and so affect the speed of the printer.

Other elements can affect the speed of a laser printer. The port controls how quickly data can be transmitted to a printer. The software application and microprocessor of the personal computer control how quickly data can be prepared for the printer. Each of these elements can slow the printing process. If you intend to print pages that are complex combinations of text and graphics, be sure to test the speed of this printing process. A printer rated at 8 ppm may produce only 1 page of this kind every 15 minutes.

Paper Size and Handling

Laser printers use both letter- and legal-size paper. Laser printers also offer landscape and the default portrait modes (portrait mode being normal, or vertical, printing). The number of characters you can print on a page varies by the size and type style of the characters.

Laser printers typically are best at printing on standard and legal-size paper. Paper for a laser printer is loaded into a tray placed in the printer, and you can purchase additional trays for your paper. Paper trays come in the standard letter size and legal size. If you use legal-size paper, purchasing the additional tray is much more convenient.

Keep in mind that each letter you print usually needs an envelope. A laser printer should have a way to feed one envelope or a stack of envelopes into the printer. This feature may be standard or optional. You also can purchase sheets of labels (much like the labels used for plain paper copies) to use with your laser printer.

Some laser printers offer double-sided printing, which enables you to print on both sides of the page without having to feed the paper through the printer twice. This feature is useful if you are printing something like manuals. If you want double-sided printing, you need to look for a model that offers this special feature, such as the LaserJet IIID from Hewlett-Packard. (The D indicates the capability to do double-sided printing.)

Control

The control panel of a laser printer helps you select printer fonts and identify problems. Many printers use an LCD panel to convey information to the user. Be wary of purchasing a printer that forces you to learn cryptic codes rather than plain English for performing normal operations.

Most PostScript printers do not have a control panel on the front. The PostScript printer operations are controlled through software.

Costs

COMPARISON

The prices of laser printers vary based on the page description language and the speed of the printer. Printers that use PCL are less expensive than printers that use PostScript. Printers that print at a rate of four pages per minute (often referred to as personal printers) are less expensive than printers that print at eight pages per minute or more. Printers with fast, high-performance microprocessors are more expensive than printers with slower processors. A personal laser printer with the PCL language costs about $1,000. A PostScript printer with a high-performance microprocessor costs about $5,000.

Laser printers have much in common with copy machines. Like a copy machine, a laser printer uses a black powder called toner rather than a ribbon or ink. Because laser printers use toner, they can be costly to operate. Laser printers use more electricity than other printers use. Operating a laser printer may cost two to three times more than operating a dot-matrix or inkjet printer. Other parts of the machine, such as the drum, wear out and can be costly to replace. Drums can vary in price from less than $50 to more that $200. Yields vary, however, keeping the cost per copy similar for most lasers.

Printer Manufacturers

When you choose a printer model, consider the company that manufactures the printer. When you use a printer with a software program, you need to enter into the program information concerning the make and model of the printer you intend to use. For this reason, make sure that your software supports the printer model you are considering.

Dot-Matrix Printers

EPSON has set the dot-matrix printing standards for many years. For this reason, almost all software programs for IBM and compatible computers support EPSON printers. This fact does not mean that you must buy a dot-matrix printer from EPSON, but you should purchase a dot-matrix printer that offers EPSON emulation.

Inkjet and Thermal Printers

Not many inkjet or thermal printer models are on the market. The most popular inkjet printers for IBM and compatible computers are the Hewlett-Packard DeskJet and the Canon Bubble Jet; a popular thermal printer is the IBM QuietWriter. For Macintosh computers, Hewlett-Packard makes an inkjet printer called the DeskWriter, and Apple makes one called the StyleWriter. Hewlett-Packard sets the standards for inkjet printers for IBM and compatible computers. If you buy another model, make sure that your software supports that printer.

Laser Printers

The most popular laser printer brand for IBM and compatible computers is Hewlett-Packard. If you are considering a PCL printer other than the HP LaserJet series II or III, make sure that the printer can emulate one of these models. The most popular laser printer brand for Apple Macintosh computers is Apple. If you are considering a PostScript printer other than one of the Apple LaserWriters, make sure that the printer can emulate one of the LaserWriter models. Apple LaserWriters work not only with Macintosh computers but also with IBM and compatible computers.

The internal parts of a laser printer, the printer engine, can differ from printer to printer. Canon, IBM, Kyocera Unison, Ricoh, Sharp, and other companies make the engines. Laser printers from two different companies may use the same printer engine or different printer engines. Knowing which engine a laser printer uses is important because the toner cartridge and other parts that may need to be replaced fairly often differ from engine to engine. If you are thinking of buying a laser printer, make sure that you find out how to replace the toner and parts that wear out, such as the OPC (optical photo coupler). Also make sure that these items are readily available.

Chapter Summary

As you have seen in this chapter, much technology is available to get thoughts and ideas from the computer to paper. Dot-matrix printers offer you the widest use, being able to print text and graphics on many different types and sizes of paper, as well as on multiple part forms. For high quality, quiet printing, however, inkjet, thermal, and laser printers are the best choice. Of course, laser printers offer the best quality and the highest performance.

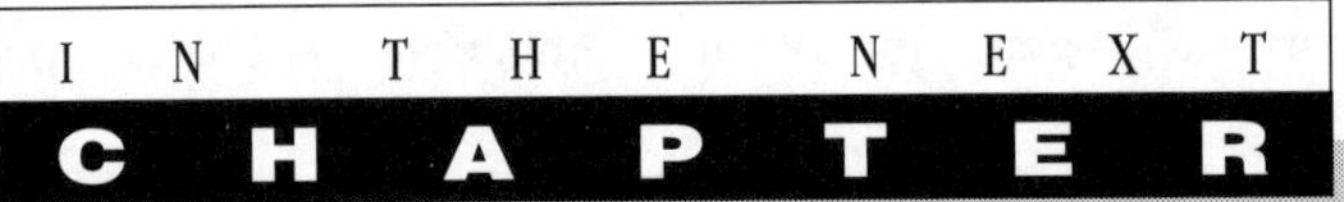

Although this chapter gives you the mechanics of printers and explains the different types of printers you may choose from, you still must decide what type of printer is best for you. The real way to make that decision is based on how you will use the printer and what applications you will print from. The next chapter discusses how you may use your printer and helps you make the best selection for you.

CHAPTER EIGHT

Deciding What Printer Model You Need

Deciding which printer to buy is not just a matter of checking cost or technology. You also should think about how you will use the printer. This chapter tells you what kinds of jobs require which kinds of printers, and which kinds of printers are best suited to particular kinds of software packages. This chapter also gives you information on specific printers and recommends which ones may best suit your needs. When you want to compare prices and other specifications of printers, see Chapter 9.

Determining Your Required Output

When purchasing a printer, you should have a clear idea of the kinds of documents you want to print. For example, desktop publishing is meant to be done with a laser printer—you can do only a crude job with a dot-matrix printer. You can print banners and very wide spreadsheets, however, only on tractor-feed dot-matrix printers. This section makes recommendations based on the output you produce.

Printing Internal Reports

Internal reports, such as budget figures that you pass around to various members in a department, are not meant to look impressive. Rather, these reports should communicate information clearly and efficiently. Internal reports often are printed on tractor-feed paper that isn't torn apart. In fact, the fanfold paper helps keep the pages in order. Usually, printing speed is more important than type quality, so a fast dot-matrix printer with a tractor-feed mechanism is the best choice. Select a 24-pin or a 9-pin dot-matrix printer with a narrow or a wide carriage, depending on the job you want to do.

Printing Letters, Resumes, and Papers

Business and professional documents such as letters, resumes, and lengthy papers usually are printed in a standard pica font, such as Courier. This kind of font is smart-looking but not too fancy. Some 24-pin dot-matrix printers produce the quality needed for these documents. You may want to print on continuous-form paper that tears apart or on single sheets fed into the printer with a sheet-feeding mechanism.

If you want to feed single sheets of paper into the printer, check whether the printer model you are considering has a cut-sheet feeder as an optional accessory. You can buy cut-sheet feeders that hold 100 or more sheets of paper. If you often feed letterhead paper as your first sheet and then feed blank sheets for subsequent pages, determine whether the printer has this kind of cut-sheet feeder as an optional accessory. Finally, if you want to feed envelopes into the printer, find out whether the printer model you are considering has as an optional accessory, such as a cut-sheet feeder that feeds paper plus envelopes into the printer.

If the standard Courier font is not sufficient for your work, consider a printer with other font choices, such as Times Roman, Gothic, and so forth. If you want a dot-matrix printer to provide a variety of fonts, be sure to check some sample printouts before you make a purchase. A dot-matrix printer, even one with 24 pins, may not be capable of giving you the print quality you want. On the other hand, thermal transfer and laser printers offer very high quality. Be sure to check the standard fonts that come with the printer model you are considering. Although the printer may be capable of printing many different fonts, the kind you want may be an optional rather than a standard feature of the printer.

Remember that laser printers have different paper-handling capabilities than dot-matrix models have. Laser printers almost exclusively use single sheets of paper rather than fanfold paper. A laser printer model may not have as a standard feature the paper-handling feature you need but may offer the feature as an optional accessory. For example, a laser printer may have a paper tray that holds only 50 sheets of paper. If you want a paper tray that holds more paper (usually 250 sheets), you need to purchase this tray as an optional accessory. The same holds true for envelopes. Check how many envelopes the paper tray that comes with the printer can hold (typically 5 envelopes), and how many envelopes the optional paper tray can hold (typically 50 envelopes). If you expect to print a large quantity of letters, you will want the printer to store as much paper as possible. A large paper tray eliminates the need to constantly add paper to the paper tray. If you need to feed legal-size paper into a laser printer, check whether you need a special paper tray for this purpose. If you plan to print multipage documents where the first page is letterhead, purchase a printer that supports multiple bins. With multiple-bin printers, you can place two different types of paper in the printer at a time.

Printing Mailing Labels

Mailing labels rarely need high-quality print output, so you can use the least expensive 9-pin dot-matrix printer you can find. Printing long lists on mailing labels, however, can reduce a printer's life span. (Both the print motor and print head heat up with extended use.) To print long mailing lists, you need a rugged 9-pin printer that can handle the work. The more work a printer can handle, the more it costs.

The labels may jam when you print a long mailing list. This jamming happens more often if the printer feeds labels from the back and the labels must curl around the platen. To avoid this curling, you need a printer that feeds labels through a slot at the bottom of the printer.

If you will print very long mailing lists on labels, keep in mind the printer's speed. Check a printer's rated speed at the size of print you prefer to use. For example, a printer manufacturer may quote a fast speed for draft print, but the size of the print may be very small, for example, 15 characters per inch. If you prefer the standard size, 10 characters per inch, be sure to compare printer speeds at this size. An average speed for draft printing at 10 characters per inch is 120 characters per second (cps). A slow printer may be 100 cps or less, and a fast printer is 160 cps or greater.

Make sure that the printer has a tractor-feed mechanism you can adjust to fit the width of the mailing labels. You can purchase labels that are one, two, or more labels across a page. If you purchase a wide-carriage printer, you can print on sheets containing three or more labels across a page. When you print labels that are more than one across, you increase the speed of printing labels.

If you are considering a laser printer for other printing purposes, you may wonder whether you can use it to print mailing labels, too. You can if you purchase sheets of labels that can withstand the considerable heat generated inside a laser printer. Sheets of labels designed to work with laser printers cost about double the price of those designed for dot-matrix printers.

If you frequently print mailing labels, you may want to purchase a 9-pin dot-matrix printer just for this purpose. This way, you can leave the fanfold sheets of labels in the printer and always be ready to print. If you add a second printer, however, you may need to add a second port or adapter to your computer. Although many computers have two or three ports that can be used for printers, other devices such as a mouse or modem may be attached to these ports. If you have no free ports on your computer, you must add the port.

Printing Banners

Banners generally are used for signs or for special events, such as parties. To create banners, you need special software and a dot-matrix printer. Banners are pages of fanfold paper that have not been torn apart and that have letters printed sideways along the continuous sheets. For example, one sentence printed across the sheets of paper can create a banner 12 feet long. Because banners are printed in graphics mode (one line of dots at a time), the kind of dot-matrix printer you use does not matter; 9-pin and 24-pin models work equally well. Just make sure that the banner program supports the printer you are considering.

To jazz up the banner, you may want to purchase a dot-matrix printer with color capability. You have two ways to print in color. You can substitute the black ribbon with a single-color ribbon such as red. In this case, you do not need a printer with color capability, you simply need a source of color ribbons. A printer with color capability uses a ribbon with four colors on the same ribbon. If you want to print in color with a color-capable printer, make sure that the banner program supports the printer you are considering.

To print banners with a laser printer, you need a banner program that supports a laser printer. Be advised, however, that you will need to tape single sheets together to create the banner.

Printing Wide Spreadsheets

You can print wide spreadsheets (spreadsheets that are more than 132 characters wide) in several ways. You can use a wide-carriage dot-matrix printer and 11-by-14-inch fanfold paper to print wide spreadsheets in draft mode or letter-quality print. Most wide-carriage printers can print about 300 characters across a sheet if you use condensed mode (17 characters per inch) and if the software supports this amount.

You can print wide or very wide (more than 300 characters across) spreadsheets sideways on a narrow carriage or wide-carriage dot-matrix printer. To print spreadsheets sideways, you must use a spreadsheet program that includes this feature, or you must purchase special software for sideways printing, such as Sideways from Frank Software. Examine the print quality of sideways printing before making a decision; sideways print quality normally is inferior to standard print quality.

If the required font is built into a laser printer or on a plug-in cartridge, laser printers can print spreadsheet data in landscape mode (across a page) as well as portrait mode (down a page). If you use 8 1/2-by-14-inch paper in a laser printer and print in landscape mode, you can print a spreadsheet across the 14-inch length of the page. With a font that prints at 17 characters per inch in landscape mode, you can fit more characters across a page than with a font that prints at 10 characters per inch. On the 14-inch page, at 17 characters per inch, you can fit more than 225 characters on a line.

Printing Forms

You can print forms, such as invoices, on any kind of printer. Two kinds of forms are available. You can use preprinted forms in a printer and print only the data (client name, products sold, amounts, and so on). Alternatively, you can create forms entirely on the printer. The printer prints the form from scratch, which includes the company logo, lines, shaded areas, and so forth. If a form is complicated, with many tiny characters and shaded areas, you need a laser printer to print a nice-looking form. For simpler form layouts, dot-matrix and inkjet printers are sufficient. If the software application you use does not enable you to print an entire form, special software (such as Formbase from Ventura Software for IBM and compatibles or Fast Forms from Power Up! for the Macintosh) is available for this task.

You must use a dot-matrix printer to print on multipart forms because dot-matrix printers form characters by impact, transferring the characters from carbon to carbon. When you purchase a dot-matrix printer for this purpose, ask how many copies it can print successfully.

Look for a printer that feeds forms from the bottom of the printer rather than one that rolls them around the printer's platen. Multipart forms fed from the bottom rather than around the platen are less likely to jam in the printer. Also, a blank form curled around the platen while the printer is stopped remains curled after you print the form. Check whether you can cut the form at the perforation without advancing the form past the printer's paper bail. If you advance a form to remove it, you may not be able to print on the next blank form. Some printers advance the form automatically to a place where you can tear it off and then retract the next form before printing on it.

You can print preprinted forms, such as checks, invoices, and so forth, on laser printers and other printers that accept only single sheets. In this case, you purchase the appropriate forms on single sheets rather than on fanfold sheets.

Printing Newsletters, Brochures, and Other High-Quality Documents

You should print newsletters, brochures, and other documents that demand high print quality on a laser printer. To create special typographical effects or to use large-sized fonts for headlines, you need a laser printer that uses the PostScript page description language or a PCL page description language laser printer with a PostScript add-in board. Printers with the PCL 5 page description language, namely the Hewlett-Packard LaserJet III series, perform almost as well as PostScript printers but do not have the wide support from application software enjoyed by PostScript printers.

If your needs are less demanding, you can use a PCL laser printer with an IBM or compatible computer, or a QuickDraw printer with a Macintosh (see "QuickDraw Page Printers" in this chapter).

With the advent of System 7.0 on the Macintosh and a font type manager called TrueType, many printers not previously capable of producing scalable fonts (characters at any size) can do so now. If you use Microsoft Windows, you can use a type manager program such as Adobe Type Manager to produce scalable fonts even on a dot-matrix printer. With a type manager, you can create typefaces and type styles that may not be built into your printer.

You can print newsletters with a dot-matrix printer, but print quality suffers. Although some dot-matrix printers print at 360 dots per inch, the printed page does not look as sharp and crisp as pages printed on a 300 dpi laser printer. The dot-matrix dots are thick, overlapping, and uneven.

If you find the initial cost of a laser printer too high, an inkjet printer may be an acceptable compromise. For example, Hewlett-Packard's DeskJet 500 and DeskWriter printers are inkjet printers that produce near-laser-quality output. The price range for inkjet printers falls between the prices of a dot-matrix printer and a laser printer.

Determining the Right Printer for Your Applications

Different personal computer applications use printers in different ways. To decide what kind of printer you need, consider the printer requirements of your software packages. The following sections break down applications by group and examine their typical printer requirements.

Spreadsheet Applications

Spreadsheets are composed almost entirely of columns of numbers. In most cases, spreadsheet programs have simple printer requirements. A simple font like Courier, dot-matrix draft print, or dot-matrix condensed print is often all you need. With condensed fonts, you can print many more numbers on a page than you can with standard-size fonts.

The print quality of a spreadsheet is not usually an issue. A good printout makes the rows and columns of numbers easy to read. Printing speed is not usually important, except when you print large spreadsheets or multiple copies. A 9- or 24-pin wide-carriage printer is best for basic spreadsheet printing.

Many spreadsheet programs now offer a feature called spreadsheet publishing. With this feature, you can combine numbers and text in a variety of fonts, and add graphs and images. A laser printer is best for black-and-white spreadsheet publishing. To print in color, consider a color inkjet printer.

Database Applications

Database applications have simple printing requirements. A wide-carriage 9-pin dot-matrix printer is sufficient for most database printing. Speed, however, is usually a concern: printing one sales invoice may not require great speed, but printing a large number of records does. The time needed to print a large mailing list varies noticeably with even small differences in printer speed. Compare your needs with the information given in Chapter 9 to see what speed printer you need.

If you link your database application to a program that creates forms, you need a laser printer for best results. Laser printers also are best for printing statistics from a database and publishing them in a newsletter.

To add pizzazz to your database reports, you may need more than your database application. You may need to move the information from your database to a spreadsheet (with spreadsheet publishing features), a word processor, a graphics program, or a desktop publishing program. For high-quality printouts from any of these sources, you need a laser printer.

Word Processing Applications

Word processors work with all types of printers. Almost any printer can make a printed page look as if it came from a typewriter. For school reports and some business correspondence, a 9-pin dot-matrix printer with near-letter-quality print is sufficient. For business letters and internal business reports, 24-pin dot-matrix, inkjet, thermal transfer, and PCL laser printers are best.

Today, some word processing programs have desktop publishing features that enable you to use a variety of fonts and to incorporate images into a word processing document. A PCL or PostScript laser printer is the recommended choice if you use your word processor in this way.

To print with proportional rather than monospaced (each letter takes up the same width of space) fonts, your printer must support the font you want to use. Most printers support proportional fonts, but some do a better job of this than others. Check the printer's output before you make a purchase. Keep in mind that many word processors for IBM and compatible computers do not support proportional fonts on-screen. Through special preview modes, the word processor approximates the correct spacing between letters. Ultimately, however, the spacing depends on which font the printer uses. If you intend to print with proportional fonts and want your screen display to match your printer output, look for WYSIWYG (what-you-see-is-what-you-get) word processors for IBM and compatible computers. Macintosh word processors show monospaced and proportional fonts on-screen.

Desktop Publishing Applications

Desktop publishing applications run the gamut from low-end packages that create single-page newsletters and fliers to high-end packages that satisfy almost any publishing need. The printer to choose depends on the desktop publishing application you use and the type of output you need. If you will do serious desktop publishing, you probably want to select a PostScript laser printer, because you can use this kind of printer to manipulate type and work with fonts of virtually any size. If you do not need these features or cannot afford the cost of a PostScript laser printer, desktop publishing programs work with other kinds of printers, too—for example, a dot-matrix printer with a high graphics resolution, such as 360 by 180, or a 300 dpi inkjet printer. The best solution might be an inexpensive laser printer such as Hewlett-Packard IIP, Hewlett-Packard IIIP, Okidata 400, or EPSON EPL 7000 for an IBM or compatible or a QuickDraw printer for the Mac.

Accounting Applications

Accounting applications have simple printing requirements. Accounting reports are usually for internal use, so print quality is not an issue. A 9-pin dot-matrix printer should meet most accounting needs. If you print long reports, look for a printer with speed and a tractor-feed mechanism. When printing yearly information, you may need a wide page. Consider a wide-carriage dot-matrix printer for this application.

Graphics and Drawing Applications

Popular graphics and drawing applications support all kinds of printers. For reliable, consistent, high-quality graphics printing, however, you should use a laser printer. Make sure that the laser printer you are considering has enough memory to print the kind of graphics you want to print. One to two megabytes of memory should be sufficient for most applications. For less stringent graphics printing, a dot-matrix or inkjet printer is sufficient. Check the resolution of the printer and look at some sample printouts before you make a purchase.

To print color graphics, choose a dot-matrix printer with color capability. Also make sure that your graphics or drawing program supports the printer and that four-color ribbons are easy to get. For better quality color printouts, consider a color inkjet printer. A color thermal transfer printer offers the best quality, but this kind of printer is much more expensive than the others, usually costing between $5,000 and $15,000.

Educational Applications

Many educational applications do not have a printing option, and most applications with printing options support only 9-pin dot-matrix printers. If you want to use a particular educational program with a 24-pin or laser printer, make sure that the software works with the printer.

Determining the Printer You Need

Deciding on a specific brand and model of printer can be a daunting task if you are not sure what kind of printer you want and what features you need. The preceding chapter and preceding sections should help you narrow your choices based on the kinds of printers available, printer features, required output, and the kinds of applications used. The following sections give you information about the manufacturers and price ranges of printers in specific categories.

9-Pin Dot-Matrix Printers

If you buy a low-end Apple Macintosh computer such as the Macintosh Classic and want to connect the computer to a dot-matrix printer, the Apple ImageWriter II is a logical choice. This 9-pin dot-matrix printer prints in black or in color and sells for around $450. A lower cost alternative is the Seikosha SP1000, which sells for about $225.

For IBM and compatible computers, you have a large selection of 9-pin dot-matrix printers. EPSON, once the recognized leader in this category, now has stiff competition. If you want an inexpensive 9-pin printer, the EPSON LX810, Panasonic KX-P1180, and Star Micronics NX-1000 Multifont II are all good choices that sell for less than $200. If you want more features than these models have, more sophisticated 9-pin printers (which can cost several hundred dollars more) are available from these and other companies.

24-Pin Dot-Matrix Printers

The leading low-cost 24-pin dot-matrix printers are the EPSON LQ-510 and Panasonic KX-P1124, either of which you can purchase for less than $300. If these models do not satisfy your need for speed, paper handling, ruggedness, and other features, you can choose among other models in these company's lines as well as among fine 24-pin printers from companies such as IBM, Okidata, Toshiba, and NEC. Keep in mind that many reputable companies manufacture 24-pin dot-matrix printers. If a printer has the features you are looking for at the right price, and the print quality is top-notch, you are likely to be happy with your purchase.

Inkjet Printers

If you want an inkjet printer, you have only a few models from which to choose. For IBM and compatible computers, the Hewlett-Packard DeskJet 500 and Canon BJ-130 are the popular models. These two printers cost approximately $800 and $1,100, respectively. The Hewlett-Packard DeskWriter and Apple StyleWriter are the choices for Macintosh computers. The former costs approximately $1,000, and the latter is priced aggressively at $599. An advantage of the StyleWriter is its capability to use TrueType outline fonts, even if you do not use the Macintosh System 7 operating system.

The Canon BJ-10e and Kodak Diconix 150 Plus are portable inkjet printers for IBM and compatible computers. The Diconix 150M Plus is a portable inkjet printer for the Macintosh. These printers range in price from about $400 to $600.

PCL Laser Printers

COMPARISON

Hewlett-Packard created the standards for laser printing for IBM and compatible computers. HP still sets the standards with its newest model, the LaserJet Series III, which retails for approximately $2,400. This model features variable-sized dots and scalable fonts. Depending on your needs and the amount of money you can spend, you can choose the IIID (for double-sided printing) or the IIIP (for personal printing). The IIIP is half as fast as the III but retails for only $1,595.

Laser printers for IBM and compatible computers also are available from many other companies. Almost all these models are PCL printers, which means that they are compatible with Hewlett-Packard LaserJet Series II printers. You may want to wait to buy this kind of printer until newer models appear with LaserJet Series III compatibility.

For standard business applications, a PCL laser printer does the job just as well as a PostScript printer. If cost is an issue, note that some PostScript laser printers cost two to three times the amount of a PCL printer.

PostScript Laser Printers

COMPARISON

The standard-setting PostScript laser printer is the Apple LaserWriter II NTX. Advertised prices for this model are approximately $4,500. Many competitors, however, are selling true Adobe PostScript laser printers (such as the Texas Instruments MicroLaser 35) and compatible PostScript printers. Prices for these printers are in the $2,000 to $3,000 price range. The best choice among these models depends on the features you want and the price you are willing to pay.

If you want PostScript capability but cannot afford a PostScript printer, you have some alternatives. You can add PostScript to many PCL printers by installing a circuit board inside the printer or by plugging in a cartridge. If this option appeals to you, make sure that the PCL printer you are considering can be expanded by one of these methods. Another alternative is to buy a software program that enables your printer to work like a PostScript printer; for example, GoScript from LaserGo, Inc., translates PostScript files and prints them on a printer. (A software solution also can give PostScript compatibility to other types of printers, such as dot matrix or inkjet.)

These alternatives differ in performance and cost, with the add-in card offering the best performance at the highest cost. For example, the retail price of a QMS PS810 PostScript printer is $3,995. This printer is not only PostScript but is also compatible with the Hewlett-Packard LaserJet II. If you equip a Hewlett-Packard LaserJet III with a PostScript cartridge, an extra 1M of memory, and an AppleTalk interface card to attach the printer to a Macintosh, the retail price is $3,595, a savings of $400.

Not all application programs work with PCL or PostScript printers. If you use a particular application program, be sure that the program supports the PCL or PostScript printer you are considering before you purchase the printer.

QuickDraw Page Printers

Some page printers designed to work with Apple Macintosh computers use the QuickDraw program built into the Apple Macintosh ROM rather than a page description language. QuickDraw printers are designed for individuals who own Macintosh computers but do not need the power of or cannot afford a PostScript laser printer. Keep in mind that QuickDraw laser printers are designed for Macintosh computers, whereas PCL printers are designed for use with IBM and compatible computers.

The Apple Personal LaserWriter SC and GCC PLP IIS are two good choices in this category. Each of these printers sells for less than $2,000.

Color Printers

Color printers are available at prices from $350 to more than $10,000, depending on the technology. Dot-matrix color printers are the least expensive. Almost all dot-matrix printer manufacturers have color models.

The most popular inkjet models are the Hewlett-Packard PaintJet for IBM and compatible computers and the PaintWriter for Macintosh computers. Retail prices for these printers are about $1,400. Kodak Diconix also sells a model called the Color 4 that can be used with Macintosh and IBM and compatible computers. This printer retails for about $1,500.

Because of their advanced technology, thermal transfer color printers have the best output, but they cost significantly more than the rest. Two good choices are the Tektronix Phaser PX and the QMS ColorScript 100. Color thermal transfer printers range from about $5,000 to $15,000.

Chapter Summary

This chapter describes how your required output—internal reports, letters, papers, banners, wide spreadsheets, forms, newsletters, or brochures—affects the kind of printer you should consider. The chapter then shows you which kinds of printers are best for applications such as spreadsheets, databases, word processors, desktop publishing, accounting, graphics, drawing, and education. Finally, the chapter recommends specific printer models in each printer category.

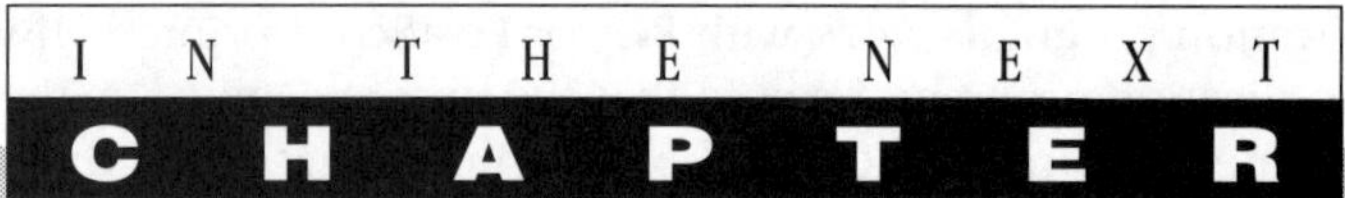

The next chapter lists printers you may want to consider for purchase. It also includes information that explains the entries in the list.

CHAPTER NINE

Listing of Printers

No doubt, in your desk or in your pencil holder, you have a variety of writing instruments. Perhaps you have your Number 2 pencil, which you use for much of your work, knowing that this pencil is inexpensive and gives you flexibility. You also keep your old, trusty ballpoint pen, which also is flexible. The ballpoint, however, is a bit more permanent than the pencil; and the ink commands more attention than pencil lead does. Finally, for special documents, you keep your roller-ball pen. This pen flows across the paper nicely and makes your words look smoother than does either the ballpoint pen or your old faithful Number 2 pencil. Of course, with each increment of writing device, the cost increases. But the cost of each is worthwhile because different results are necessary.

Choosing to use one of your writing instruments takes much the same kind of forethought as choosing a printer requires. Will you need an old Number 2 pencil, analogous to a dot-matrix printer? Will you go with the ballpoint pen, typical of an inkjet printer? Or do you require the elegance of a laser printer, compared to the smooth-flowing roller-ball pen?

This chapter contains three tables, which give you specifications on a variety of printers. Table 9.1 provides many specifications of dot-matrix printers. Table 9.2 gives you much of what you need to know to select an inkjet printer. Finally, table 9.3 informs you about specifications of different laser printers. Each table is preceded by text that explains the contents and organization of that table.

Dot-Matrix Printer Listing

Dot-matrix printers are good all-around printers. Their uses range from printing mailing labels, to printing multiple-part forms, to printing correspondence. To help you make a good choice, table 9.1 includes specifications for more than 60 different dot-matrix printers. The printers are sorted according to the number of pins found in the print head and then by manufacturer.

Looking at the table, you first see the manufacturer, model, and number of print head pins for a given printer. Next are the print speeds of the printer, both draft speed and letter-quality speed, expressed in characters per second (cps). Some printers, however, are fast enough to measure in lines per minute (lpm). The next column shows the number of built-in fonts from which you can select. Because dot-matrix printers are often used for printing graphics, *GRAPHICS RESOLUTION* is shown in dots per inch (dpi). The greater the number of dots per inch, the denser the print and the better quality the graphics will be. Many printers are capable of custom configuration by means of buttons on the front panel. So the column *FRONT PANEL CONFIG* lets you see which printers have this capability. The *PAPER FEED* column shows you what types of paper the printer can use. Most dot-matrix printers have tractors for continuous-feed paper. Many printers have a platen for friction-feeding single sheets of paper. And a few dot-matrix printers have cut-sheet feeders that enable you to place a stack of paper (letterhead, for example) in a bin and feed each sheet when necessary.

For compatibility reasons, many printers emulate, or act like, other printers; the *EMULATION* column shows which printers each model emulates. The *ADD-ON FONTS* column shows you whether you can get additional fonts besides the built-in fonts. Sometimes, you may want to use wide, 11-by-14-inch, paper instead of the standard 8 1/2-by-11-inch paper. The *PAPER SIZE* column shows which printers accommodate wide paper. The *PORTS* column indicates how the printer attaches to your computer. The last two columns give the retail price of the printer and other information that may help you select the best dot-matrix printer for you.

Table 9.1. List of Dot-Matrix Printers Sorted by Number of Pins and Company

COMPANY	MODEL	PINS	DRAFT SPEED (cps)	LQ SPEED (cps)	NUMBER FONTS	GRAPHICS RESOLUTION (dpi)	FRONT PANEL CONFIG	PAPER FEED
Apple Computer	ImageWriter II	9	250	45	1 plus var width	72 to 160	No	Tractor, sheet, friction
Citizen	200GX	9	213	40	3 LQ/2 draft	240 x 216	Yes	Tractor (push, pull), friction
Citizen	200GX 15	9	213	40	3 NLQ/2 draft	240 x 216	Yes	Tractor (push, pull), friction
Citizen	HSP-500	9	300	66	2 NLQ/2 draft	240 x 216	No	Tractor (push, pull), friction
Citizen	HSP-550	9	300	66	2 NLQ/2 draft	240 x 216	No	Tractor (push, pull), friction
Data Products	9030	9	300	50	2	60/120/240 x 72	No	Cut sheet, tractor (push, pull)
Data Products	9040	9	300	50	2	60/120/240 x 72	No	Cut sheet, tractor (push, pull)
Datasouth	XL 300	9	300	62	6 std/ 2 opt	240 x 216	Yes	Tractor (pull)
Datasouth	XL 300 DD	9	300	62	6 std/ 2 opt	240 x 216	Yes	Tractor (push)
EPSON	DFX-8000	9	1066	160	4	240 x 216	No	Tractor (push)
EPSON	FX-1050	9	220	45	3	240 x 216	Yes	Tractor, sheet, friction
EPSON	FX-850	9	220	45	3	240 x 216	Yes	Tractor, sheet, friction
EPSON	LX-810	9	200	25	3	240 x 216	Yes	Tractor, sheet, friction
IBM	IBM 4226 Model 302	9	533	533	4	240 x 72	Yes	Tractor
IBM	IBM Personal Printer Series II/2380	9	320	65	4	144 x 240	Yes	Tractor, sheet, friction
IBM	IBM Personal Printer Series II/2381	9	320	65	4	144 x 240	Yes	Tractor, sheet, friction
NCR	NCR 6421	9	250	60		240 x 72	No	Cut sheet, tractor (push, pull)
Panasonic Office Automation	KX-P1180	9	160	32	4	240 x 216	Yes	Tractor (push, pull)
Data Products	8070 Plus	18	480	300	2	70/140/82.5/165 x 82.5	No	Cut sheet, bidirectional tractor
Data Products	8500	18	520	133	2	240 x 72	No	Tractor, friction, cut sheet

EMULATION	ADD-ON FONTS	PAPER SIZE	PORTS	WARRANTY (years)	RETAIL PRICE	OTHER INFORMATION
		Standard	Serial	1	$595.00	Color cap, 4-carbon-copy cap
Citizen 200GX, EPSON FX, IBM ProPrinter	No	Standard,	Parallel, serial	2	$299.00	Color & other options available
Citizen 200GX, EPSON FX, IBM ProPrinter	No	Standard, wide	Parallel, serial	2	$499.00	Color & other options available
Citizen HSP, EPSON FX, IBM ProPrinter	No	Standard	Parallel, serial	2	$499.00	Color & other options available
Citizen HSP, EPSON FX, IBM ProPrinter	No	Standard, wide	Parallel, serial	2	$699.00	Color & other options available
IBM ProPrinter, EPSON FX86e, FX286e	Yes	Standard	Parallel, serial	1	$748.00	Other options available
IBM ProPrinter, EPSON FX86e, FX286e	Yes	Standard	Parallel, serial	1	$899.00	Color & other options available
EPSON FX, DEC LAIZO, Datasouth 180	No	Standard, wide	Parallel, serial, opt TX, CX	1		Bar code & other options available
EPSON Fx, DEC LAIXO, Datasouth 180	No	Standard, wide	Parallel, serial, opt TX, CX	1		Bar code & other options available
IBM ProPrinter XL		Standard, wide	Parallel, serial	1	$3,699.00	Other options available
		Standard, wide	Parallel	1	$799.00	Other options available
		Standard, wide	Parallel	1	$549.00	Other options available
		Standard, wide	Parallel	1		Other options available
IBM 4202 ProPrinter, EPSON DFX-5000	No	Standard, wide	Parallel, serial	1	$2,295.00	Other options available
IBM ProPrinter 4201, 4202, EPSON FX 850, 1050	No	Standard	Parallel, opt serial	1	$499.00	Multi-paper path, other options available
IBM ProPrinter 4201, 4202, EPSON FX 850, 1050	No	Standard, wide	Parallel, opt serial	1	$699.00	Multi-paper path, other options available
IBM ProPrinter, EPSON FX86e, EPSON FX286e, C.Itoh 8510, 1550	No	Standard, wide	Parallel, serial	1		Multi-paper path, other options available
EPSON FX 86c, IBM ProPrinter II		Standard, wide	Parallel, opt serial	2	$269.95	Other options available
IBM Color, IBM Graphics, Dataproducts P-series	No	Standard	Parallel, serial	1	$1,795.00	Color standard
EPSON FX-1050, IBM ProPrinter LIXL		Standard, wide	Parallel, serial	1	$2,195.00	Cut sht feed & other options available

continues

Table 9.1. Continued

COMPANY	MODEL	PINS	DRAFT SPEED (cps)	LQ SPEED (cps)	NUMBER FONTS	GRAPHICS RESOLUTION (dpi)	FRONT PANEL CONFIG	PAPER FEED
Datasouth	Performax A600	18	622	117	13	60/72/80/90/120/ 240 x 72/216	Yes	Tractor, cut sheet
Datasouth	XL 400	18	400	120	6 std/ 2 opt	240 x 216	Yes	Tractor
Citizen	GSX-130	24	180	60	4 LQ/1 draft	360 x 360	Yes	Tractor (push, pull), friction
Citizen	GSX-140 PLUS	24	220	72	6 LQ/2 draft	360 x 360	Yes	Tractor (push, pull), friction
Citizen	GSX-145	24	192	64	4 LQ/2 draft	360 x 360	Yes	Tractor (push, pull), friction
Data Products	9034	24	300	83	2	60/80/90/120/180/ 240/360 x 180	No	Cut sheet, tractor (push)
Data Products	9044	24	300	83	2	60/80/90/120/180/ 240/360 x 180	No	Cut sheet, tractor (push, pull)
EPSON	LQ-1010	24	150	50	5	360 x 360	Yes	Tractor, sheet, friction
EPSON	LQ-1050	24	300	82	11 LQ/1 draft	360 x 360	Yes	Tractor, sheet, friction + auto single
EPSON	LQ-200	24	160	53	7	360 x 180	Yes	Tractor, sheet, friction
EPSON	LQ-2550	24	333	111	7	360 x 360	Yes	Tractor, sheet, friction
EPSON	LQ-510	24	160	53		360 x 360	No	Tractor, sheet, friction
EPSON	LQ-850	24	300	82	11 LQ/1 draft	360 x 360	Yes	Tractor, sheet, friction+auto single
EPSON	LQ-860	24	300	82	4	360 x 360	Yes	Tractor, sheet, friction
GCC Technologies	Write Impact	24	192		22	360 x 180	No	Tractor, sheet, friction
Hewlett-Packard	HP Rugged Writer 480	24	480	240	3	PCL to 180 x 180, EPSON to 360 x 180	Yes	Tractor, cut sheet, friction
IBM	4207-002 ProPrinter X24E	24	240	80	4	60/120/180/240/ 360 x 180	Yes	Tractor, sheet, friction
IBM	4208-002 ProPrinter XL24E	24	240	80	4	60/120/180/240/ 360 x 180	Yes	Tractor, sheet
IBM	4212-001 ProPrinter 24P	24	160	53	7	360 x 180	Yes	Tractor, sheet, friction
IBM	5204-1	24	330	55	8	360 x 180	Yes	Friction

EMULATION	ADD-ON FONTS	PAPER SIZE	PORTS	WARRANTY (years)	RETAIL PRICE	OTHER INFORMATION
EPSON FX, DEC LAIZO, IBM Graphics Printer, IBM ProPrinter	No	Standard, wide	Parallel, serial, opt TX, CX	1		Print bar codes, other options available
IBM ProPrinter, EPSON FX, DEC LAIZO	No	Standard, wide	Parallel, serial, opt TX, CX	1		Print bar codes, other options available
Citizen GSX, EPSON LQ, IBM ProPrinter X24	No	Standard	Parallel, serial	2	$399.00	Color & other options available
Citizen GSX, EPSON LQ, IBM ProPrinter XL24	No	Standard	Parallel, serial	2	$499.00	Color & other options available
Citizen GSX, EPSON LQ, IBM ProPrinter XL24	No	Standard, wide	Parallel, serial	2	$649.00	Color & other options available
EPSON LQ800, LQ 1000, Diablo 630	Yes	Standard	Parallel, serial	1	$899.00	
EPSON LQ800, LQ1000, Diablo 630	Yes	Standard	Parallel, serial	1	$1,099.00	Color & other options available
		Standard, wide	Parallel, opt serial	1	$699.00	Other options available
		Standard	Parallel, serial	2	$1,099.00	Other options available
		Standard	Parallel	2	$399.00	Other options available
		Standard, wide	Parallel, serial	2		Other options available
		Standard, wide	Parallel	2	$499.00	Other options available
		Standard	Parallel, serial	2	$749.00	Other options available
		Standard, wide	Parallel, serial	1	$949.00	Color cap, other options available
	No	Standard	Serial	1	$699.00	Other options available
EPSON Esc, P (LQ-1000, LQ-1500)	Yes	Standard, wide	Parallel, serial, HP IB	1		Other options available
IBM ProPrinter	No	Standard	Parallel, opt serial	1	$859.00	Other options available
IBM ProPrinter	No	Standard, wide	Parallel, opt serial	1	$1,099.00	Other options available
IBM ProPrinter	No	Standard	Parallel	1	$499.00	Other options available
IBM ProPrinter & IBM QuietWriter III	Yes	Standard, wide	Parallel, serial	1	$1,765.00	Other options available

continues

Table 9.1. Continued

COMPANY	MODEL	PINS	DRAFT SPEED (cps)	LQ SPEED (cps)	NUMBER FONTS	GRAPHICS RESOLUTION (dpi)	FRONT PANEL CONFIG	PAPER FEED
NEC	P9300 Pinwriter	24	400	111	8	360 x 360	Yes	Tractor
NEC	Pinwriter P3200	24	216	60	7	360 x 360	Yes	Tractor
NEC	Pinwriter 6200	24	300	83	8	360 x 360	Yes	Tractor
NEC	Pinwriter 6300	24	300	83	8	360 x 360	Yes	Tractor
NEC	Pinwriter P3300	24	216	60	7	360 x 360	Yes	Tractor
NEC	Pinwriter P5200	24	265	75	7	360 x 360	Yes	Tractor
NEC	Pinwriter P5300	24	265	75	7	360 x 360	Yes	Tractor
Panasonic Office Automation	KX-P1123	24	160	53	4	360 x 360	Yes	Tractor (push, pull)
Panasonic Office Automation	KX-P1124i	24	250	83	7/1 SLQ	360 x 360	Yes	Tractor (push, pull)
Panasonic Office Automation	KX-P1624	24	160	53	5	360 x 360	Yes	Tractor (push, pull)
Panasonic Office Automation	KX-P1654	24	250	83	8	360 x 360	Yes	Tractor (push, pull)
Panasonic Office Automation	KX-P1695	24	275	55	6	240 x 216	Yes	Tractor (push, pull)
Tandy	DMP 2103	24	225	90	7	360 x 360	No	Tractor, sheet, friction
Tandy	DMP 2130	24	480	66	6	240 x 216	No	Tractor, sheet, friction
Tandy	DMP 240	24	192	64	6	360 x 360	No	Tractor, sheet, friction
Tandy	DMP 302	24	270	75	7	360 x 360	No	Tractor, sheet, friction
Toshiba America Information Systems	ExpressWriter 420	24	240	80	7	180 x 180, 180 x 360	Yes	Tractor, sheet, friction
Toshiba America Information Systems	ExpressWriter 440	24	240	80	7	180 x 180, 180 x 360	Yes	Tractor, sheet, friction
IBM	5202-001 QuietWriter III	40	160	80	4	60/72/120/240/60 x 60, 120 x 120, 240 x 240	Yes	Friction
Data Products	LX Series		600 lpm	220 lpm		120 x 144	No	Tractor

EMULATION	ADD-ON FONTS	PAPER SIZE	PORTS	WARRANTY (years)	RETAIL PRICE	OTHER INFORMATION
NEC Pinwriter, EPSON LQ	Yes	Standard, wide	Parallel, opt serial	1	$1,395.00	Other options available
EPSON LQ	Yes	Standard, wide	Parallel, opt serial	1	$429.00	Auto paper load, park, other options available
NEC Pinwriter, EPSON LQ	8 types	Standard, wide	Parallel, opt serial	1	$749.00	Cut sht feed & other options available
NEC Pinwriter, EPSON LQ	8 types	Standard, wide	Parallel, opt serial	1	$999.00	Cut sht feed & other options available
EPSON LQ	Yes	Standard, wide	Parallel, opt serial	1	$599.00	Auto paper load, park, other options available
EPSON LQ	Yes	Standard, wide	Parallel, opt serial	1	$729.00	Other options available
EPSON LQ	Yes	Standard, wide	Parallel, opt serial	1	$899.00	Other options available
EPSON LQ-850, IBM ProPrinter X24		Standard, wide	Parallel, opt serial	2	$399.95	Other options available
EPSON LQ-850, IBM ProPrinter X24		Standard, wide	Parallel, opt serial	2	$499.95	Other options available
EPSON LQ 2500, IBM ProPrinter X24		Standard, wide	Parallel, opt serial	2	$649.95	Other options available
IBM XL24E, EPSON LQ-1050		Standard, wide	Parallel, serial	2	$949.95	Other options available
IBM ProPrinter IIXL, EPSON FX-1050		Standard, wide	Parallel	2	$699.95	Other options available
IBM ProPrinter XL24, EPSON LQ-1050	No	Standard, wide	Parallel	1	$899.00	Other options available
IBM ProPrinter XL, EPSON FX 286e	No	Standard, wide	Parallel	1	$1,199.00	Other options available
IBM ProPrinter X24, EPSON LQ-500, 850, EPSON LQ2500	No	Standard	Parallel	1	$549.95	Other options available
IBM ProPrinter X24, EPSON LQ-850	No	Standard	Parallel	1	$599.00	Other options available
IBM ProPrinter X24, EPSON LQ 850	No	Standard	Parallel, serial	2		4-part forms, other options available
IBM ProPrinter XL24 & EPSON LQ 1050	No	Standard, wide	Parallel, serial	2		4-part forms,other options available
IBM ProPrinter	Yes	Standard, wide	Parallel	3 mos	$1,815.00	Other options available
Dataproducts LB Series, Printronix P Series		Standard, wide, multi-part form	Parallel, serial	1	$4,395.00	Demand doc options, 0 tear form-saving

continues

Table 9.1. Concluded

COMPANY	MODEL	PINS	DRAFT SPEED (cps)	LQ SPEED (cps)	NUMBER FONTS	GRAPHICS RESOLUTION (dpi)	FRONT PANEL CONFIG	PAPER FEED
NCR	NCR 6450-0101 Shuttle Matrix Line Printer	shuttle	240 lpm	65 lpm		180/ 240 x 72	Yes	Forward, backward
NCR	NCR 6450-0201 Shuttle Matrix Line Printer	shuttle	480 lpm	130 lpm		180/ 240 x 72	Yes	Forward, backward

EMULATION	ADD-ON FONTS	PAPER SIZE	PORTS	WARRANTY (years)	RETAIL PRICE	OTHER INFORMATION
Resident Printronix P-series	No	Standard, wide	Parallel, serial	1		Other options available
Resident Printronix P-series	No	Standard, wide	Parallel, serial	1		Other options available

Inkjet Printer Listing

Inkjet printers often serve a useful purpose; they give you near laser-quality printing, but often they are small or even portable, and less expensive than laser printers. Table 9.2 gives you the specifications of several different inkjet printers.

Table 9.2 has been sorted by computer compatibility and then by manufacturer. Computer compatibility, represented by the tenth column of the table, *IBM/MAC COMPATIBLE*, tells you whether the printer is designed to operate with an IBM-compatible computer, a Macintosh computer, or both. The first two columns list the manufacturer and the model of the inkjet printer being described. Next is the resolution of the printer. The greater the number of dots per inch shown, the greater the resolution. The next two columns list the speed of the printer in characters per second when printing in draft mode and letter-quality mode. Because of the fast speed of some printers, their speed is expressed in pages per minute (ppm) rather than characters per second. The next column displays the number of built-in fonts that the printer has. *FRONT PANEL CONFIG* shows you whether you can customize the printer by means of buttons on the front or top of the printer. *PAPER FEED* tells you what type of paper the printer supports, for example, continuous-feed paper or cut-sheet paper.

Because most printers emulate the most popular printers, the ninth column shows you which printers each inkjet printer emulates. Some printers support additional fonts by adding them to the printer. The column *FONT CARTRIDGE SUPPORT* gives this information. *PAPER SIZE* specifies the different sizes of paper you can use with a printer, and *PORTS* tells you how the printer attaches to the computer. Because printing is done by spraying ink onto the page, if you do much printing you will have to replace the ink cartridge. The fourteenth column lets you know how long you can expect an ink cartridge to last. This rating is generally based on printing 10 pica characters per inch on an 8 1/2-by-11-inch piece of paper, 60 lines of 65 characters per line. The final three columns show the warranty of each printer, the retail price, and other information that may help you select the best inkjet printer for you.

Table 9.2. Listing of Inkjet Printers Sorted by Computer Compatibility and Company

COMPANY	MODEL	RESOLUTION (dpi)	DRAFT SPEED (cps)	LQ SPEED (cps)	INTERNAL FONTS	FRONT PANEL CONFIG	PAPER FEED	EMULATION
Canon	Canon BJ-10e	360	83	83	2		Friction	IBM ProPrinter X24E, Canon BJ 130e
Eastman Kodak Company	KODAK Diconix 150 Plus	192 x 192	180	52	2	Yes	Tractor, friction	EPSON 80/85, IBM ProPrinter
Hewlett-Packard	HP DeskJet 500	300	3 ppm	120	4	Yes	Cut sheet	EPSON FX-80, IBM ProPrinter III
Hewlett-Packard	HP PaintJet	180		1/4 ppm	3	No	Tractor, friction, cut sheet	
Hewlett-Packard	HP PaintJet XL	300		3/4 ppm	3	Yes	Cut sheet	
IBM	4072 ExecJet	360 x 360	600	150	18	Yes	Tractor, friction, sheet	IBM ProPrinter XL 24E, EPSON LQ1050, IBM
Sharp Electronics	JX-730 Color	180	70				Friction	
Canon	Canon BJ-300	360	300	150	2	No	Tractor, friction	IBM ProPrinter X-24e, EPSON LQ-850
Canon	Canon BJ-330	360	300	150	3	No	Tractor, friction	IBM ProPrinter XL24e, EPSON LQ1050
Eastman Kodak Company	KODAK Diconix Color 4	192 x 192	125	28	3	Yes	Tractor, cut sheet	HP PaintJet
Tektronix, Inc.	ColorQuick 4697SI	216	1 ppm	1/2 ppm	1	Yes	Friction, cut sheet	Tek 4696
Tektronix, Inc.	Phaser Jet PXi 4698PXi	300	1 ppm	1/2 ppm	39	Yes	Friction, cut sheet	PostScript Level 2, HP-GL
Apple Computer	Apple Stylewriter	360	1 ppm	1/2 ppm	4		Detachable cut sheet	
GCC Technologies	Write Move	192 x 192	Varies		22	No	Tractor, friction, sheet	
Hewlett-Packard	HP Deskwriter	300	2 ppm	1 ppm	4	No	Cut sheet	
Hewlett-Packard	HP PaintWriter	180		1/4 ppm	4	No	Tractor, friction, cut sheet	
Hewlett-Packard	HP PaintWriter XL	180		3/4 ppm	4	No	Tractor, friction, cut sheet	

IBM/MAC COMPATIBLE	FONT CARTRIDGE SUPPORT	PAPER SIZE	PORTS	INK CARTRIDGE LIFE	WARRANTY (years)	RETAIL PRICE	OTHER INFORMATION
IBM	No	Std, lgl, trans, A4	Parallel	700K char	1	$499.00	Options cut-sheet feeder
IBM	No	Std	Parallel, serial optional	500 pgs	1	$519.00	3.75 lbs with batt
IBM	Yes	Std, lgl	Parallel, serial	500K char	3		Other options available
IBM	Yes	Std	Parallel, serial, HP-IB	1,100K char	1		Other options available
IBM	Yes	Std, wide	Parallel, serial, HP-IB	1,100K char	1		Other options available
IBM	Yes	Std, wide, lgl	Parallel, serial opt	2,000K char	1	$1,099.00	64 jets
IBM		Std, wide	Parallel		1	$2,195.00	4 ink clr, 7 prt clr, 48 jets, replace depleted colors
IBM (Mac optional)	Yes	Std, lgl, trans, A4	Parallel, serial optional	1,000K char	1	&799.00	Options cut-sheet feeder
IBM (Mac optional)	Yes	Std, lgl, trans, A4	Parallel, serial optional	1,000K char	1	$940.00	Options cut-sheet feeder
IBM, Mac	Yes	Std	Parallel, serial optional	500 pgs	1	$1,495.00 IBM, $1,595.00 Mac	
IBM, Mac	Soft fonts	Roll paper, trans 11"	Parallel, SCSI	120 pgs	90 days on-site	$2,495.00	TekColor Color Match for Mac, tractor options
IBM, Mac	Soft fonts	Std, trans	Parallel, serial, AppleTalk	200 pgs	1	$9,995.00	TekColor Color Match for Mac
Mac	Yes	Std, lgl, trans, A4	Serial	500 pgs	1	$599.00	Acc kit, software bundles
Mac	No	Std	Serial	400 pgs	1	$399.00	
Mac	Soft fonts	Std, lgl	Serial, AppleTalk	500K char	1		Other options available
Mac	Soft fonts	Std	Serial	1,100K char	1		Other options available
Mac	Soft fonts	Std, wide	Serial, AppleTalk	1,100K char	1		Other options available

9

Laser Printer Listing

Like that wonderful-to-use roller-ball pen that makes your writing look superb, a laser printer provides both high-quality printing and speed. If you need a laser printer, scan the listings in table 9.3.

As you look through table 9.3, you will find more than 70 printers listed by order of computer compatibility and manufacturer. Printers that work with IBM-compatible computers are listed first, followed by printers that work with both IBM-compatible and Macintosh computers, and then printers that work with only Macintosh computers. You first see the manufacturer of each laser printer, followed by the model of the printer. Next, you see the resolution of the printing expressed in dots per inch. Most laser printers print at least 300 dpi, and some have even greater resolutions. Expect the price to rise with resolution.

The next two columns show you information about the printer's engine, such as who makes it, what type it is, and how much printing you can expect out of the engine before service is needed. The *TYPE* is included because some printers use different technology, such as LED rather than laser. The *ENGINE LIFE* is expressed in number of pages. The *PRINT SPEED* tells you the number of pages per minute that printer can output. This rating is based on the built-in Courier font and is given simply as a reference point. Most laser printers come with multiple typefaces created in different manners. The *TYPEFACES, FONTS* column shows the number of built-in typefaces and indicates how the fonts are created.

Before a page is printed, it must be built in the printer's RAM. The more complicated a page is, the more RAM is required. So the eighth column tells you how much RAM comes with the printer and the maximum to which you can expand the printer's RAM. The most common printer languages are PCL and PostScript, but other languages exist. The *PRINTER LANGUAGE* column shows you which language each printer supports. As with other classes of printers, laser printers emulate some of the most popular printers. The *EMULATION* column shows you which popular printer each model emulates. Laser printers generally print on 8 1/2-by-11-inch paper, which is loaded into a paper tray that accompanies the printer. Because different sizes of paper are available, legal, for example, you may want to purchase additional trays. The tray that comes with the printer may hold only a small number of pages, while added trays hold larger amounts of paper. The twelfth column shows you how much paper the original tray holds and whether additional trays are available. Laser printers, like copiers, use toner to make images on the paper. Some printers use a specially designed toner cartridge, while others are made so that you pour toner into the printer. The next two columns tell you how toner is replenished in the printer, how many pages can generally be printed before replacing toner, and how much the toner replacement costs. The last three columns show the warranty of each printer, the retail cost, and other information you may need to know about a printer before making a decision.

Table 9.3. Laser Printer Listings Sorted by Computer Compatibility and by Company

COMPANY	MODEL	RESOLUTION (dpi)	ENGINE MAKER, TYPE	ENGINE LIFE (pgs)	PRINT SPEED (ppm)	TYPEFACES, FONTS	RAM MIN, MAX (bytes)	PRINTER LANGUAGE
Eastman Kodak	KODAK EKTAPLUS 7008	300	TEC, Laser	Infinite	8	14 Bit map	1.5M, 2.5M	PCL4, HP-GL
EPSON	EPL-7000	300	Minolta, Laser	180,000	6	14 Bit map	512K, 6M	PCL4
IBM	3812-002 PagePrinter	240	IBM, LED		12	62 Bit map	1M	
IBM	3816-01D Duplex	240	IBM, LED		24		4.5M	Other
IBM	3816-01S Single Side	240	IBM, LED		24		3.5M	Other
IBM	4019-001 LaserPrinter	300	IBM, Laser		10	4 Bit map	512K, 4M	PCL4, PostScript optional
IBM	4019-E2 LaserPrinter	300	IBM, Laser		5	4 Bit map	512K, 4M	PCL4, PostScript optional
NCR	6436-301	300	IBM, Laser	1,500,000	15	36 Scalable	2M, 4M	
Packard Bell	PB 9815	300	Laser		8	8 Bit map	1.5M, 4.5M	
Panasonic Office Automation	KX-P4420	300	Panasonic, Laser	180,000	8	22 Bit map	512K, 4.5M	
Panasonic Office Automation	KX-P4450i	300	Panasonic, Laser	300,000	11	28 Bit map	512K, 4.5M	
Sharp Electronics	JX-9500 PostScript printer	300	Laser		6	35 PostScript		PostScript
Tandy	Tandy LP950	300	Sharp, Laser	200,000	6	6 Bit map	512K, 2M	PCL4
Abaton	LaserScript LX	300	TEC, Laser	300,000	6	35 Bitstream, 24 Bit map	2.5M, 4.5M	PCL4, PostScript
Apple Computer	LaserWriter IINT	300	Canon, Laser		8	11 PostScript	2M	PostScript
Apple Computer	LaserWriter IINTX	300	Canon, Laser		8	35 PostScript	2M, 12M	PostScript
Apple Computer	Personal LaserWriter NT	300	Canon, Laser	150,000	4	37 PostScript	2M	PostScript
Canon	Canon LBP-4	300	Canon, Laser	Indefinite	4	9 Scalable	512K, 2M	Proprietary
Canon	Canon LBP8 Mark III	300	Canon, Laser	Indefinite	8	9 Scalable	1.5M	Proprietary
Canon	Canon LBP8 Mark III R	300	Canon, Laser	Indefinite	8	9 Scalable	1.5M	Proprietary

9

IBM, MAC COMP	EMULATION	PAPER CAP (pgs), OPT TRAY	TONER	TONER LIFE (pgs), COST	WARRANTY (years)	RETAIL PRICE	OTHER INFORMATION
IBM	HP LaserJet IIP, HP 7475A plotter	200, No	Separate toner, drum	1,500, $29	1	$2,095.00	
IBM	EPSON FX, LQ	250, Yes	Toner cartridge	6,000, $175	2	$1,399.00	Can support 2 users
IBM	IBM Graphics Printer	500, Yes	Toner cartridge	16,500, $48	3 months	$10,790.00	Optional printer-sharing card
IBM	IBM QuietWriter III, 5202	500, Yes	Toner cartridge	18,000, $49	3 months	$23,470.00	
IBM	IBM QuietWriter III, 5202	500, Yes	Toner cartridge	18,000	3 months	$18,010.00	
IBM	IBM ProPrinter, HP LaserJet II, IBM, HP Plotters	200, Yes	Toner cartridge	10,000	1	$2,395.00	Includes automatic emulation switching
IBM	IBM ProPrinter, HP LaserJet II, IBM, HP Plotters	500, Yes	Toner cartridge	10,000	1	$1,495.00	Includes automatic emulation switching
IBM	HP LaserJet II, Diablo 630, EPSON FX-86, 286e, IBM ProPrinter XL, HP 7475 Plotter	500/500, Included					
IBM	HP LaserJet II, IBM ProPrinter, Y24E, YC24 Packard Bell Proprietary, Diablo 630	250	Toner cartridge	3,000	1	$1,995.00	
IBM	HP LaserJet II	250, No	Separate toner, drum	3,000, $49		$1,395.00	
IBM	HP LaserJet II	250, Yes	Separate toner, drum	5,000, $45	1	$2,095.00	
IBM						$3,495.00	
IBM	HP LaserJet II, Diablo 630, EPSON FX-80, IBM ProPrinter, IBM Graphics Printer	250, Yes	Toner cartridge	3,000, $65	1	$1,599.00	
IBM, Mac	Apple LaserWriter, HP LaserJet II	150, No	Separate toner, drum	Toner-1,500, 2-$79, Drum-10,000, $150	1, 90 days on-site	$1,995.00	2 serial, 1 parallel, 1 AppleTalk port
IBM, Mac	Diablo 630	200, Yes	Toner cartridge	3,500, $129	1	$3,999.00	Includes LaserWriter Fonts, Install disk
IBM, Mac	HP LaserJet Plus, Diablo 630	200, Yes	Toner cartridge	3,500, $129	1	$4,999.00	Includes LaserWriter Fonts, Install disk
IBM, Mac	HP LaserJet Plus, Diablo 630	250, Yes	Toner cartridge	3,500, $99	1	$2,599.00	Includes LaserWriter Fonts, Install disk
IBM, Mac		50, Yes	Toner cartridge	3,500, $95	1	$1,545.00	
IBM, Mac	Diablo 630	200, No	Toner cartridge	4,000, $125	1	$2,495.00	Optional printer emulations
IBM, Mac	Diablo 630	200/bin, 2 bins, No	Toner cartridge	4,000, $125	1	$3,795.00	Optional printer emulations

continues

Table 9.3. Continued

COMPANY	MODEL	RESOLUTION (dpi)	ENGINE MAKER, TYPE	ENGINE LIFE (pgs)	PRINT SPEED (ppm)	TYPEFACES, FONTS	RAM MIN, MAX (bytes)	PRINTER LANGUAGE
Canon	Canon LBP8 Mark III T	300	Canon, Laser	Indefinite	8	9 Scalable	1.5M	Proprietary
Data Products	LZR 1230	300	Laser	25,000 pgs/mo	12	12 Bit map	512K	
Data Products	LZR 1260i	300	Laser	25,000 pgs/mo	12	36 Bit map	4M	
Data Products	LZR 1650	300	Laser	30,000 pgs/mo	15.8	100 Bit map	512K	PCL4
Data Products	LZR 2455	300	Laser	120,000 pgs/mo	24	24 PostScript	2M	PostScript
Data Products	LZR 2455D	300	Laser	120,000 img/mo	24 images/min	24 PostScript	2M	PostScript
Data Products	LZR 2620	300	Laser	100,000 pgs/mo	26	16 Bit map	512K	
Data Products	LZR 2630	300	Laser	100,000 pgs/mo	26	5 Bit map	512K	
Data Products	LZR 2655	300	Laser	100,000 pgs/mo	26	5 Bit map	512K	
Data Products	LZR 2655/LJ	300	Laser	100,000 pgs/mo	26	34 Bit map	512K	
Data Products	LZR 2655/LN	300	Laser	100,000 pgs/mo	26	17 Bit map	512K	
Data Products	LZR 2665	300	Laser	100,000 pgs/mo	26	13 PostScript	2M	PostScript
Data Products	LZR 650	300	Laser	3,000 pgs/mo	6	16 Bit map	512K, 4.5M	PCL4
Data Products	LZR 960	300	Laser	3,000 pgs/mo	9	35 PostScript	2M, 10M	PostScript
Eastman Kodak	KODAK EKTAPLUS 7016	300	Eastman Kodak Co., LED	Infinite	Printer-16 Copier-6	30 Bitstream	2M, 4M	PCL4, HP-GL
Eastman Kodak	KODAK EKTAPLUS 7016PS	300	Eastman Kodak Co., LED	Infinite	Printer-16 Copier-6	30 Bitstream	2M, 6M	PCL4, PostScript, HP-GL
EPSON	EPL-7500	300	Minolta, Laser	180,000	6	35 PostScript	2M, 6M	PostScript
Everex	LaserScript FAX	300	TEC, Laser	300,000	6	35 Bitstream, 24 Bit map	4M, 8M	PCL4, PostScript
GCC Technologies	BLP II	300	OKI Electric, LED	180,000	4	35 PostScript	2M, 4M	PostScript
GCC Technologies	BLP IIS	300	OKI Electric, LED	300,000	8	35 PostScript	2M, 4M	PostScript

9

IBM, MAC COMP	EMULATION	PAPER CAP (pgs), OPT TRAY	TONER	TONER LIFE (pgs), COST	WARRANTY (years)	RETAIL PRICE	OTHER INFORMATION
IBM, Mac	Diablo 630	200/bin, 2 bins, No	Toner cartridge	4,000, $125	1	$3,295.00	Optional printer emulations
IBM, Mac	HP LaserJet Plus, Diablo 630, EPSON FX80	250, Yes				$3,695.00	Includes 2 serial, 1 parallel port
IBM, Mac	HP LaserJet PLUS	250, Yes				$5,995.00	Includes serial, parallel, AppleTalk port
IBM, Mac	HP LaserJet II	500/200, Included				$3,695.00	Optional envelope tray, 2,500-sheet feeder
IBM, Mac	HP LaserJet, DEC LNO3 PLUS, Diablo 630	550/250, Included				$14,995.00	Standard int 3.5" disk drive, opt 1,200-sheet feeder, 1,400-sheet stacker
IBM, Mac	HP LaserJet, DEC LNO3 PLUS, Diablo 630	550/250, Included				$19,995.00	Standard internal 3.5" disk drive, optional 1,200-sheet feeder, 1,400-sheet stacker
IBM, Mac	TEK 4010, 4014	250/500, Included				$9,995.00	Bar codes, OCR, block chars, opt 10-bin sorter, collator, 1,500-sheet feeder
IBM, Mac	Diablo 630	250/500, Included				$9,495.00	Legal chars, optional 10-bin sorter, collator, 1,500-sheet feeder
IBM, Mac	TEK 4010, 4014, Diablo 630	250/500, Included				$10,495.00	Optional 1,500-sheet feeder
IBM, Mac	HP LaserJet 2000	250/500, Included				$9,995.00	Optional 1,500-sheet feeder
IBM, Mac	DEC LNO3 PLUS	250/500, Included				$9,995.00	Optional 1,500-sheet feeder
IBM, Mac		250/500, Included				$11,495.00	Optional 1,500-sheet feeder
IBM, Mac	HP LaserJet II, Diablo 630, EPSON FX-80, IBM ProPrinter, IBM Graphics Printer	250, Yes				$1,695.00	
IBM, Mac	PostScript Level 2, HP LaserJet II	250, Yes				$2,995.00	SCSI standard, serial, parallel, AppleTalk port
IBM, Mac	HP LaserJet II, EPSON FX-80, IBM ProPrinter	250/250, Included	Separate toner, drum	4,000, $130	90 days on-site	$5,495.00	Can support 4 users or 4 networks
IBM, Mac	HP LaserJet II, EPSON FX-80, IBM ProPrinter	250/250, Included	Separate toner, drum	4,000, $130	90 days on-site	$6,995.00	Can support 4 users or 4 networks
IBM, Mac	HP LaserJet II	250, Yes	Toner cartridge	6,000, $175	2	$2,999.00	
IBM, Mac	Apple LaserWriter, HP LaserJet II	150, No	Separate drum	Toner-1,500, 2-$79, Drum-10,000, $150	1, 90 days on-site		Built-in fax capabilities
IBM, Mac		200, No	Toner cartridge	2,500, $33	1	$1,999.00	
IBM, Mac		200, No	Toner cartridge	2,500, $33	1	$2,899.00	

continues

Table 9.3. Continued

COMPANY	MODEL	RESOLUTION (dpi)	ENGINE MAKER, TYPE	ENGINE LIFE (pgs)	PRINT SPEED (ppm)	TYPEFACES, FONTS	RAM MIN, MAX (bytes)	PRINTER LANGUAGE
GCC Technologies	GLP Elite	300	OKI Electric, LED	180,000	4	17 PostScript	2M, 4M	PostScript
Hewlett-Packard	LaserJet III	300	Canon, Laser	Indefinite	8	14 Bit map, 8 scalable	1M, 5M	PCL5
Hewlett-Packard	LaserJet IIID	300	Canon, Laser	Indefinite	8	14 Bit map, 8 scalable	1M, 5M	PCL5
Hewlett-Packard	LaserJet IIIP	300	Canon, Laser	Indefinite	4	14 Bit map, 8 scalable	1M, 5M	PCL5
Hewlett-Packard	LaserJet IIISi	300	Canon, Laser	Indefinite	17	14 Bit map, 8 scalable	1M, 17M	PCL5
Hewlett-Packard	LaserJet IIP	300	Canon, Laser	Indefinite	4	14 Bit map	512K, 4.5M	PCL4
NEC	Silentwriter 2 LC 890XL	300	NEC, LED	600,000	8	35 PostScript	4M, 8M	PCL4, PostScript
NEC	Silentwriter 2 Model 90	300	Minolta, Laser	180,000	6	35 PostScript	2M, 4M	PCL4, PostScript
NEC	Silentwriter 2 Model 990	300	Canon UX, Laser	300,000	8	35 PostScript	2M, 4M	PCL4 PostScript
NewGen Systems Corp.	TurboPS/1200T	1200 x 600	Copal, Laser	10,000 pgs/mo	12	35 PostScript	20M, 48M	PCL4, PCL5, PostScript
NewGen Systems Corp.	TurboPS/300	300	Canon, Laser	5,000 pgs/mo	8	35 PostScript	2M, 5M	PCL4, PCL5, PostScript
NewGen Systems Corp.	TurboPS/300P	300	Canon, Laser	3,500 pgs/mo	4	35 PostScript	2M, 16M	PCL4, PCL5, PostScript
NewGen Systems Corp.	TurboPS/360	600 x 300	Canon, Laser	5,000 pgs/mo	8	35 PostScript	3M, 5M	PCL4, PCL5, PostScript
NewGen Systems Corp.	TurboPS/400	400	Canon, Laser	5,000 pgs/mo	8	35 PostScript	3M, 5M	PCL4, PCL5, PostScript
NewGen Systems Corp.	TurboPS/400P	400	Canon, Laser	3,500 pgs/mo	4	35 PostScript	2M, 16M	PCL4, PCL5, PostScript
NewGen Systems Corp.	TurboPS/480	800 x 400	Canon, Laser	5,000 pgs/mo	8	35 PostScript	5M	PCL4, PCL5, PostScript
NewGen Systems Corp.	TurboPS/600T	600	Copal, Laser	10,000 pgs/mo	12	35 PostScript	2M, 48M	PCL4, PCL5, PostScript
Panasonic Office Automation	KX-P4455	300	Panasonic, Laser	300,000	11	39 PostScript	2M, 4M	PostScript
QMS	QMS ColorScript 100 Model 10	300	Mitsubishi G370, Thermal	72,000 prints	1	35 PostScript	5M, 10M	PostScript, HP-GL
QMS	QMS ColorScript 100 Model 10p	300	Mitsubishi G370, Thermal	72,000 prints	1	35 PostScript	4M, 8M	PostScript, HP-GL optional

IBM, MAC COMP	EMULATION	PAPER CAP (pgs), OPT TRAY	TONER	TONER LIFE (pgs), COST	WARRANTY (years)	RETAIL PRICE	OTHER INFORMATION
IBM, Mac		200, No	Toner cartridge	2,500, $33	1	$1,599.00	
IBM, Mac		200, Yes	Toner cartridge	4,000, $125	1		
IBM, Mac		200/200, Included	Toner cartridge	4,000, $125	1, on-site		
IBM, Mac		70, Yes	Toner cartridge	3,500, $95	1		Optional 250-sheet lower tray
IBM, Mac		500, Yes	Toner cartridge	8,000, $169	1, on-site		
IBM, Mac		50, Yes	Toner cartridge	3,500, $95	1		Optional 250-sheet lower tray
IBM, Mac	HP LaserJet Plus, Diablo 630	250, Yes	Toner cartridge	5,000, $24	1	$5,995.00	
IBM, Mac	HP LaserJet IIP	250, Yes	Toner cartridge	6,000, $200	1	$2,495.00	
IBM, Mac	HP LaserJet IIP	200, Yes	Toner cartridge	4,000, $125	1	$4,495.00	
IBM, Mac	HP LaserJet II, HPGL Plotter	Yes	Separate toner, drum	5,000, $249	1	$16,995.00	
IBM, Mac	HP LaserJet II, HPGL Plotter, EPSON LQ-800	Yes	Toner cartridge	5,000, $199	1	$4,495.00	Upgradable to 600 x 300 dpi
IBM, Mac	HP LaserJet II, HPGL Plotter	50, Yes, 250 pgs	Toner cartridge	3,500, $99	1	$2,495.00	
IBM, Mac	HP LaserJet II, HPGL Plotter, EPSON LQ-800	Yes	Toner cartridge	5,000, $199	1	$4,995.00	
IBM, Mac	HP LaserJet II, HPGL Plotter, EPSON LQ-800	Yes	Toner cartridge	5,000, $199	1	$5,495.00	Upgradable to 800 x 400 dpi
IBM, Mac	HP LaserJet II, HPGL Plotter, EPSON LQ-800	50, Yes	Toner cartridge	3,500, $99	1	$2,995.00	
IBM, Mac	HP LaserJet II, HPGL Plotter, EPSON LQ-800	250, Yes	Toner cartridge	5,000, $199	1	$7,495.00	
IBM, Mac	HP LaserJet II, HPGL Plotter, EPSON LQ-800	250, Yes	Separate toner, drum	5,000, $249	1	$14,995.00	
IBM, Mac	HP LaserJet II, Diablo 630	250, Yes	Separate toner, drum	5,000, $45		$3,495.00	
IBM, Mac	HPGL Plotter	100, No	Ink roll	100 prints	1	$8,995.00	Panatone approved, serial, parallel, AppleTalk port
IBM, Mac		100, No	Ink roll	100 prints	1	$6,995.00	Panatone approved, serial, parallel, AppleTalk port

continues

Table 9.3. Concluded

COMPANY	MODEL	RESOLUTION (dpi)	ENGINE MAKER, TYPE	ENGINE LIFE (pgs)	PRINT SPEED (ppm)	TYPEFACES, FONTS	RAM MIN, MAX (bytes)	PRINTER LANGUAGE
QMS	QMS ColorScript 100 Model 30i	300	Mitsubishi G650, Thermal	300,000 prints	1	35 PostScript	8M	PostScript, HP-GL
QMS	QMS ColorScript 100 Model 30si	300	Mitsubishi G650, Thermal	300,000 prints	1	35 PostScript	12M	PostScript, HP-GL
QMS	QMS-PS 410	300	Canon LX, Laser	360,000	4	45 PostScript	2M, 6M	PCL4, PostScript, HP-GL optional
QMS	QMS-PS 810	300	Canon SX/TX, Laser	750,000	8	35 PostScript	2M, 3M	PostScript, PCL4, HPGL, Diablo
QMS	QMS-PS 815	300	Canon SX/TX, Laser	750,000	8	45 PostScript	2M, 8M	PCL4, PostScript, HPGL optional
QMS	QMS-PS 820	300	Canon SX/TX, Laser	750,000	8	35 PostScript	2M, 3M	PostScript, PCL4, HPGL, Diablo
QMS	QMS-PS 825	300	Canon SX/TX, Laser	750,000	8	45 PostScript	2M, 8M	PCL4, PostScript, HPGL optional
Seiko	CH5500 Series Color Printer A-size	300	Thermal		55 sec/pg			
Seiko	CH5500 Series Color Printer B-size	300	Thermal		55 sec/pg			
Seiko	ColorPoint PS Model 14	300	Thermal		75 sec/pg	35 PostScript	6M, 34M	PostScript
Seiko	ColorPoint PS Model 4	300	Thermal		55 sec/pg	35 PostScript	6M, 34M	PostScript
Texas Instruments	microLaser	300	Sharp, Laser	40,000	6	14 Bit map	512K, 4.5M	
Texas Instruments	microLaser XL	300	Sharp, Laser	Indefinite	16	14 Bit map	512K, 4.5M	PCL4
Toshiba America	PageLaser 6	300	TEC, Laser	200,000	6	8 Bit map	512K, 4.5M	PCL4
Apple Computer	Apple Personal LaserWriter LS	300	Canon, Laser	150,000	4	4 TrueType	512K	
GCC Technologies	PLP II S	300	OKI Electric, LED	300,000	8	40 Quickdraw	1M	Quickdraw
GCC Technologies	PLPII	300	OKI Electric, LED	180,000	4	22 Quickdraw	1M	Quickdraw

IBM, MAC COMP	EMULATION	PAPER CAP (pgs), OPT TRAY	TONER	TONER LIFE (pgs), COST	WARRANTY (years)	RETAIL PRICE	OTHER INFORMATION
IBM, Mac	HPGL Plotter	150, No	Ink roll	180 prints	3 months	$10,995.00	Panatone approved, serial, parallel, AppleTalk port
IBM, Mac	HPGL Plotter	150, No	Ink roll	180 prints	3 months	$12,995.00	11 x 17 full bleeds, Panatone approved except for 11 x 17 3-color ink roll
IBM, Mac	HP LaserJet II	50, Yes	Toner cartridge	3,500 prints	1	$2,795.00	Emulation-sensing processor
IBM, Mac	HP LaserJet, HP 7475A, Diablo 630	200, No	Toner cartridge	4,000 prints	1		ASAP hardware for faster "first-page-out" perf
IBM, Mac		200, No	Toner cartridge	4,000 prints	1		Emulation-sensing processor
IBM, Mac	HP LaserJet, HP 7475A, Diablo 630	200/200, Included	Toner cartridge	4,000 prints	1		ASAP hardware for faster "first-page-out" perf
IBM, Mac		200/200, Included	Toner cartridge	4,000 prints	1		Emulation-sensing processor
IBM, Mac			YMC, YMCK, 1 color ink				Full-size image, over 16M colors, auto cutter
IBM, Mac			YMC, YMCK, 1 color ink				Full-size image, over 16M colors, auto cutter
IBM, Mac		Roll paper, No	YMC, YMCK, 1 color ink		90 days on-site		Color thermal transfer, up to 16.7M colors-PANTONE
IBM, Mac		Roll paper, No	YMC, YMCK, 1 color ink		90 days on-site		Color thermal transfer, up to 16.7M colors-PANTONE
IBM, Mac	HP LaserJet II	250, Yes	Toner cartridge	3,000, $60	1	$1,449.00	
IBM, Mac	HP LaserJet II, Diablo 630, EPSON 850, 1050	250, Yes	Toner cartridge	6,000, $95	1	$3,449.00	Compact, 262 sq in
IBM, Mac	HP LaserJet II	150, No	Separate toner, drum	6,000, 2-$49	1		
Mac		50, Yes	Toner cartridge	3,500, $99	1	$1,299.00	Includes Install disk, TrueType Fonts, Mac Prn Tools
Mac		200, Yes	Toner cartridge	2,500, $33	1	$1,499.00	
Mac		200, Yes	Toner cartridge	2,500, $33	1	$999.00	

CHAPTER

TEN

Deciding What Extras You Need

After you have decided on a personal computer system, you may want to consider additional pieces of equipment, such as a modem, a pointing device, a CD ROM drive, a tape-backup device, or a scanner. The following sections describe these products and tell you about key features to look for in each. Product recommendations are made for each type of product.

Modems

A modem is a device for sending information from one computer to another over telephone lines. You can use a modem to share programs and data with other computer users. With a modem, you can *upload* (send) information to or *download* (receive) information from another computer. You also can chat, which means that you can type on your keyboard, and the words are transmitted to the person at the other end of the phone line. That person, in turn, responds by typing a message to you.

Other popular uses for modems include connecting to bulletin board systems (BBSs), on-line services (such as CompuServe and Prodigy), electronic mail services (such as MCI Mail), electronic databases (such as Dialog), and electronic stock market services (such as the Dow-Jones News/Retrieval Service).

Like most other computer products, speed is a major issue with modems. You pay for the telephone call you make with a modem just as you do for a voice call. If you are downloading a large spreadsheet from a distant location during business hours, you want to transfer the information as quickly as possible. The speed of a modem is defined by its baud rate (the number of data bits per second that the modem can send or receive). A 2400-baud modem, for example, is twice as fast as a 1200-baud modem. The only modems you need to consider are 2400-baud and 9600-baud models, because these two types are the most common today.

A 2400-baud modem, also known as a V.22bis modem, gives you reasonable speed at a reasonable price and is sufficient for most applications. This kind of modem can cost anywhere from $60 to $600, depending on features and the manufacturer of the device. If you plan to send or receive large files regularly, you may want to consider a 9600-baud modem, also known as a V.32 modem. These modems are in the $600 to $1,200 range, again depending on features and manufacturer. Keep in mind that both sending and receiving modems must operate at the same rate—in this case, 9600 baud.

Two features that add to the cost of a modem are data compression and error correction. To increase the speed of data transfers, some modems compress the information before sending it. Features such as MNP5 or V.42bis mean that a modem compresses data before sending it. (MNP5 is Microcom's Networking Protocol Class 5; V.42bis is a communications standard developed by the CCITT—Consultative Committee of International Telephone and Telegraph.) Compressed data must be expanded again after being received at the other end of the connection. For this expansion to occur, you need to send information to an MNP5 or V.42bis modem. In other words, the modem at each end of the connection must use the same communications standard. When a modem compresses data before transmission, the modem appears to work much more quickly than its rated speed for most kinds of information. For example, a 2400-baud modem with MNP5 data compression may appear to send data as fast as 4800 baud.

Modems that feature MNP5 or V.42bis also provide error correction. Error correction attempts to ensure that the information sent is the same as the information received.

Features like high speed, data compression, and error correction make a modem more costly, but the hardware can pay for itself if you telecommunicate often. If you don't plan to use a modem extensively, or plan to use it only for working with on-line services, a simple 2400-baud modem without enhanced features is sufficient. These basic modems cost less than $100. Remember that both the host and remote modems must adhere to the same standards. If the modem that you will communicate with is only a 2400-baud modem without compression, you have no need for the compression feature.

If you purchase a 2400-baud modem without advanced features, you can use the error-correction (and sometimes data-compression) features provided in many communications programs. Programs such as Crosstalk and PROCOMM PLUS enable you to access your modem for dialing and connecting to another computer and for transferring files. Files are transferred using *transfer protocols* such as Xmodem. Xmodem is an example of an error-correcting protocol included with most communications programs to transfer a file and to make sure that none of the file becomes corrupted during the transfer.

A modem faster than 2400 baud does not always save money. If you connect to an on-line service and spend time exploring the available features, reading menus, reading messages, and so forth, you usually are charged for the time you are connected to the service, regardless of how fast information is sent back and forth. Sometimes an information service even charges you a premium for using a faster modem.

External modems connect to a serial port on your computer. Internal modems connect to an expansion slot on the system board. The modem you choose may depend on which means of connection is available in your system: a port or a slot. For IBM and compatible computers with an ISA or EISA bus, an internal modem must be designed for the ISA bus. For IBM PS/2 computers with a Micro Channel bus, an internal modem must be designed for the Micro Channel bus. For Macintosh computers, you are not likely to have a slot available for an internal modem unless you have a Macintosh II or a Macintosh Portable; you therefore need to consider an external modem. For laptop and notebook computers, a good choice for an external modem is a "pocket" modem, because portability is a key concern. Make sure that any internal modem you consider for a laptop or notebook computer is designed to work with the laptop or notebook computer you have.

To ensure compatibility between the modem and the communications software you use, make sure that the software supports the modem you intend to buy. If the software doesn't support the modem directly, check whether the software supports Hayes-compatible modems. A Hayes-compatible modem is one that uses the Hayes AT command set (most modems use these commands), and generally responds just the way a Hayes modem does.

Some other features to look for when considering a modem are a volume control and the capability to switch between voice and data. Some modem manufacturers include communications software such as Hayes Smartcom II or PROCOMM PLUS (from DATASTORM TECHNOLOGIES), which saves you an additional expense.

Manufacturers sometimes put more than one communication device on a board. Some products work as modems and fax machines; some work as modems, fax machines, and answering machines; and some have more than one modem built into the circuit board. Multiple-modem boards are useful if you want to set up your computer as an electronic bulletin board.

Reviewing Modem Manufacturers

Hayes Microcomputer Products has set the standards for personal computer modems for many years. Unfortunately, Hayes sells its modems for a premium price when compared to its competitors. If you want to buy a name-brand modem and don't mind spending the money, Hayes is a good choice. If you want to save some money without sacrificing much in the way of performance and reliability, you can choose from many manufacturers. Some companies that sell good, low-cost modems are Zoom Telephonics, US Robotics, Practical Peripherals, ATI Technologies, and Computer Peripherals. Most modem companies sell both internal and external models.

Modem Listings

In table 10.1, you see a list of many different modems available for IBM-compatible and Macintosh computers. Many varieties are listed to fit nearly any need. The modems listed range in transmission speeds from 1200 baud to 38,400 baud. The modems also support many different compression specifications, and some include fax capabilities.

To use table 10.1, notice that the modems have been sorted by baud rate and then alphabetically by company within each baud-rate range. You will find information about what compression specification the modem supports, if any; whether the modem is internal or external; and whether any software is included with the modem. One column specifies whether the modem supports fax and, if the modem supports fax, whether the modem sends only or sends and receives, as well as gives the speed of fax transmission. Finally, the last two columns list the retail price of the modem and other information that may help you determine which modem is best for you.

Table 10.1. Listing of Modems Sorted by Baud Rate and Company Name

COMPANY	MODEL	MAX BAUD RATE	COMPRESSION	INTERNAL, EXTERNAL	SOFTWARE INCLUDED	FAX MODEM, BAUD	RETAIL PRICE	OTHER INFORMATION
Applied Engineering	Datalink 1200	1200		Internal	OnLine 64		$119.00	
Multitech Systems	MT212PC5 MultiModem PC5	1200		Internal	PROCOMM		$229.00	PC half card
Practical Peripherals	Practical Modem 1200	1200		Internal	Yes			
Practical Peripherals	Practical Modem 1200SA Mini	1200		External				
Altec	Wiz	2400	MNP4	Internal	VCOM		$65.00	
Apple Computer	Apple Data Modem 2400	2400	MNP				$349.00	
Apple Computer	Macintosh Portable Data Modem 2400	2400					$449.00	For Mac Portable, 4 oz
Applied Engineering	Datalink Mac II	2400	MNP5	Internal	Terminal, AE Send Fax	Send only, 4800	$349.00	
Applied Engineering	DataMac Portable Modem	2400	MNP5	Internal	Terminal, AE Send Fax	Send only, 4800	$299.00	
ATI Technologies	2400 ETC E	2400	V.42, V.42bis, MNP5	External		Send only, 9600	$239.00	Ext vol ctrl, 24-hr BBS, free tech support
ATI Technologies	2400 ETC I	2400	V.42, V.42bis, MNP5	Internal	Yes	Send only, 9600	$199.00	24-hr BBS, free tech support
Cardinal	2400 MNP	2400	MNP5	External			$229.00	Asynch, synch comm
Cardinal	2400 V42	2400	V42, V42bis, MNP5	External			$289.00	Asynch, synch comm
Cardinal	2450 MNP	2400	MNP5	Internal	FLASHlink		$189.00	Auto speed adj
Cardinal	2450 V42	2400	V.42, V.42bis, MNP5	Internal	FLASHlink		$249.00	Auto speed adj
Cardinal	MB2250F	2400	MNP with FLASHlink	Internal	Yes	Send only, 4800/9600		Large on-board speaker
Cardinal	MB2296F	2400	MNP with FLASHlink	Internal	Yes	Send only, 4800/9600		Large on-board speaker
Cardinal	MB2296SR	2400	MNP with FLASHlink	Internal	Yes	Send/ Receive, 4800/9600		Large on-board speaker
Cardinal	MB2400EX	2400	MNP with FLASHlink	External			$179.00	Auto speed adjust
Cardinal	MB2450	2400	MNP with FLASHlink	Internal	FLASHlink		$159.00	Assign COM 1-4

continues

Table 10.1. Continued

COMPANY	MODEL	MAX BAUD RATE	COMPRESSION	INTERNAL, EXTERNAL	SOFTWARE INCLUDED	FAX MODEM, BAUD	RETAIL PRICE	OTHER INFORMATION
Cardinal	MB2450	2400	MNP with FLASHlink	Internal	Bitcom		$129.00	Assign COM 1-4
Cardinal	MC2450	2400	MNP with FLASHlink	Internal	FLASHlink		$189.00	Microchannel
Everex	Abaton Interfax 24/96	2400	MNP 5	External	Yes	Send/ Receive, 9600	$595.00	Macintosh comp only
Everex	MD2400	2400	MNP 5	External	No		$299.00	Macintosh comp only
Hayes	Personal Modem 2400lus	2400		External	SmartcomEZ, Smartcom II Mac	Send only		Fax via modem & info service
Hayes	Pocket Edition 2400	2400		External	SmartcomEZ	Send only		Uses pwr from phone line & PC, 3 oz, 3 in
Hayes	Smartmodem 2400	2400		External		Send only		Fax via modem & info service
Hayes	Smartmodem 2400B	2400		Internal	Smartcom III, Smartcom II	Send only		Fax via modem & info service
Hayes	V-Series Smartmodem 2400	2400	V.42bis, MNP5, Hayes Adp comp	External	Smartcom III	Send only		Fax via modem & info src, X.25, AutoSync, AutoStream
Hayes	V-Series Smartmodem 2400M	2400	V.42bis, MNP5, Hayes Adp comp	Internal	Smartcom II Mac	Send only		Fax via modem & info src, X.25, AutoSync, AutoStream, Mac
Hyundai	HMD-2404M	2400	MNP5	External	Yes		$189.00	
Hyundai	HMD-2404MP	2400	MNP5	Internal	Yes		$159.00	PC half card
IBM	5853-1	2400	MNP3	External			$813.00	
IBM	Modem/A (1755)	2400	MNP3	Internal			$462.00	
Intel	Intel 2400EX MNP	2400	MNP5	External	METZ			
Intel	Intel SatisFAXtion	2400	MNP5	Internal	FaxPop	Send/ Receive, 9600		Built-in scanner port, background operation
Multitech Systems	MT224AH MultiModem 224	2400		External			$449.00	Support synch, async
Multitech Systems	MT224EC MultiModem 224EC	2400	MNP5	Internal	PROCOMM		$399.00	
Multitech Systems	MT224EC7B MultiModem 224EC7B	2400	V.42bis, MNP5	Internal	PROCOMM		$449.00	
Multitech Systems	MT224EH MultiModem 224E	2400	V.42, MNP5	External			$499.00	Support synch, async

COMPANY	MODEL	MAX BAUD RATE	COMPRESSION	INTERNAL, EXTERNAL	SOFTWARE INCLUDED	FAX MODEM, BAUD	RETAIL PRICE	OTHER INFORMATION
Multitech Systems	MT224EH7 MultiModem 224E7	2400	V.42, MNP5, MNP7	External			$549.00	Support synch, async
Multitech Systems	MT224EH7B MultiModem 224E7B	2400	V.42, V.42bis, MNP5	External			$549.00	Support synch, async
Multitech Systems	MT224EM MultiModem 224E for Mac	2400	V.42, MNP5	External	Quick-Link II		$499.00	Support synch, async
Multitech Systems	MT224EM7 MultiModem 224E7 for Mac	2400	V.42, MNP5, MNP7	External	Quick-Link II		$549.00	Support synch, async
Multitech Systems	MT224EM7B MultiModem 224E7 for Mac	2400	V.42, V.42 bis, MNP5	External	Quick-Link II		$549.00	Support synch, async
Multitech Systems	MT224ES MultiModem 224ES	2400	MNP5	Internal	PROCOMM		$449.00	Auto-switching speeds, callback sec, remote config
Multitech Systems	MT224ES7B MultiModem 224ES7B	2400	V.42bis, MNP5	Internal	PROCOMM		$499.00	Auto-switching speeds, callback sec, remote config
Multitech Systems	MT224PC MultiModem 224PC	2400		Internal	PROCOMM		$349.00	Auto-switching speeds, callback sec, remote config
Multitech Systems	MT224PS MultiModem 224PS	2400		Internal	PROCOMM		$399.00	Microchannel
Multitech Systems	MultiModemB MT224EA76	2400	V.42bis, MNP5	External			$549.00	Callback sec, remote config
Outbound Systems	Pocket Port Modem	2400		External	Pocket Comm			2.2 x 3.1 x .8 in, Mac comp, line powered
Practical Peripherals	Laptop 2400	2400		Internal	Yes			Toshiba or NEC laptop
Practical Peripherals	Laptop 2400 MNP/5	2400	MNP5	Internal	Yes			Toshiba or NEC laptop
Practical Peripherals	Laptop 2400 SendFAX	2400		Internal	Yes	Send/ Receive, 4800		Toshiba or NEC laptop
Practical Peripherals	Practical Modem 2400	2400		Internal	Yes			Select as COM1-COM4.
Practical Peripherals	Practical Modem 2400 PS/2	2400		Internal	Yes			Auto COM selection, MicroChannel
Practical Peripherals	Practical Modem 2400SA	2400		External				
Practical Peripherals	Practical Modem PM2400 SendFAX	2400		Internal	Yes	Send only, 4800		Auto adaptive eq, non-volatile RAM
Practical Peripherals	Practical Pocket Modem	2400		External	CompuServe			Software speaker
Practical Peripherals	SmartPack 2400 For The Macintosh	2400		External	Smartcom II Mac			Automatic adaptive equalization

continues

Table 10.1. Continued

COMPANY	MODEL	MAX BAUD RATE	COMPRESSION	INTERNAL, EXTERNAL	SOFTWARE INCLUDED	FAX MODEM, BAUD	RETAIL PRICE	OTHER INFORMATION
Swan Technologies	2400 bps MNP Internal/ SW2MI	2400	MNP5	Internal	BitCom		$99.00	Tech support available
Swan Technologies	2400 bps MNP External/ SW2ME	2400	MNP5	External	BitCom		$139.00	Tech support available
Swan Technologies	Sendfax Modem/ SSFM9	2400		Internal	BitCom, BitFax	Send only, 9600	$109.00	Tech support available
Swan Technologies	Swan 2400 bps External/ SW24E	2400		External	BitCom		$89.00	Tech support available
Swan Technologies	Swan 2400 bps Internal/SW241	2400		Internal	BitCom		$69.00	Tech support available
Tandy	2400 BPS Half Card Modem	2400		Internal			$149.95	
US Robotics	Sportster 2400MNP	2400	MNP5	Internal, External	Prodigy		$249.00	
Zoom	FC9624	2400		Internal	PROCOMM, Bitfax	Send/ Receive, 9600	$199.00	
Zoom	FX9624	2400		External	PROCOMM, Bitfax	Send/ Receive, 9600	$199.00	
Zoom	HC2400A	2400		Internal	PROCOMM, Bitfax		$129.00	
Zoom	HCSF48	2400		Internal	PROCOMM, Bitfax	Send only	$149.00	
Zoom	HCSF96	2400		Internal	PROCOMM, Bitfax	Send only	$169.00	
Zoom	MX2400A	2400		External			$129.00	
Zoom	MXSF48	2400		External	PROCOMM, Bitfax or QLII Mac	Send only	$149.00	
Zoom	MXSP96	2400		External	PROCOMM, Bitfax or QLII Mac	Send only	$169.00	
Zoom	V42X	2400	V.42bis, MNP 5	External			$300.00	
Applied Engineering	LC Modem	9600	MNP5	Internal	Terminal, AE Send Fax	Send only, 9600	$349.00	V.42 opt $79, Rec Fax opt $79
ATI Technologies	9600 ETC E	9600	V.42, V.42bis, MNP5	External			$499.00	24-hr BBS, free tech support
Cardinal	9600 V42	9600	V.32, V.42, V.42bis, MNP5	External			$699.00	Asynch, synch comm
Cardinal	9650 V32	9600	V.32, MNP5	Internal	FLASHlink		$599.00	Assign COM 1-4

COMPANY	MODEL	MAX BAUD RATE	COMPRESSION	INTERNAL, EXTERNAL	SOFTWARE INCLUDED	FAX MODEM, BAUD	RETAIL PRICE	OTHER INFORMATION
CompuCom	SpeedModem Challenger	9600	V.32, V.42, V.42bis, MNP5	Internal		Send/ Receive, 9600	$678.00	Data speed with comp: 14,400 - 57,600 bps
CompuCom	SpeedModem Challenger	9600	V.32, V.42, V.42bis, MNP5	External		Send/ Receive, 9600	$728.00	Data speed with comp: 14,400 - 57,600 bps
CompuCom	SpeedModem Challenger	9600	V.32, V.42, V.42bis, MNP5	External			$629.00	Data speed with comp: 14,400 - 57,600 bps
CompuCom	SpeedModem Challenger	9600	V.32, V.42, V.42bis, MNP5	Internal			$579.00	Data speed with comp: 14,400 - 57,600 bps
CompuCom	SpeedModem Combo	9600	MNP5, CSP3	External	Yes	Send/ Receive, 9600	$339.00	Data speed with comp: 38,400 bps
CompuCom	SpeedModem Combo	9600	MNP5, CSP3	Internal			$199.00	
CompuCom	SpeedModem Combo	9600	MNP5, CSP3	Internal	Yes	Send/ Receive, 9600	$299.00	Data speed with comp: 38,400 bps
CompuCom	SpeedModem Combo	9600	MNP5, CSP3	External			$239.00	
CompuCom	SpeedModem Storm	9600	V.32, V.42, V.42bis, MNP5	External		Send/ Receive, 9600	$508.00	Data speed with comp: 38,400 bps
CompuCom	SpeedModem Storm	9600	V.32, V.42, V.42bis, MNP5	Internal			$359.00	Data speed with comp: 38,400 bps
CompuCom	SpeedModem Storm	9600	V.32, V.42, V.42bis, MNP5	External			$409.00	Data speed with comp: 38,400 bps
CompuCom	SpeedModem Storm	9600	V.32, V.42, V.42bis, MNP5	Internal		Send/ Receive, 9600	$458.00	Data speed with comp: 38,400 bps
Hayes	Smartmodem 9600	9600						Autosync
Hayes	Ultra 96	9600	V.42bis, MNP5, Hayes Adp comp	External		Send only		Fax via modem & info src, X.25, AutoSync, AutoStream
Hayes	V-Series Smartmodem 9600	9600	V.42bis, MNP5, Hayes Adp comp	External		Send only		Fax via modem & info src, X.25, AutoSync, AutoStream
Hayes	V-Series Smartmodem 9600B	9600	V.42bis, MNP5, Hayes Adp comp	Internal	Smartcom III	Send only		Fax via modem & info src, X.25, AutoSync, AutoStream
Multitech Systems	MT696EA MultiModem 696E	9600	MNP6	External			$795.00	Auto-switching speeds, callback sec, remote config
Multitech Systems	MT932EA MultiModem V32	9600	V.32, V.42, MNP5	External			$869.00	Auto-switching speeds, callback sec, remote config
Multitech Systems	MT932EAB MultiModem V32	9600	V.32, V.42, V.42bis, MNP5	External			$899.00	Auto-switching speeds, callback sec, remote config
Multitech Systems	MT932EC MultiModem V32EC	9600	V.32, V.42, MNP5	Internal	QModemSST		$869.00	Auto-switching speeds, callback sec, remote config

continues

Table 10.1. Concluded

COMPANY	MODEL	MAX BAUD RATE	COMPRESSION	INTERNAL, EXTERNAL	SOFTWARE INCLUDED	FAX MODEM, BAUD	RETAIL PRICE	OTHER INFORMATION
Multitech Systems	MT932ECB	9600	V.32, V.42bis, MNP5	Internal	QModemSST		$899.00	Callback sec, remote config
Multitech Systems	MT932ECB MultiModem V32EC	9600	V.32, V.42, V.42bis, MNP5	Internal	QModemSST		$899.00	Auto-switching speeds, callback sec, remote config
Multitech Systems	MT932EM MultiModemV32 for the Mac	9600	V.32, V.42, MNP5	External	Quick-Link II		$869.00	Auto-switching speeds, callback sec, remote config
Multitech Systems	MT932EMB MultiModem V32 Mac	9600	V.32, V.42, V.42bis, MNP5	External	Quick-Link II		$899.00	Auto-switching speeds, callback sec, remote config
Practical Peripherals	Practical Modem 9600SA	9600	V.32, V.42, V.42bis, MNP5	External	CompuServe			Data buffering, stores 4 numbers
Practical Peripherals	Practical Modem PM2400	9600	V.42, V.42bis, MNP5, LAPM	Internal	Yes			Auto adaptive eq, non-volatile RAM
Practical Peripherals	Practical Modem PM2400SA	9600	V.42, V.42bis, MNP5, LAPM	External	CompuServe			Auto adaptive eq, non-volatile RAM
Practical Peripherals	SmartPack 9600 For The Macintosh	9600	V.32, V.42, V.42bis, MNP5	External	Smartcom II Mac			Automatic speed buffering
Swan Technologies	Swan 9600 bps External/ SW96E	9600	V.42bis	External	FLASHLINK		$449.00	Tech support available
Swan Technologies	Swan 9600 bps Internal/SW96I	9600	V.32bis	Internal	BitCom		$399.00	Tech support available
UDS	Fastalk FAX 32	9600	V.42, V.42bis, MNP5	External		Send/ Receive, 9600		
US Robotics	Sportster V.32	9600	V.42bis, MNP5	Internal, External	Prodigy		$595.00	
US Robotics	WorldPort 9600 V.32	9600	MNP4	External	Yes		$699.00	
Zoom	V32/V42	9600	V.42bis, MNP 5	External			$599.00	Up to 38,400 bps
US Robotics	Courier HST	14.4K	V.42, V.42bis, MNP5	Internal, External			$995.00	
US Robotics	Courier HST Dual Standard	14.4K	V.42, V.42bis, MNP5	Internal, External			$1,295.00	
US Robotics	Courier V.32bis	14.4K	V.42, V.42bis, MNP5	Internal, External			$995.00	
Multitech Systems	MultiModem V32BL 1432L8	14.4K	V.32bis, V.42bis, MNP5	External			$1,199.00	Auto-switching speeds, callback sec, remote config
Multitech Systems	MultiModem V32B MT14322EAB	14.4K	V.42bis, MNP5	External			$1,099.00	Callback sec, remote config
Intel	Intel 9600 EX Modem	38.4K	V.42bis, MNP5	External	Crosstalk (MK.4)			

Pointing Devices

Chapter 2 describes the mouse and trackball. These devices can move a cursor around the screen, and they are especially helpful when you are operating a computer with a graphical user interface. If a traditional mouse or trackball does not serve your needs, however, you have some other options.

One option is a cordless mouse. A cordless mouse operates much like a standard mouse, but a wire between the mouse and the computer is not needed. Instead, a cordless mouse sends infrared signals to a receiver attached to the computer (much the way a remote-control unit for a television works). A cordless mouse may be preferable to a traditional mouse if you need to stand farther away from the computer than usual. Distances of more than 10 feet are possible, but the display is difficult to read that far away. You may prefer a cordless mouse if you often use a computer for presentations.

A mouse pen works like a mouse, but is handled like a pen. A typical mouse pen is shown in figure 10.1. You may prefer a mouse pen to a mouse if you work with a portable computer while traveling. A mouse pen does not need a tabletop; it works on many types of surfaces and at different angles. For example, you can use a mouse pen on your leg or on the back of an airplane seat. You also may want to use a mouse pen for ergonomic reasons, because you may prefer the feel of a pen to the feel of a mouse.

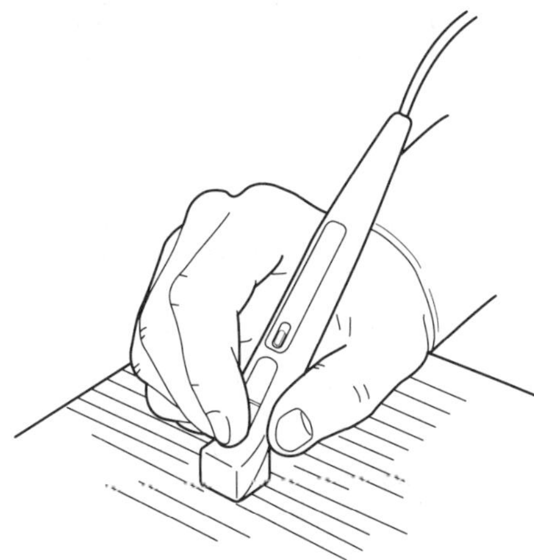

Fig. 10.1. *A mouse pen.*

Another option is a mouse tablet, such as the one shown in figure 10.2. With a mouse tablet, sliding your index finger over the tablet moves the cursor on-screen. Pressing on the tablet is like clicking a mouse button. (If you do not want to use your finger with the tablet, you can substitute a stylus.) A feature of a mouse tablet, not available with a traditional mouse, is the capability to program the tablet. For example, you can program the tablet to perform several functions in an application program. To activate the program, you press a specific area of the tablet.

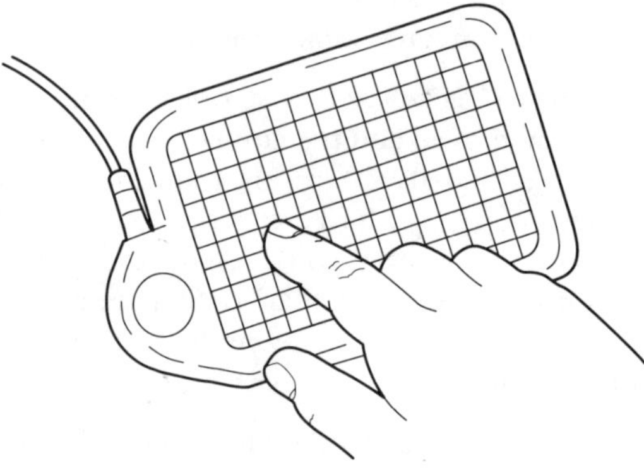

Fig. 10.2. *A mouse tablet.*

One other option is a miniature trackball, such as the one shown in figure 10.3. This device is small enough to attach to a keyboard or a portable computer, yet flexible enough to use at a distance from the computer. A miniature trackball works very much like a standard-size trackball. To move the cursor on the screen, you roll the ball with your thumb. To click, you click one of the buttons on the device.

Fig. 10.3. *A miniature trackball.*

Many pointing devices have a feature that enables you to control the speed of the cursor on the screen. This feature is especially useful for precise control in paint and draw programs.

Most kinds of pointing devices work with IBM and compatible computers or Apple Macintosh computers. When buying one of these devices, make sure that you specify which type of computer you have.

Reviewing Manufacturers of Pointing Devices

Two major manufacturers of the traditional mouse for IBM and compatible computers are Microsoft and Logitech. A Microsoft Mouse, which sells for about $100, is an excellent choice. Naturally, if the system you are considering comes with a mouse, you likely will choose to use it instead. For Apple Macintosh computers, Apple provides a mouse.

Trackballs are manufactured by a number of companies, including Microsoft, Kensington Microware, Kraft, and others. A standard trackball costs about $110. A trackball for a laptop or notebook portable costs about $10 more.

The cordless mouse is manufactured by companies such as Lightwave Technologies, Numonics, and Practical Solutions. A cordless mouse costs about $25 more than a traditional mouse.

You can buy a mouse pen from manufacturers such as International Machine Control Systems and Appoint. A mouse pen costs about the same as a traditional mouse.

A mouse tablet called the UnMouse is available from Micro Touch Systems. This device sells for about $200. A thumb-operated mouse called Thumbelina is available from Appoint. This device costs about the same as trackballs for portable computers.

Mouse and Trackball Listing

Although all mice and trackballs (pointing devices) serve the same basic purpose, each device has a feature that may make a specific pointing device more appealing to you. Table 10.2 gives a listing of many different pointing devices. Also listed are features of each pointing device that will help you make the best selection for your use.

To use table 10.2, note that each pointing device is listed alphabetically by the manufacturer's name and then by the model. Next are lists of pertinent hardware features about each pointing device, such as how many buttons are on the device and whether the device is mechanical or optomechanical. Also given is the resolution of the device, that is, how quickly the mouse pointer moves when you move the mouse or roll the ball. The last hardware specification tells how the device attaches to the computer. Also listed are the software that accompanies the device and the popular mouse the pointing device emulates, or acts like, (even trackballs emulate specific mice). Finally, you see the warranty information, and the last two columns list the retail price of the mouse or trackball and give other information that may help you determine which pointing device is best for you.

Table 10.2. Listing of Pointing Devices in Order of Manufacturer

COMPANY	MODEL	BUTTONS	TYPE	RESOLUTION (dpi)	INTERFACE
Altec	Genius	3	Mech	200-1,200	Serial
CompuAdd	CompuAdd Mouse	2	Mech		Serial
Datadesk	Switchball	3	Optomech	200	Serial
Everex	EMAC Silhouette Trackball	3	Optomech	200	ADB
IBM	PS/2 Mouse	2	Mech		PS/2
Insight	Insight	3	Optomech	290-1,450	Serial
Kensington	Expert Mouse/ Trackball	2	Optomech	200	Serial, PS/2
Kensington	Expert Mouse/ Trackball	2	Optomech	200	Serial
Logitech	MouseMan, left hand	3	Optomech	200-400	Mouse port, serial
Logitech	MouseMan, right hand	3	Optomech	200-400	Mouse port, serial, bus
Logitech	MouseMan, cordless	3	Radio	200-400	Serial
Logitech	Track Man	3	Optomech	300	Serial, bus
Logitech	TrackMan Stationary Mouse for Mac	3	Optomech	150-300	ADB
Logitech	TrackMan Portable	3	Optomech	200	Serial
Microsoft	Microsoft BallPoint Mouse	2	Mech	12-22,400	Combo serial, PS/2
Microsoft	Microsoft Mouse	2	Mech	12-22400	Serial, bus, PS/2
Microspeed	Mac TRAC ADB/ PD-340	3	Optomech	200	ADB
Microspeed	Mac TRAC DB9/PD-330	3	Optomech	200	Serial
Microspeed	PC-TRAC Bus/ PD-240	3	Optomech	50-1,000	Bus
Microspeed	PC-TRAC PS/2/PD-250	3	Optomech	50-1,000	PS/2

SOFTWARE	EMULATION	WARRANTY (years)	RETAIL PRICE	OTHER INFORMATION
Genius mouse driver	Mouse Systems, Microsoft	1	$25.00	Track ball avail also
Mouse driver	Microsoft	1	$24.95	
Mouse driver	Microsoft	3		Y-shaped cord
Mouse driver		2	$99.95	Special contour to rest wrist
IBM Mouse driver	IBM	1 carry-in	$101.00	
Mouse driver/Prog interface	Microsoft	1	$29.00	
Mouse driver	Microsoft, Mouse Systems, IBM		$149.95	Click-lock for click and drag function/Chording feature for 3rd button emulation
Mouse driver	Microsoft, Mouse Systems, IBM		$179.95	Click-lock for click and drag function/Chording feature for 3rd button emulation
Mouseware utils	Microsoft, IBM	Limited lifetime	$119.00	
Mouseware utils	Microsoft, IBM	Limited lifetime	$119.00	Bus mouse: $129.00
Mouseware utils	Microsoft, IBM	Limited lifetime	$199.00	
Mouseware utils		Limited lifetime		Thumb-operated trackball technology
		Limited lifetime	$149.00	
Yes	Microsoft, IBM	Limited lifetime	$169.00	Nylon taffeta carrying case/Vertical desktop capable
Menumaker, menus, mouse drivers	Microsoft	1, 30 days refund	$175.00	Supports DOS, Windows, and OS/2
Menumaker, menus, mouse drivers	Microsoft	Limited lifetime	$125.00	Software bundles available
No		1		Drag Lock
No		1		Drag Lock
Yes	Microsoft	1		Drag Lock/Keyboard Emulator
Yes	IBM	1		Drag Lock/Keyboard Emulator

continues

Table 10.2. Concluded

COMPANY	MODEL	BUTTONS	TYPE	RESOLUTION (dpi)	INTERFACE
Microspeed	PC-TRAC Serial/PD-230	3	Optomech	50-1,000	Serial
Mouse Systems	A 3	3	Optical	300 adj	ADB
Mouse Systems	Little Mouse A+	1	Optical	300 adj	Serial
Mouse Systems	Little Mouse/ADB	1	Optical	300 adj	Apple ADB
Mouse Systems	Little Mouse/PC	2	Optical	30-30,000	Serial, PS/2
Mouse Systems	Omnimouse II	2	Optomech	20-64,000	Serial, PS/2
Mouse Systems	PC Mouse III	3	Optical	30-30,000	Serial, PS/2
Mouse Systems	PC Mouse III (Bus)	3	Optical	30-30,000	Bus
Mouse Systems	PC Trackball	3	Optomech	20-6,400	Serial, PS/2
Mouse Systems	PC Trackball/Bus	3	Optomech	20-6,400	Bus
Mouse Systems	Trackball/ADB	2	Optomech	200 adj	ADB
Mouse Systems	White Mouse	3	Optomech	20-20,000	Serial, PS/2
Mouse Systems	White Mouse/Bus	3	Optomech	20-20,000	Bus
Swan Technologies	Swan Mouse	2	Optomech	400	Serial
Tandy	Tandy Serial Mouse	2	Mech	200	Serial
Tandy	Two-Button Mouse	2	Optomech	200	PS/2

SOFTWARE	EMULATION	WARRANTY (years)	RETAIL PRICE	OTHER INFORMATION
Yes	Microsoft	1		Drag Lock/Keyboard Emulator
Nu-Paint DA/3 button power CDEV	Apple	Lifetime		Prog button func generate up to 32 key strokes
Nu-Paint DA	Apple	Lifetime		
Nu-Paint DA	Apple	Lifetime		
Yes	Microsoft, IBM	Lifetime		Software bundles included
Yes	Microsoft, Mouse Systems, IBM	Lifetime		Software bundles included
Yes	Microsoft, Mouse Systems, IBM	Lifetime		Software bundles included
Yes	Microsoft, Mouse Systems, IBM	Lifetime		Software bundles included
Yes	Microsoft, Mouse Systems, IBM	Lifetime		Software bundles included
Yes	Microsoft, Mouse Systems, IBM	Lifetime		Software bundles included
Nu-Paint desk accessory	Apple	Lifetime		Right button functions as a cursor lock
Yes	Microsoft, Mouse Systems, IBM	Lifetime		Software bundles included
Mouse driver	Microsoft, Mouse Systems, IBM	Lifetime		Software bundles included
Basic mouse software	Microsoft	2	$49.00	
Yes	Microsoft	30 days	$49.95	
Yes	Microsoft	30 days	$49.95	

CD ROM Drives

A CD ROM (compact disk read-only memory) disk is a special kind of computer disk that stores an enormous amount of information. For example, a typical 5 1/4-inch CD ROM disk can store more than 500M of information. Compare that amount to a typical 5 1/4-inch double-density floppy disk that can hold just 0.36M. A single CD ROM disk can store an entire encyclopedia with text, images, and even sounds. Currently, almost 2,000 CD ROM disks are available, covering all kinds of topics. To use these disks, you need to attach a CD ROM drive to your personal computer.

The first thing to decide about a CD ROM drive is whether you want an internal CD ROM drive to mount inside the computer or a separate external drive. An internal drive costs about $50 to $100 less than an external drive. An external drive has its own case and includes its own power supply.

If you want a CD ROM drive for an IBM or compatible computer, you must insert a board into an expansion slot in the computer. Some CD ROM drives include a proprietary controller board in the package. Other drives are designed to connect to an SCSI (small computer system interface) adapter, which the computer manufacturer may or may not provide. A SCSI adapter typically costs about $125. Most IBM-compatible computers require a SCSI adapter card because the SCSI is not built into the computer. If you are considering a CD ROM drive for a Macintosh, you don't have to worry about installing a board. A CD ROM drive can be connected to the built-in SCSI port on the Macintosh.

CD ROM drives typically include stereo headphone jacks so that you can listen to any audio accompaniment that the disk provides. You also may want to play the audio through a sound system. In this case, the CD ROM drive must have jacks that provide audio output. Keep in mind that a CD ROM drive can play not only CD ROM disks, but also the audio compact disks that you buy in a music store.

CD ROM drives come in all shapes and sizes. Internal models are about the same size as a typical 5 1/4-inch floppy disk drive. External models, however, can vary considerably. Some models enable you to insert a disk just as you insert a disk into a floppy drive. With other models, the top of the drive opens up, and you place the disk into the drive. Some models hold more than one disk (often called "jukebox" drives). Some other CD ROM drives are small portable models that look very much like the portables that play music compact disks. You may want to consider a portable if you often need to carry the drive to different locations.

If you expect to build up a library of CD ROM disks, you may want to take advantage of a company's bundling arrangement. Some companies sell a CD ROM drive and include a selection of CD ROM disks in the package.

Like any disk drive, a CD ROM drive needs time to find information on the disk, and the amount of time required (the *access time*) can vary considerably from drive to drive. Typical access times for CD ROM drives are 350 and 500 milliseconds. If you are concerned about the time element, make sure that you check the average access time for each drive you are considering.

Sometimes a company that offers a database service on CD ROM disk also can sell you a CD ROM drive. Before accepting an offer of this kind, make sure that the price of the CD ROM drive is comparable to one that you can purchase on your own.

Reviewing CD ROM Drive Manufacturers

Manufacturers of CD ROM drives include Sony, NEC, Hitachi, Philips, Pioneer, Toshiba, and others. Most of these companies sell standard CD ROM drives, both internal and external models. Standard CD ROM drives vary in price from about $450 to about $800. NEC also sells portable CD ROM drives priced under $400. Pioneer sells a drive called the Minichanger, which holds multiple disks; its cost is about $1100. Sony and NEC are examples of companies that bundle CD ROM disks with their CD ROM drives.

CD ROM Drive Listing

The CD ROM drive is becoming increasingly popular because large amounts of information can be stored on a CD. You can store both computer information and sound. A few computers now come standard with a CD ROM drive. To aid you in selecting a CD ROM drive for your computer, table 10.3 lists many different models of CD ROM drives from quite a few manufacturers.

To aid you in selecting a CD ROM drive, table 10.3 has been sorted by manufacturer and lists much of the information that you need to know to select a CD ROM drive. Notice an individual entry in table 10.3. First listed are the manufacturer and model of the CD ROM drive. Next you see the type. The next columns specify whether the drive can be installed inside a computer or must remain external. The next column shows the capacity of CD the drive supports, rated in megabytes (M) of information. *AVERAGE ACCESS* gives you an idea of how quickly the drive searches for the information and is rated in milliseconds, or thousandths of a second. The transfer rate, rated in kilobytes per second, shows the rate that information is sent from the drive to the computer. The *ADAPTER TYPE* and *OPERATING SYSTEM* columns show you what type of adapter is required to run the drive and tell what operating system is supported. *CD AUDIO* tells you whether the drive supports audio CDs, and *CD ROM STANDARD* provides standards information. Often, CD ROM drives come bundled with CDs, so the next columns gives you this information. Finally, the table shows the warranty length, retail price, and other pertinent information that will help you decide which CD ROM drive is right for you.

Table 10.3. Listing of CD ROM Drives Sorted by Manufacturer

COMPANY	MODEL	TYPE	CAPACITY (M)	AVG. ACCESS (ms)	TRANSFER RATE (K/sec)	ADAPTER TYPE	OPERATING SYSTEM
Apple Computer	AppleCD SC M2700/B		656 (Mode 1), 748 (Mode 2)	500	150 (Mode 1), 171 (Mode 2)	SCSI	Macintosh
CD Technology		Both	683	325	150	SCSI (others available)	OS/2, DOS, Windows, Macintosh
Chinon	CDA-431	External	660	350	150	SCSI	DOS
Chinon	CDC-431	External	660	350	180	SCSI	DOS, Macintosh
Chinon	CDS-431	Internal	660	350	150	SCSI	DOS, Macintosh
Chinon	CDX-431	External	660	350	150	SCSI	DOS
Corel Systems Corporation	Pioneer DRM600 CD-ROM Minichanger	External	680	0.6 sec	1.5M/sec	SCSI	DOS and Novell NetWare 386 file server
Corel Systems Corporation	Sony CDU 6211 drive	External	680	0.38 sec	150	SCSI	DOS and Novell NetWare 386 file server
Denon America	DRD 253 for AT	External	680	400	153 , 1.6M/sec burst	SCSI	DOS, Macintosh, OS/2
Denon America	DRD 253 for MAC	External	680	400	153 , 1.6M/sec burst	SCSI	Macintosh
Everex	EMAC Metro CD	External	540 (formatted capacity)	.5 sec	150	SCSI	Macintosh
Genesis Integrated Systems	GenSTAR 2000	External	680	450	150	Proprietary	DOS
IBM	3.5" Rewritable Optical Drive	Internal	128	66	4.35M/sec	SCSI	DOS, OS/2, AIX
IBM	3510-1	External	600	380	150 , 1.5M/sec burst	SCSI	DOS, OS/2, ACX
IBM	Internal CD-ROM	Internal	600	380	150 , 1.5M/sec burst	SCSI	DOS, OS/2, AIX
Insight	Pioneer DRM-600/610 changer, A600 magazine	External	540	600	153 , 1.5M/sec burst	SCSI	
Laser Magnetic Storage Int'l	CM 50 portable	External	635	800	153.6 (Mode 1), 176.4 (Mode 2)	Serial	DOS
Laser Magnetic Storage Int'l	CM202	Internal	600	350	153.6 (Mode 1), 176.4 (Mode 2)	Serial	DOS
Laser Magnetic Storage Int'l	CM214	Internal	600	350	153.6 (Mode 1), 176.4 (Mode 2)	SCSI	DOS, Macintosh, OS/2
Laser Magnetic Storage Int'l	CM221	External	600	500	153.6 (Mode 1), 176.4 (Mode 2)	Serial	DOS

CD AUDIO	CD ROM STANDARD	CD'S INCLUDED	WARRANTY (years)	RETAIL PRICE	OTHER INFORMATION
Yes	Apple II, Macintosh, High Sierra		Limited	$899.00	Requires app SCSI config, inc Owner's Guide, Apple CD Caddy, setup disks
Yes, RCA & headphone jacks	High Sierra, ISO 9660	Coupon for Image Club, Nautilus	1		120 V, 220 V power supply
Yes	High Sierra, ISO 9660, Mac HFS	Discovery Systems CD-ROM Sampler	1		Headphone jack, volume control, small footprint
Yes	High Sierra, ISO 9660, Mac HFS		1		12-func remote audio control, built-in digital disp, headphone jack, vol control
Yes	High Sierra, ISO 9660, Mac HFS		1		Headphone jack, volume control
Yes	High Sierra, ISO 9660	Discovery Systems CD-ROM Sampler	1	$569.00	Headphone jack, volume control, small footprint
Optional	High Sierra, ISO 9660		1	$796.00	CorelDRIVER for DOS offers Windows utils for CDAUDIO, inc SCSI adp
Available	ISO 9660, High Sierra Format		1	$796.00	CorelDRIVER for NetWare 386 file servers, 8 and 100 user
Yes	High Sierra, ISO 9660, Apple HFS		1	$1,054.00	MTBF 15,000 hour, 15 minute sleep mode
Yes	Apple HFS		1	$940.00	MTBF 15,000 hour, 15 minute sleep mode
Yes	High Sierra, ISO 9660	Nautilus	2	$799.00	
Yes, audio software included	High Sierra, ISO 9660	6 with GenStar CD-ROM Bundle-$699	1	$499.00	Headphone, RCA jacks
No	SCSI X3.131-1986		1	$1,795.00	Supports either 3.5" magneto-optical cart, 3.5" optical
Yes	ISO 9660, ANSE SCSI X3.131.1986		1	$1,550.00	
Yes	ISO 9660 ANSI SCSI X3.131.1986		1	$1,250.00	
Yes	High Sierra, ISO 9660			$1,299.00	CD-ROM changer and a removable 6-disk magazine
Yes	All	Yes	1		
Yes	All	Test disk	2		
Yes	All	Test disk	2		
Yes	All	Test disk	2		

continues

Table 10.3. Continued

COMPANY	MODEL	TYPE	CAPACITY (M)	AVG. ACCESS (ms)	TRANSFER RATE (K/sec)	ADAPTER TYPE	OPERATING SYSTEM
Laser Magnetic Storage Int'l	CM231	External	600	400	153.6 (Mode 1), 176.4 (Mode 2)	SCSI	DOS, Macintosh, OS/2
Micro Design Int'l	LaserBank CD-ROM Family (600,1200, 2400)	Both	600	380	1.4M/sec	SCSI	DOS, Novell NetWare 386, OS/2, UNIX , SCO Xenix
Multimedia Systems	CD1700S (drive & CD-caddy only)	External	682 (Mode 1), 777.9 (Mode 2)	320	153.6	Hitachi bus XT/AT bus interface	DOS, optional DOS extensions disk
Multimedia Systems	CDR1700SMC (package)	External	682 (Mode 1)	320	153.6	Hitachi bus	DOS
Multimedia Systems	CDR1700SPC (package)	External	682 (Mode 1)	320	153.6	Hitachi bus, PC XT/AT proprietary	DOS
Multimedia Systems	CDR1750S (drive and caddy only)	External	682 (Mode 1)	320	153.6 , 1.3M/sec burst	SCSI	DOS, Macintosh
Multimedia Systems	CDR1750SMAC (package)	External	682 (Mode 1)	320	153.6 , 1.3M/sec burst	SCSI	Macintosh Finder 6.0 - 7.0, OS System
Multimedia Systems	CDR3600 (drive & CD caddy only)	Internal	682 (Mode 1), 777.9 (Mode 2)	450	153.6	Hitachi bus, PC bus	DOS
Multimedia Systems	CDR3600PC (package)	Internal	682 (Mode 1), 777.9 (Mode 2)	450	153.6	Hitachi bus, PC bus	DOS
Multimedia Systems	CDR3650 (drive and caddy only)	Internal	682 (Mode 1), 777.9 (Mode 2)	450	153.6 , 580 burst	SCSI	DOS, Macintosh Finder 6.0 & higher
NCR	NCR 6091 CDROM SCSI subsystem	External	553	400	153.6	SCSI	
NEC	Intersect CDR-36	External	680/12cm disk, 200/8cm disk	500	150	SCSI, parallel to SCSI host	DOS, Macintosh
NEC	Intersect CDR-73	External	680/12cm disk, 200/8cm disk	300	150	SCSI	DOS, Macintosh
NEC	Intersect CDR-83	Internal	680/12cm disk, 200/8cm disk	300	150	SCSI, parallel to SCSI host	DOS, Macintosh
Pioneer Communications of America	CD-ROM Six-Disk Minichanger	External	688	600	150	SCSI	DOS, Macintosh, TOPS, SCO Xenix, Sun OS
PLI	CD-ROM Drive	External		380	150 , 1.5M/sec burst	SCSI	DOS, Macintosh
Procom Technology	MCD-ROM 650/S	External	650	350	1.4M/sec	SCSI	DOS, Windows, NetWare, UNIX
Procom Technology	PICD650S	Internal	650	300	1.5M/sec	Proprietary	DOS
Procom Technology	PXCD650S	External	650	300	1.5M/sec	Proprietary	DOS
Reference Technology, Inc.	Hitachi CDR 1750 S	External	680	440	153.6	SCSI	DOS

CD AUDIO	CD ROM STANDARD	CD'S INCLUDED	WARRANTY (years)	RETAIL PRICE	OTHER INFORMATION
Yes	All	Test disk	2		
Yes	All		1		
Yes	High Sierra & ISO9660		1	$815.00	Optional ext, MS-DOS ext plus audio play software, stereo headphone jack
Yes, audio software included	High Sierra, ISO9660		1	$1,095.00	
Yes, audio software included	High Sierra & ISO 9660		1	$995.00	MS-DOS ext plus audio play software
Yes	CD sector level formats, CD Audio, mixed mode		1	$965.00	Stereo headphone jack, volume control, line level rear RCA jacks
Yes, audio play DA included	High Sierra, ISO9660, Apple HFS CD-Audio, mixed mode		1	$1,060.00	Stereo headphone jack, vol control, line level rear RCA jacks
Yes	High Sierra, ISO 9660, sector level formats, CD-Audio, mixed mode		1	$745.00	Stereo headphone jack, volume control, audio play software
Yes, software included	High Sierra & ISO 9660		1	$865.00	CD-ROM ext plus audio CD play software
Yes			1	$865.00	Optional MS-DOS ext disk, drivers, stereo headphone jack, volume control
Yes	High Sierra, ISO 9660, Apple HFS		2	$599.00	2.2 lbs, portable reader, opt batt pack, headphone mini-jack, vol control
Yes, Philips standard (Red book)	High Sierra, ISO 9660, Macintosh HFS		2	$949.00	64K cache mem, XA ready
Yes, Philips standard (Red book)	High Sierra, ISO 9660, Macintosh HFS		2	$849.00	64K cache mem, XA ready
Yes, RCA, headphone jacks	CD-I, DVI, Macintosh HFS, High Sierra, ISO-9660		1	$1,295.00	CD-ROM Minichanger has a six-disc removable cart
Yes	HFS, High Sierra, ISO 9660, Audio, International Formats	Nautilus MultiMedia CD	1		Switchable termination, SCSI ID Dial, metal case
Yes	High Sierra		1	$895.00	
Yes	High Sierra	Encyclopedia, U.S. & World Atlas, Reference Library	1	$399.00	
Yes	High Sierra	Encyclopedia, U.S. & World Atlas, Reference Library	1	$479.00	
Yes	High Sierra, ISO 9660		90 days + extended option		

continues

Table 10.3. Concluded

COMPANY	MODEL	TYPE	CAPACITY (M)	AVG. ACCESS (ms)	TRANSFER RATE (K/sec)	ADAPTER TYPE	OPERATING SYSTEM
Reference Technology, Inc.	Hitachi CDR 3600 u	Internal	680	550	153.6	Proprietary	DOS
Reference Technology, Inc.	Hitachi CDR 3650 u	Internal	680	550	153.6	SCSI	DOS
Reference Technology, Inc.	Hitachi CDR 700 S	External	680	440	153.6	Proprietary	DOS
Sony	CDU531	Internal	680	380	150	Proprietary	DOS
Sony	CDU535		680	340	150	Proprietary	DOS
Sony	CDU541	Internal	680	380	150	SCSI	DOS, OS/2, UNIX
Sony	CDU6201	External	680	380	150	Proprietary	DOS
Sony	CDU6211	External	680	380	150	SCSI	DOS, OS/2, UNIX
Sun Moon Star	CD Set	Both	553	550	150 , 600 burst	AT Bus	DOS
Tandy	Tandy CDR-1000	Internal	630	900	150	Proprietary	DOS 3.0
Todd Enterprises	TCDR 4000 series	External	553 (Mode 1), 630.7 (Mode 2)	300	153.6 (Mode 1), 175.2 (Mode 2)	Hitachi bus	DOS
Todd Enterprises	TCDR-3000	Double External	553 (Mode 1), 630.7 (Mode 2)	450	153.6 (Mode 1), 175.2 (Mode 2)	Hitachi bus	DOS
Todd Enterprises	TCDR-3004	Quad External	553 (Mode 1), 630.7 (Mode 2)	450	153.6 (Mode 1), 175.2 (Mode 2)	Hitachi bus	DOS
Todd Enterprises	TCDR-3600	Internal	553 (Mode 1), 630.7 (Mode 2)	450	153.6 (Mode 1), 175.2 (Mode 2)	Hitachi bus	DOS
Todd Enterprises	TCDR-6000	Single External	553 (Mode 1), 630.7 (Mode 2)	450	153.6 (Mode 1), 175.2 (Mode 2)	Hitachi bus	DOS
Toshiba America Information Systems	TXM-3301E1-Mac/PCF/PS2 (identifies kit)	External	683	325	153	SCSI-2	DOS, Macintosh
Toshiba America Information Systems	XM-3301B	Internal	683	325	153	SCSI-2	DOS, Macintosh

CD AUDIO	CD ROM STANDARD	CD'S INCLUDED	WARRANTY (years)	RETAIL PRICE	OTHER INFORMATION
Yes	High Sierra, ISO 9660		90 days + extended option		
Yes	High Sierra, ISO 9660		90 days + extended option		
Yes	High Sierra, ISO 9660		90 days + extended option		
Yes	Red & Yellow books		1	$635.00	MCA adptr avail for ext model only
Yes	Red & Yellow books		1		
Yes	Yellow & Red books		1	$795.00	MCA adptr avail for ext model only
Yes	Red & Yellow books		1	$799.95	
Yes	Yellow & Red books		1	$949.95	
Yes	High Sierra, ISO 9660	World Atlas, Illustrated Encyclopedia, Microsoft Bookshelf	18 mos	$895.00	
Yes			1	$399.00	
Yes	High Sierra, ISO 9660				
Yes	High Sierra, ISO 9660				Small footprint double CD-ROM drive, fan cooling
Yes	High Sierra, ISO 9660				Small footprint, double CD-ROM drive, fan cooling
Yes	High Sierra, ISO 9660				
Yes	High Sierra, ISO 9660				Heavy duty motor, patented lens cleaning system
Yes, Red book, Yellow book		Discovery Demo Disk	1		
Yes, Red book, Yellow book		Discovery Demo Disk	1		

Scanners

A scanner is a device that enables you to transform printed text or images into electronic text or images. The major uses for a scanner are desktop publishing, optical character recognition (OCR), and faxing. If you are creating a newsletter and want to insert a picture into the body of the copy, you can scan the picture and then use it in the program. To avoid retyping copy, you can scan a page of text and then let OCR (optical character recognition) software read and transform the image into a document that can be used with a word processor. You can use scanners with IBM-compatible and Macintosh computers.

To send text or images to another location, you can use a scanner to produce an image of the page. This image then can be transmitted by means of a fax board in your computer to any fax machine or to another computer containing a fax board.

You can choose from several types of scanners, depending on what type of material you want to scan. A flatbed scanner, such as the one shown in figure 10.4, scans documents, periodicals, and books. An overhead scanner, such as the one shown in figure 10.5, scans these items and also three-dimensional objects. A sheet-feed scanner, such as the one shown in figure 10.6, scans single sheets of paper. To scan a stack of pages, some scanners have a sheet-feeding mechanism built into the scanner or available as an option. A hand scanner, such as the one shown in figure 10.7, is an inexpensive way to scan material such as small images or columns of text.

Fig. 10.4. *A flatbed scanner.*

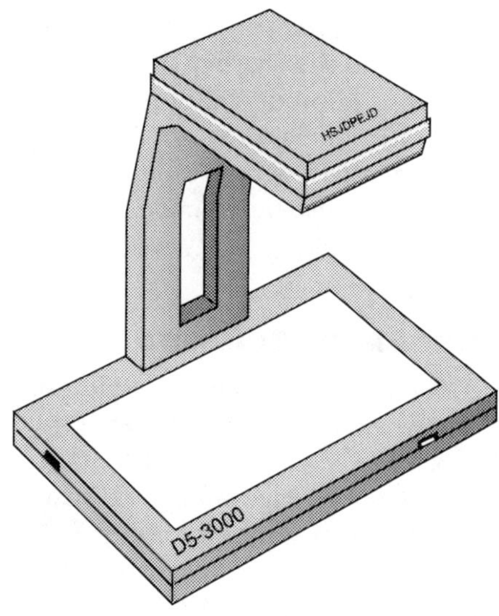

Fig. 10.5. *An overhead scanner.*

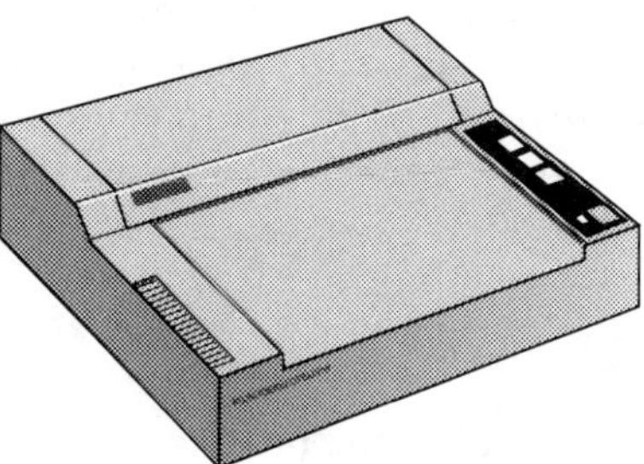

Fig. 10.6. *A sheet-feed scanner.*

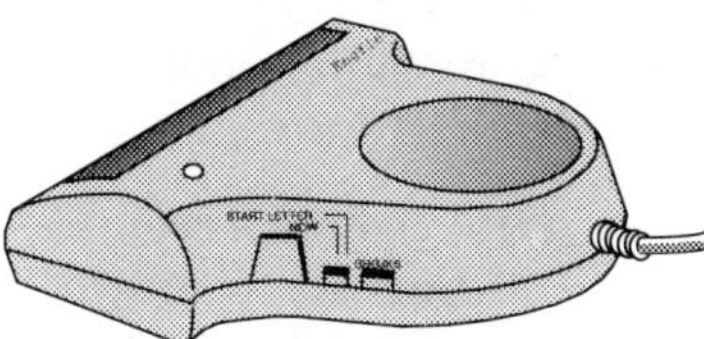

Fig. 10.7. *A handheld scanner.*

Scanners are connected to a computer through an adapter card you install in an expansion slot or through a built-in SCSI port. Most scanners include this interface hardware in the package.

Scanners scan at different resolutions. The higher the resolution, the more dots the electronic image contains and the sharper the image is. A low-cost scanner can produce images with a resolution of 300 dots per inch (dpi). This resolution is acceptable for all but the most demanding applications. More expensive scanners can produce images with much higher resolution. Most scanners produce black-and-white and half-tone images, but some expensive scanners can produce color images.

Reviewing Scanner Manufacturers

Scanners are available from companies such as Hewlett-Packard, The Complete PC, Chinon, Panasonic, Microtek, and Logitech. Hewlett-Packard's ScanJet Plus flatbed scanner sells for about $1,500, Chinon's DS-3000 overhead scanner for about $700, The Complete PC's Full-Page sheet-feed scanner for about $500, and Logitech's ScanMan Plus handheld scanner for about $175. A couple of examples of higher resolution scanners are the Microtek ScanMaker 1850, which scans 35mm slides at resolutions up to 1850 dpi ($2,995), and the ScanMaker 600Z, which scans full pages at 600-dpi resolution ($1,995).

Remember that a scanner can be used to scan images or text. If you want to scan images, you need paint software to edit and size the images after you have scanned them. If you want to scan text, you need OCR software to "read" the text so that you can use it with a word processor. Paint programs and OCR software may come bundled with the scanner, or you may have to purchase the software separately.

Scanner Listing

The scanner has two major uses. The main use is to transfer pictures to computer medium for inclusion in desktop publishing packages. The second use is for optical character recognition (OCR). Using OCR, you can scan a page of text from, for example, a magazine article and convert that image into computer-manageable text that you can import into a word processor. You also will find listed a few scanners that scan 35mm slides. Table 10.4 lists many varieties of scanners from different manufacturers.

To help you use table 10.4, the listing of scanners has been sorted by scan size and then by manufacturer within each scan size. As with other tables, this table first lists the manufacturer and model of each scanner. Next is the resolution of the scanner, in dots per inch, and the scan size. Listed are 35mm slide scanners, full-page scanners, and handheld scanners. The column *WIDTH x LENGTH* is rated in inches and shows the dimensions the scanner will scan. The *INTERFACE* column shows what type of adapter is required to attach the scanner to your computer. The next three columns tell you whether the scanner supports halftones, gray scales, and color. Although these specifications are often indicated by Yes or No, some scanners list specifically the halftone, gray scale, and color support. The next column lists any software that accompanies the scanner, and *FILE SUPPORT* shows you what graphic file specifications the scanner supports. Finally, you can see each scanner's warranty details, retail price, and other information.

Tape Backup Drives

Whenever you use a hard disk drive in a personal computer, you run the risk of someday losing all the programs and data stored on your hard disk. This loss can occur when the hard disk "crashes," or becomes inoperable. You also can lose your data if a catastrophe occurs, such as a fire or theft. To protect yourself against the loss of programs and data, you must back up your hard disk. To back up a hard disk means to make a copy of the information on the hard disk. This backup copy needs to be made at regular intervals. These intervals may be daily, weekly, or monthly, depending on how much you use the computer and how much you value the data stored in your computer.

Typically, you make a backup copy of the hard disk onto either floppy disks or magnetic tape. If you plan to back up a hard disk onto floppy disks, you don't need to worry about a tape backup drive. But if you are not too keen on the prospect of backing up a high-capacity hard disk (60M or more) onto 40 or more floppy disks, you may want to consider purchasing a tape backup drive.

Many kinds of tape backup drives are on the market. Some are meant to back up hard disks with capacities in the range of 40M to 250M. Others are intended to back up disk drives with capacities higher than 250M. This section covers tape backup drives in the first category (40M to 250M).

Tape backup drives designed to back up hard disk drives in the 40M to 250M range are called *minicartridge* tape backup drives. Both internal and external models are available. Internal drives are about the same size as a 5 1/4-inch floppy disk drive. External drives include a case and power supply and cost about $100 more than their internal counterparts.

Minicartridge tape drives use a DC2000 1/4-inch tape cartridge, which has dimensions of approximately 2 1/2 by 3 inches. The tapes come in different capacities, such as 40M, 80M, and so on. Minicartridge drives can be connected to IBM and compatible computers via the floppy disk drive controller or through a separate adapter board.

When shopping for a tape backup drive, software is a major consideration. Software to control the tape drive can vary greatly from manufacturer to manufacturer. Because you need to learn the software to use the drive, check out a demo of the software before making a purchase decision.

Table 10.4. Listing of Scanners in Order of Scan Size and Company

COMPANY	MODEL	RESOLUTION (dpi)	SCAN SIZE	WIDTH x LENGTH (inches)	INTERFACE	HALFTONE	GRAY SCALE
Howtek	Slide Scanner	2000	35mm slide	2.5 x 2.5	GPIB	Yes	Yes
Microtek	ScanMaker 1850	200-1850	35mm slide	35mm x 3mm	Proprietary		256
Microtek	ScanMaker 1850s	200-1850	35mm slide	35mm x 3mm	SCSI-Mac		256
Abaton	Scan 300/Color	72-300	Full pg	8.5 x 14	SCSI	Yes	Yes
Agfa Compugraphic	Agfa Focus 9800GSE	100-800	Full pg	8.25 x 11.5	SCSI	Yes	Yes
Agfa Compugraphic	Agfa Focus Color	100-800	Full pg	8.25 x 11.5	SCSI	Yes	Yes
Chinon	DS-2000 Image Scanner-Mac	100-200	Full pg	8.5 x 11	Serial, parallel	5 dithered	2 shades
Chinon	DS-2000 Image Scanner-PC	100-200	Full pg	8.5 x 11	Serial, parallel	5 dithered	2 shades
Chinon	DS-3000 Color Image Scanner-Mac	75-300	Full pg	8.5 x 11	SCSI		256
Chinon	DS-3000 Color Image Scanner-PC	75-300	Full pg	8.5 x 11	Parallel		256
Chinon	DS-3000 Image Scanner-Mac	75-300	Full pg	8.5 x 11	Serial, parallel	16 dithered	2 shades
Chinon	DS-3000 Image Scanner-PC	75-300	Full pg	8.5 x 11	Serial, parallel	16 dithered	2 shades
Complete PC	The Complete Page Scanner-Mac	200-300	Full pg	8.5 x 14	SCSI	3 patterns	Simulated only
Howtek	Personal Color Scanner	50-300	Full pg	8.5 x 14	Parallel	Yes	256
Howtek	Scanmaster 3	75-400	Full pg	8.5 x Var	GPIB	Yes	256
Howtek	Scanmaster 3+	75-1200	Full pg	8.5 x Var	GPIB	Yes	256
IBM	2456 Image Scanner/2456-001	100-400	Full pg	A3	SCSI		256
IBM	3117 Scanner	120-240	Full pg	8.5 x 11.5	3117 hi-spd adpt & ext	Yes	No
IBM	3118-010 Scanner	120-240	Full pg	8.5 x Var	Ser, IBM adp A	Yes	No
IBM	3118-020 Scanner	120-240	Full pg	8.5 x Var	Ser, IBM adp A	Yes	No

COLOR	SOFTWARE	FILE SUPPORT	WARRANTY (years)	RETAIL PRICE	OTHER INFORMATION
24-bit	Included	Std PC, Mac formats	90 days		Toll-free tech support
24-bit	Photostyler	TIFF, PICT2, PICT, EPS, BMP, PCX, TARGA, GIF	1	$2,995.00	
24-bit	Photoshop	TIFF, PICT2, PICT, EPS, BMP, PCX, TARGA, GIF	1	$3,195.00	
Yes	Adobe PhotoShop		1		Built-in SCSI for Mac/PC, PS/2 SCSI host adptr req
No	Optional	TIFF, PICT, EPSF	90 days	$5,495.00	
Yes	Optional	TIFF, PICT, EPSF	90 days	$7,995.00	Transparency scanning to 5 x 5 opt
	Included	TIFF, PCX, IMG, others	1	$695.00	Scans 3-D objects up to 3/4" in height
	Included	TIFF, PCX, IMG, others	1	$545.00	Scans 3-D objects up to 3/4" in height
12-bit	Colorset Software	TIFF, PCX, IMG, others	1		Scans 3-D objects up to 3/4" in height
12-bit	Colorset Software	TIFF, PCX, IMG, others	1		Scans 3-D objects up to 3/4" in height
Opt	Included	TIFF, PCX, IMG, others	1	$895.00	Scans 3-D objects up to 3/4" in height
Opt	Included	TIFF, PCX, IMG, others	1	$745.00	Scans 3-D objects up to 3/4" in height
No	SmartScan	PICT, PS, EPSF, MacPaint, TIFF	1	$999.00	Unlimited tech support 8-5 M-F
24-bit	Optional	TIFF, PICT, PICT2, EPS, VGA, TGA, PXT	1		Toll-free tech support
24-bit	Optional	Std PC, Mac formats	90 days		Toll-free tech support
24-bit	Optional	Std PC, Mac formats	90 days		Toll-free tech support
No	Optional		1	$6,995.00	Includes 50-pg doc feeder
No	Optional		1	$1,865.00	
No	Optional		1	$4,615.00	
No	Optional		1	$5,130.00	Includes 30-pg doc feeder

continues

Table 10.4. Continued

COMPANY	MODEL	RESOLUTION (dpi)	SCAN SIZE	WIDTH x LENGTH (inches)	INTERFACE	HALFTONE	GRAY SCALE
IBM	3119 Scanner-S10/B119 Pagescanner	150-300	Full pg	8.5 x 11	3119 adp A	No	128
Microtek	ScanMaker 600 G	75-600	Full pg	8.5 x 13.5	Proprietary	12 (more poss)	256
Microtek	ScanMaker 600 GS	75-600	Full pg	8.5 x 13.5	SCSI-Mac	12 (more poss)	256
Microtek	ScanMaker 600 z	75-600	Full pg	8.5 x 13.5	Proprietary	12 (more poss)	256
Microtek	ScanMaker 600 zs	75-600	Full pg	8.5 x 13.5	SCSI-Mac	12 (more poss)	256
Nikon, Inc.	Nikon Film Scanner LS-3500	4096 x 6144 pixels	Full pg	24mm x 36mm	GPIB, ser		
Pentax Technologies	SB-L301: Legal-size flatbed	39-300	Full pg	8.5 x 14	SCSI-Mac	5 patterns	16
Sharp Electronics	JX-300 Business Color Scanner	30-300	Full pg	8.5 x 11.6	GPIB		256
Sharp Electronics	JX-450 Color Scanner	30-300	Full pg	11 x 17	GPIB		256
Sharp Electronics	JX-600 Commercial Color Scanner	30-600	Full pg	17 x 11.7	GPIB		256
Varityper	1200R Reflection Scanner	1200	Full pg	11.5 x 17			1,000 levels
Varityper	3515T Slide Scanner	1024 x 1520 lpi	Full pg	35mm			black & white
Varityper	4520T Multi-format Scanner	200-2000	Full pg	4 x 5	SCSI-Mac		
Varityper	Image Scanner 1200	7.5-1200	Full pg	11.5 x 17	SCSI-Mac	256 shades	256
Xerox Imaging Systems	GS Plus		Full pg	8.5 x 14	SCSI	256	4/8 bit
Xerox Imaging Systems	K-5200	50-600	Full pg	8.25 x 14	SCSI	Yes	16 to 256
Xerox Imaging Systems	ScanWorX	200-400	Full pg	11.7 x 17	SCSI	10	16 to 256
Complete PC	The Complete Full-Page Scanner	200-300	Full pg, sheet fed	8.5 x 14	Serial	3 patterns	Simulated only
Complete PC	The Complete Page Scanner/GS	200-300	Full pg, sheet fed	8.5 x 14	Serial		256
DEST	Personal Scan	100-400	Full pg, sheet fed	8.5 x 14	Par, SCSI	64	No

10

COLOR	SOFTWARE	FILE SUPPORT	WARRANTY (years)	RETAIL PRICE	OTHER INFORMATION
	Starter program		1	$2,685.00	
No	Photostyler	TIFF, PICT, EPS, BMP, PCX, GIF	1	$1,595.00	14 brightness settings on gray scale
No	Photoshop LE	TIFF, PICT, EPS, BMP, PCX, GIF	1	$1,695.00	14 brightness settings on gray scale
24-bit	PhotoStyler	TIFF, PICT2, PICT, EPS, BMP, PCX, TARGA, GIF	1	$1,995.00	Optional SCSI adptr/14 brightness settings for each color plane
24-bit	Photoshop	TIFF, PICT2, PICT, EPS, BMP, PCX, TARGA, GIF	1	$2,195.00	14 brightness settings for each color plane
24-bit/5 filters/256 grad	Nikon ColorFlex, Letraset ColorStudio-MAC, PhotoStyler-PC	TIFF, PICT2, EPS, Raw RGB, 9 trk tape to Scitex, Crossfield	1		COLOR SCANNING: 5 filters/could substitute Adobe Photoshop for Letraset
No	Optional	Std. PC, Mac formats	1		Halftone scan: 5 def, 1 user-def dithering patterns/opt auto doc feeder
24-bit	Included	ASCII, binary		$2,345.00	
24-bit	Included	ASCII, binary		$5,995.00	Opt mirror unit to scan 35mm slides, transparencies up to 8.5 x 11
24-bit	Optional			$14,995.00	
24-bit	Optional				Transparent or reflective scanning
color	Optional		90 days		
12-bit	Optional		90 days		Contains hard disk for background scanning
No	Image Master, Super Paint, Sum Utilities	TIFF, RIFF, PICT, EPSF, others	90 days		Halftone scan: 8 bits per pixel. Special descreening filters for scanning halftones
No	Optional	Std PC, Mac formats			
No	Optional	TIFF, PCX, IGF, Xerox XPIW			
No	Optional	TIFF, IGF, Sun Rasterfile			
No	SmartScan, Wordscan OCR	TIFF, PCX, MSP, CUT, BMP, FAX	1	$899.00	Unlimited tech support 8 to 5 M-F, Spiral, Mesh, Bayer patterns
	Image-In, Wordscan	TIFF,PCX, EyeStar, BMP,MSP	2	$1,099.00	Windows 3.0 comp.
No	Recognize! OCR, Image-In	TIFF, EPS GEM, BMP, PCX, MSP	1		ASCII and RFT-DCA OCR support

continues

Table 10.4. Continued

COMPANY	MODEL	RESOLUTION (dpi)	SCAN SIZE	WIDTH x LENGTH (inches)	INTERFACE	HALFTONE	GRAY SCALE
Microtek	MSII Mac	75-300	Full pg, sheet fed	8.5 x 14	SCSI-Mac	12 (more poss)	64 simulated dither
Microtek	MSII PC	75-300	Full pg, sheet fed	8.5 x 14	Proprietary	12 (more poss)	64 simulated dither
Abaton	Scan 300 6S	72-300	Full pg, flatbed	8.5 x 14	SCSI	Yes	Yes
Abaton	TranScribe 300	72-300	Full pg, flatbed	8.5 x 14	SCSI	Yes	No
Apple Computer	Apple Scanner	75-300	Full pg, flatbed	8.5 x 14	SCSI	Yes	16
Canon	Canon IX-30F	75-300	Full pg, flatbed	216mm x 297mm	Optional	64 dithered	256
Complete PC	The Complete Flatbed Scanner	75-300	Full pg, flatbed	8.5 x 14	Serial		256
DEST	PC Scan 3000	32-300	Full pg, flatbed	8.5 x 11.7	Par, SCSI	64	256
EPSON	ES-300C	50-600	Full pg, flatbed	8.5 x 11.7	Serial, parallel	3 modes	256
Hewlett-Packard		300	Full pg, flatbed	8.5 x 14	Par, SCSI	Yes	16 & 256
Complete PC	The Complete Half-Page Scanner/400	200-400	Hand	4.1 x 14	Serial	3 patterns	Simulated only
Complete PC	The Complete Half-Page Scanner/GS	100-400	Hand	4.1 x 14	Serial		32 & 256
Complete PC	Comp Half-Pg Scanner/GS-Mac	100-400	Hand	4.1 x 14	SCSI		32 & 256
DEST	Personal Scan	100-400	Hand		Par, SCSI	64	No
Logitech	ScanMan 256	100-400	Hand	4.2 x 14		True gray scale	256 levels
Logitech	ScanMan 32 DOS	100-400	Hand	4.2 x 14	Serial	True gray scale	32
Logitech	ScanMan 32 Macintosh	100-400	Hand	4.2 x 14	SCSI	True gray scale	32
Marstek, Inc.	ColorArtist	50-400	Hand	4.13 x 24	Serial	64	64
Marstek, Inc.	M-105 WP	100-400	Hand	4.13 x 24	Serial	64	64 w/ software
Marstek, Inc.	M-800 P	100-800	Hand	4.13 x 24	Serial	64	No

10

COLOR	SOFTWARE	FILE SUPPORT	WARRANTY (years)	RETAIL PRICE	OTHER INFORMATION
No	OmniType	TIFF, PCX, PICT, BMP, GIF	1	$1,195.00	
No	OmniType	TIFF, PICT, BMP, PCX, GIF	1	$995.00	
No	Included		1		MAC, NeXT SCSI, 2 con/PC, PS/2 - SCSI host adptr req
No	OmniType by Caere	TIFF, PICT, EPS, Macpaint	1		Built-in SCSI for Mac/PC, PS/2 SCSI host adptr req/Opt auto doc feeder
No	Mac Apple Scanner, HyperScan HyperCard stack	PICT, TIFF, MacPaint	90 days	$1,799.00	3 comp modes: gray scale, line art, halftone/Full AppleFax Modem support
No	Optional		1	$1,545.00	PC adapter: $595.00
	Picture Publisher	TIFF, EPSF, PCX	1	$1,599.00	Windows 3.0 comp/opt auto feeder
No	Recognize! OCR, Image-In	TIFF,EPS, GEM, BMP, PCX, MSP	1		ASCII and RFT-DCA OCR support
24-bit	Inc with interface	TIFF,PCX, BMP, EPS, GIF, PICT, MacPaint, TGA	1	$1,699.00	PC interface inc scanning, alteration, and color software
No	HP Scanning Gallery, DeskScan	MA Paint, GEM, EPSF, PCX, TIFF, MacPaint, EPS, PICT	1		Opt 20-page auto doc feeder
	SmartScan	TIFF, PCX, MSP, CUT, BMP, FAX	2	$299.00	Wide third roller for smooth, straight scanning/Spiral, Mesh, Bayer patterns
	Image-In	TIFF, PCX, EyeStar, BMP, MSP	2	$349.00	Windows 3.0 comp.
No	SmartScan	PICT, PS, EPSF, MacPaint, TIFF	2		
No	Recognize! OCR, Image-In	TIFF, EPS GEM, BMP, PCX, MSP	1		ASCII and RFT-DCA OCR support
No	Ansel Image Editing, ScanMate	TIFF, PCX, BMP, EPS	Limited lifetime		
No	ScanMate, GrayTouch Image Editing	IMG, TIFF, PCX	1		
No	ScanMan Software	MacPaint, TIFF, PICT	Limited lifetime		
18-bit	Scankit, Rainbow Paint, Perceive Personal OCR	PCX, TIFF, TGA, MSP, CAT	1		
No	Image-In, Perceive Personal OCR	IMG, PCX, MSP, TIFF, DXF, DRW, EPS, AL, MacPaint, ASCII, WordStar, WordPerfect	1		
No	ScanKit, PC Paintbrush Plus, Perceive Personal OCR	TIFF, PCX, MSP, CUT, IMG, ASCII, WordStar, WordPerfect	1		

continues

Table 10.4. Concluded

COMPANY	MODEL	RESOLUTION (dpi)	SCAN SIZE	WIDTH x LENGTH (inches)	INTERFACE	HALFTONE	GRAY SCALE
Marstek, Inc.	M-800 WP	100-800	Hand	4.13 x 24	Serial	64	64 w/ software
Marstek, Inc.	M-800 Mac 64	100-800	Hand	4.13 x 24	SCSI	64	64 w/ software
Mouse Systems	PageBrush/32	100-400	Hand	4.13 x 12	Bus	No	32
Mouse Systems	PageBrush/ Color Mac	100-400	Hand	4.1	SCSI	No	Yes
Mouse Systems	PageBrush/ Color PC	100-400	Hand	4.1	Bus	No	Yes
Sharp Electronics	JX-100 Hand-held Color Scanner	200	Hand	4 x 6	Serial		64

Manufacturers of Tape Backup Drives

Irwin Magnetic Systems pioneered the minicartridge tape backup drive and remains the leading manufacturer in this category today. Other prominent manufacturers of these tape drives are Colorado Memory Systems and Mountain Computer. Tape drives range in cost from about $250 to $500. Tapes that hold 80M cost about $30 each.

COLOR	SOFTWARE	FILE SUPPORT	WARRANTY (years)	RETAIL PRICE	OTHER INFORMATION
No	Image-In, Perceive Personal OCR	IMG, PCX, MSP, TIFF, DXF, DRW, EPS, AL, MacPaint, ASCII, WordStar, WordPerfect	1		
No	Enhance	PICT, EPS, TIFF, MacPaint, EPS	1		
No	ScanEdit, Prodigy OCR	.PCX,.CUT,.EPS,.TIF	2		
Yes	VideoPaint	PICT, CLUT, CMYK, TIFF 5.0 (color), EPS, LZWWrite	2		
8-bit	ImageQuest, ImagePrep	CPI,.GIF, .BMP,.EPS,.PCX,.TGA	2		
6-bit	Optional			$995.00	Interface kits include software

Chapter Summary

This chapter describes some of the extras you may want to consider when you purchase a personal computer, namely modems, pointing devices, CD ROM drives, scanners, and tape backup drives. The chapter presents information about each device to help you make purchasing decisions. This chapter also lists leading manufacturers and approximate prices for the devices.

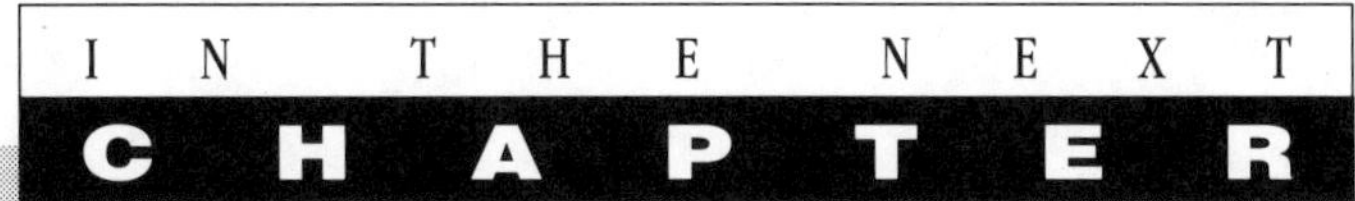

The next chapter describes personal computer software. The first part of the chapter tells you what you need to know about operating systems and graphical user interfaces. The latter part of the chapter describes application software and makes specific recommendations in a variety of application software categories.

CHAPTER ELEVEN

Determining What Software You Need

To take full advantage of the power of a personal computer, you need the proper software. In Chapter 1, you learned about different categories of software—word processors, spreadsheets, databases, and so on. In Chapter 2, you learned how to distinguish among ROM software, operating system software, and application software. This chapter gives you further information about operating system software and offers advice on selecting application software. The chapter also covers the issues of training and support, and shows how your choice of software affects your choice of hardware.

Choosing an Operating System

An important choice when you purchase a computer is the operating system software. An operating system is a level of software between an application program and the machine language used by the computer. The operating system provides services (such as storing and recalling information from a disk drive) both to you and to the application program. Besides providing services, an operating system gives you a way to interact with the computer. Nowadays, most operating systems also enable you to place a graphical user interface (GUI) between you and the operating system.

Your choice of an operating system and GUI may be determined by the computer you own. For IBM and compatibles, the most-used operating system is MS-DOS (PC DOS for IBM computers) and the most-used GUI is Microsoft Windows. Several operating systems, however, compete with MS-DOS and several GUIs compete with Windows. The most-used operating system for the Macintosh computer is the System, and its GUI is the Finder. If you purchase a Macintosh, you probably will purchase software that works with System and Finder.

When selecting an operating system and a GUI, consider whether you need to run all software at the same time or only one program at a time. To run more than one program at a time, you need an operating system or GUI that provides this feature.

In a single-tasking operating system, you run one software program at a time. For example, you use your word processor to write and print a letter. You then exit the word processor, start your spreadsheet program, and perform calculations. When you finish with the spreadsheet program, you exit and start the next program. In most cases, this mode of operation is adequate.

A single-tasking operating system generally does not need a very powerful computer or a large amount of RAM in the computer. While you run one program in a single-tasking operating system, the entire computer's processing speed is dedicated to that program. IBM and Macintosh computers both have single-tasking operating systems.

With multitasking operating systems, you can have more than one application program active at a time. For example, you can open your word processor and spreadsheet at the same time; you need not close any documents or quit any programs when you switch from one application to another. Multitasking operating systems normally provide ways to transfer data easily from one program to another. A single-tasking operating system like MS-DOS can achieve multitasking through the use of a GUI like Microsoft Windows or Quarterdeck's DESQview. The OS/2 operating system is multitasking by itself.

An operating system, like any other software product, undergoes updates and improvements over time. When you purchase a computer, purchase the latest version of the operating system. Thereafter, keep track of changes to the operating system and upgrade to a new version when warranted. For example, a change to an operating system may mean that you can use a new kind of disk drive. The following sections include information about the operating systems for IBM and compatibles and Macintosh computers.

Operating Systems for IBM and Compatible Computers

Most people who purchase an IBM or compatible computer use PC DOS (for IBM computers), MS-DOS (for IBM-compatible computers), or a version of MS-DOS (such as COMPAQ DOS) to which a compatible manufacturer has given its name. The purchase price of the computer often includes the operating system. If not, the operating system usually costs $75 to $100. The most current version of DOS (any of those just mentioned) is Version 5. If you purchase an IBM or compatible computer, make sure that you receive the latest version of DOS.

MS-DOS has competitors, such as DR DOS (see Chapter 2), that serve as direct replacements for MS-DOS and other competitors, such as OS/2, that offer advanced operating system features. The following sections describe the latest versions of MS-DOS and OS/2.

MS-DOS 5

MS-DOS is a single-tasking operating system for IBM and compatible computers. An enormous number of programs run under MS-DOS, and generally you can find an MS-DOS program to fit your needs, no matter what you want to do.

The latest version of MS-DOS is Version 5, which adds to the operating system some enhancements not present in earlier versions. Limited memory always has been a problem with MS-DOS. Application programs, along with the operating system and other kinds of programs—such as terminate-and-stay-resident programs (TSRs)—generally use the first 640K of RAM. MS-DOS 5 can use some of the memory from 640K to 1M to increase the amount of RAM available to application programs. On 80286 through 80486 computers, MS-DOS 5 can use the first 64K of extended memory to free even more conventional memory for application programs.

MS-DOS 5 includes a shell, a program to help you manage files and programs. DOS 4.01 also included this feature. The DOS 5 Shell, however, includes a task switcher, which you can use to switch programs without exiting one program and starting the other. With a task switcher, only one program operates at a time. When you switch from one program to another, the program you switch from stops operating but is ready to begin operating where you left off as soon as you switch back.

MS-DOS 5 includes important utilities, such as a program to undelete accidentally deleted files and a program to unformat an accidentally formatted disk. These programs give you a degree of safety previously available only through third-party programs. Other enhancements include support for a mouse, a new text editor, and on-line context-sensitive help.

If you decide to use MS-DOS 5, its new features may eliminate the need to buy other types of programs, such as shell, utility, and memory management programs. Any new computer usually includes a version of DOS, although sometimes at an extra cost. Make sure that you receive the latest version of DOS when you buy your computer; otherwise you will need to pay more to upgrade to DOS 5.

Que has published several excellent books about MS-DOS, including *Que's MS-DOS 5 User's Guide*, Special Edition, and *Using MS-DOS 5*. Refer to one of these books to learn more about MS-DOS.

OS/2

OS/2 is an operating system for IBM-compatible computers. Although you may not be considering OS/2, you should understand how this operating system fits into the overall picture of IBM computing. OS/2 is a multitasking operating system with a graphical user interface called the Presentation Manager (PM). The look and feel of PM is similar to Windows.

OS/2 multitasking divides a program into processes called *threads*, which are allocated processor time. A program that is sitting idle does not need processor time. OS/2 multitasking gives time to only those functions that actually need processor time. Multitasking, therefore, is very efficient.

Programs under OS/2 can communicate with each other; one program can pass results to another program. Even if you use only one program, that program can multitask—several processes within one program can run at the same time.

To run the most recent versions of OS/2, you need at least an 80286 computer and 2M to 4M of RAM plus the memory required for each program you plan to use. OS/2 needs at least 10M of hard disk space, as well.

OS/2 1.3 is the current version, but OS/2 2.0 may be released by the time you read this book. An expected major change with OS/2 2.0 is the inclusion of a new GUI called Workplace, which replaces Presentation Manager. OS/2 is not for everyone. If you think that you need more processing power than is available from DOS, OS/2 may be a solution. Most users, however, find DOS acceptable.

Apple Macintosh Operating System—System 7.0

Although the Macintosh has just one operating system, called System, it comes in many versions. The current version, System 7.0, includes features previously unavailable to Apple Macintosh users. System 7.0 is the operating system you probably will receive if you purchase an Apple Macintosh computer.

System 7.0 is the operating system that many Macintosh users have wanted for a long time. The key features of System 7.0 include support for TrueType, multitasking, publish-and-subscribe, Apple events, balloon help, file sharing, and 32-bit addressing. The following paragraphs briefly explain these features.

TrueType is Apple's outline-font technology. TrueType uses a single font-outline file to scale fonts to any size. A character can be as small as 1 point (1/72 inch) or as large as 32,768 points—on-screen and on paper. Having TrueType as a standard feature eliminates the need to purchase a font-scaling program, such as Adobe Type Manager.

Multitasking enables you to run more than one program at a time. Apple's GUI, called Finder, now includes the capability to multitask; you no longer need to invoke the MultiFinder.

With *publish-and-subscribe*, you can create a dynamic link between applications. One application, called the *publisher*, makes material, such as a pie graph or a table of numbers, available to other applications, called *subscribers*. The material copied by subscriber programs is linked to the publishing program and is updated automatically when you make a change. System 7.0 includes a set of protocols (rules for communication) called *interapplication communication (IAC)*. Apple events, which are part of IAC, enable two-way communication between applications. This communication enables the subscriber program to share the information from the publisher program.

A feature called *balloon* [illegible] ıelp in using the Apple Macintosh. Balloon help gives you info[illegible] ·oon-like balloon. You can use balloon help to gain information [illegible] ımands, dialog-box options, and so on.

If you are part of a netw[illegible] sharing to share information with other users on the netw[illegible] to use a dedicated server. If you use the Macintosh in a singl[illegible] ·nt, this System 7.0 feature is irrelevant.

You can use the 32-bit a[illegible] ·ure to break the 8M RAM barrier of previous versions of System. [illegible] ·nt this feature, you need a Macintosh that supports 32-bit addressi[illegible] LC, IIci, IIsi or IIfx. With 4M RAM SIMMs installed in these comput[illegible] example, 32-bit addressing enables you to use 10M of RAM on an LC, 1[illegible] ı a IIsi, and 32M on a IIci or IIfx.

If you decide that you need the capabilities of System 7.0, first find out whether the Macintosh model and software program you are considering takes advantage of System 7.0. Some Macintosh models cannot take advantage of 32-bit addressing. Some programs operate under System 7.0 but do not take advantage of the features. Some programs take advantage of only some features; other programs take advantage of all System 7.0's features. Before accepting a program for use with System 7.0, verify the program's compatibility level.

Graphical User Interfaces

When you choose an operating system such as OS/2 or System 7.0, you do not have to choose a graphical user interface; OS/2 currently uses the Presentation Manager, and System 7.0 uses Finder. If you choose MS-DOS, PC-DOS, or DR DOS, however, you need to choose a graphical user interface (if you want to work with one). Many GUIs are available for DOS, but only two are widely used: Microsoft Windows and Quarterdeck's DESQview. Other GUIs available for DOS are GEM by Digital Research, Deskmate by Tandy, and Ensemble (GEOWorks) from Berkeley Software.

Microsoft Windows

Microsoft Windows is the most popular graphical user interface for IBM and compatible computers. With the current version of Windows, Windows 3.0, you can start and switch among multiple DOS applications. If you are using a computer with an 80386SX, 80386, or 80486 microprocessor and have an adequate amount of memory, you can multitask DOS applications. Even if you do not need to multitask DOS applications, you can open more than one program, switch among the programs, and transfer information from one program to another.

All application programs designed to work under Windows have a similar look. If you learn how to use one, you have a head start on learning to use others. These programs also are more efficient at multitasking than programs designed with a proprietary user interface.

If you need multitasking and enjoy working with a graphical user interface, consider using Windows and Windows-specific applications. Remember, if one of the applications that meets your needs is not a Windows application but all the others are, do not rule out Windows; you can run the non-Windows application within Windows.

To use Windows adequately, you need a more powerful computer than you need to run DOS alone. You should purchase a computer with an 80386SX, 80386, 80486SX, or 80486 microprocessor. The computer that you purchase should have a high-quality display, such as VGA, and at least 2M of RAM. If you plan to multitask DOS applications under Windows, purchase at least 4M of RAM. A mouse is recommended.

Recommendations for Windows software are made later in this chapter under specific applications areas. Windows 3.0 comes with a simple word processor, drawing program, communications program, and file manager. These programs lack many features, but if your requirements are light in any of these areas, you may not need to purchase a separate program.

DESQview

In some ways, DESQview is similar to Windows 3.0. With DESQview, you can start multiple programs, switch among programs, and multitask DOS programs. Two DESQview products are available. DESQview 386 2.3 requires an 80386SX or greater microprocessor. DESQview 2.3 works with less powerful computers, such as 8088, 8086, and 80286 computers.

DESQview is designed to multitask standard DOS applications, although a few DESQview-specific applications are available. If you plan to use DESQview and need multitasking capabilities, you must have a large amount of memory in your computer. The exact amount depends on the requirements of the individual programs you multitask, plus the memory needed for DOS and DESQview. If you need only to switch among applications, you do not need as much memory. With DESQview, you also can copy information from program to program. If standard DOS applications meet your needs and you want to open multiple programs or multitask, DESQview is a fine interface to choose.

Other GUIs for IBM and Compatibles

You can buy several other graphical user interfaces for IBM-compatible computers running under DOS.

DeskMate, a GUI offered with some Tandy desktop and portable computers, has more than 100 software applications written for it, including Lotus 1-2-3 (a scaled-down version) and Symantec's popular Q&A. DeskMate comes with a simple word processor, spreadsheet, file manager, calendar, drawing program, alarm, calculator, spelling checker, and phone list. Tandy even supplies a low-end network called DeskMate Workgroup. You can start DOS applications using DeskMate and switch among these applications.

PC/GEOS is another fine graphical user interface. Applications written specifically for PC/GEOS can multitask. GeoWorks Ensemble, a program designed to run under PC/GEOS, comes with a word processor, appointment program, drawing program, communications programs, and several other utilities. These applications, although easy to use, offer many advanced features found in more expensive programs.

PC/GEOS enables you to start several DOS applications. Although you can switch from one DOS application to another, you cannot multitask DOS applications with PC/GEOS, as you can with Windows or DESQview. PC/GEOS works well on all kinds of IBM and compatible computers, including 8088-based computers. GeoWorks Ensemble, which includes PC/GEOS, sells for about $130 through mail order. A mouse is recommended.

GEM is a product of Digital Research. This graphical user interface for the IBM and compatibles offers features from other GUIs, such as a common interface, mouse support, and pull-down menus. The best-known application written to work with GEM is Ventura Publisher, a powerful desktop publishing application. Other applications are available for GEM, such as a word processor and a paint program.

Selecting Applications Software

You cannot do much with a personal computer until you purchase application software. The following sections help you select the right software package for the type of personal computer you are considering (or own) and the kind of work you want to do.

For each product recommended, a table lists the company that makes the product, the type of PC on which it runs, the kind of user interface it employs, a suggested retail price, and a typical mail order price. The table also suggests the microprocessor that works best with the application and suggests an operating system. In all cases, the operating system is the latest version at the time of this writing. If a later version appears by the time you read this, consider that instead.

Word Processors

A word processor enables you to type and manipulate text on-screen until every word, sentence, and paragraph is just right; then you can print the document. You can use word processors for any kind of writing task: memos, reports, articles, stories, books, and so on. Word processors differ in ease of use, speed of operation, advanced features, and support programs (such as a spelling checker and thesaurus). A low-end program may be easy to learn and use but may lack speed. A high-end program may be fast and have advanced features but be difficult to learn. Typically, low-end word processors support basic functions, such as moving blocks of text. Low-end word processors generally lack advanced functions, such as the automatic generation of a table of contents.

Some word processors show you a true picture of your document as you work. To see different typefaces, type styles, type sizes, and graphic elements while you work, you need a WYSIWYG (what-you-see-is-what-you-get) word processor. Word processors for IBM-compatible computers usually display characters on-screen in a monospaced font. Some word processors display a monospaced font but also offer a preview mode that shows how a document looks on paper.

Word processors can be characterized by the user interface. The majority of programs for IBM-compatible computers rely on function keys and control-key combinations to initiate commands. Many new versions of word processors, however, use pull-down menus so that you do not need to memorize many commands. WordPerfect and Microsoft Word for DOS, popular high-end word processors, recently added pull-down menus to supplement their normal user interfaces. Some word processors run under Windows 3.0 and use the graphical user interface of Windows. Word processors for the Macintosh use the computer's standard graphical user interface.

Advanced functions of word processors include the capability to apply different styles, document management, indexing and footnoting capabilities, multiple-column layouts, the capability to generate a table of contents, and the integration of graphics.

Style enables you to record text formatting on a paragraph basis. The next time you want a paragraph in that same style, you can apply the prerecorded style to the paragraph. This feature increases your productivity when you create documents that share similar styles. Some word processors can display more than one document on-screen at once. If you often move or copy text from one document to another, this *document management* feature may be a high priority.

Indexing generates an index from your documents. Tools to generate *footnotes* and a *table of contents* are useful features if you create complex documents, such as legal documents.

With *multiple-column* layouts, you can type one column, return to the top, begin typing another, and so on. This feature is useful if you create simple newsletters. (If this feature is important to you, be sure to find out the number of columns the program supports.)

Graphics integration means that you can incorporate a graph or a picture into your text—another important feature for creating newsletters or business reports.

If you want your word processor to perform a certain kind of operation, for example, mail merge, check that the word processor supports the feature. (You use mail merge to create form letters from a mailing list stored in the word processor or in a database program.)

To automate repetitive tasks, look for a word processor in which you can create macros. *Macros* are essentially miniprograms that you run by pressing a few keys instead of going through the whole procedure. Some programs have macros included with the package; others simply enable you to create your own macros.

Some support programs to look for in a word processor are a spelling checker, thesaurus, outliner, and grammar checker. When comparing spelling checkers and thesauruses, look for the total number of words included and the capability to add proper names and business-specific words to the group.

Low-end word processors are good for budget-conscious people or for home systems when you want to work on the content of a document, save the document, and bring it into the office for completion. Low-end word processors that you can run from a floppy disk are good for portable or laptop computers that lack a hard disk drive.

If you choose a low-end word processor, make sure that it can save files in ASCII format. ASCII, which stands for American Standard Code for Information Interchange, is a plain text file that contains no special formatting commands. You can easily import text saved in ASCII format into a high-end word processor for sophisticated formatting.

When considering a word processor, ask yourself the following questions:

- Is the user interface proprietary or does the program run under Windows 3.0?
- Is the program easy to use?
- Is the program fast? (You can answer this question only by comparing one word processor with another.)
- Is the program a WYSIWYG word processor?
- If the program is not a WYSIWYG word processor, does it have a preview mode?
- Does the program have style sheets?
- Can I work on more than one document at a time?
- Does the program have an indexing feature?
- Does the program support footnotes?
- Can I create multiple columns?
- Can the program generate a table of contents?
- Can I integrate graphics?
- Does the program have a mail-merge feature?
- Does the program contain a macro language?
- Does the program have an integrated spelling checker? How many words are included?

- Does the program have an integrated thesaurus? How many words are included?
- Does the program have an integrated outliner?
- Does the program have an integrated grammar checker?
- Can I create an ASCII file?

To answer these questions, you can call the company and talk to a customer service representative. You also can read the description of features on the software package, request a flier about the product from the company, and read reviews of word processors in computer magazines (see Appendix A for a discussion of computer magazines). Use the questions as a guide. The word processor you choose need not include all the features mentioned, just the features you want.

Table 11.1 gives specific recommendations for word processors based on a specific computer type, microprocessor, operating system, user interface, operating mode (WYSIWYG or monospaced), and suggested retail price.

These products all offer a good blend of features for the price. If you consider other word processors, measure them against the features and prices of the products listed in the table.

Table 11.1. Recommended Word Processors

Product	*Company*	*Computer Required*	*Operating System*	*User Interface*	*Operating Mode*	*Retail Price*
WordPerfect 5.1	WordPerfect Corporation	IBM compatible	DOS	Function keys/ pull-down menus	Monospaced font with Preview mode	$495.00
Word for Windows	Microsoft Corporation	IBM compatible	DOS	Windows 3.0	WYSIWYG	$495.00
Professional Write 2.2	Software Publishing Company	IBM compatible	DOS	Pull-down menus	Monospaced font	$249.00
LetterPerfect 1.0	WordPerfect Corporation	IBM compatible	DOS	Function keys/pull-down menus	Monospaced font	$229.00
Microsoft Word 4.0	Microsoft Corporation	Macintosh	System 7.0	Macintosh	WYSIWYG	$395.00
MacWrite II 1.1	Claris	Macintosh	System 7.0	Macintosh	WYSIWYG	$399.00
WriteNow 2.2	T/Maker Company	Macintosh	System 7.0	Macintosh	WYSIWYG	$199.00

Spreadsheet Programs

A spreadsheet program is the electronic equivalent of the sheets of paper in an accountant's analysis pad. Use spreadsheets to enter numeric data into the computer. You can create formulas that add, subtract, multiply, divide, or perform almost any other mathematical operation on the data. If you change a number or formula, all data that depends on the changed number or formula is updated automatically. For example, if you change the amount of money a business pays for rent, the amounts for total expenses and net profit change automatically. This flexibility makes spreadsheet software a valuable tool for planning and forecasting. Spreadsheets are ideal for number-oriented tasks like creating budgets, expense reports, and sales projections.

COMPARISON

Spreadsheets that run on IBM-compatible computers differ mainly in their user interface. In Lotus 1-2-3, you use a horizontal menu bar to select spreadsheet features. In other programs—for example, Quattro Pro—you use pull-down menus. In Microsoft Excel, you use the graphical user interface of the Macintosh, Windows 3.0, or OS/2.

Some spreadsheet programs can display more than one spreadsheet at a time. Lotus 1-2-3 Release 2.2 can display on-screen only one spreadsheet at a time. To see another spreadsheet, you must close the current spreadsheet and then open the one you want to see. Quattro Pro 2.0, however, can display many spreadsheets at the same time. When more than one spreadsheet is on-screen, you can easily link parts of different spreadsheets.

A related spreadsheet feature is the capability to work in three dimensions. This feature enables you to perform mathematical operations on several spreadsheets at the same time and then save the related spreadsheets together in one file. For example, with a three-dimensional spreadsheet, you can create a summary budget from the individual budgets of several different departments. Lotus 1-2-3 Release 3.1 has multiple spreadsheet and 3-D capabilities.

In addition to computational capabilities, spreadsheets can produce graphs of data. Some spreadsheets create two-dimensional graphs; others can produce two- or three-dimensional graphs. All spreadsheets can produce standard line, bar, and pie graphs, but if you are looking for a specific graph type (such as a hi-lo graph), be sure to ask whether the product supports this feature.

CHECKLIST

You can use spreadsheet publishing features to enhance a spreadsheet with a variety of typefaces and boxes and to enhance graphs with words, symbols, and pictures. Lotus 1-2-3 Releases 2.3 and 3.1 include an add-in program called WYSIWYG to provide publishing capabilities. Quattro Pro, Microsoft Excel, and Wingz have these features built into the program. You can take advantage of built-in features more easily than you can use add-in programs.

Some spreadsheets do not work with IBM-compatible computers that use an 8088 or 8086 microprocessor. See table 11.2 for personal computer recommendations.

Although many low-end spreadsheet programs were available a few years ago, most have disappeared from dealers' shelves or are difficult to find. One low-end spreadsheet still available for IBM compatibles is Borland's Quattro, the forerunner of Quattro Pro. Integrated programs, discussed later in this chapter, are also sources for low-end spreadsheets.

Ask yourself the following questions when considering a spreadsheet program:

- What is the user interface? Is it proprietary only for IBM-compatible PCs, or does the interface follow the standards set by Windows 3.0 or the Macintosh?
- Can the program display more than one spreadsheet on-screen at a time?
- Can I save related spreadsheets together in the same file (3-D capability)?
- Does the spreadsheet have publishing features?
- What kind of graph types does the program have? Can the program produce two- and three-dimensional pie graphs, line graphs, bar graphs, and so on?

To answer these questions and others, you can call the company and ask a customer service representative, ask a salesperson in a computer retail outlet, read the description of features on the software package, request a flier about the product from the company, and read reviews of spreadsheets in computer magazines (see Appendix A for a discussion of computer magazines).

Table 11.2 gives specific recommendations for spreadsheets based on a specific computer type, microprocessor, operating system, user interface, and suggested retail price.

These products all offer a good blend of features for the price. If you consider other spreadsheets, measure them against the features and prices of the products listed in the table.

Table 11.2. Recommended Spreadsheets

Product	Company	Computer Required	Operating System	User Interface	Retail Price
1-2-3 Release 2.3	Lotus Development Corporation	IBM compatible	DOS	Menu bar	$495.00
1-2-3 Release 3.1+	Lotus Development Corporation	IBM compatible	DOS	Menu bar	$595.00
Microsoft Excel 3.0 for Windows	Microsoft Corporation	IBM compatible	DOS	Windows 3.0	$495.00
Microsoft Excel 3.0 for the Mac	Microsoft Corporation	Macintosh	System 7.0	Macintosh	$395.00
Quattro Pro 3.0	Borland	IBM compatible	DOS	Pull-down menus	$495.00
Wingz 1.1	Informix	Macintosh	System 7.0	Macintosh	$395.00

Database Programs

Database programs create a structured grouping of related information, in the same way that you group related information on index cards. You can use databases to create mailing lists, to track inventory, to store information about personnel, and to store and retrieve almost any other kind of information. Two types of database programs are available: flat-file databases and relational databases.

Flat-file databases are the simplest and least expensive database programs. Flat-file databases contain all the information about a particular item (person, product, or whatever) in one record. (A record is similar to an index card of information. A set of records makes up a database file.)

Flat-file databases provide good functionality at a low cost. Sometimes called file managers, these programs enable you to create a template for a database record. You then can use the information you enter into each record to generate reports and mailing labels and to perform other database functions. An alternative to a file manager is a spreadsheet or integrated program. These programs often include features that rival those of most file managers.

Relational database programs are more complicated than flat-file databases, but you can use relational databases to link information stored in more than one file. Suppose that you have a database of client information that includes names, addresses, phone numbers, and other data. Another file stores the sales calls and purchases of clients. With a relational database, you can link the files to access a list of phone numbers of clients who have not received a sales call in the last month. To find out whether a database program is a flat-file database or a relational database, look at the packaging information, ask a sales representative, or call the company.

Databases differ in more ways than their method of handling files. As with other kinds of software for IBM-compatible computers, the user interface of databases differs from product to product. dBASE IV 1.1, for example, has two built-in user interfaces: pull-down menus and a command-line interface (you type commands to perform operations). Paradox 3.5 uses a horizontal menu bar.

An important feature to look for in a database program is its compatibility with other database programs, spreadsheets, and word processors. If you have data in dBASE IV, for example, on which you need to perform computations in 1-2-3, you need a convenient way to transfer the information from dBASE to a 1-2-3 spreadsheet. Often, the transfer method available is a translation program. Such a program can, for example, copy information from a dBASE database and place that information in a format that 1-2-3 can read. Software is becoming more advanced, enabling you to share information between programs. And GUIs are making this sharing easier, enabling you to link one application to another.

Many powerful database programs include a programming language that you can use to design and create your own applications. If you don't want to learn a programming language, make sure that you purchase a database program in which you can design custom data-entry screens, create custom reports, and do other database tasks without programming.

If you plan to incorporate pictures into a database, such as employee photos for a personnel file, make sure that the database software can accommodate pictures. Macintosh and Windows 3.0 database programs are more likely to provide this feature than DOS databases.

Ask yourself the following questions when considering a database program:

- What is the user interface? Is the program proprietary only for IBM-compatible PCs, or does it follow the standards set by Windows 3.0 or the Macintosh?
- Is the program a relational database or a flat-file database?
- Can I create data input forms, print reports, print labels, and do other database tasks without having to resort to programming?
- Can the information in the database be used by other applications, such as a word processor or spreadsheet?
- Can the database store pictures?

To answer these questions and others, you can call the company and ask a customer service representative, ask a salesperson in a computer retail outlet, read the description of features on the software package, request a flier about the product from the company, and read reviews of database software in computer magazines (see Appendix A for a discussion of computer magazines).

Table 11.3 gives specific recommendations for databases based on a specific computer type, microprocessor, operating system, user interface, level of sophistication, and suggested retail price.

These products all offer a good blend of features for the price. If you consider other databases, measure them against the features and prices of the products listed in the table.

Table 11.3. Recommended Databases

Product	Company	Computer Required	Operating System	User Interface	Retail Price
dBASE IV 1.1	Ashton-Tate	IBM compatible	DOS	Pull-down menus/ command line	$795.00
Paradox 3.5	Borland	IBM compatible	DOS	Menu bar	$725.00
FoxPro 2.0	Fox Software	IBM compatible and Macintosh	DOS and System 7.0	Pull-down menus	$795.00
SuperBase 4 for Windows	Precision Software	IBM compatible	DOS	Windows 3.0	$699.00

Financial Programs

Financial programs for PCs generally fall into three categories: high-end accounting packages, low-end accounting packages, and personal finance software. Because high-end accounting software can cost several thousand dollars, you should perform a personal, hands-on evaluation with data that reflects your business. The following sections cover low-end accounting packages and personal finance software, which can cost less than $100.

Low-End Accounting Software

Low-end accounting software typically consists of a set of accounting modules, including a general ledger, accounts receivable, accounts payable, inventory control, billing, purchasing, budgeting, auditing, and others. This software helps small businesses prepare financial reports, invoices, tax forms such as 1099s, and other business-related statements.

Low-end accounting programs for IBM-compatible computers differ in the user interface used by the program. Programs such as DacEasy Accounting and Pacioli 2000 use pull-down menus; Peachtree Complete III uses pop-up windows and function keys. The programs also differ in the number and types of modules they offer. For example, DacEasy accounting includes 11 modules; Pacioli 2000 includes 8 modules; and Peachtree Complete III has 9 modules. M.Y.O.B. for the Macintosh has 7 modules.

If you need preprinted forms such as checks, invoices, and other kinds of financial statements to use with the program, find out whether the company provides these. If not, you may be able to buy forms from a local printer or a third-party supplier such as NEBS (Groton, MA). Local retail computer stores rarely sell preprinted forms.

To move information from your accounting files to your spreadsheet, make sure that the program can export files to the spreadsheet you will be using.

Ask yourself the following questions when considering a low-end accounting program:

- What is the user interface? Is the program proprietary only for IBM-compatible PCs, or does the program follow the standards set by Windows 3.0 or the Macintosh?
- How many modules does the program have?
- Does the program have the modules I need?
- Can the program create the reports I need?
- What kind of personal computer do I need to run the software?
- Can the company supply checks and forms that work with the software?

To answer these questions and any others, you can call the company and ask a customer service representative, ask a salesperson in a computer retail outlet, read the description of features on the software package, request a flier about the product from the company, and read ads for low-end accounting software in computer magazines (see Appendix A for a discussion of computer magazines).

Table 11.4 gives specific recommendations for low-end accounting software based on a specific computer type, microprocessor, operating system, user interface, and suggested retail price.

These products all offer a good blend of features for the price. If you consider other low-end accounting packages, measure them against the features and prices of the products listed in the table.

Table 11.4. Recommended Low-End Accounting Software

Product	Computer Required	Operating System	User Interface	Retail Price
DacEasy Accounting 4.1	IBM compatible	DOS	Pull-down menus	$150.00
Peachtree Complete III	IBM compatible	DOS	Pop-up windows/function keys	$199.00
Pacioli 2000	IBM compatible	DOS	Pull-down menus	$50.00
M.Y.O.B. 2.0	Macintosh	System 7.0	Macintosh	$295.00
Business Sense	Macintosh	System 7.0	Macintosh	$199.00
Peachtree Crystal Accounting	IBM compatible	DOS	Pull-down menus	$249.00

Personal Finance Software

Personal finance software helps you with financial matters such as balancing a check book, itemizing expenses, analyzing and planning expenditures, tracking investments, and planning for retirement. Some personal finance programs are powerful enough to double as a small-business accounting program.

With a good checkbook program, you can set up accounts and current balances for checking, credit cards, IRS funds, and money market funds. You then can set up budget categories such as income, expense, asset, or liability. You can design monthly budgets for checking or charge accounts. By establishing income and expense categories, you can play forecasting games. The program should generate constant income and expenses for several months. With some programs, you can create charts showing expenses compared to budgets, for example.

Some programs perform double-entry bookkeeping, in which expense transactions are listed in your expense category, tax records, monthly budget, and so on. Double-entry bookkeeping requires extra work from you, however. You need to set goals for what you want the package to do and use its features accordingly. You still have to set up accounts and categories. If you want a year-end record of all tax-deductible expenditures, you must describe and mark each tax-deductible expense category in accordance with Schedule C, and so on. You must know enough about your tax situation to know how much is deductible.

Personal finance programs should accommodate your need to print checks. Generally, you purchase checks from a third party. Often, the software company has information on where to obtain special forms, and usually this information is included in the software package. Find out whether the program works with your printer.

You can use the data in your personal finance program for income taxes and banking. Find out whether your tax preparer can use the program's files to submit your taxes electronically. Find out whether the program supports electronic banking at the bank where you do your business.

Remember that these programs cannot teach you how to manage your personal finances—don't make the mistake of thinking that software products can think for you! Programs are tools that structure your data to help you do the thinking. If you set up your personal accounting system correctly, a personal finance program tracks, categorizes, and catches your budget when it slips out of line. Two examples of this type of program are Quicken and Managing Your Money, which are available for the IBM and the Macintosh.

Ask yourself the following questions when considering a personal finance program:

- What is the user interface? Is the program proprietary only for IBM-compatible PCs, or does it follow the standards set by Windows 3.0 or the Macintosh?
- Does the program have a checkbook register?
- Does the program track investments?
- Does the program keep track of charge accounts?
- Does the program do single- or double-entry bookkeeping?
- Can the program's files be used by the person who prepares my taxes?
- What kinds of printers does the program support?
- Can the program print checks?
- Can the company supply checks that work with the software?
- Does the program support electronic banking at my bank?

All these questions may not apply to your situation. You can find answers for those that do by calling the company and asking a customer service representative, asking a salesperson in a computer retail outlet, reading the description of features on the software package, requesting a flier about the product from the company, and reading ads for personal finance software in computer magazines (see Appendix A for a discussion of computer magazines).

Table 11.5 gives specific recommendations for personal finance software based on a specific computer type, microprocessor, operating system, user interface, and suggested retail price.

These products all offer a good blend of features for the price. If you consider other personal finance packages, measure them against the features and prices of the products listed in the table.

Table 11.5. Recommended Personal Finance Software

Product	Company	Computer Required	Operating System	User Interface	Retail Price
Quicken 4.0	Intuit	IBM compatible	DOS	Function keys	$60.00
Managing Your Money 7.0	Meca Ventures	IBM compatible	DOS	Function keys	$220.00
Quicken 1.5	Intuit	Macintosh	System 7.0	Macintosh	$60.00
Managing Your Money 3.0	Meca Ventures	Macintosh	System 7.0	Macintosh	$220.00

Desktop Publishing Software

Desktop publishing software tackles page layout, producing attractive pages for newsletters, brochures, fliers, magazines, newspapers, manuals, and books. High-end and low-end desktop publishing programs are available, and some word processors can double as desktop publishing programs.

Desktop publishing programs combine text created in a word processor, graphics created in a drawing program, and tables and graphs created in a spreadsheet program. Check whether the desktop publishing program you are considering supports your other software.

With a desktop publishing program, you can manipulate text, graphics, and tables until you create the effect you want. Generally, the layout tools of high-end programs offer more flexibility and control than tools of low-end programs.

If you create complex or long documents, consider a high-end program. When comparing high-end programs, note that some are better suited for certain tasks. If you intend to publish very long documents or need sophisticated features such as color separation, check whether the program can accommodate these needs.

Low-end desktop publishing programs are best suited for simple newsletters and fliers. If you go beyond a page, you may have problems when stories that start on page 1 are continued on other pages of the newsletter, especially if you have to make changes to the text. Low-end programs usually force you to compromise on typographical features such as kerning, leading, and the way text wraps around graphic images. (*Kerning* is the capability to vary the spacing between individual letters; *leading* is the capability to vary the spacing between lines. If these term are unfamiliar, you may want to brush up on the basics of typography, especially if you intend to publish a professional-looking newsletter.)

If your typographical needs aren't too stringent, and you don't mind using tools not specifically designed for the task, you can use a high-end word processor such as WordPerfect 5.1, Ami Professional 1.2, or Word for Windows 1.1. One of these programs may fit your needs better than a low-end desktop publishing program.

The quality of output depends on your printer. If you intend to use a laser printer or a PostScript laser printer, make sure that the program you choose can take advantage of the printer. Some low-end desktop publishing programs, for example, do not support PostScript printers.

Ask yourself the following questions when considering a desktop publishing program:

- What is the user interface? Is the program proprietary only for IBM-compatible PCs, or does it follow the standards set by Windows 3.0 or the Macintosh?
- Do I want to create short publications such as newsletters and fliers or longer ones such as magazines, newspapers, manuals, and textbooks?
- Does the desktop publishing program support my word processor, drawing program, and spreadsheet program?
- Does the program offer control of kerning and leading?
- Will the program wrap type around graphic images?
- Does the program allow for easy changes when stories jump from page to page?
- Does the program provide advanced technical features such as color separations?
- What kind of personal computer do I need to run the software?
- What kinds of printers does the program support? Does the program support a PostScript printer?
- How difficult is the program to learn and use?

To answer these and other questions, you can call the company and ask a customer service representative, ask a salesperson in a computer retail outlet, read the description of features on the software package, request a flier about the product from the company, and read reviews of desktop publishing software in computer magazines (see Appendix A for a discussion of computer magazines).

Table 11.6 gives specific recommendations for desktop publishing programs based on a specific computer type, microprocessor, operating system, user interface, type of task, and suggested retail price.

These products all offer a good blend of features for the price. If you consider other desktop publishing packages, measure them against the features and prices of the products listed in the table.

Table 11.6. Recommended Desktop Publishing Software

Product	Company	Computer Required	Operating System	User Interface	Type of Tasks	Retail Price
PageMaker 4.0	Aldus	Macintosh	System 7.0	Macintosh	Newsletters, magazines, newspapers	$795.00
QuarkXpress	Quark	Macintosh	System 7.0	Macintosh	Newsletters, magazines, newspapers	$795.00
FrameMaker 2.1	Frame Technology	Macintosh	System 7.0	Macintosh	Manuals, textbooks	$995.00
Springboard Publisher II	Springboard Software	IBM compatible	System 7.0	Macintosh	Newsletters, fliers	$200.00
PageMaker 4.0	Aldus	IBM compatible	DOS	Windows 3.0	Newsletters, magazines, newspapers	$795.00

Communications Software

Communications software usually connects two computers over telephone lines by modem. Communications software links the computers so that you can send or receive files created with a word processor, spreadsheet, or other software. The computers do not have to be the same type—a Macintosh can be linked through a modem to an IBM compatible, for example. You can connect to an on-line service such as Prodigy or an electronic mail service such as MCI Mail. When connected to an on-line service, you can browse, exchange messages with other members of the service, download (receive) programs, shop electronically, and use many other services. You also can send electronic mail to or receive it from any other member of the service.

Communications software can be classified as standard, remote control, or designed for an on-line service. Standard communications programs offer similar kinds of features but differ in the extent to which they support certain features. For example, all programs support communications protocols such as Xmodem, a popular error-correcting protocol. (The purpose of a protocol is to send files quickly and without errors.) Some programs support a whole range of protocols; others support just a few. Xmodem is sufficient for most file transfers, but if you need another protocol to communicate with a certain host program, you should check whether the program provides it.

Another feature most programs include is some way to automate communications, usually with a proprietary programming language. Generally, when you communicate with another computer, you must read prompts on the screen, answer questions, and type commands to control the computer with which you are communicating. Often, a communications program has a built-in language that you can program to call another computer and to issue the commands necessary to get the information from the computer with which you are communicating. The language is proprietary, meaning that the language is not another standard programming language like BASIC. If you are interested in this automating of communications, be sure to find out how difficult the language is to learn and use and also how powerful it is.

Remote-control programs enable you to control another computer over the phone lines. You can use programs like pcAnywhere III to control your office PC from your PC at home. You need the same program at both ends of the line for remote communications. (Some companies require you to buy two copies of the software!) Some standard communications programs also include remote features but may provide limited control.

Some communications programs are designed for use with specific on-line services, such as CompuServe. These programs, such as the CompuServe Information Manager or TAPCIS, help you navigate through the various parts of the service. Standard communications programs can connect to almost any on-line service, but they contain no special navigation aids. Some on-line services require special communications programs and do not work with a standard communications program. Prodigy and America On-line are two such services. When you subscribe to these services, however, you receive the software at no additional cost.

Communications software often is provided with the purchase of a modem. If you use Windows 3.0, remember that this environment includes a program called Terminal with limited communications features.

Ask yourself the following questions when considering communications software:

- What is the user interface? Is the program proprietary only for IBM-compatible PCs, or does it follow the standards set by Windows 3.0 or the Macintosh?
- Does the program use the Xmodem protocol? What other protocols does it have?
- How difficult is automating communications?
- Does the program offer remote-control capability? Are two copies of the program required?
- Does the program help me navigate through an on-line service?
- What kind of personal computer do I need to run the software?
- How difficult is the program to learn and use?

To answer these questions and others, you can call the company and ask a customer service representative, ask a salesperson in a computer retail outlet, read the description of features on the software package, request a flier about the product from the company, and read reviews of communications software in computer magazines (see Appendix A for a discussion of computer magazines).

Table 11.7 gives specific recommendations for communications software based on a specific computer type, microprocessor, operating system, user interface, type of task, and suggested retail price.

These products all offer a good blend of features for the price. If you consider other communications packages, measure them against the features and prices of the products listed in the table.

Table 11.7. Recommended Communications Software

Product	Company	Computer Required	Operating System	User Interface	Type of Tasks	Retail
PROCOMM PLUS 1.1	DATASTORM Technologies	IBM compatible	DOS	Alt-key/menu bar	Standard Communications	$99.00
SmartCom III 1.2	Hayes Microcomputer Products	IBM compatible	DOS	Pull-down menus	Standard Communications	$249.00
pcAnywhere III	Dynamic Microcomputer Associates	IBM compatible	DOS	Proprietary	Remote Communications	$145.00
Microphone III 3.0	Software Ventures	Macintosh	System 7.0	Macintosh	Standard Communications	$295.00

Integrated Software

An integrated program combines several applications in one package. Typical applications include word processing, spreadsheet, database management, graphics, and communications. With integrated software, you can write memos, create budgets, send electronic mail, maintain a list of client names, and so on, without having to learn a new program or user interface for each module. Another advantage of an integrated package is the capability to move information from one application to another. You easily can copy a table or graph created in the spreadsheet, for example, to a document in the word processor. If data changes, both portions are updated automatically.

The popularity of high-end integrated software has declined in recent years. Many people prefer the power of a high-end stand-alone product like WordPerfect to the overall functionality of a high-end integrated program like Lotus Symphony.

Low-end integrated programs are still popular. These programs offer as many as eight functions and usually sell through mail order for less than $100. If you have basic computing needs, consider purchasing a low-end IBM-compatible or Macintosh computer and a low-end integrated software package like PFS: First Choice, Lotus Works, or Microsoft Works.

Ask yourself the following questions when considering integrated software:

- What is the user interface? Is the program proprietary only for IBM-compatible PCs, or does it follow the standards set by Windows 3.0 or the Macintosh?
- How many modules does the program have?
- Do any individual modules rival the power of a stand-alone program?
- Does the word processor have a spelling checker?
- Does the communications module enable me to automate communications?
- What kind of personal computer do I need to run the software?
- How difficult is the program to learn and use?

To answer these questions and others, you can call the company and ask a customer service representative, ask a salesperson in a computer retail outlet, read the description of features on the software package, request a flier about the product from the company, and read reviews of integrated software in computer magazines (see Appendix A for a discussion of computer magazines).

Table 11.8 gives specific recommendations for integrated software based on a specific computer type, microprocessor, operating system, user interface, and suggested retail price.

These products all offer a good blend of features for the price. If you consider other integrated packages, measure them against the features and prices of the products listed in the table.

Table 11.8. Recommended Integrated Software Packages

Product	Company	Modules	Computer Required	Operating System	Retail Price
Symphony 2.2	Lotus Development Corporation	Spreadsheet, word processor, database, graphing, communications	IBM compatible	DOS	$695.00
Microsoft Works 2.0	Microsoft Corporation	Spreadsheet (with graphing), word processor, database, communications	IBM compatible	DOS	$150.00
PFS: First Choice 3.1	Software Publishing Company	Spreadsheet, word processor, spelling checker, outliner, database, graphing, communications, desktop	IBM compatible	DOS	$150.00
Better Working-Eight-in-One	Spinnaker	Spreadsheet, word processor, spelling checker, outliner, database, graphing, communications, desktop	IBM compatible	DOS	$60.00
Microsoft Works 2.0	Microsoft Corporation	Spreadsheet (with graphing), word processor, database, communications	Macintosh	System 7.0	$295.00

Paint and Drawing Programs

You use paint and drawing programs for personal computers to create and manipulate images. With a paint program, you create images as you create them with painting tools like pencils, pens, brushes, and paint. Paint programs can simulate paintings done with water colors, oil paints, or acrylic paints. Paint programs create a bit-mapped image formed by a pattern of pixels (dots). The drawback of images created with paint programs is that the images degrade if you try to enlarge them.

With a drawing program, you create images like those you create using illustration tools such as technical pens, French curves, and transfer screens. These vector images are formed on-screen by controlling an electron gun, and they stretch as you enlarge them, maintaining their resolutions and ratios at any size.

Paint programs differ in the user interface, the number of colors available, the resolution of the image, and the painting tools available. A big difference among these programs is the file format the program uses. The most popular file format for IBM-compatible computers is the PCX format found in programs such as PC PaintBrush IV Plus. For Macintosh computers, the MacPaint format is the most popular.

Some differences among drawing programs are the user interface, the drawing tools available, and color support. As with paint programs, a big difference among drawing programs is the file format the program uses. The most popular file format is CGM, found in programs such as CorelDRAW! and Adobe Illustrator.

Be sure to find out what kind of input and output devices paint and drawing programs support. If you intend to use a mouse or a graphics tablet for input, make sure that the program supports the model you have (or plan to buy). If you intend to use a printer to print your drawings or illustrations, make sure that the program supports the model you have (or plan to buy).

Most drawing programs and some paint programs are targeted for graphic arts professionals. Low-end paint programs often are bundled or included with the purchase of a mouse or a graphical user interface such as Windows 3.0.

Ask yourself the following questions when considering paint and drawing software:

- What is the user interface? Is the program proprietary only for IBM-compatible PCs, or does it follow the standards set by Windows 3.0 or the Macintosh?
- What kinds of painting or drawing tools does the program have?
- How many colors does the program support?
- What is the image resolution (for paint programs only)?
- What kind of input devices does the program support?
- What kind of output devices, such as laser printers and color printers, does the program support?
- What file format does the program use? What file formats can be imported into and exported out of the program?
- What kind of personal computer do I need to run the software?
- How difficult is the program to learn and use?

To answer these questions and others, you can call the company and ask a customer service representative, ask a salesperson in a computer retail outlet, read the description of features on the software package, request a flier about the product from the company, and read reviews of paint and drawing software in computer magazines (see Appendix A for a discussion of computer magazines).

Table 11.9 gives specific recommendations for paint and drawing software based on a specific computer type, microprocessor, operating system, user interface, type of program, and suggested retail price.

These products all offer a good blend of features for the price. If you consider other paint and draw packages, measure them against the features and prices of the products listed in the table.

Table 11.9. Recommended Paint and Drawing Software

Product	Company	Computer Required	Operating System	User Interface	Program Type	Retail Price
PC PaintBrush IV 1.0	ZSoft	IBM compatible	DOS	Pull-down menus	Paint	$199.00
Corel Draw! 2.0	Corel Systems	IBM compatible	DOS	Windows 3.0	Draw	$495.00
DeskPaint/ DeskDraw 3.01	Zedcor	Macintosh	System 7.0	Macintosh	Paint and draw	$200.00
Adobe Illustrator 3.0	Adobe Systems	Macintosh	System 7.0	Macintosh	Draw	$595.00

Music Sequencing and Notation Software

Music sequencing software enables a personal computer to act like a tape recorder to record one or more tracks of music information. You enter music into a computer with an instrument like a keyboard synthesizer. After the music is in RAM, you can manipulate the music with sequencing software. You can think of sequencers as word processors for music. After you edit, you can play the music again through the synthesizer.

Music notation software translates music entered into the computer into standard music notation. You can enter music into a computer through the computer's keyboard or an instrument such as a keyboard synthesizer. The programs produce sheet music on a printer.

You normally use music sequencing and notation software in combination with a Musical Instrument Digital Interface (MIDI) system such as the one shown in figure 11.1. The figure shows a personal computer connected to a MIDI-compatible keyboard synthesizer, which is connected to an amplifier connected to speakers.

For IBM compatibles, you can insert a MIDI adapter board into an expansion slot and connect the keyboard to the board's MIDI port. For Macintoshes, you can place a MIDI interface box between the keyboard and the computer. The keyboard connects to the interface, and the interface connects to a serial port of the computer.

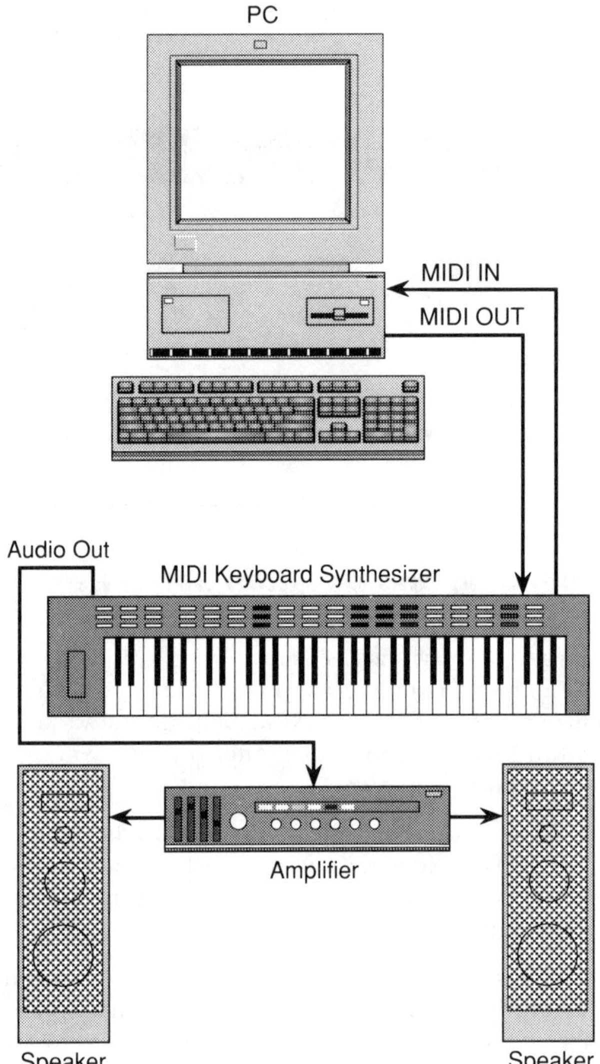

Fig. 11.1. *A typical MIDI system.*

Music sequencing programs differ in the user interface, the method of displaying notes and tracks, the number of tracks supported, editing capabilities, and other features. Music notation programs differ in the user interface, the method of displaying notes, editing capabilities, number of pages per musical score, sequencing software supported, printers supported, and other features. Music sequencing and notation programs are targeted for professional musicians, although some companies offer apprentice versions of their products. Some music programs combine the capabilities of sequencing and notation software into one product.

Ask yourself the following questions when considering sequencing and notation software:

- What is the user interface? Is the program proprietary only for IBM-compatible PCs, or does it follow the standards set by Windows 3.0 or the Macintosh?
- How does the program display musical notes and tracks?
- What editing features does the program have?
- How many tracks does the program support?
- What sequencing software does the notation software support?
- What is the maximum number of pages per musical score?
- What kind of dot-matrix, inkjet, and laser printers does the program support?
- What kind of personal computer do I need to run the software?
- How difficult is the program to learn and use?
- Is any technical support available with the program?

To answer these questions and others, you can call the company and ask a customer service representative, ask a salesperson in a computer retail outlet, read the description of features on the software package, request a flier about the product from the company, and read reviews of sequencing and notation software in computer and electronic music magazines (see Appendix A for a discussion of computer magazines).

Table 11.10 gives specific recommendations for music sequencing and notation software based on a specific computer type, microprocessor, operating system, user interface, type of program, and suggested retail price.

These products all offer a good blend of features for the price. If you consider other music sequencing and notation packages, measure them against the features and prices of the products listed in the table.

Table 11.10. Recommended Music Sequencing and Notation Software

Product	Company	Computer Required	Operating System	User Interface	Program Type	Retail Price
Cakewalk Professional 3.0	Twelve Tone Systems	IBM compatible	DOS	Pull-down menus	Music sequencing	$249.00
Copyist DTP	Dr. T's Music Software	IBM compatible	DOS	Pull-down menus	Music notation	$399.00
The Musicator	Musicator	IBM compatible	DOS	Pull-down menus	Music sequencing and notation	$545.00
Performer 3.5	Mark of the Unicorn	Macintosh	System 7.0	Macintosh	Music sequencing	$495.00
Finale	Coda Music Software	Macintosh	System 7.0	Macintosh	Music notation	$749.00

Educational and Game Programs

Educational and game programs for personal computers fall into several categories. Most educational programs can be classified as arcade, simulation, role-play, adventure, interactive drill, and reference programs. Most game programs can be classified as arcade, simulation, adventure, sports, board, game show, or casino games.

Game and educational programs differ in graphics quality. If you have fairly sophisticated graphics available on your computer, a VGA adapter on an IBM-compatible computer, for example, look for programs that support VGA with the appropriate driver set. One of the most popular educational programs—Where in the World is Carmen San Diego?—recently was updated to include digitized photographs of various geographic locations taken from *National Geographic* magazine.

Programs also use different sound effects. Macintosh and some IBM-compatible computers, such as the Tandy 1000 series, contain electronic circuits to produce synthesized sound. If you own or intend to buy one of these computers, look for programs that take advantage of this feature. You can insert special sound boards, such as the Sound Blaster, into an expansion slot of most IBM-compatible computers.

Other differences to watch for are the level and content of the software. Educational programs are designed for different learning levels, from preschool to adult. Game programs run the gamut of human experience; the packaging shows the subject matter of a game.

For the most part, educational and game programs are designed to run on low-end computers, although many support complete lines of computers. Many game and educational programs have versions for different types of computers. Some programs demand a special piece of equipment; for example, an educational reference program, such as an electronic encyclopedia, usually requires a CD-ROM drive.

If you are interested in educational software developed by educators, check out software by MECC (Minnesota Educational Computing Corporation), some of whose products have won awards. For example, The Oregon Trail is a role-playing program that teaches decision making and survival skills as you experience a pioneer lifestyle that includes hunting buffalo, rafting down rivers, visiting trading posts, acquiring supplies, and dealing with Indians and midnight robbers.

Ask yourself the following questions when considering educational or games software:

- Into what category does the program fall? For games, is the category arcade, simulation, adventure, sports, board, card, or casino game? For education, is the category arcade, simulation, role-play, adventure, or reference?
- What kind of graphics does the program support?
- Does the program have sound effects?
- If the program is an educational program, what is the subject and learning level?
- If the program is a game, what is the subject matter?
- What kind of personal computer do I need to run the software?
- Is any special equipment required?
- How difficult is the program to learn and use?
- Does the company provide customer support?

To answer these questions and others, you can call the company and ask a customer service representative; ask a salesperson in a computer retail outlet; read the description of features on the software package; request a flier about the product from the company; and read reviews of game and educational software in computer, educational, and electronic games magazines (see Appendix A for a discussion of computer magazines).

Like all other kinds of software, game and educational programs differ in quality. Too many game and educational programs exist to list even a small portion of them. Deciding on a game or educational program is to a great extent a matter of personal preference. At a retail store or at a friend's house, try any programs you are considering. Check which educational programs are used at the local schools. Finally, magazines that cover educational and game software often include top ten lists or editor's favorites. These lists give you an indication of the current hot titles.

Shareware

Shareware is software developed by independent programmers who let you try the program before you buy it. Shareware programs cover the whole spectrum of software, from word processors and spreadsheets to games and educational programs. Most shareware programs are significantly less expensive than commercial products.

The easiest way to obtain a shareware program is to send away for one through mail order. A shareware disk costs anywhere from $1 to $4. If you decide to buy the program after you try it, you send additional money to the author of the program (the program specifies the amount to pay). Paying the fee normally gives you some additional benefits, such as documentation, technical support, and notification of updates to the program. The whole concept of shareware is based on an honor system—no one forces you to pay the program's author.

You also can obtain shareware through on-line services and bulletin board systems. Use your modem to download any programs you want. If you like the program, you send money to the author.

Some shareware programs are great, and others are awful. Because so many titles exist, you often have to find good programs by trial and error. You are unlikely to see reviews of shareware programs in computer magazines.

A related group of programs is public domain software. Any program or program file in the public domain is free; you pay only for obtaining the disk. You are not likely to find full-blown word processors and spreadsheets in the public domain, but you may find interesting utility programs, graphics, games, and educational programs.

Although you may have plenty of questions about various shareware and public domain programs, the answers aren't easy to find. Try locating books or magazines dedicated to shareware, but be aware that these may not provide detailed up-to-date information. Probably the best way to find out about these programs is to ask opinions of the other users of bulletin boards and on-line systems. You can do this by leaving messages for all users of the system to read. The following list gives one shareware program in each major category that may suit your needs.

Word processor:	PC Write 3.03
Spreadsheet:	As-Easy-As
Database:	PC-File 5.0
Communication:	PROCOMM
Accounting:	Painless Accounting
Educational:	PC FastType
Games:	Caddyshack (Golf)

This list can get you started on the right track with shareware. Although these programs are for IBM-compatible computers, shareware and public domain software are available for Macintosh computers, too. Remember, shareware programs give you the opportunity to try before you buy—the fun is in trying.

Considering Training and Support

No matter what software program you choose, you have to learn how to use it. If you think that you need training to learn how to use a particular software package, you can investigate some avenues before you make a software purchase. Many computer stores and schools hold software seminars and classes. The more popular software packages naturally attract more training companies and schools. You easily can find outside training for Lotus 1-2-3 and WordPerfect 5.1. If you learn well on your own, investigate whether a software package includes a tutorial or other learning aids. Companies sometimes produce video tapes to help you learn the software. If a video tape is not available from the company, you often can find tapes from third-party sources. Finally, books such as *Que's Using 1-2-3 Release 3.1*, *Using WordPerfect 5.1*, and many others, can help you learn a particular software package.

When you purchase software, also consider the availability of support. Sometimes you may know what you want to do, but you cannot figure out how to do it—even after you become proficient with the program. If a company offers good support, you can call the company and ask how to implement a particular feature. Some companies offer free lifetime support. Others offer free support for a short time and then charge you for continued support. A few companies have toll-free numbers. The documentation or packaging often spells out the company's support policy.

Company support should extend to program upgrades. Most programs are upgraded periodically. New features may be added, and existing features may be increased or made easier to use. The company should keep you informed about all program upgrades and offer you the chance to make the upgrade. Ask about a company's upgrade policy before you purchase a program.

Determining Your Hardware Configuration

Obviously, software not designed for your computer will not run on your computer. Macintosh software, for example, cannot run on IBM computers. Software designed to run on your computer brand, however, may not run on your particular computer system if your system does not meet the software's minimum requirements.

Almost all software packages carry a label listing the system requirements. The system requirements tell you the minimum requirements your system needs to run the program. The following system requirements apply to Lotus 1-2-3 Release 2.2:

- IBM PC and Lotus-certified compatibles
- DOS Version 2.0 or above
- Minimum of 320K bytes of system RAM required
- 512K bytes recommended
- Hard disk and 512K bytes of system RAM required for Allways

The IBM PC mentioned in the requirements is the original IBM model with the 8088 microprocessor. This requirement, therefore, can be met by any IBM-compatible system. (Don't worry about Lotus certification. The term is a hold-over from the days when some IBM compatibles weren't very compatible.) The requirements specify that you must have at least 320K to operate the program. Remember, however, that this amount is the minimum. Generally, the more memory you have available, the better. Notice that Lotus recommends 512K of memory. Notice, too, that you must have a hard disk to use the Allways program that accompanies Lotus 1-2-3 Release 2.2.

Contrast the requirements of Lotus 1-2-3 Release 2.2 with the requirements of Lotus 1-2-3 Release 3.1:

- IBM PC AT and Lotus-certified compatibles, including most IBM PS/2 and COMPAQ models
- Hard disk with 5M available
- EGA, VGA, high-resolution CGA, or Hercules graphics adapter for WYSIWYG display
- DOS 3.0 or higher
- 1M of available system RAM

Notice that Lotus 1-2-3 Release 3.1 requires at least an IBM PC AT, a personal computer with an 80286 microprocessor. This version of Lotus 1-2-3 does not run on an IBM or compatible with an 8088 or 8086 microprocessor, but this version runs fine on an 80286 through 80486 IBM and compatible computers.

Also notice that the minimum DOS requirement is different. At least DOS Version 3.0 is required, rather than DOS Version 2.0. Also specified is the type of video adapter, the minimum amount of RAM, and a hard disk. Although the minimum memory specification is 1M, you are better off purchasing more memory.

Programs for other computers usually suggest similar requirements. For example, a program may require a specific version of the operating system or a certain amount of memory.

If you know which software programs you need, you can select a personal computer that meets the hardware requirements of the software. Remember that the minimum requirements generally are conservative. Although the program operates with the minimum specifications, you may find the program faster and more capable of meeting your needs if your hardware exceeds these specifications.

Chapter Summary

This chapter provides an overview of different kinds of personal computer software you may consider. The chapter describes operating system software and graphical user interfaces. The chapter then delves into a variety of software categories. For each category, this chapter defines the type of software, explains differences among products, gives a list of questions to consider, and provides a table of recommended products. These recommendations should provide a firm foundation for making software purchasing decisions. The chapter then considers software and training and support, and provides information about determining the correct computer configuration you need to run different kinds of software.

You now have some ideas about the personal computer you want, and you know which company or group of companies you are considering. The next chapter recommends various models and prices for particular applications. Chapter 12 also describes portable computers and the differences among the various styles. Finally, Chapter 12 makes suggestions about purchasing a used computer.

PART III

Making the Purchase

Includes

Choosing a System To Fit Your Needs

Making the Purchase

CHAPTER TWELVE

Choosing a System To Fit Your Needs

As you shop for a computer, you not only are faced with a bewildering array of computer brand names, you also discover that each computer manufacturer offers a variety of models. This chapter helps you decide which model is appropriate for running specific software applications, such as word processors, spreadsheets, databases, graphics, and electronic communications. The chapter also gives you guidelines about which model to choose if you want a computer flexible enough to run several different applications.

Although most people assume that personal computers are always desktop machines, PCs come in all shapes and sizes. This chapter shows you how luggables, laptops, and notebook computers may fit your computing plans. This chapter also explains how to save money by buying a good second-hand computer at the right price.

Selecting a Model Based on an Application

If you are purchasing a computer to run a single application, selecting a specific model is easy. The following sections correlate specific recommendations with particular software applications.

Computers without hard disks are not recommended (except for some laptop models). A hard disk may add $200 or more to the cost of a PC, but the convenience is definitely worth the extra expense. A hard disk adds a great deal of storage capacity to the system and significantly improves the speed of such disk operations as saving and retrieving files.

For IBM and IBM-compatible computers, VGA is the current color standard. A VGA adapter and monitor may add $150 or more to the cost of a color system. The system is worth the money, however, because VGA produces sharp, clear text and provides many more colors than CGA or EGA.

Note that, although 8088 and 8086 computers are slow and cannot run some of the latest software, they are low in cost. An 8088 or 8086 computer is a reasonable choice for a student or for someone using only such applications as word processing and entertainment packages. Most computer companies are no longer selling the 8088 and 8086 machines. The prices of the 286 machines are as low as the 8088 prices were last year. For an IBM compatible, however, a computer based on at least the 80286 microprocessor is a better choice, even for only word processing.

The prices given are advertised prices—not suggested retail. These prices, which were gleaned from local newspapers and computer magazines, are rounded to the nearest $10, depending on the price of the item. The systems and prices are shown only to represent sample computers so that you can get a feel for what you will spend. Keep in mind that the cost of computer equipment varies from place to place and store to store, and that the price of computer equipment usually decreases with time.

Recommendations for particular computer models, printers, and software products are examples of equipment and software worth considering. Even if you choose products that are not included in the list, you can compare your selections with the components suggested in the appropriate classification.

Word Processing

Word processing can be simple or sophisticated, depending on what program features you use. For simple word processing, the speed at which the computer works is not important. You can type, save, and print your work on any low-end computer model from any manufacturer.

A more sophisticated word processor may include such features as a spelling checker, an electronic thesaurus, or the capability to integrate pictures in a document. If you need these features, you will be happier with a more powerful—and more expensive—system.

A word-processing program that shows you on-screen exactly how your document will look on paper (WYSIWYG—what you see is what you get), requires more computing power than a word processor that works only in text mode.

Low-End Word Processing Systems

The following configurations are recommended as simple word processing systems.

IBM-Compatible Computer

80286 AT computer, such as EPSON Equity 286 Plus	$ 1,004.00
1M of RAM	
5 1/4-inch, 1.2M floppy disk drive	
VGA monochrome monitor	
Built-in VGA video adapter	
20M hard disk drive	$ 200.00
9-pin dot-matrix printer, such as EPSON LX-810	$ 150.00
Word processing software, such as Professional Write 2.2	$ 165.00
Total cost	$ 1,519.00

This configuration, which combines the least-expensive IBM-compatible components with a reputable word processor, is appropriate for the home or for a college student. If you substitute a 24-pin dot-matrix printer, such as the EPSON LQ-510, which sells for about $250, you can use this system in a small office.

Apple Macintosh Computer

8 MHz 68000 Macintosh Classic	$ 1,250.00
2M of RAM	
3 1/2-inch, 1.44M floppy disk drive	
Monochrome monitor with built-in video	
40M hard disk drive	
9-pin dot-matrix printer, such as Apple ImageWriter II	$ 470.00
Word processing software, such as WriteNow 2.2	$ 120.00
Total cost	$ 1,840.00

This configuration, which combines the least-expensive Macintosh components with a reputable word processor, is appropriate for the home or a small office.

High-End Word Processing Systems

The following configurations are recommended as sophisticated word processing systems.

IBM-Compatible Computer

16 MHz 80386SX computer, such as EPSON Equity 386-SX+	$ 1,950.00
1M of RAM	
3 1/2-inch, 1.44M floppy disk drive	
VGA monochrome monitor and VGA video adapter	
40M hard disk drive	
DOS 4.0	$ 100.00
24-pin dot-matrix printer, such as EPSON LQ-1050	$ 600.00
Word processing software, such as WordPerfect 5.1	$ 250.00
Total cost	$ 2,900.00

This configuration, which combines a more powerful IBM-compatible computer with a more durable printer and a superior word processor, is appropriate for a small business that relies on word processing. If you prefer a printer like the Hewlett-Packard LaserJet III, the cost increases by about $1,000.

IBM Computer

16 MHz 80386SX PS/2 Model 55SX	$ 2,600.00
2M of RAM	
3 1/2-inch floppy disk drive	
VGA color monitor with built-in VGA video	
80M hard disk drive	
DOS 5.0	$ 110.00
Laser printer, such as Hewlett-Packard LaserJet III	$ 1,600.00
Word processing software, such as WordPerfect 5.1	$ 250.00
Total cost	$ 4,560.00

This configuration, which combines brand-name computer and printer components with a superior word processor, is appropriate for small- or medium-size businesses and for professionals who need crisp-looking correspondence and don't mind spending the extra upkeep money that a laser printer demands.

Apple Macintosh Computer

16 MHz 68020 Macintosh LC	$ 2,634.00
4M of RAM	
3 1/2-inch, 1.44M floppy disk drive	
12-inch color monitor with built-in video	
80M hard disk drive	
Keyboard	$ 95.00
Laser printer, such as GCC Technologies PLP II	$ 1,400.00
Word processing software, such as Microsoft Word 4.0	$ 250.00
Total cost	$ 4,379.00

This configuration, which combines a more powerful computer system than the low-cost Macintosh version, a laser printer, and a sophisticated word processor, is appropriate for small- or medium-size businesses that want quality components and can afford the cost. You can reduce the total system cost by about $800 by substituting the Apple StyleWriter inkjet model or the Hewlett-Packard DeskWriter for the laser printer.

Spreadsheets

Spreadsheets can be simple or sophisticated, depending on the features the program offers and whether you take advantage of these features. To create, save, and print a simple spreadsheet, any computer model from any manufacturer will do. You will not notice how slowly the computer operates unless you build large spreadsheets with many formulas and links to other spreadsheets.

A spreadsheet program, however, that integrates text with graphs and pictures and requires high-quality output takes more computing power. Spreadsheet programs use RAM to store the data and formulas you enter. When you enter too many numbers and formulas, you run out of memory. To create large, complex spreadsheets, you need a fast computer with a coprocessor with a great deal of memory.

Low-End Spreadsheet Systems

The following configurations are recommended as systems for simple spreadsheet work.

IBM-Compatible Computer

80286 AT computer, such as EPSON Equity 286 Plus	$ 1,004.00
1M of RAM	
5 1/4-inch, 1.2M floppy disk drive	
VGA monochrome monitor	
Built-in VGA video adapter	
20M hard disk drive	$ 200.00
9-pin dot-matrix printer, such as EPSON LX-810	$ 150.00
Spreadsheet software, such as Quattro	$ 100.00
Total cost	$ 1,454.00

This configuration combines the least-expensive IBM-compatible components with a basic spreadsheet program. Such a low-budget system is appropriate for the home. If you want to print wide spreadsheets, substitute a wide-carriage printer. If you discover, after using Quattro for a while, that you would like a more powerful product, you can purchase the more powerful Quattro Pro ($350), which runs fairly well on this system.

Apple Macintosh Computer

8 MHz 68000 Macintosh Classic	$ 1,400.00
2M of RAM	
3 1/2-inch, 1.44M floppy disk drive	
Monochrome monitor with built-in video	
40M hard disk drive	
9-pin dot-matrix printer, such as Apple ImageWriter II	$ 470.00
Spreadsheet software, such as Microsoft Excel 3.0	$ 325.00
Total cost	$ 2,195.00

This configuration, which combines the least-expensive Macintosh components with a quality spreadsheet, is appropriate for the home or a small office where computing expenses must be kept to a minimum.

Medium-Level Spreadsheet Systems

The following configurations are recommended as medium-level spreadsheet systems.

IBM-Compatible Computer

20 MHz 80386SX computer, such as CompuAdd 320sc	$ 2,515.00
2M RAM	
32K Cache RAM	
3 1/2-inch, 1.44M floppy disk drive	
VGA color monitor and built-in VGA video	
80M hard disk drive	
24-pin wide-carriage printer, such as EPSON LQ-1050	$ 600.00
Spreadsheet software, such as Lotus 1-2-3 Release 3.1	$ 450.00
Total cost	$ 3,565.00

This configuration uses a powerful IBM-compatible computer, with enough additional RAM to run large spreadsheets and a large hard disk for ample storage capacity. The printer has a wider carriage and is of higher quality than the printer recommended for the lower-cost system. The spreadsheet software uses a DOS extender that accesses all the memory in the system. The software also has advanced spreadsheet-publishing features. To take advantage of these features, substitute a laser printer—the Hewlett-Packard LaserJet III, for instance—for the 24-pin printer. This system is appropriate for a small business.

IBM Computer

16 MHz 80386SX PS/2 Model 55SX	$ 2,600.00
2M of RAM	
3 1/2-inch floppy disk drive	
VGA color monitor with built-in VGA video	
80M hard disk drive	
DOS 5.0	$ 110.00
24-pin wide-carriage printer, such as EPSON LQ-1050	$ 600.00
Spreadsheet software, such as Lotus 1-2-3 Release 3.1	$ 450.00
Total cost	$ 3,760.00

This configuration, which combines brand-name computer and printer components with a superior spreadsheet program, is appropriate for small- or medium-size businesses that want quality products and can afford the cost.

Apple Macintosh Computer

16 MHz 68020 Macintosh LC	$ 2,634.00
4M of RAM	
3 1/2-inch, 1.4M floppy disk drive	
12-inch color monitor with built-in video	
80M hard disk drive	
Keyboard	$ 95.00
24-pin wide-carriage printer, such as EPSON LQ-2550	$ 1,000.00
Spreadsheet software, such as Microsoft Excel 3.0	$ 325.00
Total cost	$ 4,054.00

High-End Spreadsheet Systems

33 MHz 80486 computer, such as Dell System 433P	$ 4,999.00
2M of RAM	
3 1/2-inch floppy disk drive	
VGA color monitor with built-in VGA video	
100M hard disk drive	
2M of additional RAM	$ 180.00
Laser printer, such as Hewlett-Packard LaserJet III	$ 1,600.00
Spreadsheet software, such as Lotus 1-2-3 Release 3.1	$ 450.00
Total cost	$ 7,229.00

This configuration uses an IBM compatible equipped with Intel's fastest and most powerful microprocessor. The math coprocessor, which is installed on the chip, significantly speeds spreadsheet calculations. This configuration also provides enough memory to run large spreadsheets and includes a hard disk with ample storage capacity. The spreadsheet software, which uses a DOS extender to access all the memory in the system, takes full advantage of the capabilities of the printer. This system is appropriate for any company that needs a high-performance system to run powerful spreadsheet software.

Apple Macintosh Computer

40 MHz 68030 Macintosh IIfx	$ 6,000.00
4M of RAM	
68882 math coprocessor	
3 1/2-inch, 1.44M floppy disk drive	
80M hard disk drive	
Keyboard	$ 150.00
Multiscanning monitor, such as 14-inch Sony 1304 HG	$ 800.00
8-bit video adapter	$ 450.00
Laser printer, such as Apple LaserWriter II NT	$ 2,900.00
Spreadsheet software, such as Microsoft Excel 3.0	$ 320.00
Total cost	$10,620.00

At a somewhat higher cost, this configuration provides more memory, a larger hard disk, and a laser printer—and you can run spreadsheet software in color. This system is appropriate for small- or medium-size businesses that can afford the cost. You can significantly reduce the cost by substituting a PostScript-compatible laser printer or a high-quality dot-matrix model.

Databases

As with word processors and spreadsheets, your database needs may be modest or demanding. For modest needs, such as tracking a few thousand names for a mailing list or a few hundred items from a baseball-card collection, any low-end PC can do the job.

If you want to develop a more sophisticated database, and possibly incorporate pictures, you need a more powerful system with a fast, large-capacity hard disk. Because a database program continually scans the database for records, a hard disk with a fast access time gets the job done more quickly.

Low-End Database Systems

The following configurations are recommended for database systems with simple requirements.

IBM-Compatible Computer

80286 AT computer, such as EPSON Equity 286 Plus	$ 1,004.00
1M of RAM	
5.25-inch, 1.2M floppy disk drive	
VGA monochrome monitor	
Built-in VGA video adapter	
20M hard disk drive	$ 200.00
9-pin dot-matrix printer, such as EPSON LX-810	$ 150.00
Database software, such as PC-File 5.0	$ 80.00
Total cost	$ 1,434.00

This configuration, which combines a reputable database with the least-expensive IBM-compatible components available, is appropriate for the home or small office. If you plan to print wide reports, you may want to substitute a 24-pin dot-matrix printer, such as the EPSON LQ-510, which sells for about $250.

Apple Macintosh Computer

8 MHz 68000 Macintosh Classic	$ 1,275.00
2M of RAM	
3 1/2-inch, 1.44M floppy disk drive	
Monochrome monitor with built-in video	
40M hard disk drive	
9-pin dot-matrix printer, such as Apple ImageWriter I	$ 470.00
Database software, such as FileMaker Pro	$ 220.00
Total cost	$ 1,965.00

This configuration, which combines the least-expensive Macintosh components with a reputable database, is appropriate for the home or a small office where expenses must be kept to a minimum.

Medium-Level Database Systems

The following configurations are recommended as medium-level database systems.

IBM-Compatible Computer

20 MHz 80386SX computer, such as CompuAdd 320sc	$ 2,245.00
2M RAM	
3 1/2-inch, 1.44M floppy disk drive	
Monochrome monitor	
Hercules-compatible video adapter	
80M hard disk drive	
9-pin wide-carriage printer, such as EPSON FX-1050	$ 410.00
Database software, such as dBASE IV 1	$ 500.00
Total cost	$ 3,155.00

This configuration, which combines a more powerful IBM-compatible computer, a high-capacity hard disk, and a wide-carriage printer with a superior database program, is appropriate for a small business. If you want to integrate pictures into the database, substitute a VGA or a multiscanning color monitor.

IBM Computer

16 MHz 80386SX PS/2 Model 55SX	$ 2,600.00
1M of RAM	
3 1/2-inch floppy disk drive	
VGA color monitor with built-in VGA video	
80M hard disk drive	
DOS 5.0	$ 110.00
9-pin wide-carriage printer, such as EPSON FX-1050	$ 410.00
Database software, such as dBASE IV 1.1	$ 500.00
Total cost	$ 3,620.00

This configuration, which combines brand-name computer and printer components with a superior database program, is appropriate for small- to medium-size businesses.

Apple Macintosh Computer

16 MHz 68020 Macintosh LC	$ 2,634.00
4M of RAM	
3 1/2-inch, 1.44M floppy disk drive	
12-inch monitor with built-in video	
80M hard disk drive	
Keyboard	$ 95.00
24-pin wide-carriage printer, such as EPSON LQ-2550	$ 1,000.00
Database software, such as 4th Dimension V2.01	$ 475.00
Total cost	$ 4,204.00

This configuration, which combines the SE/30 computer (a more powerful model than the Macintosh Classic), a high-capacity hard disk, and a wide-carriage dot-matrix printer with a sophisticated database program, is appropriate for small- to medium-size businesses that can afford the cost. If you need color, you can upgrade by adding a color adapter board and a color monitor.

High-End Database Systems

The following configurations are recommended as high-end database systems.

33 MHz 80486 computer, such as Dell System 433P	$ 4,999.00
2M of RAM	
3 1/2-inch floppy disk drive	
VGA color monitor with built-in VGA video	
100M hard disk drive	
2M of additional RAM	$ 180.00
Laser printer, such as Hewlett-Packard LaserJet III	$ 1,600.00
Database software, such as dBASE IV 1.1	$ 500.00
Total cost	$ 7,279.00

This configuration uses an IBM-compatible computer that is equipped with Intel's fastest, most powerful microprocessor and an ample hard disk. The monitor provides a color display of business forms—or of images available in the database. The high-quality printer produces attractive forms. This system is appropriate for a company that needs a high-performance system to run powerful database software.

Apple Macintosh Computer

40 MHz 68030 Macintosh IIfx	$ 6,400.00
4M of RAM	
68882 math coprocessor	
3 1/2-inch, 1.44M floppy disk drive	
160M hard disk drive	
Keyboard	$ 150.00
Multiscanning monitor, such as 14-inch Sony 1304 HG	$ 800.00
8-bit video adapter	$ 450.00
Laser printer, such as Apple LaserWriter II NT	$ 4,200.00
Database software, such as 4th Dimension 2.01	$ 475.00
Total cost	$12,475.00

This configuration, which has ample memory, a large hard disk, a laser printer, and color display, is appropriate for small- or medium-size businesses that can afford the cost. You can significantly reduce the cost by substituting a PostScript-compatible laser printer or a high-quality dot-matrix model.

Graphics

Graphics programs, such as paint, drawing, presentation graphics, and computer-aided design (CAD) programs, demand a large volume of computing power. A low-end system will not run a graphics program, but a mid-range computer is sufficient to run paint and presentation programs.

A top-of-the-line PC is the best choice to run drawing and CAD programs because these programs often perform complex functions, like rotation and redrawing. You may be dismayed, however, by the cost of high-end systems. If these prices are not within your budget, you can run drawing and CAD programs on a less powerful computer, but you pay a penalty each time you wait for the computer to complete a task. Additional hardware, such as a graphics coprocessor board, can expedite drawing or CAD programs, but the additional hardware is expensive.

The following configurations are recommended as systems for running paint and presentation software.

IBM-Compatible Computer

20 MHz 80386SX computer, such as CompuAdd 320sc		$ 2,515.00
2M of RAM		
3 1/2-inch, 1.44M floppy disk drive		
VGA color monitor and built-in VGA video		
80M hard disk drive		
Color inkjet printer, such as Hewlett-Packard PaintJet		$ 795.00
Paint software, such as PC Paintbrush IV Plus, or		$ 125.00
Presentation software, such as Freelance Plus 3.01		$ 350.00
Total cost		$ 3,435.00
	or	$ 3,660.00

This system, which gives you enough computing power and hard-disk capacity to run paint or presentation programs, is suitable for a small business. You may save approximately $450 on this system by substituting a 24-pin dot-matrix printer with color capability. A similar system that uses an IBM 55SX computer costs approximately $1,300 more.

Apple Macintosh Computer

16 MHz LC 68020 computer		$ 2,700.00
2M of RAM		
3 1/2-inch, 1.44M floppy disk drive		
40M hard disk drive		
12-inch RGB Display		
Color inkjet printer, such as Hewlett-Packard PaintWriter		$ 795.00
Paint software, such as Pixel Paint Professional, or		$ 400.00
Presentation software, such as Microsoft PowerPoint		$ 250.00
Total cost		$ 3,895.00
	or	$ 3,745.00

This configuration, the least-expensive Macintosh color system, is suitable for a small business. You may save approximately $200 by substituting the Apple ImageWriter II printer, which has color capability.

The most powerful systems for running drawing and CAD software may cost more than $10,000 (sometimes more than $20,000), particularly if you use very high-resolution graphics adapters, large-screen monitors, and thermal color printers. If you are considering a purchase of this kind, ask an experienced person to assist you. If you are interested in less costly systems for this kind of work, you may want to consider one of the systems listed in the following paragraphs.

The following configurations are recommended as systems for running drawing and CAD software.

IBM-Compatible Computer

33 MHz 80486 computer, such as Dell System 433P	$ 4,999.00
2M of RAM	
3 1/2-inch floppy disk drive	
VGA color monitor with built-in VGA video	
100M hard disk drive	
2M of additional RAM	$ 180.00
Laser printer, such as Hewlett-Packard LaserJet III	$ 1,600.00
Drawing software, such as Corel Draw (and Microsoft Windows) or	$ 450.00
CAD software, such as Generic CADD 5.0	$ 250.00
Total cost	$ 7,229.00
	or $ 7,029.00

This system uses the fastest and most powerful Intel microprocessor. Substituting the more popular and more powerful AutoCAD will increase the cost of the system by about $2,000.

Apple Macintosh Computer

40 MHz 68030 Macintosh IIfx	$ 6,400.00
4M of RAM	
3 1/2-inch, 1.44M floppy disk drive	
68882 math coprocessor	
160M hard disk drive	
Keyboard	$ 150.00
Multiscanning monitor, such as 14-inch Sony 1304 HG	$ 800.00
8-bit video adapter	$ 450.00
Laser printer, such as Apple LaserWriter II NT	$ 2,900.00
Drawing software, such as Adobe Illustrator 88, or	$ 275.00
CAD software, such as Generic CADD Level 3	$ 325.00
Total Cost	$10,975.00
	or $11,025.00

Electronic Communications

Electronic communications depend on the modem, not on the type of computer you use. If you want to connect to an on-line service, such as CompuServe or Prodigy, you need only a low-end computer (like those recommended for low-end word processing), communications software, and a standard modem.

The following configurations are recommended for simple electronic communication.

2400-baud modem	$ 100.00
Communications software, such as	
CompuServe Navigator, or	$ 50.00
PROCOMM PLUS 1.1	$ 70.00

PROCOMM PLUS is a more general communications program than CompuServe Navigator. A modem sometimes includes communications software.

If you are interested in high-speed communication, you need a high-speed modem and such special features as data compression and data correction. The computer you use is not of paramount concern.

The following configuration is recommended for high-speed electronic communication.

9600-baud modem, such as Intel 9600EX MNP	$600.00

To perform special communications tasks, such as using one computer to control another computer by telephone, you can use any modem—if you install the proper software.

The following configuration is recommended for remote communication.

Remote-control software, such as PC Anywhere III	$60.00

Desktop Publishing

Desktop publishing software demands a high level of computing and printing power. You need a superior PC and a powerful laser printer, and this combination can be costly. Because desktop publishing products are in high demand, software companies have responded with products that work with inexpensive computers and printers. The finished products—newsletters, for instance—suffer from a lack of quality but seem to satisfy market demand.

The recommendations given here reflect the diversity of the desktop publishing market. If you want professional desktop publishing, don't buy a low-end system. Apple Macintosh computers are better suited for desktop publishing than IBM and IBM-compatible computers, even when both systems run the same software. This difference is true of PageMaker, for example, which Aldus produces in both Macintosh and IBM formats.

Low-End Desktop Publishing

Inexpensive desktop publishing systems for IBM-compatible and Apple Macintosh computers can be identical to systems for word processing—with different software, of course.

The following low-cost desktop publishing software programs are recommended for desktop publishing software.

IBM-Compatible Computer

Publish It! 1.2	$140.00

Apple Macintosh Computer

Publish-It!	$225.00

High-End Desktop Publishing

For professional desktop publishing, you need a system as powerful as the following:

Apple Macintosh Computer

40 MHz 68040 Macintosh IIfx 4M of RAM 3 1/2-inch, 1.44M floppy disk drive 68882 math coprocessor 160M hard disk drive	$ 6,400.00
Keyboard	$ 150.00
PostScript laser printer, such as Texas Instruments MicroLaser with 4.5M of RAM	$ 2,500.00
Additional full-page monochrome monitor and adapter, such as 15-inch Sigma Designs PageView	$ 1,050.00
Desktop publishing software, such as PageMaker 4.0	$ 500.00
Word processing software, such as Microsoft Word 4.0	$ 250.00
Drawing software, such as Adobe Illustrator 88	$ 275.00
Total cost	$11,125.00

High-quality desktop publishing programs can retrieve images from a drawing program, as well as text from a word processor. These requirements, however, add to the cost of the total package. Professional desktop publishing, for instance, requires a full-page display monitor and a laser printer. (The Apple LaserWriter II NT adds about $2,000 to the cost of the system.) A PostScript laser printer is the best choice for desktop publishing. However, because the Hewlett-Packard LaserJet III supports scalable fonts and can be upgraded to support PostScript, the HP printer may suit your needs.

For IBM and IBM-compatible computers, an alternative desktop publishing configuration uses a high-end word processor, such as WordPerfect 5.1. Except for the laser printer, the system configurations are the same as those listed for word

The following is the configuration for a word processing system to be used for desktop publishing.

IBM and IBM-compatibles

20 MHz 80386SX computer, such as CompuAdd 320sc 2M of RAM 3 1/2-inch, 1.44M floppy disk drive VGA monochrome monitor and built-in VGA video 40M hard disk drive	$ 1,975.00
Word processing software, such as WordPerfect 5.1	$ 250.00
Laser printer, such as HP LaserJet III	$ 1,600.00
Total cost	$ 3,825.00

WordPerfect and other advanced word processors like it offer many features of a desktop publishing program, such as building tables and inserting graphics into the document. These word processing programs also support features of a laser printer, such as switching among type styles and fonts. You get very nice results by using this IBM computer with a laser printer.

Education

Educational software usually is designed to work with low-end computers. For IBM and IBM-compatible computers, plan to buy a VGA color system, because most programs use color. This caveat is not true for the Macintosh, however; educational software works well with the monochrome Macintosh Classic.

The following configurations are recommended as low-cost systems to run educational software.

IBM-Compatible Computer

10 MHz 8088 XT computer, such as Tandy 100RC HD	$ 1,299.00
640K of RAM	
3 1/2-inch, 720K floppy disk drive	
Color display and adapter	
20M hard disk drive	
VGA monitor	
9-pin dot-matrix printer, such as EPSON LX-810	$ 150.00
Educational software: four titles at $40 each	$ 160.00
Total cost	$ 1,609.00

This configuration, which uses an inexpensive IBM-compatible computer with a VGA color adapter and color monitor, is appropriate for the home and can be used for applications other than education.

Apple Macintosh Computer

8 MHz 68000 Macintosh Classic	$ 1,400.00
2M of RAM	
3 1/2-inch, 1.44M floppy disk drive	
Monochrome monitor with built-in video	
40M hard disk drive	
9-pin dot-matrix printer, such as Apple ImageWriter II	$ 230.00
Educational software: four titles at $40 each	$ 160.00
Total cost	$ 1,790.00

This configuration, which uses the most inexpensive Macintosh components, is appropriate for the home and can be used for applications other than education.

As an alternative, you may consider a more advanced computer for education: the Macintosh LC.

16 MHz 68020 Macintosh LC	$ 2,434.00
2M of RAM	
3 1/2-inch, 1.44M floppy disk drive	
12-inch color monitor with built-in video	
40M hard disk drive	

Keyboard	$ 95.00
Apple IIe emulation card	$ 149.00
9-pin dot-matrix Apple ImageWriter II	$ 230.00
Educational software: four titles at $40.00 each	$ 160.00
Total cost	$ 3,068.00

This system enables you to run software designed for the Apple IIe. A great deal of software was created for this computer, including much educational software.

Accounting

Accounting programs for businesses are often specialized databases. Although some businesses use off-the-shelf accounting packages, many companies design their own accounting systems and database software. Accounting programs cost from one hundred to several thousand dollars, depending on the needs of the business. See the database section for information on purchasing a PC system for accounting.

Building a General-Purpose PC

You may have one specific application in mind when you shop for a personal computer, but remember that a PC is flexible. If you think that you may use a system for a variety of applications, consider building a general-purpose computer. Building does not mean putting together a computer kit or even buying all the parts separately and putting them together yourself. In this case, building means that you select components which are useful for a variety of applications. The general-purpose configurations in the following sections are for IBM, IBM-compatible, and Macintosh.

IBM General-Purpose Computer

Unless you need more power for a particular application, the IBM PS/2 55SX is currently the best IBM model. This reasonably priced computer is appropriate for today's software—and for future applications. The IBM PS/2 55SX has built-in VGA color circuitry and a high-performance hard disk drive, the two primary features needed for general-purpose computing.

The following is the configuration for the general-purpose IBM model.

IBM Computer

20 MHz 80386SX PS/2 Model 55SX	$ 2,700.00
4M of RAM	
3 1/2-inch, 2.88M floppy disk drive	
Built-in VGA video	
80M hard disk drive	
VGA or multiscan monitor	$ 500.00
Mouse	$ 100.00
Total cost	$ 3,300.00

IBM-Compatible General-Purpose Computer

IBM-compatible computers come in many different configurations. If you are interested in purchasing one of these computers, arm yourself with a list of specifications before you go to a computer store or call a computer mail-order company. Most parts for IBM-compatible computers are interchangeable, so you should get exactly what you want. If one company cannot give you what you want, shop somewhere else.

The following is the configuration for the general-purpose IBM-compatible computer.

IBM-Compatible Computer

20 MHz 80386SX computer	$ 1,300.00
2M of RAM	
3 1/2-inch, 1.44M floppy drive	
80M IDE hard disk with IDE adapter	$ 680.00
Super VGA Adapter	$ 300.00
14-inch multiscan color monitor	$ 500.00
Mouse	$ 100.00
Total cost	$ 2,880.00
Same system with 6M of RAM	$ 3,280.00

This system gives you the blend of microprocessor speed, hard disk speed and capacity, and high-resolution color graphics you need to run software under MS-DOS or Microsoft Windows 3.0.

Macintosh General-Purpose Computer

If you want to use a Macintosh as a general-purpose computer, your best bet is one of the Macintosh II computers that features color support and NuBus expandability.

The following is the recommended configuration for the general-purpose Macintosh model.

Apple Macintosh computer Macintosh IIci	$ 5,050.00
5M of RAM	
3 1/2 inch, 1.44M floppy disk drive	
Built-in 8-bit color	
Mouse	
101-key keyboard	$ 150.00
14-inch multiscan color monitor	$ 500.00
105M SCSI hard disk drive	$ 830.00
Total cost	$ 6,530.00

Buying a Portable Computer

Buying a portable computer is much like buying a desktop model. You need to consider the microprocessor, memory, floppy disks, hard disks, and video display. A portable computer, however, differs from a desktop model in four significant ways:

- *Size*. Portables can be as large as a piece of luggage or as small as a notebook. Portable computer sizes are categorized as luggable, laptop, and notebook. These sizes are described in more detail in the sections that follow.
- *Video display*. Most portables do not use the kind of picture tube found in video monitors. Instead, they use a flat-panel display, generally monochrome. Flat-panel color displays are available, but they can add as much as $5,000 to the cost of a system.
- *Keyboard*. Many portables have an integrated keyboard—usually much smaller than desktop computer keyboards.
- *Power source*. Some portables use AC power exclusively, some use battery power exclusively, and some can use either energy source.

Decide first what size portable you want. Then carefully examine the display. Some displays are hard to read, particularly if room lighting is not perfect. More information about displays is given in the following sections.

Try out the keyboard next. To keep the machine small, manufacturers of portable computers make tradeoffs in keyboard configuration. Applications such as WordPerfect 5.1 use function keys extensively, yet some portable keyboards do not have a separate row of function keys. You need to know what kind of portable keyboard you want.

If the size of the portable, the video display, the keyboard, and the power source (AC or battery) are all satisfactory, ask about the microprocessor, RAM, disk drives, and other features you need.

Luggables

Luggables—portable computers that are not especially easy to carry around—come in several shapes. One is the lunch-box shape (see fig. 12.1), which weighs approximately 20 pounds and comes in two different styles. The key difference between styles of lunch-box-shaped computers is display flexibility. One type enables you to tilt the display. The other type enables you to move the display up and over the top of the case. See figure 12.2 for a comparison of the two types. The video display of the computer on the left can be raised. One style is not better than the other, so choosing between the two styles is simply a matter of preference.

Another type of luggable, which weighs from 14 to 18 pounds and looks like an oversized laptop, is more suitable for a desk than a lap. Figure 12.3 shows a size comparison between a laptop computer and a luggable look-alike.

Fig. 12.1. *A lunch-box-shaped luggable computer.*

Fig. 12.2. *The two different lunch-box styles.*

Fig. 12.3. *A luggable computer (left) and a laptop computer (right).*

Because luggables can be as powerful as desktop computers, they often are used for giving presentations at different locations.

If you are considering a luggable, choose one that has a microprocessor at least as powerful as a 16 MHz 80386SX, a hard disk of 40M or larger, and a VGA-compatible display. The most readable luggable computer displays are yellow-and-black DC-plasma displays or orange-and-black gas-plasma displays.

Unlike smaller portables, luggables have keyboards much like those used with desktop models. Luggables can work from AC power or battery power, but battery power lasts only a couple of hours.

Luggables are costly, especially such brand-name luggables as COMPAQ and Toshiba. The Toshiba Model 3100SX, for example, costs approximately $4,000. You can purchase alternative brands of luggables for about $3,000 from some mail-order manufacturers.

If you are interested in a luggable Macintosh, Apple offers the Macintosh Portable. This computer has a 16 MHz 68000 microprocessor, a liquid crystal display, and a keyboard with an integrated trackball that serves as a mouse. This computer, which sells for approximately $3,200, is the only Apple portable currently available.

Laptops

Laptop computers are small enough and light enough—10 to 15 pounds—to sit comfortably on your lap. A laptop enables you to work while you travel or are away from your office or are at home.

Laptops are actually small IBM-compatible computers. The most commonly used microprocessor is the 80286; however, the 80386SX and 80386 are also used. Some laptops even are designed around the 80486 microprocessor. Although some laptops offer hard disk drives, others have only floppy disk drives.

Laptop computers often allow for expansion, enabling you to attach external disk drives or a larger capacity hard disk, upwards of 100M. Some laptops even offer at least one expansion slot for plug-in cards.

Apple offers a Macintosh laptop. This computer comes with at least 2M of RAM and a 40M hard disk. Also built into this model is a trackball. A trackball, described in Chapter 10, is like an upside-down mouse. You roll a built-in ball to move an arrow on the screen and press a button near the ball to make a selection.

Laptops have become very popular in our mobile society. Even more popular are small laptop computers called notebooks, described in the following section.

Notebooks

Notebook portables put the power of a desktop computer into a lightweight package you can carry under your arm. A notebook computer generally weighs less than 10 pounds. Notebook computers are the wave of the future in portable computing. If you are interested in a high-powered portable computer, a good choice is a notebook computer with the following features:

> Display: super-twist liquid crystal display; VGA compatible; edge lit, back lit, or side lit; 10-inch diagonal

Processor: 20 MHz 80386SX microprocessor

Hard disk drive: 20M (or greater)

Floppy disk drive: 3 1/2-inch 1.44M

Memory: 2M

Notebook computers with these features cost approximately $2,400 and higher and are available from such companies as CompuAdd and Dell. (A name brand model, like COMPAQ or IBM, costs about $1,000 to $2,000 more.) Figure 12.4 shows a notebook computer that fits easily inside a briefcase.

Fig. 12.4. *A notebook computer.*

Some notebook computers lack a floppy disk drive. To use software applications, such as a word processor, you must transfer the software directly from a desktop computer to the notebook computer's hard disk or RAM. You make the transfer by connecting the serial ports of the two computers, using a cable and a software-transfer program like LapLink. Notebook computers that do not have a floppy disk come with MS-DOS and a software-transfer program built into ROM or installed on the hard disk. If you don't want to use a transfer program, look for a notebook computer with an internal or optional external floppy disk drive (which costs about $225).

At the time of this writing, a new microprocessor from Intel, the 80386SL, promises to give notebook computers better power management capabilities. Because power management is so crucial to portable computer operation, expect a wave of notebook computers that use this microprocessor.

Buying a Used Computer

Because new IBM-compatible systems—complete with printer and software—are available for less than $1,000, price and brand name are the only reasons you should purchase a used computer. You should be able to buy a used IBM system computer for less than $1,000 or a used IBM-compatible for less than $600. If you don't benefit in brand name or price, buying a used computer doesn't make sense.

Purchasing a used computer can be dangerous. An old system may be ready to quit. An oddball system may leave you on a computing island, with no one to help you when you encounter problems.

If you are thinking of buying a used computer, be sure to do the following:

- Obtain documentation for the computer.
- Obtain documentation for any boards added to the computer.
- Obtain documentation for any software.
- Determine the age of the computer.
- Determine a fair market price.

When you look at a used computer, begin by making sure that the system works. Then ask about the microprocessor, RAM, disk drives, video adapter, and video display. Make sure that an IBM or compatible computer system has at least 640K of RAM. (Most of the newer programs cannot run on a system with 256K of RAM.) Don't buy a used computer that does not have a hard disk drive. A hard disk is indispensable to computing performance.

Most dealers will check out used systems, for a charge, to make sure that the computer is in working order. You may want to take the computer you are interested in buying to a computer dealer's service center. You will have to pay for the service but the money may be spent well.

Avoid paying a premium price for a CGA or EGA adapter and monitor. These video standards are out of date. You get more for your money if the system uses a Hercules or Hercules-compatible monochrome graphics adapter and a monochrome display.

Check prices with the *Computer Blue Book Price List*, published by the National Association of Computer Dealers ($15.95 at bookstores). This 364-page book provides a list of prices for computer products and a directory of the computer industry.

Purchasing a Used IBM Computer

IBM has manufactured many computer models since the IBM PC was introduced in 1981. Compatibility is the strongest benefit of purchasing an IBM computer. When you buy an IBM computer, you don't have to worry about whether a circuit board or a software program will work—they are designed for IBMs. Furthermore, an IBM keyboard is considered by many users to be the best keyboard made for personal computers. Compatibility and quality are the two characteristics the IBM name guarantees.

IBM PC

A used IBM PC typically has just two floppy disk drives. You cannot install a hard disk drive in an IBM PC without adding a stronger power source—perhaps even new ROM. If the IBM PC has been upgraded with a hard disk and a new power supply, consider purchasing it. If you cannot find out whether these options have been added, however, forget the computer.

IBM PC XT

A used IBM PC XT may be an excellent choice for several reasons. The XT has none of the problems associated with the PC, and you can upgrade the XT when you feel the need for more power. By simply adding a circuit board, such as the Intel Inboard 386, you can change the IBM PC XT (4.77 MHz 8088) to a 16 MHz 80386 computer.

IBM AT

The IBM AT computer is a slow 6 or 8 MHz 80286 computer. A used IBM AT may cost several hundred dollars more than a used XT. You receive some immediate performance benefits in the short term, but you probably will want more performance in the long term. When you upgrade either an AT or an XT to 80386, you have essentially the same computer, except that the AT has a somewhat faster hard disk performance. Consider purchasing a used AT only if a more economical XT is not available.

IBM PS/2

Used PS/2 Models 25, 30, or 30/286 are not easy to upgrade. A used PS/2 with an 80286 CPU, such as the Model 50, is also difficult to upgrade. If you lock yourself into a computer with an 80286 CPU, you will not be able to run software designed for more advanced processors. The price must be very low for you to consider purchasing one of the IBM PS/2 80286 models. If you have an opportunity, however, to purchase at a significantly low price a used IBM PS/2 model with an 80386SX or 80386 CPU, grab the used model.

Purchasing a Used IBM Compatible

Of all the computers you can purchase, a used IBM compatible may give you the most trouble. Older IBM compatibles notoriously are incompatible with circuit boards and software designed for IBM computers. If you are not careful, you may buy a computer with a proprietary design that does not accept standard add-on cards. The AT&T 6300, for example, is an older IBM compatible that cannot use

VGA adapter boards or any other kind of color adapter designed for IBM computers. Be certain that any used compatible you are considering can accept standard circuit boards and can run software designed for IBM computers. Ask for help if you need it.

Remember that new IBM compatibles are the least expensive PCs available—and prices are dropping all the time. Check the prices of comparable new compatibles before considering a used model.

Purchasing a Used Macintosh

Like IBM, Apple has manufactured many different models of computers. Unlike IBM, which began a whole industry of compatible computers, Apple is the sole supplier of Macintosh computers; no compatibles are currently available. When IBM makes a drastic design change, such as switching its bus design to Micro Channel, older computer models are not adversely affected because many other companies are still selling computers with the older ISA bus. When Apple makes a change, however, older computer models are greatly affected.

If you are considering a used Macintosh, therefore, you should check the prices and features of Apple's current Macintosh line. At this writing, the Apple Macintosh line includes

Macintosh Classic
Macintosh SE/30
Macintosh LC
Macintosh IIsi
Macintosh IIci
Macintosh IIfx
Macintosh Portable

All current Macintosh models have a 1.44M floppy disk drive and 512K of ROM. In effect, these specifications are the new standards for Macintosh computing. To make your used Macintosh compatible with the newest models, you eventually will have to upgrade the older Macintosh to these standards. You can purchase the upgrade through an Apple dealer for $300 to $700, depending on the model and the age of your machine.

Before you purchase a used Macintosh, do two things:

1. Check the price of a comparable new model.
2. Check the cost of making the used model compatible with the new model. If the cost of the used model plus the upgrade saves you money, the used model is worth considering.

Purchasing Another Kind of Used Computer

Many other brands of computers are available besides the brands discussed in this book. You may find a used Commodore 64, Apple II Plus, Coleco Adam,

Timex Sinclair, or other brand. Unless you have some special interest in one of these models, don't consider any of them. Although any computer has some merit as a computing device, some are very slow and difficult to upgrade.

Finding a Used Computer

After you decide to purchase a used computer, the problem is finding one. The first—and probably the best place to look is in the computer section of your newspaper's classified ads. Find out why the advertiser wants to sell the computer. If the reason for selling is that the owner needs money, you can probably negotiate the price down 20 percent. If the computer is available because the seller has just bought a new system, watch out. Don't buy someone else's troubles.

Look next in the business section of the newspaper for names of computer-brokerage services. If you decide to use a computer broker, however, remember that you are dealing with a business person who is trying to make a profit on the deal. The Boston Computer Exchange is a well-known brokerage that tries to match sellers with buyers. For details on this operation, call (617) 542-4414.

Your local computer store is another place to look for used computers. These stores sometimes accept, refurbish, and resell trade-ins. A computer store also may purchase manufacturer's close-outs. Remember, however, that when you deal with a business, you may not get as good a bargain as when you deal with an individual.

If you live in a large city you may find a good buy at a flea market or computer swap meet—a good place to find good contacts for computer support.

You occasionally may find a used computer for sale in a computer magazine, but because these publications usually are distributed nationwide, you may not find sellers in your area. You also might check with members of local user groups.

Evaluating a Used Computer

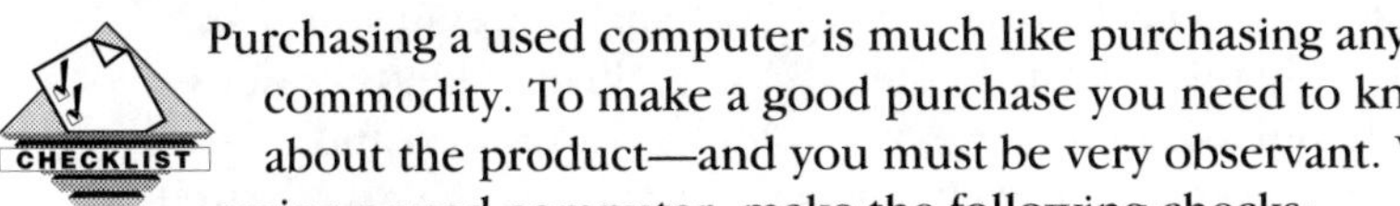

Purchasing a used computer is much like purchasing any other used commodity. To make a good purchase you need to know something about the product—and you must be very observant. When you examine a used computer, make the following checks:

- Turn on the machine.

  Is the display crisp and clear? Do you see any waviness? Are there any lines on the display that don't belong there?

- Inspect the keyboard.

  Is it clean? Does it look like it has been well cared for? Press each key, making sure that every letter or number appears on-screen. If possible, try out one of your own software programs on the computer. How does the keyboard action feel to you?

- Check the system unit.

  Try to copy files from the hard disk to the floppy disk drive. How do the disk drives sound? Noisy disk drives are a bad sign—especially a noisy hard disk.

- Ask the owner to remove the cover of the system unit.

  The cover should come off easily. Look inside. Is the system board clean, or is there dust and dirt everywhere? Keep in mind that a hair lying across a computer circuit has the same effect as a tree fallen across a road.

If everything seems to work and your overall impression is that the system has been well cared for, you probably have found a good used computer.

Chapter Summary

This chapter presents specific recommendations for buying desktop personal computers for a variety of applications, such as word processing, spreadsheets, databases, graphics, electronic communication, desktop publishing, education, and accounting. For each application, the text recommends typical IBM, Apple, and IBM-compatible systems for the home or for a small business. Personal computer systems for general-purpose use also are suggested. The chapter covers the different types of portable computers and suggests ways to choose a specific portable model. The text also discusses laptop and notebook computers. Finally, the chapter explains how to find and evaluate used computers.

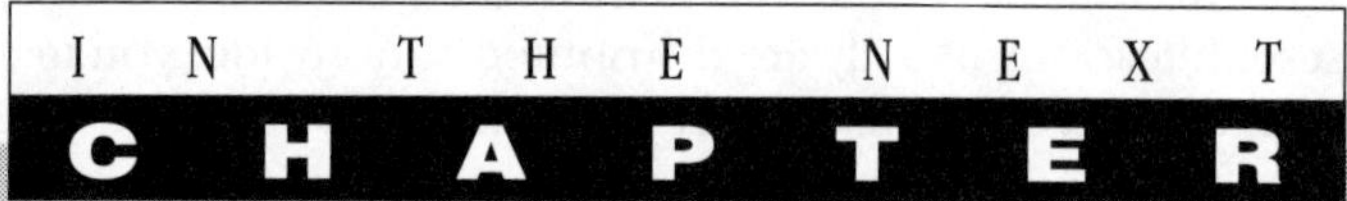

Chapter 13 explains how to purchase a computer and describes the different places you can shop for a system—such as retail stores and mail order companies. That chapter also explains the kinds of questions you should ask about support, training, warranties, and other important buying issues. The chapter encourages you to do research before making a purchase and tells you where to find the information you need. The chapter also gives advice on evaluating a computer vendor.

CHAPTER THIRTEEN

Making the Purchase

By now you probably have an idea of the type of personal computer system and printer you want. This chapter gives you advice about where to purchase a computer, whether from a computer store, an electronics store, a department store, or a mail-order company. The chapter lists the questions you should ask concerning support, training, warranties, and package deals. This chapter also discusses the type of research you should do and how to find the best computer vendor to serve you. Finally, the chapter gives you tips to ensure that you purchase all the pieces of equipment and parts you need.

Where Do I Purchase a Computer?

You purchase a computer in a store or through the mail, as you would any other piece of electronic equipment. Some stores specialize in computers and associated products, such as printers and software. Electronics stores sell computers and other kinds of electronic products, including calculators, video cameras, stereos, and VCRs. Other stores sell computers and many other kinds of merchandise. If you plan to purchase equipment through mail-order suppliers, you can find many computer companies from which to choose.

The kind of computer you want to buy determines the kind of store you should patronize. If you want a brand-name computer, such as IBM, COMPAQ, or Apple, check the telephone book or the business section of your local newspaper for authorized dealers. ComputerLand, the Computer Factory, MicroAge, and Sears Business Systems Centers are authorized sellers of IBM and COMPAQ computers. Connecting Point and ComputerLand sell Apple Macintosh computers.

Some stores sell only one brand of computer. Radio Shack, which sells the Tandy line of computers, has business computer centers in addition to its consumer electronics stores. CompuAdd sells its line of IBM-compatible computers through CompuAdd Superstores and through mail order.

If you plan to purchase an IBM-compatible computer or a portable, you can shop in computer stores, consumer electronics stores, or through mail order. Look in a telephone book or newspaper for stores that sell the compatible you are seeking.

Computer Stores

If you intend to purchase a brand-name computer, such as IBM, COMPAQ, or Apple, an authorized dealer (ComputerLand, Connecting Point, and so on) often is the only place you can shop. These stores traditionally charged premium prices for the products, but recently have been forced to be more price-competitive. These stores also offer benefits, such as leasing and financing plans, training, and on-site service contracts. (If you purchase an on-site service contract, a repair person comes to your place of business to diagnose and repair problems that occur with your system.)

If you buy an IBM, Apple, or other computer in a computer store, you are not forced to purchase an all-IBM or all-Apple system. You can purchase monitors and printers made by other manufacturers.

Computer stores often set up systems in the store. You can sit down in front of the computer, try the keyboard, examine the monitor, and look at the print quality of pages printed by a printer. If you have little experience with computers, this hands-on use can help you develop a feel for what the system offers.

Salespeople in computer-specialty stores do not necessarily have more computer expertise than salespeople in other kinds of stores. Depending on the size of the store and how it is run, you may deal with a salesperson who has little knowledge of PCs. On the other hand, you may deal directly with the store owner, who knows the products inside and out. The only way to determine the quality of store personnel is to ask technical questions, such as, "What is the speed of this computer?" If the salesperson responds with a vague answer, such as, "It's very fast," you know that technical expertise could be lacking. You should receive a specific answer for every question you ask.

Computer Superstores

Superstores, such as CompUSA, BizMart, and CompuAdd, sell desktop and portable computers, monitors, printers, software, and other computer-related items in stores modeled on warehouse-sized consumer electronics stores. These stores usually offer discounted prices on a wide selection of hardware and software, but often lack some of the services that are available at a computer store, such as software training and network support. If you are looking for a place to do comparison shopping, a superstore may be the place for you. Until recently, name-brand products, such as IBM and Apple, were not sold in superstores. New agreements, however, will allow low-end computers from IBM, Apple, and COMPAQ to be sold in some of these stores. (CompuAdd superstores carry only

CompuAdd desktop and portable computers, but sell equipment such as monitors, video adapters, and printers from a variety of well-known manufacturers.)

Consumer Electronics Stores

If you plan to purchase an IBM-compatible computer, such as EPSON, NEC, AST, Leading Edge, Packard Bell, Vendex, ALR, Panasonic, or Everex, you should shop at your local electronics retailer. These stores also carry portables made by companies such as Toshiba, Mitsubishi, Zenith, and Sharp. You often find the best deals in large electronics stores, because these stores sell all kinds of electronics at very low prices. Some electronics retailers, however, advertise low prices and then persuade you to buy more expensive items. This selling technique is known as bait and switch. Don't fall for it. In fact, this technique may be illegal in your area and at the very least is disreputable. If you are being pressured to buy a more expensive system than you want, try another store.

Consumer electronics stores often advertise complete systems, but don't let this stop you from buying the kind of equipment you want. Ask about every part of the system—microprocessor, hard disk drive, video adapter, video monitor, and so on. If you don't like the hard disk drive or monitor or any other component of the system, ask the salesperson to exchange it for a component you do like. For example, if the store packages a system with a VGA adapter, and you want a SuperVGA adapter, tell the salesperson. Making this kind of exchange is easy enough. Of course, a better component adds to the cost of the system.

Consumer electronics stores often bundle software with the computers they sell. Ask about this possibility. You may receive a free copy of MS-DOS, Windows, Microsoft Works, or other software.

Electronics stores usually have a service center you can turn to if you have problems with your PC. Obtain as many details as possible about the repair services the store provides. This information will help you avoid unpleasant surprises if you need to use the service center. Ask about repair policies. Are repairs done at the store, or is the equipment shipped back to the manufacturer? How long do you have to wait for a typical repair? Do you have to pay for shipping costs if the product is sent back to the manufacturer? Do you have to deliver the equipment to the store, or do you deal directly with the manufacturer? If the store's repair facility does not meet your expectations, you should consider purchasing your equipment elsewhere.

Department Stores

A computer sold in a department store usually is a low-performance IBM-compatible model at a premium price. These stores are unlikely to have a service center on the premises. Unless you have a particular reason for buying a computer at a department store, you should make your purchase at a computer store, computer superstore, or electronics store.

The IBM PS/1 computer is being sold in department stores such as Sears, which has a good reputation for supporting the products it sells. If you are considering buying a PS/1 in a department store, ask specifically about the store's computer support policy.

Mail-Order Companies

Like many other products, you can get the best prices on personal computers by buying through mail order. If you know someone who can help you put together a system and if you don't mind dealing with any hassles that may arise, then you should take advantage of lower mail-order prices. If you don't know anyone who can help you or if you're not willing to deal with potential problems, you probably should avoid this kind of purchase.

Depending on the mail-order company, you can order an advertised system or one that you specify component-by-component. Many mail-order companies include a statement in their advertisements saying that they provide custom configurations.

To buy a computer from a mail-order company successfully, first check with the Better Business Bureau or a consumer protection agency in the company's area. Many mail-order firms experience problems, even if they are well known. If possible, talk to people who have done business with the company and find out about their experience in dealing with it. The Better Business Bureau can tell you whether any problems have developed in that company. You should feel confident about buying equipment from a company before you place an order.

Next, check to see whether the system you want is in stock. If your choice is unavailable, ask when the system will be sent to you. Pay by credit card and find out when you will be charged. Charges should be applied only after a product is actually shipped; check the charge date on your bill. Ask about the mail-order company's return policy. Some companies offer extended warranties and money-back guarantees with no questions asked. Ask what shipping charges you will be expected to pay. Some companies charge a restocking fee if you return a product. Find out how much this fee is and decide whether you are willing to pay it.

Paying by credit card offers you some measure of protection against problems that may occur with a mail-order company. Check with your credit card issuer to find out the procedure for filing a claim, in case the need arises.

Don't worry about being left to fend for yourself if you have problems with your computer system. Mail-order companies have some of the best support people in the personal computer industry. Find out whether the company offers toll-free technical support and what the hours are. Some companies offer 24-hour, 365-days-a-year telephone support; others confine support to normal business hours. If you depend on the company for repairs, ask about repair policies. Some companies offer on-site service; others replace defective parts through the mail. Ask about replacement policies and the average repair turn-around time.

When you purchase through mail order, you choose the method of payment and the method of shipment. Find out whether the company accepts credit cards; if so, does the company accept the kind of credit card you have? Does the mail-order company impose a surcharge for using a credit card? Check to see whether you can order products COD. Find out whether the company ships through Federal Express, UPS, or another carrier. Does the company ship overnight? How much does shipping cost?

Some mail-order companies issue you their own credit cards—if you qualify. If you use this service, find out what interest rate the company charges. Some mail-order companies also will lease you a computer—if you meet certain credit qualifications.

The Direct Marketing Association suggests that if you have a problem with a mail-order company, you deal first with the seller. If you cannot resolve the problem, you can write to the following address:

Mail Order Action Line
c/o DMA
6 E. 43rd Street
New York, NY 10017

How Do I Find a Vendor?

If you plan to buy from a computer store, you can find a vendor's products in several ways. The yellow pages and local newspapers are the first places to look. Computer stores advertise in the business, computer, or science sections of the paper. Electronics stores usually advertise on certain days of the week; ask your newspaper sales representative. Retail stores and regional chains that sell one brand of computer usually advertise in catalogs and fliers that are sent through the mail or included with Sunday newspapers.

To purchase a computer through mail order, look for company advertising in computer magazines. Certain magazines cover certain computers: *PC Magazine* and *PC World* cover IBM computers and compatibles; *MacUser* and *Macworld* cover Macintosh computers. Some magazines are directed at people who buy through mail order: *Computer Shopper*, *Computer Monthly*, *Computer Buying World*, and *PC Sources*.

When you consider computer warranties and on-site service, remember that personal computers and other components, such as printers, monitors, video adapters, and hard disks, are reliable and may not require servicing for several years. When you purchase a computer with a one-year warranty, you are protecting yourself against defects in materials or workmanship, which usually appear right away. After you turn on a PC for the first time, for example, the video adapter or another component may die an hour or a day later. The warranty protects you against these defects. If a component malfunctions, call the store where you made the purchase and ask them to replace the defective part. If you want protection against any possible problem, you should look for products with money-back guarantees. A typical 30-day money-back guarantee enables you to return equipment if you are dissatisfied.

You should ask the following questions about warranties:

- Where do I take the system for repair? Do I have to take it back to the store or mail it back to the manufacturer?
- What happens after the warranty expires? Can I extend the warranty?
- Do warranties cover the entire system or just specific parts? (The entire system should be warranted, not specific parts.)
- When does the warranty start? The date the computer is manufactured, the date it is shipped to the distributor, the date it is sold in the store, or the date it is delivered to me? (The warranty should start on the date the computer is delivered to you.)
- Are the warranties advertised yours, the manufacturer's, or some third-party service organization's? (Advertised warranties should be the manufacturer's or manufacturer's plus the seller's.)
- Who tracks the warranty: the store, the distributor, or the manufacturer? (The store should track the warranty.)
- What does the warranty cover? (The warranty should cover everything, including software.)
- What is the money-back period? (The money-back period should be at least 30 days.)
- What is the period for immediate replacement from store inventory? If a product fails right away, do I get a new product, or is the defective product repaired? (You should receive immediate replacement from store inventory within the first 90 days of purchase.)
- What is the guaranteed turn-around time for damaged parts sent in for repair?
- Are repairs done at the dealer's site, or is equipment shipped back to the manufacturer? (Repairs should be done at the dealer's site.)
- If a damaged component must be replaced, does the component need to be received by the dealer or the manufacturer before a new component is sent? (You should not have to wait to have a damaged component replaced.)
- Who pays for shipment of the damaged part? (The dealer should pay.)
- Who pays for shipment of the good replacement part? (The dealer should pay.)

- How quickly are parts shipped?
- What is the labor charge for out-of-warranty service?

Ask the following questions about on-site (user's site) service:

- What level of training or certification do you require of the technicians you employ? (Technical training supplied by the manufacturer is best.)
- What is the response time for on-site service?

Ask these questions about warranties and on-site service to discover what level of service you are purchasing. A portion of the initial purchase price of a computer goes for service. If you are getting a good deal—the printer is on sale, for example—ask whether you receive the same level of service. Sometimes sale items are "special buy" pieces of equipment that the dealer doesn't support on a day-to-day basis.

Who Does Setup and Training?

When the computer arrives, you have to set it up. Connecting the components is not difficult. These physical connections are comparable to putting a stereo system together or hooking up a VCR. Some people prefer to do the setup themselves; others request a friend's help or hire someone to set up the system to make certain it works correctly.

A computer system includes hardware and software. You cannot begin to work with the system until you load the operating system and application software. A dealer or mail-order supplier can configure a system to load the operating system and present you with a selection of applications from which to choose. If no one does this setting up for you, you must do it yourself, which takes time and effort. You need time to read the manuals for the operating system and the application software. To get started right away, make sure that the dealer or mail-order supplier takes care of this task for you.

If you want training, you can take personal computer classes offered through computer stores, training companies, colleges, high schools, and user groups. You can find out about these training opportunities in fliers, newspaper ads, or by asking the salesperson where you purchase the computer. The least expensive options are adult education classes given in high schools and community colleges.

If you learn well on your own, look in your favorite bookstore for books on personal computing. You also can find videotapes that explain PC hardware and teach you how to use popular software. For system repair information, you should consider the book *Upgrading and Repairing PCs*, written by Scott Mueller and published by Que Corporation.

How Do I Make the Big Purchase?

After you have done your research by reading this book, looking at ads in newspapers, scanning computer magazines, talking to friends, and visiting computer stores, you should have a clear vision of what you want to purchase. Before you leave for the store or make that phone order, complete a checklist, such as the one shown in table 7.1.

CHECKLIST

This list gives you a method for comparing prices. You want a quote on everything. If the salesperson baits you with a $200 printer but requires that you purchase an $80 cable with it, you are smarter to buy a printer and cable for $250 elsewhere. The table also includes the small items not discussed in this chapter.

Table 7.1. PC Buyer's Checklist

Number/ Description	*Cost**
PERSONAL COMPUTER	
Model ____________	$ _____
CPU ____________	
Speed (MHz) ____________	
RAM ____________	
Cache RAM ____________	
Floppy disk drive size(s) ____________	
Floppy drive capacity ____________	
Hard disk size ____________	$ _____
Hard disk capacity ____________	
Hard disk/controller ____________	
Video adapter ____________	$ _____
Case style ____________	
Keyboard ____________	$ _____
Mouse ____________	$ _____
Power cord ____________	
Serial port(s) ____________	
Parallel port(s) ____________	
Other ____________	
MONITOR	
Model ____________	$ _____
Type ____________	
Cable ____________	
Tilt and swivel base ____________	
Power cord ____________	

Number/Description	*Cost**
PRINTER	
Model ____________	$ _____
Type ____________	
Parallel cable ____________	$ _____
Power cord ____________	
MODEM	
Model ____________	$ _____
Type ____________	
Modem power cord ____________	
Modem phone wire ____________	
Serial cable (for external modems) ____	$ _____
WARRANTY	
Standard warranty ____________	
Extended warranty ____________	$ _____
SOFTWARE	
Operating system disks ____________	$ _____
Diagnostic disks ____________	
System setup disks ____________	
Utility disks ____________	
Video adapter disks ____________	
Application 1 (e.g., word processor) ___	$ _____
Application 2 (e.g., spreadsheet) _____	$ _____
Application 3 (e.g., database) ________	$ _____
SUPPLIES	
Floppy disks ____________	$ _____
Paper ____________	$ _____
Mailing labels ____________	$ _____
Extra ribbons or toner for printer _____	$ _____
MISCELLANEOUS	
Mouse pad ____________	$ _____
Power strip/surge protector _________	$ _____
Keyboard cover ____________	$ _____
Total	$ _____

*Certain parts of the system may be included in a total system price.

Make copies of the checklist and compare several different personal computer systems. Using the checklist also ensures that you purchase all the parts and pieces you need to begin computing.

After you complete the checklist, follow these steps to purchase your computer:

1. Call the Better Business Bureau. Ask whether the store or company has any outstanding complaints.
2. Write down the name, address, and phone number of the store, as well as the name of the salesperson you deal with (this information may be on the invoice). Ask for copies of the refund policy and warranty. Inquire about service by using the questions given in this chapter.
3. Pay for your microcomputer and accessories with a credit card, if possible. When you get your new computer, put it together immediately and try it out. Examine everything closely. Try all the components, such as floppy disk drives, to make sure that they are working correctly. Format a floppy disk. Check to make sure that the capacity of the disk matches the type of disk drive you ordered (for example, a 1.44M floppy drive formats floppy disks with 1.44M of storage capacity). Look for an indication that the amount of RAM in the computer is the amount you ordered. For example, IBM and compatible computers display on-screen the amount of RAM in the system when you start up the system. Check the amount of space on the hard disk (if you don't know how, check your operating system manual). Make sure that the capacity you have is the capacity you ordered. Check the monitor. Does it provide the color and resolution you expected? Look for anything odd on the screen, such as random lines that could be the result of a faulty adapter. Make sure that all programs work as expected.
4. If you determine that the system is working properly, pay the entire credit card bill, if possible, to avoid significant interest charges. If the computer you receive, however, isn't what you actually ordered, or if you think something is wrong with any hardware or software component, call the dealer or mail-order company immediately to discuss the problem. If you are unsuccessful at resolving the problem, you can contest the charge for the entire computer system with your credit card company. Most credit card companies refuse to make payment on a bill if you provide written documentation of a legitimate grievance you have with the charged product. Many credit card companies also will negotiate a resolution with the company that has sold you the item in question.

In addition to helping you guard against possible problems with a computer store or company, you have another good reason for buying with a credit card—to take advantage of credit card promotions. For example, some credit card companies double the length of a warranty when you purchase products with its card. In most of these programs, the credit card company pays the cost of necessary repairs after the warranty expires until the warranty extension runs out.

Don't think, however, that only credit card buyers have advantages when purchasing a computer. One reason you may want to consider paying cash for your computer is that some computer stores offer additional discounts for cash. Use the method of payment that works best for you.

Chapter Summary

This chapter explains where to purchase a computer system: computer stores, computer superstores, consumer electronics stores, department stores, or through mail-order companies.

After suggesting where to buy, the chapter explains how to find a personal computer from a particular vendor. This chapter then provides questions to ask about warranties and on-site service. Finally, the chapter furnishes a checklist to use when making the big purchase.

APPENDIX A

Planning for the Future

After you purchase a system and have it working properly, you want to keep it running smoothly. This appendix describes products that help you keep your system unit, disk drives, keyboard, mouse, monitor, and printer in top condition. In the following sections, you also learn about in-warranty and out-of-warranty repairs. Finally, this appendix describes ways to keep track of what is going on in the personal computer industry and recommends magazines and on-line sources of up-to-date computing information.

Maintaining Your Computer

Like a car, your computer needs periodic maintenance. To keep your car in good working order requires regular oil changes, the right fuel, frequent cleaning and washing, and periodic inspections of parts—such as brakes and windshield wipers. Proper maintenance helps you avoid costly repairs.

Periodic preventive maintenance is as important for your computer as for your car. By keeping your computer in tip-top condition, you can avoid costly repair bills, as well as loss of valuable data.

Maintaining the System Unit

The computer system unit needs little maintenance. If you work in a dusty or smoky environment, open the case every two months and vacuum the inside of the unit. (Vacuuming does not remove the smoke residue but is your best defense against it.) A blanket of dust or smoke residue acts as an insulator on the chips, causing them to run at higher temperatures. In a normal environment, you can avoid heat-induced chip failure by cleaning the chips once a year with canned compressed air or a hand vacuum designed for electronic components.

Many computer systems contain one or more batteries. IBM-compatible and IBM AT computers use a battery to power the CMOS chip, which holds the setup information needed to operate the computer. Your computer cannot start correctly when the battery is dead. To restore the setup information that your computer needs, replace the battery and run a setup program. The setup program can reside in ROM or on a setup disk. If the setup program is in ROM, you start the setup program by turning on your computer and pressing a combination of keys. Typically, the setup program determines the setup information. You may need to supply the information if the program cannot determine the correct setup procedure. Battery life varies from one to five years. Your dealer can give you some idea about probable battery life and about the cost and availability of replacement batteries.

Maintaining the Disk Drives

The disk drives in the system unit need occasional maintenance. Although the floppy disk drive needs physical maintenance, the hard disk drive needs only software maintenance, such as reformatting and data protection. Proper maintenance preserves the usefulness of the drives and ensures their capability to record your data correctly.

Maintaining Floppy Disk Drives

Clean the magnetic heads in the floppy drive once a year. Cleaning is simple when you use a kit from a company like Curtis Manufacturing. Cleaning kits for 5 1/4-inch or 3 1/2-inch floppy disk drives are available at computer retail stores and cost approximately $10. Make sure that the cleaning system is a wet system rather than a dry system. A dry system may damage your disk drive recording heads.

Maintaining Hard Disk Drives

The hard disk is the most vulnerable part of a personal computer system. If your hard disk crashes, you may lose the use of your hard disk and all or part of the data on the disk. (The term *crash* originally meant that the head on a hard disk hit a platter, causing irreparable damage to the disk and its data. Today, the term more loosely describes any problem that causes the hard disk to stop working.) To ensure against the loss of important data and programs because of an unexpected crash, keep floppy disk backup copies of the data on your hard disk.

PC Fullback+ 1.12 (West Lake Data) and Fastback Plus 3.0 (Fifth Generation Systems) are programs that back up hard disks for IBM and compatible computers. PC Tools Deluxe Version 7.0 (Central Point Software), a collection of useful disk utilities, also includes hard disk backup software. In general, these programs are faster and easier to use than BACKUP, the program that accompanies DOS. Because the third-party programs also compress data, you can store the contents of your hard disk on fewer floppy disks.

Retrospect 1.3 (Dantz Development) is a good backup program for Macintosh hard disks. Fastback Mac III 2.5 (Fifth Generation Systems), a cousin product to Fastback Plus 3.0, is another good backup program for Macintosh computers. Mac Tools Deluxe (Central Point Software) and Sum II (Symantec) provide hard disk backup capability, as well as many other disk utilities.

For best results, back up your hard disk daily, weekly, or monthly, depending on how much data you enter and how costly the loss of the data would be. Hard disks, on the whole, are reliable and work for many years, depending on how much you use your computer. Your backup strategy should reflect this level of dependability, as well as the amount and value of data on your computer.

Several products for IBM and IBM-compatible computers prevent hard disk failure by examining the surface of the hard disk platter for defects. SpinRite II (Gibson Research) is one example of a preventive program. Nothing, however, should replace making regular backups.

Computer viruses recently have received a great deal of press. A virus may be nondestructive, causing minor annoyances such as messages on your screen. A virus, however, could destroy some or all data on your hard disk. If you download programs by modem from information services or bulletin-board systems, or exchange disks with someone who does, you are susceptible to a computer virus. To protect yourself from computer viruses, purchase one of the following antiviral software programs: Norton Antivirus (Symantic) or Virex 1.1 (Microcom) for IBM and compatibles; AntiVirus for Mac, Version 3.0 (Symantec) or Virex 2.71 (Microcom) for the Macintosh.

The more you use a hard disk, the more slowly the disk operates. This slowdown is caused by file fragmentation, which occurs when program and data files are divided and distributed randomly over available space on the hard disk. To bring your disk up to speed again, you need an optimizing program. Disk-optimizing software collects the scattered pieces of a program or file into one block on the hard disk. Good choices for disk-optimizing software are OPTune (Gazelle Systems) and Norton Utilities 5.0 (Symantec) for IBM and compatibles and Disk Express II (ALSoft) and Mac Tools Deluxe (Central Point Software) for the Macintosh. Run a disk-optimizing program every two months.

No matter how much data your hard disk can hold, you eventually will fill the disk to capacity. How quickly or slowly you fill your hard disk depends on the number of software programs you install on the hard disk and the size of the files you create with those programs. You occasionally need to reorganize the files to keep from overloading the hard disk. You can move some files from the hard disk to floppy disks for archival storage, or you can erase unnecessary files.

If you work only with MS-DOS on an IBM or compatible computer, these housekeeping chores can be tedious. You can use a program such as XTree Pro Gold (XTree), however, to complete this task quickly and effectively. If you use Windows 3.0 on an IBM or compatible computer, or if you use a Macintosh computer, you may not need a special program to help you remove files from the hard disk. How frequently you need to do housekeeping depends on the space available on your disk and the size and number of files you create daily.

Maintaining the Keyboard, Mouse, and Video Monitor

The keyboard, mouse, and video monitor need little maintenance. You can clean the keyboard surface as needed with a cloth dampened with a mild cleaning solvent. (Never spray a solvent directly on the keyboard.) Remove and clean the mouse ball with a mild solvent every six months. At the same time, clean the rollers that come into contact with the mouse ball with a cotton swab and a mild solvent. Clean the monitor display area (with the monitor turned off) once a week with ordinary glass cleaner. If the glass is covered with an antiglare coating, use a special screen cleaner such as Clean Screen (Curtis Manufacturing Company). The documentation that comes with the monitor tells you whether the screen is coated.

Maintaining the Printer

Printers need periodic maintenance, primarily by replacing ribbons and cartridges. If you have a dot-matrix printer with a nylon ribbon, the print becomes lighter with use. Print a page when the ribbon is new, and use that page as a visual guide to indicate when you should replace the ribbon.

Clean your dot-matrix printer each time you change the printer ribbon. Use a vacuum to clean out the paper dust that tends to collect in the printer. Periodically, perhaps every fifth time you change the ribbon, you should use a cotton swab and mild solvent to clean the printer head; then use a soft cloth to clean the platen (the rubber-like cylinder against which the paper rests).

A laser or inkjet printer signals you when to replace the toner cartridge or ink cartridge. Because the black toner powder spreads through the machine, you need to clean the inside of a laser printer regularly. The documentation for the laser printer gives you the proper cleaning procedures. Inkjet printers do not require much maintenance. As with a dot-matrix printer, clean your laser or inkjet printer each time you change the toner or ink cartridge. Plan to keep an extra toner or ink cartridge handy. These printers do not give you much warning before the ink runs dry. For example, an inkjet printer signals you only a few pages before the ink runs out.

Long-Term Troubleshooting Strategies

After your system is up and running, you may not experience problems with components for several months, or even years. If you suspect a problem, however, the diagnostic software that comes with your computer can pinpoint the problem for you. Although you may not be able to solve the problem, you will have information to give to your dealer or a technical support person. The documentation that accompanies the computer should discuss how to operate the diagnostic software.

For an IBM or compatible computer, you can purchase diagnostic software that is more thorough and easier to use than the software that comes with the system. A good choice is Check It (TouchStone Software). Check It tests the system unit board, RAM, hard disk drive, floppy disk drive, video circuits, serial and parallel ports, keyboard, mouse, joystick, and printer. Check It also indicates whether the problem is caused by hardware or software. If Check It locates a problem, you can give the information to a repair person or use the information to repair the computer yourself. Macintosh computers come with a program called Disk First Aid that will help you diagnose problems on your hard and floppy disk drives.

Not all computer problems are caused by system components. Problems are sometimes caused by human errors, such as erasing a file or reformatting a hard disk. Such problems can be devastating if you don't have the appropriate software to rescue you. Utility software is designed to perform several important tasks: to recover erased files, to reverse problems caused by reformatting a hard disk, to reconstruct damaged files, and to repair a corrupted hard disk.

When you look for utility software, notice what features the program offers. A unique feature may make one utility program more suitable for your purposes than another program. Utility software includes maintenance programs. For IBM and compatible computers, utility options include, for example, PC Tools Deluxe 6.0 (Central Point Software), Norton Utilities 5.0 (Symantec), and Mace Utilities 1990 (Fifth Generation Systems). For Macintosh computers, choose a utility program like Sum II (Symantic), Mac Tools Deluxe (Central Point Software), or Norton Utilities for the Macintosh.

Repairing a Personal Computer System

Personal computer systems are inherently reliable and can give you many years of trouble-free service; nevertheless, electronic components are susceptible to breakdown. During the warranty period, you need only return the computer to the dealer for repair or contact the manufacturer. When the computer or components are out of warranty, you have several options.

In-Warranty Repairs

The warranty period differs among components and from computer to computer. Most computer manufacturers offer one-year warranties; a few offer longer warranties. The warranty period may be longer for additional components you buy for your computer—such as a modem—than for the computer. Keep accurate records of purchase dates and warranty periods; make sure that you have dated copies of your receipts. You must prove that your computer or component is in warranty to obtain a warranty repair.

Keep a record of procedures to follow if your computer or a component breaks down during warranty. For best repair service, return the computer to the dealer from whom you purchased your computer or component or to an authorized dealer repair center. IBM, COMPAQ, and Apple, for example, have authorized dealer repair centers that honor the manufacturer's warranties.

Your warranty may provide on-site service for a period of time. Having the repair person come to your business or home to repair your computer eliminates the need to disconnect and move the computer. If your warranty provides on-site service, find out what procedures you must follow when you need a repair person.

If you purchased your computer through the mail with no provision for service or if you are not located near an authorized service center, you may need to mail the computer or the component to the manufacturer for repair. Sending your computer away for repairs is not as difficult as it sounds. Find out whether the manufacturer offers telephone support to help you verify that your computer really needs repair. Make sure that you have proper authorization from the company to return the computer. The manufacturer also may recommend a carrier or a means of shipment. If possible, pack your computer in the original packing cartons. Some, but not all, manufacturers may return the repaired components to you by air.

Ask your dealer or the manufacturer if a warranty repair extends the warranty. The replacement part may carry a warranty of its own. For example, suppose that your computer carries a one-year warranty and you need to replace the disk drive after six months. If the new disk drive carries a one-year warranty of its own, it may have six months of coverage beyond the computer warranty. Keep all documentation relating to warranty repairs.

Out-of-Warranty Repairs

When you need to repair your computer after the warranty period, be selective about the repair service you choose. Your dealer may charge a premium price for the repair. Find a good technical repair shop that charges reasonable rates, or consider making the repair yourself.

Finding a Reliable Repair Center

The dealer who sold you your system may not be the only reliable service center in your area. Other repair shops may have better prices or offer bonuses that your dealer does not offer. For example, some repair shops offer loaner or rental equipment while your computer or component is being repaired.

Where do you look for repair shops? Ask a friend or someone you trust. Word of mouth often is the best way to find reputable service centers. Check the yellow pages under *Computers & Computer Equipment—Service & Repair*. Many service centers advertise this way. Their ads may tell you which computers and other products they service. Check the prices and the services available at several service centers near you. Ask the following questions:

- Do you charge by the hour or by the job?
- Do you provide loaner or rental equipment?

- Do you use replacement parts from the original manufacturer?
- Do you provide on-site service?
- Do you provide pick-up and delivery services?
- What do you charge for on-site service or pick up and delivery?
- How long will the repair take?
- Will you guarantee a time for completion?
- Do you offer a warranty on the repair?

Generally, the cost is less—and easier for you to budget—when a repair is charged by the job. Loaner or rental equipment can help you keep up your productivity, especially if the repair takes several days or longer.

Major computer manufacturers, such as IBM, Apple, and COMPAQ, have specially designed components in their systems. These components often are sized or shaped so that only parts from the original manufacturer work well in the computers. Discuss the options with your repair center before you decide whether to use original manufacturer components or generic, or third-party, components made by other manufacturers.

On-site service usually is the fastest way to have your computer fixed and to keep computer downtime to a minimum, although you pay a premium price. A service center that picks up and delivers also saves you travel time.

An estimate of how much time the repair will take can help you make decisions, especially if your business depends on your computer. If the repair takes less than two days, you may not need to borrow or rent another computer. When your computer goes down in the middle of a time-essential task, however, you may have no other choice than to rent a replacement for the duration of the repair. Rentals can be expensive, so shop around for the facility that offers the fastest repairs and for a rental company that offers the most reasonable rates.

Repairing Your Computer Yourself

Computers are modular. A computer is made up of a main circuit board with smaller circuit cards attached to it, so you don't have to wade through an intricate maze of wiring. The video circuitry, for example, often resides on a video card (although this circuitry may be on the motherboard). Your computer may fail to display anything on-screen for several reasons: the monitor is unplugged; the monitor is not turned on; the monitor is faulty; or the video card is faulty. If the problem is not with the monitor, check the video card. (The video card is the one where you attach the cable from the monitor.)

Opening an IBM or compatible computer system unit is simple. Usually, two to five screws on the rear of the computer hold the case together; other models have removable tops. After you remove the screws, the cover slides off. Opening a Macintosh Plus, Classic, SE, or SE/30 requires special tools and is more difficult than opening a standard PC. You can pop off the top of the Mac II line by removing one screw and releasing two thumb latches. Check the manufacturer's documentation to make sure that you don't void any warranties by opening your computer. Make sure that you don't open any units sealed with a label because you may void your warranty if you do.

If you plan to make repairs yourself, look for software and books to help you. Check It (TouchStone Software) is an aid to diagnosing computer problems. An excellent do-it-yourself repair book is *Upgrading and Repairing PCs*, written by Scott Mueller and published by Que Corporation.

Keeping Pace with New Developments

Flexibility makes buying a personal computer different from buying any other piece of electronic equipment. A personal computer is not limited to one purpose. For example, you can use a personal computer you buy for word processing for spreadsheets, as well. You can use the computer to manage your personal finances or to play games. For this reason, you should keep abreast of new developments in personal computer components and software. Computer magazines and on-line services are two good ways to keep current with developments in the personal computer industry.

Subscribing to Computer Magazines

Many computer magazines are available, each devoted to a different aspect of computing. *PC Magazine*, for instance, has many comparative reviews of similar products in each issue. *PC Magazine*, however, is geared toward the person who buys equipment and software for corporations, so the information can be overwhelming to a novice. *Computer Shopper* and similar magazines specialize in ads from hundreds of mail-order suppliers of personal computer systems, components, and software. *Computer Craft* is a good source of information for anyone interested in upgrading or enhancing a personal computer system.

Some magazines focus on a specific product. For example, *Lotus* magazine publishes many articles about Lotus 1-2-3, and *WordPerfect* magazine concentrates on articles about the WordPerfect word processing program. If you are interested in a specific area of computing such as desktop publishing or music, look for magazines like *Publish* and *Electronic Musician*.

When you consider buying or subscribing to a magazine, keep in mind the magazine's slant—what readers the magazine addresses. Some magazines are intended for computer technicians, whereas others are aimed more toward the general reader. A quick glance through the table of contents of a magazine should give you a feel for its audience.

Some magazines cover only one kind of computer. For example, *PC Magazine* and *PC World* cover IBM and compatible computers; *Mac World* and *Mac User* cover the Macintosh computer. All these magazines are good sources of information for using and buying products associated with a particular brand of personal computer.

Joining an On-Line Service

You may want to contact other people who have similar computer systems and software in order to ask them questions or to discuss a particular topic. Consider signing up for an on-line service such as CompuServe, GEnie, Prodigy, or America On-Line. These services have hundreds of special interest groups (SIGs), where you can leave messages and get responses to questions about computing topics. You also can "chat" with other members of the service. Chatting takes place when you connect your computer with another on-line service user's computer and you both type messages to each other.

To connect to an on-line service, you need communications software and a modem, and you pay an hourly fee for using the service, besides long distance telephone rates if the call is not local. The information you receive, however, can be well worth the cost. Find out what hours are peak and off-peak for calling the service; peak rates can be two to three times the cost of off-peak rates.

Although CompuServe and GEnie may be too expensive for you, other on-line sources may interest you. Prodigy, sponsored by IBM and Sears, is an on-line service that charges a flat monthly fee rather than a fee for on-line time. Prodigy offers services such as on-line shopping, national weather reports, and airline reservations. Another service is the local bulletin-board service (BBS). BBSs often keep a computer on-line so that you can leave messages at any time. Others in the user group can then read and respond to your messages. Some BBSs cater to IBM and compatibles only, Macintosh only, or other special areas—even noncomputer related areas. Contact your local user groups to find out about BBSs.

Summary

This appendix offers advice for planning for the future in two key areas: maintenance and repair. The first section includes advice on how to maintain the different components of a computer system; the second section explains what to do when your computer needs repair—with and without a warranty in effect. The last section describes two ways to keep abreast of new products introduced for personal computers: computer magazines and on-line services. These sources help you obtain information about computing and locate people with interests similar to yours.

APPENDIX B

Vendor Information

Abaton (Subsidiary of Everex Systems, Inc.)
48431 Milmont Drive
Fremont, CA 94538
PHONE: 800/444-5321
FAX: 415/683-2151

Acer America Corporation
401 Charcot Avenue
San Jose, CA 95131
PHONE: 800/733-2237
FAX: 408/922-0176

Advanced Logic Research, Inc.
9401 Jeronimo
Irvine, CA 92718
PHONE: 800/444-4257
FAX: 714/581-9240

Agfa Corporation
200 Ballardvale Street, MS 200-4-7D
Wilmington, MA 01887
PHONE: 800/288-4089
FAX: 508/658-0200 ext. 5460

Altec Technology Corporation
18555 East Gale Avenue
City of Industry, CA 91748
PHONE: 800/255-9971
FAX: 818/912-8048

Altima Systems, Inc.
1390 Willow Pass Road, Suite 1050
Concord, CA 94520
PHONE: 800/356-9990
FAX: 510/356-2408

Apple Computer, Inc.
20525 Mariani Avenue
Cupertino, CA 95014
PHONE: 408/996-1010

Applied Engineering
3210 Beltline Road
Carrollton, TX 75234
PHONE: 214/241-6060
FAX: 214/484-1365

ARES
24762 Crestview Court
Birmington Hills, MI 48335
PHONE: 800/322-3200
FAX: 313/473-4450

AST Research, Inc.
16215 Alton Parkway, P.O. Box 19658
Irvine, CA 92713-9658
PHONE: 800/876-4278
FAX: 714/727-9355

ATI Technologies, Inc.
3761 Victoria Park Avenue
Scarborough, Ontario M1W 3S2
Canada
PHONE: 416/756-0711 (Support)
416/756-0718 (Office)
FAX: 416/756-0720

Austin Computer Systems
10300 Metric Boulevard
Austin, TX 78758
PHONE: 800/752-1577 (Sales)
800/752-4171 (Tech. Support)
FAX: 512/454-1357

C D Technology, Inc.
766 San Aleso Avenue
Sunnyvale, CA 94086
PHONE: 408/752-8500
FAX: 408/752-8501

Canon U.S.A., Inc.
One Canon Plaza
Lake Success, NY 11042
PHONE: 800/848-4123 (Dealer)

Cardinal Technologies, Inc.
1827 Freedom Road
Lancaster, PA 17601
PHONE: 800/233-0187
FAX: 717/293-3104

Chinon America, Inc.
660 Maple Avenue
Torrance, CA 90503
PHONE: 800/441-0222
213/533-0274
FAX: 213/533-1727

Citizen America Corporation
P.O. Box 4003
Santa Monica, CA 90411-4003
PHONE: 213/453-0614 ext. 435 (Support)
800/556-1234 ext. 34 (Literature)
FAX: 213/453-2814

Club American Technologies
3401 West Warren Avenue
Fremont, CA 94539
PHONE: 415/683-6688
FAX: 415/490-2687

COMPAQ Computer Corporation
20555 SH 249
Houston, TX 77070
PHONE: 800/231-0900 (Dealer)
800/345-1519 (Tech. Support)

CompuAdd Corporation
12303 Technology Boulevard
Austin, TX 78727
PHONE: 800/627-1967
FAX: 512/331-6236

Compucom Corporation
1180-J Miraloma Way
Sunnyvale, CA 94086
PHONE: 800/228-6648
FAX: 408/732-4570

Corel Systems Corporation
1600 Carling Avenue
Ottawa, Ontario K1Z 8R7
Canada
PHONE: 613/728-8200
FAX: 613/761-9177

CTX International, Inc.
20530 Earlgate Street
Walnut, CA 91789
PHONE: 714/595-6146
FAX: 714/595-6293

Data World
3733 San Gabriel River Parkway
Pico Rivera, CA 90660-1404
PHONE: 800/736-3282 ext. 222
FAX: 213/695-7016

Datadesk International, Inc.
9330 Eton Avenue
Chatsworth, CA 91311
PHONE: 800/328-2337
FAX: 818/998-0330

Dataproducts Corporation
6219 DeSoto Avenue, P.O. Box 746
Woodland Hills, CA 91365-0746
PHONE: 800/334-3174
FAX: 818/887-4789

Datasouth Computer Corporation
4216 Stuart Andrew Boulevard
Charlotte, NC 28217
PHONE: 800/476-2120
704/523-8500
FAX: 704/523-9298

Dell Computer Corporation
9505 Arboretum Boulevard
Austin, TX 78759-7299
PHONE: 800/879-3366
FAX: 512/338-8700

Denon America, Inc.
222 New Road
Parsippany, NJ 07054
PHONE: 201/575-7810
FAX: 201/808-1608

DTK Computer Inc.
17700 Castleton Street, Suite 300
City of Industry, CA 91748
PHONE: 818/810-8880
FAX: 818/810-5233

E-Machines
9305 S.W. Gemini Drive
Beaverton, OR 97005
PHONE: 800/344-7274
FAX: 503/641-0946

Eastman Kodak Company,
Printer Products Division
901 Elmgrove Road
Rochester, NY 14653-6305
PHONE: 800/344-0006

Ehman Incorporated
97 South Red Willow Road
Evanston, WY 82930
PHONE: 800/257-1666
FAX: 307/789-4656

EPSON America, Inc.
20770 Madrona Avenue
Torrance, CA 90509-2842
PHONE: 800/922-8911

Ergo Computing, Inc.
One Intercontinental Way
Peabody, MA 01960
PHONE: 800/633-1925
FAX: 508/535-7512

Everex Systems, Inc.
48431 Milmont Drive
Fremont, CA 94538
PHONE: 800/821-0806

Falco Data Products, Inc.
440 Potrero Avenue
Sunnyvale, CA 94086
PHONE: 800/325-2648
408/745-7123
FAX: 408/745-7860

Gateway 2000
610 Gateway Drive
North Sioux City, SD 57049
PHONE: 800/523-2000
FAX: 605/232-2023

GCC Technologies, Inc.
580 Winter Street
Waltham, MA 02154
PHONE: 800/422-7777
FAX: 617/890-0822

Genesis Integrated Systems
1000 Shelard Parkway, Suite 270
Minneapolis, MN 55426
PHONE: 800/325-6582
FAX: 612/544-4347

Hayes Microcomputer Products, Inc.
P.O. Box 105203
Atlanta, GA 30348
PHONE: 404/441-1617

Hewlett-Packard Company
19310 Pruneridge Avenue
Cupertino, CA 95014
PHONE: 800/752-0900

Hitachi Home Electronics Inc.,
Multimedia Systems
401 West Artesia Boulevard
Compton, CA 90220
PHONE: 800/369-0422
FAX: 213/515-6223

Howtek, Inc.
21 Park Avenue
Hudson, NH 03051
PHONE: 800/444-6983
FAX: 603/880-3843

Hyundai Electronics America
166 Baypointe Parkway
San Jose, CA 95134
PHONE: 800/727-6972 (Sales)
FAX: 408/473-9349

IBM (International Business Machines
Corporation)
P.O. Box 92835
Rochester, NY 14692
PHONE: 800/445-2426

Insight Distribution Network, Inc.
1912 West Fourth Street
Tempe, AZ 85281
PHONE: 800/767-3475 (Hard Drives)
800/776-7600 (Systems)
FAX: 602/829-9193

Intel Corporation
5200 Elam Young Parkway
M.S. C03-07
Hillsboro, OR 97124-6497
PHONE: 800/538-3373
503/629-7354
FAX: 800/525-3019

Kensington Microware Limited
2855 Campus Drive
San Mateo, CA 95054
PHONE: 800/535-4242
FAX: 415/572-9675

Laser Magnetic Storage International
4425 ArrowsWest Drive
Colorado Springs, CO 80907
PHONE: 800/777-5674
FAX: 719/593-4597

Leading Edge Computer
Products, Inc.
117 Flanders Road
Westboro, MA 01581
PHONE: 800/874-3340
FAX: 508/836-4504

Logitech, Inc.
6505 Kaiser Drive
Fremont, CA 94555
PHONE: 800/231-7717
415/795-8500 (Corporate)
FAX: 415/792-8901

Marstek, Inc.
15225 Alton Parkway
Irvine, CA 92718
PHONE: 800/366-4620
FAX: 714/833-7813

Micro Design International, Inc.
6985 University Boulevard
Winter Park, FL 32792
PHONE: 407/677-8333
FAX: 407/677-8365

Microlab
23976 Freeway Park Drive
Farmington Hills, MI 48335
PHONE: 800/677-7900 (Systems)
800/288-7828
(Components)
FAX: 313/474-0843

Microsoft Corporation
One Microsoft Way
Redmond, WA 98052-6399
PHONE: 800/426-9400
FAX: 206/883-8101

Microspeed, Inc.
44000 Old Warm Springs Boulevard
Fremont, CA 94538
PHONE: 800/232-7888
415/490-1403
FAX: 415/490-1665

Microtek Lab, Inc.
680 Knox Street
Torrance, CA 90502
PHONE: 800/654-4160
FAX: 213/538-1193

Mirror Technologies
2644 Patton Road
Roseville, MN 55113
PHONE: 800/654-5294
FAX: 612/633-3136

MIS Computer Systems
935 Benecia Avenue
Sunnyvale, CA 94086
PHONE: 800/733-9188
FAX: 408/730-5933

Mouse Systems Corporation
47507 Seabridge Drive
Fremont, CA 94538
PHONE: 415/656-1117
FAX: 415/770-1924

Multi-Tech Systems, Inc.
2205 Woodale Drive
Mounds View, MN 55112
PHONE: 800/328-9717
612/785-3500
FAX: 612/785-9874

NCR Corporation
1700 South Patterson Boulevard
Dayton, OH 45479
PHONE: 800/225-5627
513/445-5000
(Computer Systems)

NEC Technologies, Inc.
1414 Massachusetts Avenue
Boxborough, MA 01719
PHONE: 800/632-4636
508/264-8000

New Dest Corporation
1015 East Brokaw Road
San Jose, CA 95131
PHONE: 408/436-2700
FAX: 408/436-2750

NewGen Systems Corporation
17580 Newhope Street
Fountain Valley, CA 92708
PHONE: 800/888-1689
FAX: 714/436-5189

Nikon Electronic Imaging
1300 Walt Whitman Road
Melville, NY 11747
PHONE: 800/526-4266
FAX: 516/547-0305

Northgate Computer Systems, Inc.
7075 Flying Cloud Drive
Eden Prairie, MN 55344
PHONE: 800/548-1993
FAX: 612/943-8338

Outbound Systems, Inc.
4840 Pearl East Circle
Boulder, CO 80301
PHONE: 800/444-4607
FAX: 303/786-8611

Packard Bell
9425 Canoga Avenue
Chatsworth, CA 91311
PHONE: 800/733-5858
818/773-4400 ext. 407

Panasonic Communications
& Systems Company
185 Hansen Court
Wood Dale, IL 60191
PHONE: 800/447-4700 (Service)
800/222-0584 (Tech. Support)

PC Brand, Inc.
877 Supreme Drive
Bensenville, IL 60106
PHONE: 800/722-7263 ext. 1114
FAX: 800/722-7392

Pentax Technologies Corporation
100 Technology Drive
Broomfield, CO 80021
PHONE: 303/460-1600
FAX: 303/460-1628

Pioneer Communications of America
600 East Crescent Avenue
Upper Saddle River, NJ 07458
PHONE: 800/527-3766

PLI
47421 Bayside Parkway
Fremont, CA 94538
PHONE: 800/288-8754 EXT. 426
FAX: 415/683-9713

Practical Peripherals, Inc.
31245 La Baya Drive
Westlake Village, CA 91362
PHONE: 800/442-4774
FAX: 818/706-2474

Procom Technology
200 McCormick
Costa Mesa, CA 92626
PHONE: 800/800-8600
FAX: 714/549-0527

QMS, Inc.
One Magnum Pass
Mobile, AL 36618
PHONE: 205/639-4400
FAX: 205/633-4866

Radius Inc.
1710 Fortune Drive
San Jose, CA 95131
PHONE: 800/227-2795
FAX: 408/434-0127

Reference Technology, Inc.
5775 Flatiron Parkway, Suite 220
Boulder, CO 80301
PHONE: 800/345-9569
FAX: 303/442-1816

Samsung Information Systems
America, Inc.
3655 North First Street
San Jose, CA 95134-1713
PHONE: 800/624-8999 ext. 851
FAX: 408/434-5653

Seiko Instruments USA, Inc.
1130 Ringwood Court
San Jose, CA 95131
PHONE: 800/553-5312 (Sales/Supply)
408/922-1917 (Tech. Support)
FAX: 408/922-5840

Sharp Electronics
Sharp Plaza
Mahwah, NJ 07430
PHONE: 201/529-9600
FAX: 201/529-9454

Sigma Designs, Inc.
46501 Landing Parkway
Fremont, CA 94538
PHONE: 800/845-8086
FAX: 415/770-2640

Sony Corporation of America
655 River Oaks Parkway
San Jose, CA 95134
PHONE: 408/432-0190
FAX: 408/432-0253

Standard Computer
12803 Schabarum Avenue
Irwindale, CA 91706
PHONE: 800/662-6111
FAX: 818/337-2626

Sun Moon Star
1941 Ringwood Avenue
San Jose, CA 95131
PHONE: 408/452-7811 (Dealer)

SuperMac Technology
485 Potrero Avenue
Sunnyvale, CA 94086
PHONE: 408/245-2202
FAX: 408/735-7250

Swan Technologies
3075 Research Drive
State College, PA 16801
PHONE: 800/468-9044
FAX: 814/237-4450

Tandon Corporation
405 Science Drive
Moorpark, CA 93021
PHONE: 800/800-8850
FAX: 805/529-8408

Tandy Corporation
1800 One Tandy Center
Fort Worth, TX 76102
PHONE: 817/390-3011

Tangent Computer
197 Airport Boulevard
Burlingame, CA 94010
PHONE: 800/223-6677
FAX: 415/342-9380

Taxan America, Inc.
161 Nortech Parkway
San Jose, CA 95134
PHONE: 800/648-2926
FAX: 408/942-1201

Tektronix, Inc.
P.O. Box 1000, 26600 S.W. Parkway, MS 63-630
Wilsonville, OR 97070-1000
PHONE: 800/835-6100
FAX: 503/685-3063

Texas Instruments Incorporated
P.O. Box 202230
Austin, TX 78720-2230
PHONE: 800/527-3500

The Complete PC
1983 Concourse Drive
San Jose, CA 95131
PHONE: 408/434-0145
800/229-1753
FAX: 408/434-1048

Todd Enterprises, Inc.
224-49 67th Avenue
Bayside, NY 11364
PHONE: 800/445-8633
718/343-1040
FAX: 718/343-9180

Toshiba America Information Systems
9740 Irvine Boulevard
Irvine, CA 92718
PHONE: 800/745-4745

Tri-Star Computer Corporation
140 South Weber Drive
Chandler, AZ 85226
PHONE: 800/678-2799
FAX: 602/345-0110

U.S. Robotics, Inc.
8100 North McCormick Boulevard
Skokie, IL 60076
PHONE: 800/342-5877
FAX: 708/982-5058

UDS Motorola
5000 Bradford Drive
Huntsville, AL 35805
PHONE: 800/451-2369
FAX: 205/430-8926

Ultra-Comp
3801 Ultra-Comp Drive
Earth City, MO 63045

USA Flex
135 North Brandon Drive
Glen Ellyn, IL 60139
PHONE: 800/872-3539
FAX: 708/351-7204

Varityper, Inc.
11 Mount Pleasant Avenue
East Hanover, NJ 07936
PHONE: 800/631-8134
FAX: 201/884-6311

Wyse Technology, Inc.
3471 North First Street
San Jose, CA 95134
PHONE: 800/438-9973

Xerox Imaging Systems, Inc.
9 Centennial Drive
Peabody, MA 01960
PHONE: 800/248-6550 (Sales)
508/977-2117
FAX: 508/977-2150

Zenith Data Systems
2150 East Lake Cook Road
Buffalo Grove, IL 60089
PHONE: 800/553-0331

Zeos International, Ltd.
530 5th Avenue, N.W.
St. Paul, MN 55112
PHONE: 800/423-5891
612/633-4591
FAX: 612/633-1325

Zoom Telephonics
207 South Street
Boston, MA 02111
PHONE: 800/666-6191
FAX: 617/423-9231

INDEX

K–L

M

P

T

U

V

W

X–Z

Complete Coverage From A To Z!

Que's Computer User's Dictionary

Que Development Group

This compact, practical reference contains hundreds of definitions, explanations, examples, and illustrations on topics from programming to desktop publishing. You can master the "language" of computers and learn how to make your personal computers more efficient and more powerful. Filled with tips and cautions, *Que's Computer User's Dictionary* is the perfect resource for anyone who uses a computer.

IBM, Macintosh, Apple, & Programming

Order #1086 **$10.95 USA**

0-88022-540-8, 500 pp., 4 3/4 x 8

The Ultimate Glossary Of Computer Terms— Over 200,000 In Print!

"Dictionary indeed. This whammer is a mini-encyclopedia...an absolute joy to use...a must for your computer library...."

Southwest Computer & Business Equipment Review

To Order, Call:
(800) 428-5331 OR (317) 573-2510

Teach Yourself
With QuickStarts From Que!

The ideal tutorials for beginners, Que's QuickStart books use graphic illustrations and step-by-step instructions to get you up and running fast. Packed with examples, QuickStarts are the perfect beginner's guides to your favorite software applications.

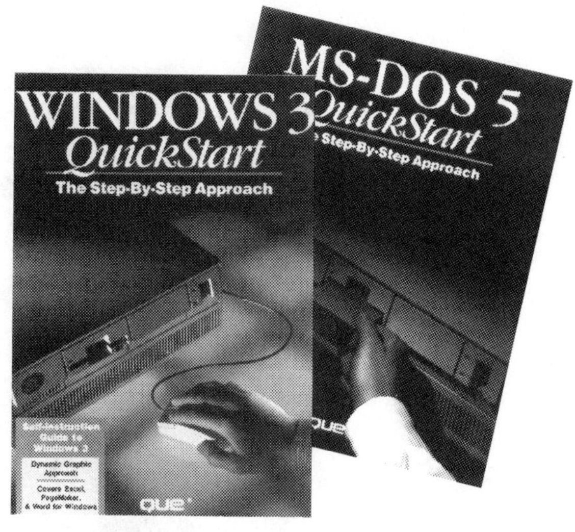

1-2-3 Release 2.2 QuickStart, 2nd Edition
Releases 2.01 & 2.2
Order #1207 **$19.95 USA**
0-88022-612-9, 400 pp., 7 3/8 x 9 1/4

1-2-3 Release 3.1 QuickStart, 2nd Edition
Releases 3 & 3.1
Order #1208 **$19.95 USA**
0-88022-613-7, 400 pp., 7 3/8 x 9 1/4

dBASE IV QuickStart
dBASE IV
Order #873 **$19.95 USA**
0-88022-389-8, 384 pp., 7 3/8 x 9 1/4

dBASE IV QuickStart, 2nd Edition
Through Version 1.1
Order #1209 **$19.95 USA**
0-88022-614-5, 400 pp., 7 3/8 x 9 1/4

Excel QuickStart
IBM Version 1 & Macintosh Version 2.2
Order #957 **$19.95 USA**
0-88022-423-1, 334 pp., 7 3/8 x 9 1/4

MS-DOS QuickStart, 2nd Edition
Version 3.X & 4.X
Order #1206 **$19.95 USA**
0-88022-611-0, 400 pp., 7 3/8 x 9 1/4

Q&A QuickStart
Versions 3 & 4
Order #1264 **$19.95 USA**
0-88022-653-6, 400 pp., 7 3/8 x 9 1/4

Quattro Pro QuickStart
Through Version 2.0
Order #1305 **$19.95 USA**
0-88022-693-5, 450 pp., 7 3/8 x 9 1/4

WordPerfect QuickStart
WordPerfect 5
Order #871 **$19.95 USA**
0-88022-387-1, 457 pp., 7 3/8 x 9 1/4

WordPerfect 5.1 QuickStart
WordPerfect 5.1
Order #1104 **$19.95 USA**
0-88022-558-0, 427 pp., 7 3/8 x 9 1/4

Windows 3 QuickStart
Ron Person & Karen Rose

This graphics-based text teaches Windows beginners how to use the feature-packed Windows environment. Emphasizes such software applications as Excel, Word, and PageMaker and shows how to master Windows' mouse, menus, and screen elements.

Version 3
Order #1205 **$19.95 USA**
0-88022-610-2, 400 pp., 7 3/8 x 9 1/4

MS-DOS 5 QuickStart
Que Development Group

This is the easy-to-use graphic approach to learning MS-DOS 5. The combination of step-by-step instruction, examples, and graphics make this book ideal for all DOS beginners.

DOS 5
Order #1293 **$19.95 USA**
0-88022-681-1, 400 pp., 7 3/8 x 9 1/4

To Order, Call:
(800) 428-5331 OR (317) 573-2510